Make the Grade.
Your Atomic Dog Online Edition.

The Atomic Dog Online Edition includes proven study tools that expand and enhance key concepts in your text. Reinforce and review the information you absolutely 'need to know' with features like:

- **Review Quizzes**
- Key term Assessments
- Interactive Animations and Simulations
- Notes and Information from Your Instructor
- Pop-up Glossary Terms
- A Full Text Search Engine

D0580212

Ensure that you 'make the grade'. Follow your lectures, complete assignments, and take advantage of all your available study resources like the Atomic Dog Online Edition.

How to Access Your Online Edition

If you purchased this text directly from Atomic Dog ....
Visit atomicdog.com and enter your email address and password in the login box at the top-right corner of the page.

If you purchased this text NEW from another source....
Visit our Students' Page on atomicdog.com and enter the **activation key located below** to register and access your Online Edition.

If you purchased this text USED from another source....
Using the Book Activation key below you can access the Online Edition at a discounted rate. Visit our Students' Page on atomicdog.com and enter the **Book Activation Key in** the field provided to register and gain access to the Online Edition.

Be sure to download our *How to Use Your Online Edition* guide located on atomicdog.com to learn about additional features!

This key activates your online edition. Visit atomicdog.com to enter your Book Activation Key and start accessing your online resources. For more information, give us a call at (800) 310-5661 or send us an email at support@atomicdog.com

160IFM72J

PKG

CENGAGE
Learning™

Research Methods Knowledge Base

THIRD EDITION

William M.K. Trochim

James P. Donnelly

Atomic Dog
A part of Cengage Learning

CENGAGE
Learning™

Australia • Brazil • Japan • Korea • Mexico • Singapore • Spain • United Kingdom • United States

CONTENTS

PART 3:   OBSERVATION AND MEASUREMENT

PART 4:   DESIGN AND STRUCTURE

PART 5:   ANALYSIS

You can approach the study of research methods in many different ways. Here I'm going to give you two metaphors to use for thinking about how you might work your way through the material in this book.

The Road to Research

Remember all those Bob Hope and Bing Crosby films, such as *The Road to Singapore* and *The Road to Morocco?* Of course you don't; you're much too young! Well, two old guys made a whole bunch of movies just after they started doing talkies, and each of the movies had a "road to" title. These guys always managed to get themselves into a terrible jam (along with their beautiful female companion, Dorothy Lamour), but things invariably worked out both comically and musically (in those days, people actually used to sing in movies). Research is a lot like those old movies. No, really. You're going to have fun. Honest.

Well, I thought it might be useful to visualize the research endeavor sequentially, like taking a trip, like moving down a road—the Road to Research. Figure 1 shows an applied way to view the content of this text that helps you consider the research process as a practical sequence of events. You might visualize a research project as a journey where you pass certain landmarks along your way. Every research project needs to start with a clear problem formulation. As you develop your project, you will find critical junctions where you will make choices about how to proceed. Consider issues of sampling, measurement, design, and analysis, as well as the theories of validity behind each step. In the end, you will need to think about the whole picture and write up your findings. You might even find yourself backtracking from time to time and reassessing your previous decisions! This is a two-way road; planning and reflection are critical and interdependent. Think of the asphalt of the road as the foundation of research philosophy and practice. Without consideration of the basics in research, you'll find yourself bogged down in the mud!

The Yin and the Yang of Research

Another way to look at research is illustrated in Figure 2. The figure shows one way of structuring the material in the Knowledge Base. The left side of the figure refers to the theory of research. The right side of the figure refers to the practice of research. The yin-yang figure in the center links you to a theoretical introduction to research on the left and to the practical issue of how to formulate research projects on the right.

The four arrow links on the left describe the four types of validity in research. The idea of validity provides a unifying theory for understanding the criteria for good research. The four arrow links on the right point to the research practice

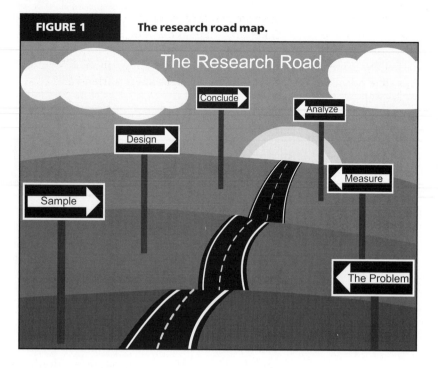

FIGURE 1   The research road map.

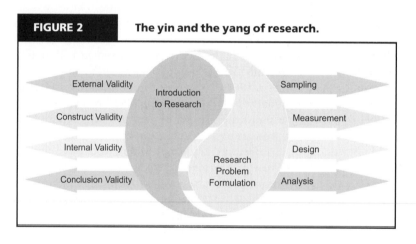

FIGURE 2   The yin and the yang of research.

areas that correspond with each validity type. For instance, external validity is related to the theory of how to generalize research results. Its corresponding practice area is sampling methodology, which is concerned with how to draw representative samples so that generalizations are possible.

The figure as a whole illustrates the yin and yang of research—the inherent complementarities of theory and practice—that I try to convey throughout this book. If you can come to an understanding of this deeper relationship, you will be a better researcher, one who is able to create research processes, rather than simply use them.

"Two Shorten the Road" (The Social Nature of Social Science)

There is an old Irish proverb which advises "Two shorten the road." Having been down the research road a few times I've learned that the Irish saying applies quite well to the research journey. At its best social research is a very social activity. You can go more places, move more quickly and have more fun if you travel the research road with others. This is true when conducting a single study, when trying to learn about research methods as a student, and when writing about research methods. So this time down the research road I've brought along a friend and collaborator, Jim Donnelly.

About 15 years ago Jim got interested in my work in concept mapping and in the interim we've been able to collaborate on a number of projects, including a workbook for the Concise version of this text. I knew that as a teacher of research methods and long time user of the *Knowledge Base,* he might like to join me in developing the Third edition of the book. He heartily accepted my invitation. So this volume extends both the content of the book as well as the authorship, reflecting some important changes in the field and also my belief in collaboration. We must note that our collaboration brought us to one interesting choice point having to do with the issue of "voice."

Readers of the previous volumes know that this book has taken a conversational tone. This has been well received by faculty and students over the years. Many of the stories and the lighter comments would have been lost if we had written this new volume as "we." Therefore, *we* decided to retain the singular voice in order to maintain the conversational flow of the previous volumes. So from here on, *we* will become *I* and *you* can sign up for a metaphysics course to ponder how *we* did it . . . .

What's New?

The Research Methods Knowledge Base, Third Edition, builds upon the strengths of the previous edition and significantly extends and enhances its coverage of applied social research methods. Four new chapters have been added that address several critically important topics in research design, analysis, and synthesis. The 16 chapters in the present volume cover everything from the development of a research question to the writing of a final report, describing both practical and technical issues of sampling, measurement, design, analysis, and on into research synthesis and evidence-based practice.

Okay now, it's time for you to sit cross-legged and meditate on the yin and yang of it all as we start down the road to research . . . .

Additional resources are provided in the Online Edition of this text. Login to your Online Edition at www.atomicdog.com to find these additional resources located in the Study Guide at the end of each chapter. These resources include Key Terms/Key Terms Matching, Chapter Summary, Suggested Web Sites, and a Practice Quiz.

Acknowledgments

Bill Trochim:

This work, as is true for all significant efforts in life, is a collaborative achievement. I want to thank especially the students and friends who assisted and supported me in various ways over the years.

I especially want to thank Dominic Cirillo, who labored tirelessly over several years on the original web-based and printed versions of *The Research Methods Knowledge Base* and without whom I simply would not have survived. There are also the many graduate teaching assistants who helped me make the transition to a web-based course and contributed their efforts and insights to this work and the teaching of research methods.

The *Knowledge Base* has grown from a simple web site to a real text in both electronic and hard-copy versions. For that I need to thank all of my friends at Atomic Dog who supplied the enthusiasm and vision to move this effort to the next step as well as their successors at Cengage. The list must begin with Alex von Rosenberg, who encouraged me to take this step and convinced me that his dog would indeed hunt. Thanks to Chris Morgan for putting up with all of my questions and concerns. I'd also like to thank Nicole Bauer for the wonderful graphics work she has done, and I especially want to thank Dreis vanLanduyt, Sydney Jones, Laura Pearson, Christine Abshire, Kendra Leonard, Laureen Ranz, and K.A. Espy for their tireless efforts to edit this text into something readable. We appreciate the efforts of Cadmus/KGL for their composition services. We do indeed know we live in a digital age when we can collaborate on a project like this without ever having met! You deserve all of the credit and none of the blame.

And, of course, I want to thank all of the students, both undergraduate and graduate, who participated in my courses over the years and used the *Knowledge Base* in its various incarnations. You have been both my challenge and inspiration.

Jim Donnelly:

I would like to echo the expression of gratitude to our colleagues at Atomic Dog and Cengage as well as the wonderful graduate students I've known at the University at Buffalo. Most of all, I want to thank Bill Trochim for the ongoing lessons in methodology, for the opportunity to collaborate on this edition of the *Knowledge Base*, and for the vitally personal and professional inspiration and support he's provided over the last 15 years.

About Atomic Dog

Atomic Dog is faithfully dedicated to meeting the needs of today's faculty and students, offering a unique and clear alternative to the traditional textbook. Breaking down textbooks and study tools into their basic 'atomic parts' we were able to recombine them and utilize rich digital media to create a "new breed" of textbook.

This blend of online content, interactive multimedia, and print creates unprecedented adaptability to meet different educational settings and individual learning styles. As a part of Cengage Custom Solutions, we offer even greater flexibility and resources in creating a learning solution tailor-fit to your course.

Atomic Dog is loyally dedicated to our customers and our environment, adhering to three key tenets:

Focus on Essential & Quality Content: We are proud to work with our authors to deliver you a high-quality textbook at a lower cost. We focus on the essential information and resources students need and present them in an efficient but student friendly format.

Value and Choice for Students: Our products are a great value and provide students more choices in 'what and how' they buy—often at a savings of 30–40% versus traditional textbooks. Students who chose the online edition may see even greater savings compared to a print textbook. Faculty play an important and willing roll—working with us to keep costs low for their students by evaluating texts online and supplementary material.

Reducing Our Environmental 'Paw-Print': Atomic Dog is working to reduce its impact on our environment in several ways. Our textbooks and marketing materials are printed on recycled paper and we will continue to explore environmentally friendly methods. We encourage faculty to review text materials online instead of requesting a print review copy. Students who buy the online version do their part by going 'paperless' and eliminating the need for additional packaging or shipping. Atomic Dog will continue to explore new ways that we can reduce our 'paw print' in the environment and hope you will join us in these efforts.

Atomic Dog is dedicated to faithfully serving the needs of faculty and students—providing a learning tool that helps make the connection. We know that after you try our texts that Atomic Dog—like a great dog—becomes your faithful companion.

Online and In Print

Atomic Dog publishes unique products that give you the choice of both online and print versions of your text materials. We do this so that you have the flexibility to choose which combination of resources works best for you. For those who use the online and print versions together, we don't want you getting lost as you move between the web and print formats, so we numbered the primary heads and subheads in each chapter the same. For example, the first primary head in Chapter 1 is labeled 1-1, the second primary head in this chapter is labeled 1-2, and so on. The subheads build from the designation of their corresponding primary head: 1-1a, 1-1b, etc.

This numbering system is designed to make moving between the online and print versions as seamless as possible. So if your instructor tells you to read the material in 2-3 and 2-4 for tomorrow's assignment, you'll know that the information appears in Chapter 2 of both the web and print versions of the text, and you can then choose the best way for you to complete your assignment. For your convenience, the Contents for both the web and print versions also show the numbering system.

PART 1

Foundations

CHAPTER 1

Foundations

KEY TERMS

alternative hypothesis
anonymity
attribute
cause construct
concept mapping
conclusion validity
confidentiality
constructivist
correlational relationship
critical realism
cross-sectional
deductive
dependent variable
ecological fallacy
effect construct
empirical
epistemology
evidence-based practice
exception fallacy
exhaustive
hierarchical modeling
hypothesis
hypothetical-deductive model
independent variable
inductive
informed consent
Institutional Review Board (IRB)
longitudinal
methodology
mixed methods

mutually exclusive
natural selection theory of
  knowledge
negative relationship
null hypothesis
one-tailed hypothesis
operationalization
positive relationship
positivism
post-positivism
qualitative data
qualitative variable
quantitative data
quantitative variable
relationship
repeated measures
Requests for Proposals (RFPs)
research question
right to service
subjectivist
theoretical
third-variable problem
threats to validity
time series
two-tailed hypothesis
unit of analysis
validity
variable
voluntary participation

You have to begin somewhere. Unfortunately, you can only be in one place at a time and, even less fortunately for you, you happen to be right here right now, so you may as well consider this a place to begin, and what better place to begin than an introduction? Here's where I cover all the stuff you think you already know, and probably should already know, but most likely don't know as well as you think you do.

Let's begin with the big historical picture before you get started in your study of how things are currently done. For now, we might suggest that the beginning lies in the struggle of our species to survive and that our current point of view results from the evolution of learning to survive via that most basic of research strategies: trial and error. It may be coincidental, but at present one of the most important research designs is called the *clinical trial* in which clinical researchers attempt to establish control over sources of *error* in their methods and results. Philosophy is another long-term influence on how research is done. Philosophy has always been a critical aspect of the sorting and rating of "truth" whether in science, politics, religion, or other domains. For example, if you have heard any discussion of whether "intelligent design" should be included in school curricula, you know that philosophy remains very much a part of the public discussion of what we might call our cultural knowledge base.

Fast-forwarding to the here and now, it is clear that modern research involves an eclectic blending of an enormous range of skills and activities. To be a good social researcher, you must be able to work well with a variety of people, understand the specific methods used to conduct research, understand the core of the subject that you are studying as well as its boundaries, convince someone to give you the funds to study it, stay on track and on schedule, speak and write persuasively, and on and on. You'll be challenged to learn and apply language, concepts, and skills in the context of complex environments that include your study participants, fellow students, research advisors, ethical and scientific review boards, funding agencies and the general public. Few paths are more difficult, interesting, or potentially worthwhile.

Perhaps language acquisition is the most fundamental step needed to get your foot in the door of modern research methods. This chapter begins with the basic language of research, the introductory vocabulary you need to read the rest of the text. With the basic terminology under your belt, I'll show you some of the underlying philosophical issues that drive the research endeavor. Social research always occurs in a social context. It is a human endeavor. I'll point out the critical ethical issues that affect the researcher, research participants, and the research effort generally. For instance, you'll consider how much risk your research participants can be placed under and how you must ensure their privacy. In the section on conceptualization, I answer questions such as where do research problems come from and how do I develop a research question?

That ought to be enough to get you started. At least it ought to be enough to get you thoroughly confused. But don't worry, there's stuff that's far more confusing than this yet to come.

1-1 The Language of Research

Learning about research is a lot like learning about anything else. To start, you need to learn the jargon people use, the big controversies they fight over, and the different factions that define the major players. For example, there has been a tendency for researchers to classify methods as either qualitative or quantitative (basically words versus numbers). Recently, more attention has been paid to the "debate" about the relative merits of various approaches under these headings due to the emergence of qualitative methods into the mainstream of social science methodology. Yet, as we will see, qualitative versus quantitative is a very limited dichotomy, whether we are discussing types of data or types of research strategies. There is now recognition of the value of using **mixed methods**, depending on the nature of the study goals or research questions. The term *mixed methods* means that more that one kind of method, most often a combination of qualitative and quantitative methods, is used in the study.

mixed methods
Any research that uses multiple research methods to take advantage of the unique advantages that each method offers. For instance, a study that combines case study interviews with an experimental design can be considered mixed methods.

1-1a Types of Studies

Research projects take three basic forms:

1. *Descriptive* studies are designed primarily to describe what is going on or what exists. Public opinion polls that seek only to describe the proportion of people who hold various opinions are primarily descriptive in nature. For instance, if you want to know what percent of the population would vote for a Democrat or a Republican in the next presidential election, you are simply interested in describing something.
2. *Relational* studies look at the relationships between two or more variables. A public opinion poll that compares what proportion of males and females say they would vote for a Democratic or a Republican candidate in the next presidential election is essentially studying the relationship between gender and voting preference.
3. *Causal* studies are designed to determine whether one or more variables (for example, a program or treatment variable) causes or affects one or more outcome variables. If you performed a public opinion poll to try to determine whether a recent political advertising campaign changed voter preferences, you would essentially be studying whether the campaign (cause) changed the proportion of voters who would vote Democratic or Republican (effect).

The three study types can be viewed as cumulative. That is, a relational study assumes that you can first describe (by measuring or observing) each of the variables you are trying to relate. A causal study assumes that you can describe both the cause and effect variables and that you can show that they are related to each other. Causal studies are probably the most demanding of the three types of studies to perform.

Probably the vast majority of applied social research consists of descriptive and relational studies. So why should we worry about the more difficult studies? Because for most social sciences, it is important to go beyond simply looking at the world or looking at relationships. Instead, you might like to be able to change the world, to improve it, and eliminate some of its major problems. If you want to change the world (especially if you want to do this in an organized, scientific way), you are automatically interested in causal relationships—ones that tell how causes (for example, programs and treatments) affect the outcomes of interest. In fact, the era of **evidence-based practice**, described fully in the final chapter, has elevated the status of causal studies in every field and in every part of the world. Evidence-based practice means that what we do to intervene in the lives of others is a result of studies that have given us a strong empirical base for predicting that a program or treatment will cause a specific kind of change in the lives of participants, clients, or patients.

evidence-based practice
The use of the best available programs or treatments based on careful evaluation using critically reviewed research.

1-1b Time in Research

Time is an important element of any research design, and here I want to introduce one of the most fundamental distinctions in research design nomenclature: cross-sectional versus longitudinal studies. A **cross-sectional** study is one that takes place at a single point in time. In effect, you are taking a slice or cross-section of whatever it is you're observing or measuring. A **longitudinal** study is one that takes place over time—you have at least two (and often more) waves (distinct times when observations are made) of measurement in a longitudinal design.

A further distinction is made between two types of longitudinal designs: repeated measures and time series. There is no universally agreed upon rule for distinguishing between these two terms; but in general, if you have two or a few waves of measurement, you are using a **repeated measures** design. If you have many waves of measurement over time, you have a **time series**. How many is many? Usually, you wouldn't use the term *time series* unless you had at least twenty waves of measurement, and often far more. Sometimes the way you distinguish between these is with the analysis methods you would use. Time series analysis requires that you have at least twenty or so observations over time. Repeated measures analyses aren't often used with as many as twenty waves of measurement.

1-1c Types of Relationships

A **relationship** refers to the correspondence between two variables (see the section on variables later in this chapter). When you talk about types of relationships, you can mean that in at least two ways: the *nature* of the relationship or the *pattern* of it.

The Nature of a Relationship Although all relationships tell about the correspondence between two variables, one special type of relationship holds that the two variables are not only in correspondence, but that one *causes* the other. This is the key distinction between a simple correlational relationship and a causal relationship. A **correlational relationship** simply says that two things perform in a synchronized manner. For instance, economists often talk of a correlation between inflation and unemployment. When inflation is high, unemployment also tends to be high. When inflation is low, unemployment also tends to be low. The two variables are correlated; but knowing that two variables are correlated does not tell whether one *causes* the other. It is documented, for instance, that there is a correlation between the number of roads built in Europe and the number of children born in the United States. Does that mean that if fewer children are desired in the United States there should be a cessation of road building in Europe? Or, does it mean that if there aren't enough roads in Europe, U.S. citizens should be encouraged to have more babies? Of course not. (At least, I hope not.) While there is a relationship between the number of roads built and the number of babies, it's not likely that the relationship is a causal one.

This leads to consideration of what is often termed the **third-variable problem**. In this example, it may be that a third variable is causing both the building of roads and the birthrate and causing the correlation that is observed. For instance, perhaps the general world economy is responsible for both. When the economy is good, more roads are built in Europe and more children are born in the United States. The key lesson here is that you have to be careful when you interpret correlations. If you observe a correlation between the number of hours students use the computer to study and their grade point averages (with high computer users getting higher grades), you *cannot* assume that the relationship is causal—that computer use improves grades. In this case, the third variable might be socioeconomic status—richer students, who have greater resources at their disposal, tend to both use computers and make better grades. Resources drive both use and grades; computer use doesn't cause the change in the grade point averages.

cross-sectional
A study that takes place at a single point in time.

longitudinal
A study that takes place over time.

repeated measures
Two or more waves of measurement over time.

time series
Many waves of measurement over time.

relationship
Refers to the correspondence between two variables.

correlational relationship
Two variables that perform in a synchronized manner.

third-variable problem
An unobserved variable that accounts for a correlation between two variables.

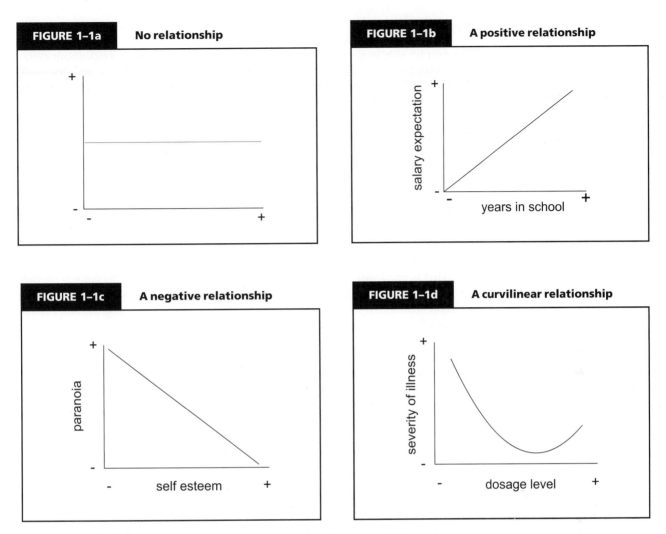

FIGURE 1–1a   No relationship

FIGURE 1–1b   A positive relationship

salary expectation

years in school

FIGURE 1–1c   A negative relationship

paranoia

self esteem

FIGURE 1–1d   A curvilinear relationship

severity of illness

dosage level

Patterns of Relationships Several terms describe the major different types of patterns one might find in a relationship. First, there is the case of *no relationship* at all. When there is no relationship between two variables, if you know the values on one variable, you don't know anything about the values on the other. For instance, I suspect that there is no relationship between the length of the lifeline on your hand and your grade point average. If I know your GPA, I don't have any idea how long your lifeline is. Figure 1–1a shows the case where there is no relationship.

Then, there is the **positive relationship**. In a positive relationship, high values on one variable are associated with high values on the other and low values on one are associated with low values on the other. Figure 1–1b shows an idealized positive relationship between years of education and the salary one might expect to be making.

On the other hand, a **negative relationship** implies that high values on one variable are associated with low values on the other. This is also sometimes termed an *inverse* relationship. Figure 1–1c shows an idealized negative relationship between a measure of self-esteem and a measure of paranoia in psychiatric patients.

These are the simplest types of relationships that might typically be estimated in research. However, the pattern of a relationship can be more complex than these. For instance, Figure 1–1d shows a relationship that changes over the range of both variables, a curvilinear relationship. In this example, the horizontal axis represents dosage of a drug for an illness and the vertical axis represents a severity of illness measure. As the dosage rises, the severity of illness goes down; but at some point, the patient begins to experience negative side effects associated with too high a dosage, and the severity of illness begins to increase again.

positive relationship
A relationship between variables in which high values for one variable are associated with high values on another variable, and low values are associated with low values.

negative relationship
A relationship between variables in which high values for one variable are associated with low values on another variable.

1-1d Variables

variable
Any entity that can take on different values. For instance, age can be considered a variable because age can take on different values for different people at different times.

quantitative variable
Data in the form of numbers.

qualitative variable
A variable that is not in numerical form.

You won't be able to do much in research unless you know how to talk about variables. A **variable** is any entity that can take on different values. Okay, so what does that mean? Anything that can vary can be considered a variable. For instance, *age* can be considered a variable because age can take different values for different people or for the same person at different times. Similarly, *country* can be considered a variable because a person's country can be assigned a value.

Variables aren't always **quantitative data** or numerical. The variable *gender* consists of two text values: *male* and *female*, which we would naturally think of as a **qualitative variable** because we are distinguishing between qualities of a variable rather than quantities. If it is useful, quantitative values can be assigned instead of (or in place of) the text values, but it's not necessary to assign numbers for something to be a variable. It's also important to realize that variables aren't the only things measured in the traditional sense. For instance, in much social research and in program evaluation, the treatment or program is considered to consist of one or more variables. (That is, the cause can be considered a variable.) An educational program can have varying amounts of time on task, classroom settings, student-teacher ratios, and so on. Therefore, even the program can be considered a variable, which can be made up of a number of subvariables.

attribute
A specific value of a variable. For instance, the variable sex or gender has two attributes: male and female.

An **attribute** is a specific value on a variable. For instance, the variable *sex* or *gender* has two attributes: male and female, or, the variable *agreement* might be defined as having five attributes:

1 = strongly disagree
2 = disagree
3 = neutral
4 = agree
5 = strongly agree

Another important distinction having to do with the term *variable* is the distinction between an independent and dependent variable. This distinction is particularly relevant when you are investigating cause-effect relationships. It took me the longest time to learn this distinction. (Of course, I'm someone who gets confused about the signs for arrivals and departures at airports—do I go to arrivals because I'm arriving at the airport or does the person I'm picking up go to arrivals because they're arriving on the plane?) I originally thought that an independent variable was one that would be free to vary or respond to some program or treatment and that a dependent variable must be one that *depends* on my efforts (that is, it's the *treatment*). However, this is entirely backward! In fact *the **independent variable** is what you (or nature) manipulates*—a treatment or program or cause. The **dependent variable** *is what you presume to be affected by the independent variable*—your effects or outcomes. For example, if you are studying the effects of a new educational program on student achievement, the program is the independent variable and your measures of achievement are the dependent ones.

independent variable
The variable that you manipulate. For instance, a program or treatment is typically an independent variable.

dependent variable
The variable affected by the independent variable; for example, the outcome.

exhaustive
The property of a variable that occurs when you include all possible answerable responses.

mutually exclusive
The property of a variable that ensures that the respondent is not able to assign two attributes simultaneously. For example, gender is a variable with mutually exclusive options if it is impossible for the respondents to simultaneously claim to be both male and female.

Finally, there are two traits of variables that should always be achieved. Each variable should be **exhaustive**, meaning that it should include all possible answerable responses. For instance, if the variable is *religion* and the only options are *Protestant*, *Jewish*, and *Muslim*, there are quite a few religions that haven't been included. The list does not exhaust all possibilities. On the other hand, if you exhaust all the possibilities with some variables—religion being one of them—you would simply have too many responses. The way to deal with this is to explicitly list the most common attributes and then use a general category like *Other* to account for all remaining ones. In addition to being exhaustive, the attributes of a variable should be **mutually exclusive**, meaning that no respondent should be able to have two attributes simultaneously. While this might seem obvious, it is often rather tricky in practice. For instance, you might be tempted to represent the variable *Employment Status* with the two attributes *employed* and *unemployed*. However, these attributes are not necessarily mutually exclusive—a person who is looking for a second job while employed might be able legitimately to check both attributes! But don't researchers often use questions on surveys that ask the respondent to check all that apply and then list a series of categories? Yes, but technically speaking, each of the categories in a question like that is its own variable and is treated dichotomously as either checked or unchecked—as attributes that *are* mutually exclusive.

1-1e Hypotheses

A **hypothesis** is a specific statement of prediction. It describes in concrete (rather than theoretical) terms what you expect to happen in your study. Not all studies have hypotheses. Sometimes a study is designed to be exploratory (see Section 1-2b, Deduction and Induction, later in this chapter). There is no formal hypothesis, and perhaps the purpose of the study is to explore some area more thoroughly to develop some specific hypothesis or prediction that can be tested in future research. A single study may have one or many hypotheses.

Actually, whenever I talk about a hypothesis, I am really thinking simultaneously about *two* hypotheses. Let's say that you predict that there will be a relationship between two variables in your study. The way to set up the hypothesis test is to formulate two hypothesis statements: one that describes your prediction and one that describes all the other possible outcomes with respect to the hypothesized relationship. Your prediction is that variable A and variable B will be related. (You don't care whether it's a positive or negative relationship.) Then the only other possible outcome would be that variable A and variable B are *not* related. Usually, the hypothesis that you support (your prediction) is called the **alternative hypothesis**, and the hypothesis that describes the remaining possible outcomes is termed the **null hypothesis**. Sometimes a notation such as H_A or H_1 is used to represent the alternative hypothesis or your prediction, and H_O or H_0 to represent the null case. You have to be careful here, though. In some studies, your prediction might well be that there will be no difference or change. In this case, you are essentially trying to find support for the null hypothesis and you are opposed to the alternative.

If your prediction specifies a direction, the null hypothesis is the no-difference prediction *and* the prediction of the opposite direction. This is called a **one-tailed hypothesis**. For instance, let's imagine that you are investigating the effects of a new employee-training program and that you believe one of the outcomes will be that there will be *less* employee absenteeism. Your two hypotheses might be stated something like this:

The null hypothesis for this study is

H_O: As a result of the XYZ company employee-training program, there will either be no significant difference in employee absenteeism or there will be a significant *increase*,

which is tested against the alternative hypothesis:

H_A: As a result of the XYZ company employee-training program, there will be a significant *decrease* in employee absenteeism.

In Figure 1–2, this situation is illustrated graphically. The alternative hypothesis—your prediction that the program will decrease absenteeism—is shown there. The null must account for the other two possible conditions: no difference, or an increase in absenteeism. The figure shows a hypothetical distribution of absenteeism differences. The term *one-tailed* refers to the tail of the distribution on the outcome variable.

When your prediction does *not* specify a direction, you have a **two-tailed hypothesis**. For instance, let's assume you are studying a new drug treatment for depression. The drug has gone through some initial animal trials but has not yet been tested on humans. You believe (based on theory and the previous research) that

hypothesis
A specific statement of prediction.

alternative hypothesis
A specific statement of prediction that usually states what you expect will happen in your study.

null hypothesis
The hypothesis that describes the possible outcomes other than the alternative hypothesis. Usually, the null hypothesis

one-tailed hypothesis
A hypothesis that specifies a direction; for example, when your hypothesis predicts that your program will increase the outcome.

two-tailed hypothesis
A hypothesis that does not specify a direction. For example, if your hypothesis is that your program or intervention will have an effect on an outcome, but you are unwilling to specify whether that effect will be positive or negative, you are using a two-tailed hypothesis.

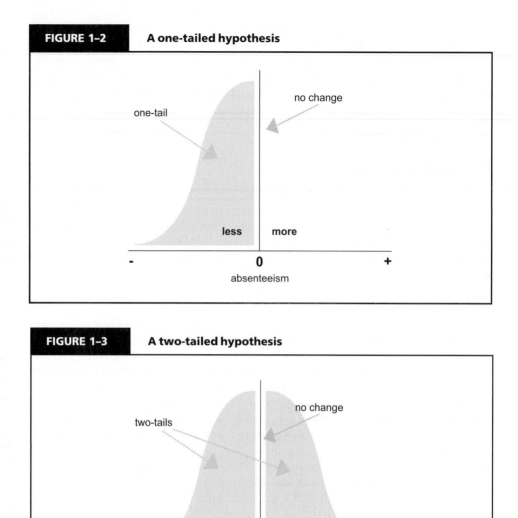

FIGURE 1–2   A one-tailed hypothesis

FIGURE 1–3   A two-tailed hypothesis

the drug will have an effect, but you are not confident enough to hypothesize a direction and say the drug will reduce depression. (After all, you've seen more than enough promising drug treatments come along that eventually were shown to have severe side effects that actually worsened symptoms.) In this case, you might state the two hypotheses like this:

The null hypothesis for this study is:

H_O: As a result of 300mg/day of the ABC drug, there will be no significant difference in depression,

which is tested against the alternative hypothesis:

H_A: As a result of 300mg/day of the ABC drug, there will be a significant difference in depression.

Figure 1–3 illustrates this two-tailed prediction for this case. Again, notice that the term *two-tailed* refers to the tails of the distribution for your outcome variable.

The important thing to remember about stating hypotheses is that you formulate your prediction (directional or not), and then you formulate a second hypothesis that is mutually exclusive of the first and incorporates all possible alternative outcomes for that case. When your study analysis is completed, the idea is that you will have to choose between the two hypotheses. If your prediction was correct, you would (usually) reject the null hypothesis and accept the alternative. If your original prediction was not supported in the data, you will accept the null hypothesis and reject the alternative. The logic of hypothesis testing is based on these two basic principles:

- Two mutually exclusive hypothesis statements that, together, exhaust all possible outcomes need to be developed.
- The hypotheses must be tested so that one is necessarily accepted and the other rejected.

Okay, I know it's a convoluted, awkward, and formalistic way to ask research questions, but it encompasses a long tradition in statistics called the **hypothetical-deductive model**, and sometimes things are just done because they're traditions. And anyway, if all of this hypothesis testing was easy enough that anybody could understand it, how do you think statisticians and methodologists would stay employed?

1-1f Types of Data

Data will be discussed in lots of places in this text, but here I just want to make a fundamental distinction between two types of data: qualitative and quantitative. Typically data is called **quantitative data** if it is in numerical form and **qualitative data** if it is not. Notice that qualitative data could be much more than just words or text. Photographs, videos, sound recordings, and so on, can be considered qualitative data.

Personally, while I find the distinction between qualitative and quantitative data to have some utility, I think most people draw too hard a distinction, and that can lead to all sorts of confusion. In some areas of social research, the qualitative-quantitative distinction has led to protracted arguments with the proponents of each arguing the superiority of their kind of data over the other. The quantitative types argue that their data is hard, rigorous, credible, and scientific. The qualitative proponents counter that their data is sensitive, nuanced, detailed, and contextual.

For many of us in social research, this kind of polarized debate has become less than productive. In addition, it obscures the fact that qualitative and quantitative data are intimately related to each other. *All quantitative data is based upon qualitative judgments; and all qualitative data can be described and manipulated numerically.* For instance, think about a common quantitative measure in social research—a self-esteem scale where the respondent rates a set of self-esteem statements on a 1-to-5 scale. Even though the result is a quantitative score, think of how qualitative such an instrument is. The researchers who developed such instruments had to make countless judgments in constructing them: how to define self-esteem; how to distinguish it from other related concepts; how to word potential scale items; how to make sure the items would be understandable to the intended respondents; what kinds of contexts they could be used in; what kinds of cultural and language constraints might be present; and so on. Researchers who decide to use such a scale in their studies have to make another set of judgments: how well the scale measures the intended concept; how reliable or consistent it is; how appropriate it is for the research context and intended respondents; and so on. Believe it or not, even the respondents make many judgments when filling out such a scale: what various terms and phrases mean; why the researcher is giving this scale to them; how much energy and effort they want to expend to complete it; and so on. Even the consumers and readers of the research make judgments about the self-esteem measure and its appropriateness in that research context. What may look like a simple, straightforward, cut-and-dried quantitative measure is actually based on lots of qualitative judgments made by many different people.

On the other hand, all qualitative information can be easily converted into quantitative, and many times doing so would add considerable value to your research. The simplest way to do this is to divide the qualitative information into categories and number them! I know that sounds trivial, but even that simple

hypothetical-deductive model
A model in which two mutually exclusive hypotheses that together exhaust all possible outcomes are tested, such that if one hypothesis is accepted, the second must therefore be rejected.

quantitative data
The numerical representation of some object. A quantitative variable is any variable that is measured using numbers.

qualitative data
Data in which the variables are not in a numerical form, but are in the form of text, photographs, sound bytes, and so on.

FIGURE 1–4	Example of how you can convert qualitative sorting information into quantitative data

Sorting of 10 qualitative items

5 8 | 6 2 1 9 | 3 4 | 10 | 7

		1	2	3	4	5	6	7	8	9	10
	1	1	1	0	0	0	1	0	0	1	0
	2	1	1	0	0	0	1	0	0	1	0
Binary	3	0	0	1	1	0	0	0	0	0	0
Square	4	0	0	1	1	0	0	0	0	0	0
Similarity	5	0	0	0	0	1	0	0	1	0	0
Matrix for the	6	1	1	0	0	0	1	0	0	1	0
sort	7	0	0	0	0	0	0	1	0	0	0
	8	0	0	0	0	1	0	0	1	0	0
	9	1	1	0	0	0	1	0	0	1	0
	10	0	0	0	0	0	0	0	0	0	1

nominal enumeration can enable you to organize and process qualitative information more efficiently. As an example, you might take text information (say, excerpts from transcripts) and pile these excerpts into piles of similar statements. When you perform something as easy as this simple grouping or piling task, you can describe the results quantitatively. For instance, Figure 1–4 shows that if you had ten statements and grouped these into five piles, you could describe the piles using a 10 × 10 table of 0s and 1s. If two statements were placed together in the same pile, you would put a 1 in their row-column juncture. If two statements were placed in different piles, you would use a 0. The resulting matrix or table describes the grouping of the ten statements in terms of their similarity. Even though the data in this example consists of qualitative statements (one per card), the result of this simple qualitative procedure (grouping similar excerpts into the same piles) is quantitative in nature. "So what?" you ask. Once you have the data in numerical form, you can manipulate it numerically. For instance, you could have five different judges sort the ten excerpts and obtain a 0-1 matrix like this for each judge. Then you could average the five matrices into a single one that shows the proportions of judges who grouped each pair together. This proportion could be considered an estimate of the similarity (across independent judges) of the excerpts. While this might not seem too exciting or useful, it is exactly this kind of procedure that is used as an integral part of the process of developing concept maps of ideas for groups of people (something that *is* useful). Concept mapping is described later in this chapter.

1-1g The Unit of Analysis

unit of analysis
The entity that you are analyzing in your analysis; for example, individuals, groups, or social interactions.

One of the most important ideas in a research project is the **unit of analysis**. The unit of analysis is the major entity that you are analyzing in your study. For instance, any of the following could be a unit of analysis in a study:

- Individuals
- Groups
- Artifacts (books, photos, newspapers)

- Geographical units (town, census tract, state)
- Social interactions (dyadic relations, divorces, arrests)

Why is it called the unit of analysis and not something else (like, the unit of sampling)? Because *it is the analysis you do in your study that determines what the unit is.* For instance, if you are comparing the children in two classrooms on achievement test scores, the unit is the individual child because you have a score for each child. On the other hand, if you are comparing the two classes on classroom climate, your unit of analysis is the group, in this case the classroom, because you have a classroom climate score only for the class as a whole and not for each individual student.

For different analyses in the same study, you may have different units of analysis. If you decide to base an analysis on student scores, the individual is the unit. However you might decide to compare average classroom performance. In this case, since the data that goes into the analysis is the average itself (and not the individuals' scores) the unit of analysis is actually the group. Even though you had data at the student level, you use aggregates in the analysis. In many areas of social research, these hierarchies of analysis units have become particularly important and have spawned a whole area of statistical analysis sometimes referred to as **hierarchical modeling**. This is true in education, for instance, where a researcher might compare classroom performance data but collect achievement data at the individual student level.

1-1h Research Fallacies

A *fallacy* is an error in reasoning, usually based on mistaken assumptions. Researchers are familiar with all the ways they could go wrong and the fallacies they are susceptible to. Here, I discuss two of the most important.

The **ecological fallacy** occurs when you make conclusions about individuals based only on analyses of group data. For instance, assume that you measured the math scores of a particular classroom and found that they had the highest average score in the district. Later (probably at the mall) you run into one of the kids from that class and you think to yourself, "She must be a math whiz." Aha! Fallacy! Just because she comes from the class with the highest *average* doesn't mean that she is automatically a high-scorer in math. She could be the lowest math scorer in a class that otherwise consists of math geniuses.

An **exception fallacy** is sort of the reverse of the ecological fallacy. It occurs when you reach a group conclusion on the basis of exceptional cases. This kind of fallacious reasoning is at the core of a lot of sexism and racism. The stereotype is of the guy who sees a woman make a driving error and concludes that women are terrible drivers. Wrong! Fallacy!

Both of these fallacies point to some of the traps that exist in research and in everyday reasoning. They also point out how important it is to do research. It is important to determine empirically how individuals perform, rather than simply rely on group averages. Similarly, it is important to look at whether there are correlations between certain behaviors and certain groups.

1-2 Philosophy of Research

You probably think of research as something abstract and complicated. It can be, but you'll see (I hope) that if you understand the different parts or phases of a research project and how these fit together, it's not nearly as complicated as it may seem at first glance. A research project has a well-known structure: a beginning, middle, and end. I introduce the basic phases of a research project in Section 1-2a, Structure of Research. Here, I also introduce some important distinctions in research: the different types of questions you can ask in a research project; and, the major components or parts of a research project.

hierarchical modeling
The incorporation of multiple units of analysis at different levels of a hierarchy within a single analytic model. For instance, in an educational study, you might want to compare student performance with teacher expectations. To examine this relationship would require hierarchical modeling because you are collecting data at both the teacher and student level.

ecological fallacy
Faulty reasoning that results from making conclusions about individuals based only on analyses of group data.

exception fallacy
A faulty conclusion reached as a result of basing a conclusion on exceptional or unique cases.

Before the modern idea of research emerged, there was a term for what philosophers used to call research: logical reasoning. So, it should come as no surprise that some of the basic distinctions in logic have carried over into contemporary research. In Section 1-2b, Deduction and Induction, I discuss how two major logical systems, the inductive and deductive methods of reasoning, are related to modern research.

Okay, you knew that no introduction would be complete without considering something having to do with assumptions and philosophy. (I thought I very cleverly snuck in the stuff about logic in the last paragraph.) All research is based on assumptions about how the world is perceived and how you can best come to understand it. Of course, nobody really *knows* how you can best understand the world, and philosophers have been arguing about that question for at least two millennia now, so all I'm going to do is look at how most contemporary social scientists approach the question of how you know about the world around you. Two major philosophical schools of thought are considered—positivism and post-positivism—that are especially important perspectives for contemporary social research. (I'm only considering positivism and post-positivism here because these are the major schools of thought. Forgive me for not considering the hotly debated alternatives like relativism, subjectivism, hermeneutics, deconstructivism, constructivism, feminism, and so on.)

Quality is one of the most important issues in research. I introduce the idea of validity to refer to the quality of various conclusions you might reach based on a research project. Here's where I have to give you the pitch about validity. When I mention validity, most students roll their eyes, curl up into a fetal position, or go to sleep. They think validity is just something abstract and philosophical (and I guess it is at some level). But I think if you can understand **validity**—the principles that are used to judge the quality of research—you'll be able to do much more than just complete a research project. You'll be able to be a virtuoso at research because you'll have an understanding of *why* you need to do certain things to ensure quality. You won't just be plugging in standard procedures you learned in school—sampling method X, measurement tool Y—you'll be able to help create the next generation of research technology.

validity
The best available approximation of the truth of a given proposition, inference, or conclusion.

1-2a Structure of Research

Most research projects share the same general structure. You might think of this structure as following the shape of an hourglass as shown in Figure 1–5. The research process usually starts with a broad area of interest, the initial problem that the researcher wishes to study. For instance, the researcher could be interested in how to use computers to improve the performance of students in mathematics, but this initial interest is far too broad to study in any single research project. (It might not even be addressable in a lifetime of research.) The researcher has to narrow the question down to one that can reasonably be studied in a research project. This might involve formulating a hypothesis or a focus question. For instance, the researcher might hypothesize that a particular method of computer instruction in math will improve the ability of elementary school students in a specific district. At the narrowest point of the research hourglass, the researcher is engaged in direct measurement or observation of the question of interest. This is what makes research **empirical**, meaning that it is based on observations and measurements of reality—on what you perceive of the world around you.

empirical
Based on direct observations and measurements of reality.

Once the basic data is collected, the researcher begins trying to understand it, usually by analyzing it in a variety of ways. Even for a single hypothesis, there are a number of analyses a researcher might typically conduct. At this point, the researcher begins to formulate some initial conclusions about what happened as a result of the computerized math program. Finally, the researcher often attempts to address the original broad question of interest by generalizing from the results of

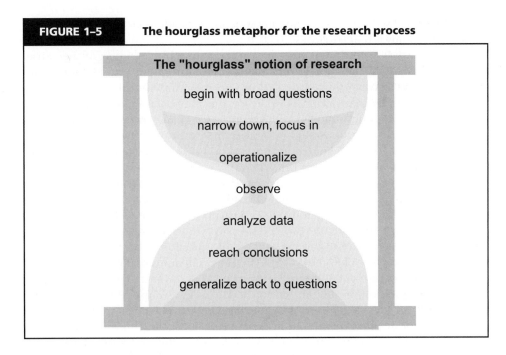

| **FIGURE 1–5** | **The hourglass metaphor for the research process** |

The "hourglass" notion of research

begin with broad questions

narrow down, focus in

operationalize

observe

analyze data

reach conclusions

generalize back to questions

this specific study to other related situations. For instance, on the basis of strong results indicating that the math program had a positive effect on student performance, the researcher might conclude that other school districts similar to the one in the study might expect similar results.

Components of a Study What are the basic components or parts of a research study? Here, I'll describe the basic components involved in a causal study. Because causal studies presuppose descriptive and relational questions, many of the components of causal studies will also be found in descriptive and relational studies.

Most social research originates from some general problem or question. You might, for instance, be interested in which programs enable the unemployed to get jobs. Usually, the problem is broad enough that you could not hope to address it adequately in a single research study. Consequently, the problem is typically narrowed down to a more specific **research question** that can be addressed. Social research is **theoretical**, meaning that much of it is concerned with developing, exploring, or testing the theories or ideas that social researchers have about how the world operates. The research question is often stated in the context of one or more theories that have been advanced to address the problem. For instance, you might have the theory that ongoing support services are needed to assure that the newly employed remain employed. The research question is the central issue being addressed in the study and is often phrased in the language of theory. For instance, a research question might be:

> Is a program of supported employment more effective (than no program at all) at keeping newly employed persons on the job?

The problem with such a question is that it is still too general to be studied directly. Consequently, in most research, an even more specific statement, called a **hypothesis** is developed that describes in *operational* terms exactly what you think will happen in the study (see Section 1-1e, Hypotheses). For instance, the hypothesis for your employment study might be something like the following:

> The Metropolitan Supported Employment Program will significantly increase rates of employment after six months for persons who are newly employed (after being out of work for at least 1 year) compared with persons who receive no comparable program.

research question
The central issue being addressed in the study, which is typically phrased in the language of theory.

theoretical
Pertaining to theory. Social research is theoretical, meaning that much of it is concerned with developing, exploring, or testing the theories or ideas that social researchers have about how the world operates.

hypothesis
A specific statement of prediction.

Notice that this hypothesis is specific enough that a reader can understand quite well what the study is trying to assess.

In causal studies, there are at least two major variables of interest: the cause and the effect. Usually the cause is some type of event, program, or treatment. A distinction is made between causes that the researcher can control (such as a program) versus causes that occur naturally or outside the researcher's influence (such as a change in interest rates, or the occurrence of an earthquake). The effect is the outcome that you wish to study. For both the cause and effect, a distinction is made between the idea of them (the *construct*) and how they are actually manifested in reality. For instance, when you think about what a program of support services for the newly employed might be, you are thinking of the construct. On the other hand, the real world is not always what you think it is. In research, a distinction is made between your view of an entity (the construct) and the entity as it exists (the **operationalization**). Ideally, the two should agree. Social research is always conducted in a social context. Researchers ask people questions, observe families interacting, or measure the opinions of people in a city. The units that participate in the project are important components of any research project. Units are directly related to the question of sampling. In most projects, it's impossible to involve all of the people it is desirable to involve. For instance, in studying a program of support services for the newly employed, you can't possibly include in your study everyone in the world, or even in the country, who is newly employed. Instead, you have to try to obtain a representative sample of such people. When sampling, a distinction is made between the theoretical population of interest and the final sample that is actually included in the study. Usually the term *units* refers to the *people* who are sampled and from whom information is gathered, but for some projects the units are organizations, groups, or geographical entities like cities or towns. Sometimes the sampling strategy is multilevel; a number of cities are selected and within them families are sampled.

In causal studies, the interest is in the effects of some cause on one or more *outcomes*. The outcomes are directly related to the *research problem*; usually the greatest interest is in outcomes that are most reflective of the problem. In the hypothetical supported-employment study, you would probably be most interested in measures of employment—is the person currently employed, or, what is his or her rate of absenteeism?

Finally, in a causal study, the effects of the cause of interest (for example, the program) are usually compared to other conditions (for example, another program or no program at all). Thus, a key component in a causal study concerns how you decide which units (people) receive the program and which are placed in an alternative condition. This issue is directly related to the research design that you use in the study. One of the central themes in research design is determining how people wind up in or are placed in various programs or treatments that you are comparing. These, then, are the major components in a causal study:

- The research problem.
- The research question.
- The program (cause).
- The units.
- The outcomes (effect).
- The design.

1-2b Deduction and Induction

In logic, a distinction is often made between two broad methods of reasoning known as the deductive and inductive approaches.

Deductive reasoning works from the more general to the more specific (see Figure 1–6). Sometimes this is informally called a *top-down approach*. You might

---

operationalization
The act of translating a construct into its manifestation—for example, translating the idea of your treatment or program into the actual program, or translating the idea of what you want to measure into the real measure. The result is also referred to as an *operationalization;* that is, you might describe your actual program as an *operationalized program*.

deductive
Top-down reasoning that works from the more general to the more specific.

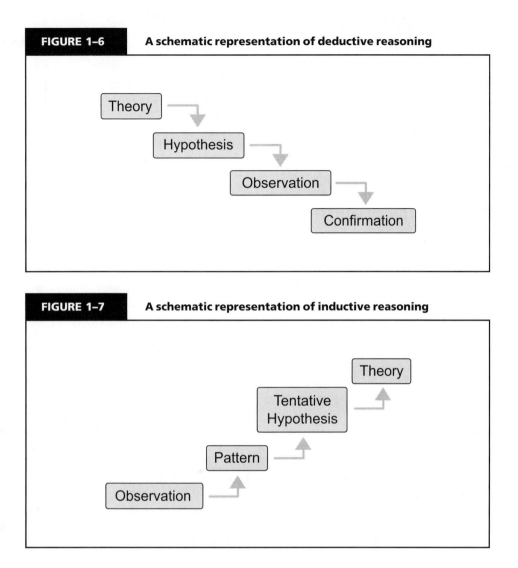

FIGURE 1–6 **A schematic representation of deductive reasoning**

Theory → Hypothesis → Observation → Confirmation

FIGURE 1–7 **A schematic representation of inductive reasoning**

Observation → Pattern → Tentative Hypothesis → Theory

begin with thinking up a *theory* about your topic of interest. You then narrow that down into more specific hypotheses that you can test. You narrow down even further when you collect *observations* to address the hypotheses. This ultimately leads you to be able to test the hypotheses with specific data—a *confirmation* (or not) of your original theories.

Inductive reasoning works the other way, moving from specific observations to broader generalizations and theories (see Figure 1–7). Informally, this is sometimes called a *bottom-up approach*. (Please note that it's bottom up and *not* bottoms up, which is the kind of thing the bartender says to customers when he's trying to close for the night!) In inductive reasoning, you begin with specific observations and measures, begin detecting patterns and regularities, formulate some tentative hypotheses that you can explore, and finally end up developing some general conclusions or theories.

Deductive and inductive reasoning correspond to other ideas that have been around for a long time: *nomothetic,* which denotes laws or rules that pertain to the general case (*nomos* in Greek); and *idiographic,* which refers to laws or rules that relate to individuals. In any event, the point here is that most social research is concerned with the nomothetic—the general case—rather than the individual. Individuals are often studied, but usually there is interest in generalizing to more than just the individual.

These two methods of reasoning have a different feel to them when you're conducting research. Inductive reasoning, by its nature, is more open-ended and

inductive
Bottom-up reasoning that begins with specific observations and measures and ends up as general conclusion or theory.

exploratory, especially at the beginning. Deductive reasoning is narrower in nature and is concerned with testing or confirming hypotheses. Even though a particular study may look like it's purely deductive (for example, an experiment designed to test the hypothesized effects of some treatment on some outcome), most social research involves both inductive and deductive reasoning processes at some time in the project. In fact, it doesn't take a rocket scientist to see that you could assemble the two graphs from Figures 1–6 and 1–7 into a single circular one that continually cycles from theories down to observations and back up again to theories. Even in the most constrained experiment, the researchers might observe patterns in the data that lead them to develop new theories.

1-2c Positivism and Post-Positivism

Let's start this brief discussion of philosophy of science with a simple distinction between epistemology and methodology. The term **epistemology** comes from the Greek word *epistêmê*, their term for knowledge. In simple terms, epistemology is the philosophy of knowledge or of how you come to know. **Methodology** is also concerned with how you come to know, but is much more practical in nature. Methodology is focused on the specific ways—the methods—you can use to try to understand the world better. Epistemology and methodology are intimately related: the former involves the *philosophy* of how you come to know the world and the latter involves the *practice*.

When most people in society think about science, they think about someone in a white lab coat working at a lab bench mixing up chemicals. They think of science as boring and cut-and-dried, and they think of the scientist as narrow-minded and esoteric (the ultimate nerd—think of the humorous but nonetheless mad scientist in the *Back to the Future* movies, for instance). Many of the stereotypes about science come from a period when science was dominated by a particular philosophy—positivism—that tended to support some of these views. Here, I want to suggest (no matter what the movie industry may think) that science has moved on in its thinking into an era of post-positivism, where many of those stereotypes of the scientist no longer hold up.

Let's begin by considering what positivism is. In its broadest sense, **positivism** is a rejection of metaphysics (I leave it to you to look up that term if you're not familiar with it). Positivism holds that the goal of knowledge is simply to describe the phenomena that are experienced. The purpose of science is simply to stick to what can be observed and measured. Knowledge of anything beyond that, a positivist would hold, is impossible. When I think of positivism (and the related philosophy of logical positivism), I think of the behaviorists in mid-20th century psychology. These were the mythical rat runners who believed that psychology could study only what could be directly observed and measured. Since emotions, thoughts, and so on, can't be directly observed (although it may be possible to measure some of the physical and physiological accompaniments), these were not legitimate topics for a scientific psychology. B. F. Skinner argued that psychology needed to concentrate only on the positive and negative reinforcers of behavior to predict how people will behave; everything else in between (like what the person is thinking) is irrelevant because it can't be measured.

In a positivist view of the world, science was seen as the way to get at truth, to understand the world well enough to predict and control it. The world and the universe were deterministic; they operated by laws of cause and effect that scientists could discern if they applied the unique approach of the scientific method. Science was largely a mechanistic or mechanical affair. Scientists use deductive reasoning to postulate theories that they can test. Based on the results of their studies, they may learn that their theory doesn't fit the facts well and so they need to revise their theory to better predict reality. The positivist believed in *empiricism*—the idea that observation and measurement was the core of the scientific endeavor. The key

epistemology
Is the philosophy of knowledge or of how you come to know.

methodology
The methods you use to try to understand the world better.

positivism
The philosophical position that the only meaningful inferences are ones that can be verified through experience or direct measurement. Positivism is often associated with the stereotype of the hard-headed, lab-coat scientist who refuses to believe in something if it can't be seen or measured directly.

approach of the scientific method is the experiment, the attempt to discern natural laws through direct manipulation and observation.

Okay, I am exaggerating the positivist position (although you may be amazed at how close to this some of them actually came) to make a point. Things have changed in the typical views of science since the middle part of the 20th century. Probably the most important has been the shift away from positivism into what is termed *post-positivism*. By post-positivism, I don't mean a slight adjustment to or revision of the positivist position; **post-positivism** is a wholesale rejection of the central tenets of positivism. A post-positivist might begin by recognizing that the way scientists think and work and the way you think in your everyday life are not distinctly different. Scientific reasoning and common sense reasoning are essentially the same process. There is no essential difference between the two, only a difference in degree. Scientists, for example, follow specific procedures to assure that observations are verifiable, accurate, and consistent. In everyday reasoning, you don't always proceed so carefully. (Although, if you think about it, when the stakes are high, even in everyday life you become much more cautious about measurement. Think of the way most responsible parents keep continuous watch over their infants, noticing details that nonparents would never detect.)

In a post-positivist view of science, certainty is no longer regarded as attainable. Thus, much contemporary social research is probabilistic, or based on probabilities. The inferences made in social research have *probabilities* associated with them; they are seldom meant to be considered as covering laws that pertain to all cases. Part of the reason statistics has become so dominant in social research is that it enables the estimation of the probabilities for the situations being studied.

One of the most common forms of post-positivism is a philosophy called **critical realism**. A critical realist believes that there is a reality independent of a person's thinking about it that science can study. (This is in contrast with a **subjectivist**, who would hold that there is no external reality—each of us is making this all up.) Positivists were also realists. The difference is that the post-positivist critical realist recognizes that all observation is fallible and has error and that all theory is revisable. In other words, the *critical* realist is critical of a person's ability to know *reality* with certainty. Whereas the positivist believed that the goal of science was to uncover the truth, the post-positivist critical realist believes that the goal of science is to hold steadfastly to *the goal of getting it right about reality, even though this goal can never be perfectly achieved.*

Because all measurement is fallible, the post-positivist emphasizes the importance of multiple measures and observations, each of which may possess different types of error, and the need to use *triangulation* across these multiple error sources to try to get a better bead on what's happening in reality. The post-positivist also believes that all observations are theory-laden and that scientists (and everyone else, for that matter) are inherently biased by their cultural experiences, worldviews, and so on. This is not cause to despair, however. Just because I have my worldview based on my experiences and you have yours doesn't mean that it is impossible to translate from each other's experiences or understand each other. That is, post-positivism rejects the relativist idea of the incommensurability of different perspectives, the idea that people can never understand each other because they come from different experiences and cultures. Most post-positivists are **constructivists** who believe that you construct your view of the world based on your perceptions of it. Because perception and observation are fallible, all constructions must be imperfect. So what is meant by *objectivity* in a post-positivist world? Positivists believed that objectivity was a characteristic that resided in the individual scientist. Scientists are responsible for putting aside their biases and beliefs and seeing the world as it really is. Post-positivists reject the idea that any individual can see the world perfectly as it really is. Everyone is biased and all observations are affected (theory-laden). The best hope for achieving objectivity is to triangulate across multiple fallible perspectives. Thus, objectivity is not the characteristic of an individual; it is inherently a

post-positivism
The rejection of positivism in favor of a position that one can make reasonable inferences about phenomena based upon theoretical reasoning combined with experience-based evidence.

critical realism
The belief that there is an external reality independent of a person's thinking (realism) but that we can never know that reality with perfect accuracy (critical).

subjectivist
The belief that there is no external reality and that the world as you see it is solely a creation of your own mind.

constructivists
Constructivist are people who hold a philosophical position that maintains that reality is a conceptual construction. In constructivism, the emphasis is placed on understanding how we construe the world. Constructivists may be realists (believe there is an external reality that we imperfectly apprehend and construct our view of) or subjectivists (believe that all constructions are mediated by subjective experience).

social phenomenon. It is what multiple individuals are trying to achieve when they criticize each other's work. Objectivity is never achieved perfectly, but it can be approached. The best way to improve objectivity is to work publicly within the context of a broader contentious community of truth-seekers (including other scientists) who criticize each other's work. The theories that survive such intense scrutiny are a bit like the species that survive in the evolutionary struggle. (This theory is sometimes called **evolutionary epistemology** or the **natural selection theory of knowledge** and holds that ideas have survival value and that knowledge evolves through a process of variation, selection, and retention.) These theories have adaptive value and are probably as close as the human species can come to being objective and understanding reality.

evolutionary epistemology or natural selection theory of knowledge
A theory that ideas have survival value and that knowledge evolves through a process of variation, selection, and retention.

Clearly, all of this stuff is not for the faint of heart. I've seen many a graduate student get lost in the maze of philosophical assumptions that contemporary philosophers of science argue about. Don't think that I believe this is not important stuff; but, in the end, I tend to turn pragmatist on these matters. Philosophers have been debating these issues for thousands of years, and there is every reason to believe that they will continue to debate them for thousands of years more. Practicing researchers should check in on this debate from time to time. (Perhaps every hundred years or so would be about right.) Researchers should think about the assumptions they make about the world when they conduct research; but in the meantime, they can't wait for the philosophers to settle the matter. After all, they do have their own work to do.

1-2d Introduction to Validity

Validity can be defined as the best available approximation to the truth of a given proposition, inference, or conclusion. The first thing to ask is: "validity of *what?*" When people think about validity in research, they tend to think in terms of research components. You might say that a measure is a valid one, that a valid sample was drawn, or that the design had strong validity, but all of those statements are technically incorrect. Measures, samples, and designs don't *have* validity—only propositions can be said to be valid. Technically, you should say that a measure leads to valid conclusions or that a sample enables valid inferences, and so on. It is a proposition, inference, or conclusion that can have validity.

Researchers make lots of different inferences or conclusions while conducting research. Many of these are related to the process of doing research and are not the major hypotheses of the study. Nevertheless, like the bricks that go into building a wall, these intermediate processes and methodological propositions provide the foundation for the substantive conclusions that they wish to address. For instance, virtually all social research involves measurement or observation, and, no matter what researchers measure or observe, they are concerned with whether they are measuring what they intend to measure or with how their observations are influenced by the circumstances in which they are made. They reach conclusions about the quality of their measures—conclusions that will play an important role in addressing the broader substantive issues of their study. When researchers talk about the validity of research, they are often referring to the many conclusions they reach about the quality of different parts of their research methodology.

Validity is typically subdivided into four types. Each type addresses a specific methodological question. To understand the types of validity, you have to know something about how researchers investigate a *research question*. Because all four validity types are really only operative when studying *causal* questions, I will use a causal study to set the context.

Figure 1–8 shows that two realms are involved in research. The first, on the top, is the land of theory. It is what goes on inside your head. It is where you keep your theories about how the world operates. The second, on the bottom, is the land of observations. It is the real world into which you translate your ideas: your programs, treatments, measures, and observations. When you conduct research, you are

---

| **FIGURE 1–8** | **The major realms and components of research** |

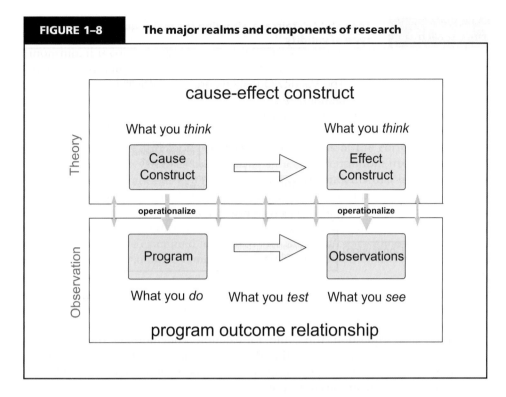

continually flitting back and forth between these two realms, between what you think about the world and what is going on in it. When you are investigating a cause-effect relationship, you have a theory (implicit or otherwise) of what the cause is (the **cause construct**). For instance, if you are testing a new educational program, you have an idea of what it would look like ideally. Similarly, on the effect side, you have an idea of what you are ideally trying to affect and measure (the **effect construct**). But each of these—the cause and the effect—have to be translated into real things, into a program or treatment and a measure or observational method. The term *operationalization* is used to describe the act of translating a construct into its manifestation. In effect, you take your idea and describe it as a series of operations or procedures. Now, instead of it being only an idea in your mind, it becomes a public entity that others can look at and examine for themselves. It is one thing, for instance, for you to say that you would like to measure self-esteem (a construct). But when you show a ten-item paper-and-pencil self-esteem measure that you developed for that purpose, others can look at it and understand more clearly what you intend by the term *self-esteem*.

Now, back to explaining the four validity types. They build on one another, with two of them (conclusion and internal) referring to the land of observation on the bottom of Figure 1–8, one of them (construct) emphasizing the linkages between the bottom and the top, and the last (external) being primarily concerned about the range of the theory on the top.

Imagine that you want to examine whether use of a World Wide Web virtual classroom improves student understanding of course material. Assume that you took these two constructs, the cause construct (the Web site) and the effect construct (understanding), and operationalized them, turned them into realities by constructing the Web site and a measure of knowledge of the course material. Here are the four validity types and the question each addresses:

- *Conclusion Validity:* In this study, is there a relationship between the two variables? In the context of the example, the question might be worded: in this study, is there a relationship between the Web site and knowledge of course material? There are several conclusions or inferences you might draw to

cause construct
Your abstract idea or theory of what the cause is in a cause-effect relationship you are investigating.

effect construct
Your abstract idea or theory of what the outcome is in a cause-effect relationship you are investigating.

against human experimentation at all costs versus allowing anyone who is willing to be the subject of an experiment.

1-3a The Language of Ethics

As in every other aspect of research, the area of ethics has its own vocabulary. In this section, I present some of the most important language regarding ethics in research.

The principle of **voluntary participation** requires that people not be coerced into participating in research. This is especially relevant where researchers had previously relied on captive audiences for their subjects—prisons, universities, and places like that. Closely related to the notion of voluntary participation is the requirement of **informed consent**. Essentially, this means that prospective research participants must be fully informed about the procedures and risks involved in research and must give their consent to participate. Ethical standards also require that researchers not put participants in a situation where they might be at *risk of harm* as a result of their participation. Harm can be defined as both physical and psychological.

Two standards are applied to help protect the privacy of research participants. Almost all research guarantees the participants **confidentiality;** they are assured that identifying information will not be made available to anyone who is not directly involved in the study. The stricter standard is the principle of **anonymity**, which essentially means that the participant will remain anonymous throughout the study, even to the researchers themselves. Clearly, the anonymity standard is a stronger guarantee of privacy, but it is sometimes difficult to accomplish, especially in situations where participants have to be measured at multiple time points (for example in a pre-post study). Increasingly, researchers have had to deal with the ethical issue of a person's **right to service**. Good research practice often requires the use of a no-treatment control group—a group of participants who do *not* get the treatment or program that is being studied. But when that treatment or program may have beneficial effects, persons assigned to the no-treatment control may feel their rights to equal access to services are being curtailed.

Even when clear ethical standards and principles exist, at times the need to do accurate research runs up against the rights of potential participants. No set of standards can possibly anticipate every ethical circumstance. Furthermore, there needs to be a procedure that assures that researchers will consider all relevant ethical issues in formulating research plans. To address such needs most institutions and organizations have formulated an **Institutional Review Board (IRB)**, a panel of persons who review grant proposals with respect to ethical implications and decide whether additional actions need to be taken to assure the safety and rights of participants. By reviewing proposals for research, IRBs also help protect the organization and the researcher against potential legal implications of neglecting to address important ethical issues of participants.

1-4 Conceptualizing

One of the most difficult aspects of research—and one of the least discussed—is how to develop the idea for the research project in the first place. In training students, most faculty members simply assume that if students read enough of the research in an area of interest, they will somehow magically be able to produce sensible ideas for further research. Now, that may be true. And heaven knows that's the way researchers have been doing this higher education thing for some time now; but it troubles me that they haven't been able to do a better job of helping their students learn *how* to formulate good research problems. One thing they can do (and some texts at least cover this at a surface level) is give students a better idea of how professional researchers typically generate research ideas. Some of this is introduced in the discussion of problem formulation that follows.

---

voluntary participation
For ethical reasons, researchers must ensure that study participants are taking part in a study voluntarily and are not coerced.

informed consent
A policy of informing study participants about the procedures and risks involved in research that ensures that all participants must give their consent to participate.

confidentiality
An assurance made to study participants that identifying information about them acquired through the study will not be released to anyone outside of the study.

anonymity
The assurance that no one, including the researchers, will be able to link data to a specific individual.

right to service
The ethical issue involved when participants do not receive a service that they would be eligible for if they were not in your study. For example, members of a control group might not receive a drug because they are in a study.

Institutional Review Board (IRB)
A panel of people who review research proposals with respect to ethical implications and decide whether additional actions need to be taken to assure the safety and rights of participants.

But maybe researchers can do even better than that. Why can't they turn some of their expertise in developing methods into methods that students and researchers can use to help them formulate ideas for research. I've been working on that area intensively for over a decade now, and I came up with a structured approach that groups can use to map out their ideas on any topic. This approach, called **concept mapping** (see Section 1-4b, Concept Mapping) can be used by research teams to help them clarify and map out the key research issues in an area, to help them operationalize the programs or interventions or the outcome measures for their study. The concept-mapping method isn't the only method around that might help researchers formulate good research problems and projects. Virtually any method that's used to help individuals and groups think more effectively would probably be useful in research formulation; but concept mapping is a good example of a structured approach and will introduce you to the idea of conceptualizing research in a more formalized way.

concept mapping
Two dimensional graphs of a group's ideas where ideas that are more similar are located closer together and those judged less similar are more distant. Concept maps are often used by a group to develop a conceptual framework for a research project.

1-4a Problem Formulation

> "Well begun is half done." —*Aristotle, quoting an old proverb*

Where Research Topics Come From So how do researchers come up with the idea for a research project? Probably one of the most common sources of research ideas is the experience of *practical problems in the field*. Many researchers are directly engaged in social, health, or human service program implementation and come up with their ideas based on what they see happening around them. Others aren't directly involved in service contexts but work with (or survey) people to learn what needs to be better understood. Many of the ideas would strike the outsider as silly or worse. For instance, in health services areas, there is great interest in the problem of back injuries among nursing staff. It's not necessarily the thing that comes first to mind when you think about the health care field; but if you reflect on it for a minute longer, it should be obvious that nurses and nursing staff do an awful lot of lifting while performing their jobs. They lift and push heavy equipment, and they lift and push heavy patients! If 5 or 10 out of every 100 nursing staff were to strain their backs on average over the period of 1 year, the costs would be enormous and that's pretty much what's happening. Even minor injuries can result in increased absenteeism. Major ones can result in lost jobs and expensive medical bills. The nursing industry figures this problem costs tens of millions of dollars annually in increased health care. In addition, the health-care industry has developed a number of approaches, many of them educational, to try to reduce the scope and cost of the problem. So, even though it might seem silly at first, many of these practical problems that arise in practice can lead to extensive research efforts.

Another source for research ideas is the *literature in your specific field*. Certainly, many researchers get ideas for research by reading the literature and thinking of ways to extend or refine previous research. Another type of literature that acts as a source of good research ideas is the **Requests for Proposals (RFPs)** that are published by government agencies and some companies. These RFPs describe some problem that the agency would like researchers to address; they are virtually handing the researcher an idea. Typically, the RFP describes the problem that needs addressing, the contexts in which it operates, the approach they would like you to take to investigate to address the problem, and the amount they would be willing to pay for such research. Clearly, there's nothing like potential research funding to get researchers to focus on a particular research topic.

Requests for Proposals (RFPs)
RFPs, published by government agencies and some companies, describe some problem that the agency would like researchers to address. Typically, the RFP describes the problem that needs addressing, the contexts in which it operates, the approach the agency would like you to take to investigate the problem, and the amount the agency would be willing to pay for such research.

Finally, let's not forget the fact that many researchers simply *think up their research* topic on their own. Of course, no one lives in a vacuum, so you would expect that the ideas you come up with on your own are influenced by your background, culture, education, and experiences.

Feasibility Soon after you get an idea for a study, reality begins to kick in and you begin to think about whether the study is feasible at all. Several major considerations come into play. Many of these involve making *trade-offs between rigor and practicality.* Performing a scientific study may force you to do things you wouldn't do normally. You might want to ask everyone who used an agency in the past year to fill in your evaluation survey only to find that there were thousands of people and it would be prohibitively expensive. Or, you might want to conduct an in-depth interview on your subject of interest only to learn that the typical participant in your study won't willingly take the hour that your interview requires. If you had unlimited resources and unbridled control over the circumstances, you would always be able to do the best quality research; but those ideal circumstances seldom exist, and researchers are almost always forced to look for the best trade-offs they can find to get the rigor they desire.

When you are determining the project's feasibility, you almost always need to bear in mind several practical considerations. First, you have to think about *how long the research will take* to accomplish. Second, you have to question whether any important *ethical constraints* require consideration. Third, you must determine whether you can acquire the *cooperation* needed to take the project to its successful conclusion. And finally, you must determine the degree to which the costs will be manageable. Failure to consider any of these factors can mean disaster later.

The Literature Review One of the most important early steps in a research project is the conducting of the literature review. This is also one of the most humbling experiences you're likely to have. Why? Because you're likely to find out that just about any worthwhile idea you will have has been thought of before, at least to some degree. I frequently have students who come to me complaining that they couldn't find anything in the literature that was related to their topic. And virtually every time they have said that, I was able to show them that was true only because they looked only for articles that were *exactly* the same as their research topic. A literature review is designed to identify related research, to set the current research project within a conceptual and theoretical context. When looked at that way, almost no topic is so new or unique that you can't locate relevant and informative related research.

Here are some tips about conducting the literature review. First, *concentrate your efforts on the scientific literature.* Try to determine what the most credible research journals are in your topical area and start with those. Put the greatest emphasis on research journals that use a blind or juried review system. In a blind or juried review, authors submit potential articles to a journal editor who solicits several reviewers who agree to give a critical review of the paper. The paper is sent to these reviewers with no identification of the author so that there will be no personal bias (either for or against the author). Based on the reviewers' recommendations, the editor can accept the article, reject it, or recommend that the author revise and resubmit it. Articles in journals with blind review processes are likely to have a fairly high level of credibility. Second, *do the review early* in the research process. You are likely to learn a lot in the literature review that will help you determine what the necessary trade-offs are. After all, previous researchers also had to face trade-off decisions.

What should you look for in the literature review? First, you might be able to find a study that is quite similar to the one you are thinking of doing. Since all credible research studies have to review the literature themselves, you can check their literature review to get a quick start on your own. Second, prior research will help ensure that you include all of the major relevant constructs in your study. You may find that other similar studies routinely look at an outcome that you might not have included. Your study would not be judged credible if it ignored a major construct. Third, the literature review will help you to find and select appropriate measurement instruments. You will readily see what measurement instruments researchers used themselves in contexts similar to yours. Finally, the literature review will help you to anticipate common problems in your research context. You can use the prior experiences of others to avoid common traps and pitfalls.

1-4b Concept Mapping

Social scientists have developed a number of methods and processes that might help you formulate a research project. I would include among these at least the following: brainstorming, brainwriting, nominal group techniques, focus groups, affinity mapping, Delphi techniques, facet theory, and qualitative text analysis. Here, I'll show you a method that I have developed, called *concept mapping* (Kane and Trochim, 2007)*, which is especially useful for research problem formulation and illustrates some of the advantages of applying social-science methods to conceptualizing research problems.

Concept mapping is a general method that can be used to help any individual or group to describe ideas about some topic in a pictorial form. Several methods currently go by names such as concept mapping, mental mapping, or concept webbing. All of them are similar in that they result in a picture of someone's ideas, but the kind of concept mapping I want to describe here is different in a number of important ways. First, it is primarily a group process, so it is especially well suited for situations where teams or groups of researchers have to work together. The other methods work primarily with individuals. Second, it uses a structured facilitated approach. A trained facilitator follows specific steps in helping a group articulate its ideas and understand them more clearly. Third, the core of concept mapping consists of several state-of-the-art multivariate statistical methods that analyze the input from all of the individuals and yield an aggregate group product. Finally, the method requires the use of specialized computer programs that can handle the data from this type of process and accomplish the correct analysis and mapping procedures.

Although concept mapping is a general method, it is particularly useful for helping social researchers and research teams develop and detail ideas for research. It is especially valuable when researchers want to involve relevant stakeholder groups in the act of creating the research project. Although concept mapping is used for many purposes—strategic planning, product development, market analysis, decision making, measurement development—I concentrate here on its potential for helping researchers formulate their projects.

So what is concept mapping? Essentially, concept mapping is a structured process, focused on a topic or construct of interest, involving input from one or more participants, that produces an interpretable pictorial view (concept map) of their ideas and concepts and how these are interrelated. Concept mapping helps people to think more effectively as a group without losing their individuality. It helps groups capture complex ideas without trivializing them or losing detail (see Figure 1–10).

A concept-mapping process involves six steps that can take place in a single day or can be spread out over weeks or months depending on the situation. The process can be accomplished with everyone sitting around a table in the same room or with the participants distributed across the world using the Internet. The steps are as follows:

- **Preparation:** Step one accomplishes three things. The facilitator of the mapping process works with the initiator(s) (those who requested the process initially) to identify who the participants will be. A mapping process can have hundreds or even thousands of stakeholders participating, although there is usually a relatively small group of between ten and twenty stakeholders involved. Second, the initiator works with the stakeholders to develop the focus for the project. For instance, the group might decide to focus on defining a

---

*Kane, M., & Trochim, W. (2007). *Concept mapping for planning and evaluation.* Thousand Oaks, CA: Sage Publications.

FIGURE 1–10	The steps in the concept-mapping process

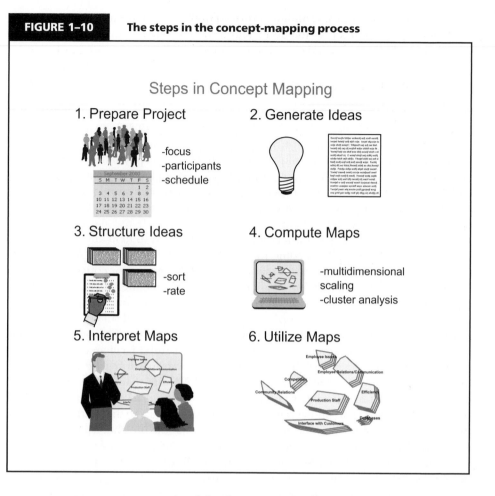

program or treatment, or it might choose to map all of the expected outcomes. Finally, the group decides on an appropriate schedule for the mapping.

- **Generation:** The stakeholders develop a large set of statements that address the focus. For instance, they might generate statements describing all of the specific activities that will constitute a specific social program, or generate statements describing specific outcomes that could result from participating in a program. A variety of methods can be used to accomplish this including traditional brainstorming, brainwriting, nominal group techniques, focus groups, qualitative text analysis, and so on. The group can generate hundreds of statements in a concept-mapping project. In most situations, around 100 statements is the practical limit in terms of the number of statements they can reasonably handle.

- **Structuring:** The participants do two things during structuring. First, each participant sorts the statements into piles of similar statements. They often do this by sorting a deck of cards that has one statement on each card, but they can also do this directly on a computer by dragging the statements into piles that they create. They can have as few or as many piles as they want. Each participant names each pile with a short descriptive label. Then each participant rates each of the statements on some scale. Usually the statements are rated on a 1 to 5 scale for their relative importance, where a 1 means the statement is relatively unimportant compared to all the rest, a 3 means that it is moderately important, and a 5 means that it is extremely important.

- **Representation:** This is where the analysis is done; this is the process of taking the sort and rating input and representing it in map form. Two major statistical analyses are used. The first—multidimensional scaling—takes the sort data across all participants and develops the basic map where each statement is a point on the map and statements that were piled together by more people are closer to each other on the map. The second analysis—cluster analysis—takes the output of the multidimensional scaling (the point map) and partitions the map into groups of statements or ideas, into clusters. If the statements describe program activities, the clusters show how to group them into logical groups of activities. If the statements are specific outcomes, the clusters might be viewed as outcome constructs or concepts.

- **Interpretation:** The facilitator works with the stakeholder group to help develop its own labels and interpretations for the various maps.
- **Utilization:** The stakeholders use the maps to help address the original focus. On the program side, stakeholders use the maps as a visual framework for operationalizing the program; on the outcome side, the maps can be used as the basis for developing measures and displaying results.

The concept-mapping process described here is a structured approach to conceptualizing. However, even researchers who do not appear to be following a structured approach are likely to be using similar steps informally. For instance, all researchers probably go through an internal exercise that is analogous to the brainstorming step described previously. They may not actually brainstorm and write their ideas down, but they probably do something like that informally. After they've generated their ideas, they structure or organize them in some way. For each step in the formalized concept-mapping process you can probably think of analogous ways that researchers accomplish the same task, even if they don't follow such formal approaches. More formalized methods like concept mapping have benefits over the typical informal approach. For instance, with concept mapping there is an objective record of what was done in each step. Researchers can be both more public and more accountable. A structured process also opens up new possibilities. With concept mapping, it is possible to imagine more effective multiple researcher conceptualization and involvement of other stakeholder groups such as program developers, funders, and clients.

1-4c Logic Models

Another method of conceptualizing research uses graphics to express the basic idea of what is supposed to happen in a program. This graphic representation can then be used to guide researchers in the process of identifying indicators or measures of the components of the graphic model. The idea is straightforward: identify the components of the program in terms of specific inputs (what goes into a program), relationships (how the components should be related to each other), and outputs (what should happen as a result of the program).

A very nice basic example of such a model was produced by the Kellogg Foundation in their Logic Model Development Guide (2004). This example is shown in Figure 1–11. Notice that the steps are shown in a left-to-right order that indicates the step-by-step logic used in planning the program, with the arrows suggesting a causal sequence of influences. A second example is shown in Figure 1–12. This model was developed to illustrate how a program could identify needs of children and families, then provide certain kinds of services, resulting in some positive

FIGURE 1–11   **A basic logic model**

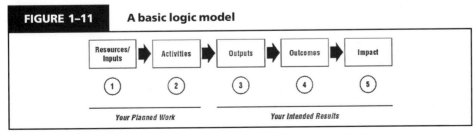

(Kellogg Foundation, 2004)

FIGURE 1–12   **A basic logic model with indicators shown**

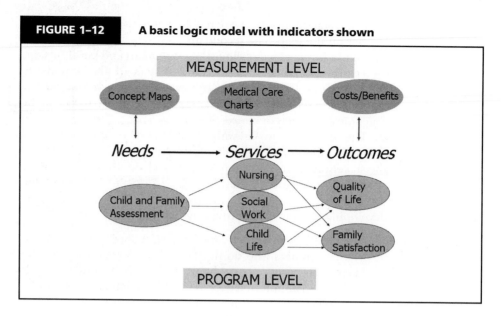

outcomes for program participants. In this model, both the program components and some indicators (measures) are shown. This figure illustrates something very general about social research, too; that we must think at two levels: the abstract idea and the observable indicator of the idea. Of course, life and research are not this simple. If you would like to read more about logic models, particularly with regard to the translation of the idea to real life, I recommend reading Renger and Hurley's paper on this topic (2006).

1-4d Summary

We've covered a lot of territory in this initial chapter, grouped roughly into four broad areas. First, we considered the language of research and enhanced your vocabulary by introducing key terms like variable, attribute, causal relationship, hypothesis, and unit of analysis. We next considered the rationale or logic of research and discussed how research is structured, the major components of a research project, deductive and inductive reasoning, several major research fallacies, and the critical topic of validity in research. This was followed by a discussion of ethics in research that introduced issues like informed consent and anonymity. Finally, we briefly considered how research is thought up or conceptualized. It certainly is a formidable agenda. But it provides you with the basic foundation for the material that's coming in subsequent chapters.

Login to the Online Edition of your text at www.atomicdog.com to find additional resources located in the Study Guide at the end of each chapter.

PART 2

Sampling

CHAPTER 2

Sampling

population
The group you want to generalize to and the group you sample from in a study.

sample
The actual units you select to participate in your study.

sampling frame
The list from which you draw your sample. In some cases, there is no list; you draw your sample based upon an explicit rule. For instance, when doing quota sampling of passersby at the local mall, you do not have a list per se, and the sampling frame consists of both the population of people who pass by within the time frame.

external validity
The degree to which the conclusions in your study would hold for other persons in other places and at other times.

validity
The best available approximation of the truth of a given proposition, inference, or conclusion.

generalizability
The degree to which study conclusions are valid for members of the population not included in the study sample.

sampling model
A model for generalizing in which you identify your population, draw a fair sample, conduct your research, and finally, generalize your results to other population groups.

proximal similarity model
A model for generalizing from your study to another context based upon the degree to which the other context is similar to your study context.

Sampling is the process of selecting units (such as people and organizations) from a **population** of interest so that by studying the **sample** you can fairly generalize your results to the population from which the units were chosen. In this chapter, I begin by covering some of the key terms in sampling like population and **sampling frame**. Then, because some types of sampling rely on quantitative models, I'll talk about some of the statistical terms used in sampling. Finally, I'll discuss the major distinction between probability and nonprobability sampling methods and work through the major types in each.

2-1 External Validity

It may seem odd to begin a chapter about sampling by discussing **external validity**. So, I want to take a minute to explain how these topics are linked. In research, our sample consists of the people who actually participate in our study. But when we conduct research, we are often interested not just in reaching conclusions about our sample in the time and place where we conducted our study but also in making some conclusions that are broader than that, in concluding what might happen with other people at other times and in other places than just our sample. When we try to reach conclusions that extend beyond the sample in our study, we say that we are generalizing. So, why is external validity so important to the issue of sampling? Because external validity is centrally related to the idea of generalizing. Recall from Section 1-3, Validity of Research, in Chapter 1, that **validity** of any type refers to the approximate truth of propositions, inferences, or conclusions. *External validity* refers to the approximate truth of conclusions that involve generalizations, or more broadly, the **generalizability** of conclusions. Put in everyday terms, *external validity* is the degree to which the conclusions in your study would hold for other persons in other places and at other times (Cook & Campbell, 1979; Shadish, Cook, & Campbell, 2002).

Science approaches the providing of evidence for a generalization in two major ways. I'll call the first approach the **sampling model**. In the sampling model, you start by identifying the population you would like to generalize to (Figure 2–1). Then, you draw a fair sample from that population and conduct your research with the sample. Finally, because the sample is representative of the population, you can automatically generalize your results back to the population. This approach has several problems. First, at the time of your study, you might not know what part of the population you will ultimately want to generalize to. Second, you may not be able to draw a fair or representative sample easily. Third, it's impossible to sample across all times that you might like to generalize to, such as next year.

The second approach to generalizing is called the **proximal similarity model** (Figure 2–2). *Proximal* means nearby and *similarity* means ... well, it means

FIGURE 2–1 The sampling model for external validity

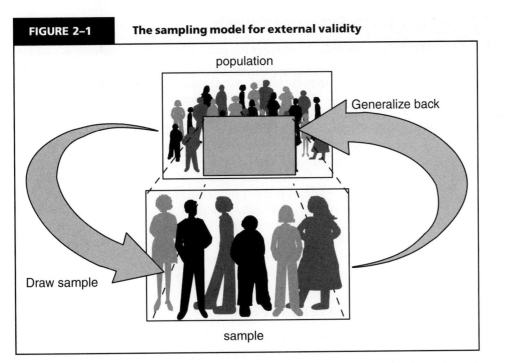

population

Generalize back

Draw sample

sample

The researcher draws a sample for a study from a defined population to generalize the results to the population.

FIGURE 2–2 The proximal similarity model for external validity

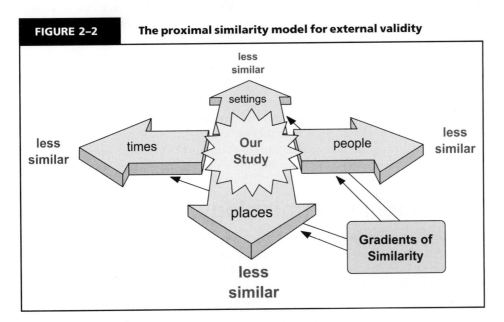

less similar

settings

less similar

times

Our Study

people

less similar

places

Gradients of Similarity

less similar

similarity. The term *proximal similarity* was suggested by Donald T. Campbell as an appropriate relabeling of the term *external validity* (although he was the first to admit that it probably wouldn't catch on). With proximal similarity, you begin by thinking about different generalizability contexts and developing a theory about which contexts are more like your study and which are less so. For instance, you might imagine several settings that have people who are more similar to the people in your study or people who are less similar. This process also holds for times and places. When you place different contexts in terms of their relative similarities, you can call this implicit theoretical dimension a **gradient of similarity**. After you develop this proximal similarity framework, you can generalize. How? You can generalize the results of your study to other persons, places, or times that are more like (that is, more proximally similar to) your study. Notice that here, you can never generalize with certainty; these generalizations are always a question of more or less similar.

gradient of similarity
The dimension along which your study context can be related to other potential contexts to which you might wish to generalize. Contexts that are closer to yours along the gradient of similarity of place, time, people, and so on can be generalized to with more confidence than ones that are further away.

2-1a Threats to External Validity

A threat to external validity is an explanation of how you might be wrong in making a generalization. For instance, imagine that you conclude that the results of your study (which was done in a specific place, with certain types of people, and at a specific time) can be generalized to another context (for instance, another place, with slightly different people, at a slightly later time). In such a case, three major threats to external validity exist because there are three ways you could be wrong: people, places, and times. Your critics could, for example, argue that the results of your study were due to the unusual type of people who were in the study, or, they could claim that your results were obtained only because of the unusual place in which you performed the study. (Perhaps you did your educational study in a college town with lots of high-achieving, educationally oriented kids.) They might suggest that you did your study at a peculiar time. For instance, if you did your smoking-cessation study the week after the Surgeon General issued the well-publicized results of the latest smoking and cancer studies, you might get different results than if you had done it the week before.

2-1b Improving External Validity

random selection
Process or procedure that assures that the different units in your population are selected by chance.

How can you improve external validity? One way, based on the sampling model, suggests that you do a good job of drawing a sample from a population. For instance, you should use **random selection**, if possible, rather than a nonrandom procedure. In addition, once selected, you should try to ensure that the respondents participate in your study and that you keep your dropout rates low. A second approach would be to use the theory of proximal similarity more effectively. How? Perhaps you could do a better job of describing the ways your contexts differ from others by providing data about the degree of similarity between various groups of people, places, and even times. You might even be able to map out the degree of proximal similarity among various contexts with a methodology like concept mapping as discussed in Chapter 1. Perhaps the best approach to criticisms of generalizations is simply to show critics that they're wrong—do your study in a variety of places, with different people, and at different times. That is, your external validity (ability to generalize) will be stronger the more you replicate your study.

2-2 Sampling Terminology

As with anything else in life you have to learn the language of an area if you're going to ever hope to use it. Here, I want to introduce several different terms for the major groups that are involved in a sampling process and the role that each group plays in the logic of sampling.

The major question that motivates sampling in the first place is: "Whom do you want to generalize to?" (Or should it be: "To whom do you want to generalize?") In most social research, you are interested in more than just the people directly participating in your study. You would like to be able to talk in general terms and not be confined to only the people in your study. Now, at times you won't be concerned about generalizing. Maybe you're just evaluating a program in a local agency and don't care whether the program would work with other people in other places and at other times. In that case, sampling and generalizing might not be of interest. In other cases, you would really like to be able to generalize almost universally.

census
A kind of survey that involves a complete enumeration of the entire population of interest.

Indeed, sometimes an actual **census** is needed. Taking a census means a counting or enumeration of every member of the population. For example, one of the main tasks undertaken by the U.S. Census Bureau is to periodically compile a record of every person living in the United States. This complete listing is necessary for the proper conduct of elections (for example, the electoral college used in

FIGURE 2–3	The different groups in the sampling model

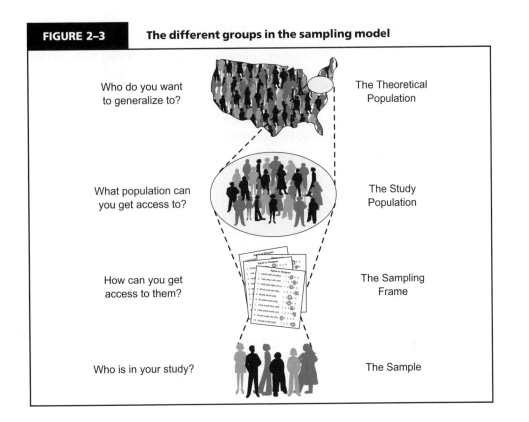

Who do you want
to generalize to?   The Theoretical
                                               Population

What population can   The Study
you get access to?   Population

How can you get   The Sampling
access to them?   Frame

Who is in your study?   The Sample

presidential elections) as well as taxation and other functions of government in which a complete record rather than an estimate is needed. (By the way the U.S. Census Bureau is a gold mine of interesting information on many aspects of the U.S. population: http://www.census.gov.)

When psychologists do research, they are often interested in developing theories that would hold for all humans; in contrast, in most applied social research, researchers are interested in generalizing to specific groups. The group you wish to generalize to is called the *population* in your study (Figure 2–3). This is the group you would like to sample from because this is the group you are interested in generalizing to. Let's imagine that you want to generalize to urban homeless males between the ages of 30 and 50 in the United States. If that is the population of interest, you are likely to have a hard time developing a reasonable sampling plan. You are probably not going to find an accurate listing of this population, and even if you did, you would almost certainly not be able to mount a national sample across hundreds of urban areas. So you probably should make a distinction between the population you would like to generalize to, and the population that is accessible to you. We'll call the former the *theoretical population* and the latter the *accessible population*. In this example, the accessible population might be homeless males between the ages of 30 and 50 in six selected urban areas across the United States.

After you identify the theoretical and accessible populations, you have to do one more thing before you can actually draw a sample: get a list of the members of the accessible population. (Or, you have to spell out in detail how you will contact them to ensure representativeness.) The listing of the accessible population from which you'll draw your sample is called the *sampling frame*. If you were doing a phone survey and selecting names from the telephone book, the phone book would be your sampling frame. That wouldn't be a great way to sample because significant subportions of the population either don't have a phone or have moved in or out of the area since the last phone book was printed. Notice that in this case, you might identify the area code and all three-digit prefixes within that area code and draw a sample simply by randomly dialing numbers (cleverly known as *random-digit-dialing*). In this case, the sampling frame is not a list *per se*, but is rather a procedure that you follow as the actual basis for sampling. Finally, you actually draw your sample (using one of the many sampling procedures described later in this chapter). The *sample* is the group of people you select to be in your study. Notice that I didn't say that the sample was the group of people who are actually in your study. You may not be able to contact or recruit all of the people you actually sample, or some could drop out over the course of the study. The group that actually completes your study is a subsample of the sample; it doesn't include nonrespondents or drop-outs. (The problem of nonresponse and its effects on a study will be addressed in Chapter 7 when discussing mortality threats to internal validity.)

People often confuse the idea of random selection with the idea of random assignment. You should make sure that you understand the distinction between random selection and random assignment described in Chapter 8.

At this point, you should appreciate that sampling is a difficult multistep process and that you can go wrong in many places. In fact, as you move from each step to the next in identifying a sample, there is the possibility of introducing systematic error or *bias*. For instance, even if you are able to identify perfectly the population of interest, you may not have access to all of it. Even if you do, you may not have a complete and accurate enumeration or sampling frame from which to select. Even if you do, you may not draw the sample correctly or accurately. And, even if you do, your participants may not all come and they may not all stay. Depressed yet? Sampling is a difficult business indeed. At times like this, I'm reminded of what one of my professors, Donald Campbell, used to say (I'll paraphrase here): "Cousins to the amoeba, it's amazing that we know anything at all!"

2-3 Statistical Terms in Sampling

Let's begin by defining some simple terms that are relevant here. First, let's look at the results of sampling efforts. When you sample, the units that you sample—usually people—supply you with one or more responses. In this sense, a **response** is a specific measurement value that a sampling unit supplies. In Figure 2–4, the person responding to a survey instrument gives a response of "4." When you look across the responses for your entire sample, you use a **statistic**. You can use a variety of statistics: mean, median, mode, and so on. In the Analysis chapter of this book (Chapter 12), you'll find more detailed information on the most commonly used statistics along with some more elaborate examples. In this example, the mean or average for the sample is 3.72; but the reason you sample is to get an estimate for the population from which you sampled. If you could, you would probably prefer to measure the entire population. If you measure the entire population and calculate a value like a mean or average, this is not referred to as a *statistic*; it is a **population parameter**.

2-3a The Sampling Distribution

So how do you get from sample statistic to an estimate of the population parameter? A crucial midway concept you need to understand is the **sampling distribution**. To understand it, you have to be able and willing to do a thought experiment. Imagine that instead of just taking a single sample like you do in a typical study, you took three independent samples of the same population. Furthermore, imagine that for each of your three samples, you collected a single response and computed a single statistic, say, the mean of the response for each sample. This is depicted in the top part of Figure 2–5. Even though all three samples came from the same population, you wouldn't expect to get the exact same statistic from each. They would differ slightly due to the random luck of the draw or to the natural fluctuations or vagaries of drawing a sample. However, you would expect all three samples to yield a similar statistical estimate because they were drawn from the same population.

response
A specific measurement value that a sampling unit supplies.

statistic
A specific value that is estimated from data.

population parameter
The mean or average you would obtain if you were able to sample the entire population.

sampling distribution
The theoretical distribution of an infinite number of samples of the population of interest in your study.

| FIGURE 2–4 | **Statistical terms in sampling** |

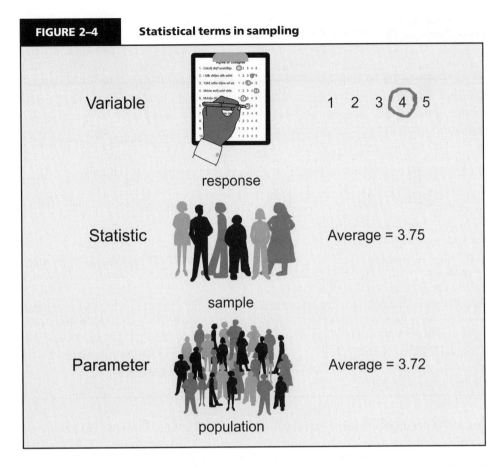

Now, for the leap of imagination! Imagine that you took an *infinite* number of samples from the same population and computed the average for each one. If you plotted the averages on a histogram or bar graph, you should find that most of them converge on the same central value and that you get fewer and fewer samples that have averages farther up or down from that central value. In other words, the bar graph would be well described by the **bell curve** shape that is an indication of a normal distribution in statistics. This is depicted in the bottom part of Figure 2–5. The distribution of an infinite number of samples of the same size as the sample in your study is known as the sampling distribution.

You don't ever actually construct a sampling distribution. Why not? You're not paying attention! Because to construct one, you would have to take an *infinite* number of samples and at least the last time I checked, on this planet infinite is not a number we know how to reach. So why do researchers even talk about a sampling distribution? Now that's a good question! Because you need to realize that your sample is just one of a potentially infinite number of samples that you could have taken. When you keep the sampling distribution in mind, you realize that while the statistic from your sample is probably near the center of the sampling distribution (because most of the samples would be there) you could have gotten one of the extreme samples just through the luck of the draw. If you take the average of the sampling distribution—the average of the averages of an infinite number of samples—you would be much closer to the true population average—the parameter of interest.

So the average of the sampling distribution is essentially equivalent to the parameter. But what is the **standard deviation** of the sampling distribution? (Okay, don't remember what a standard deviation is? This is discussed in detail in the section "Descriptive Statistics" in Chapter 10, "Analysis.") The standard deviation of the sampling distribution tells us something about how different samples would be distributed. In statistics it is referred to as the **standard error** (so you can keep it

bell curve
Smoothed histogram or bar graph describing the expected frequency for each value of a variable. The name comes from the fact that such a distribution often has the shape of a bell.

standard deviation
The spread or variability of the scores around their average in a *single sample*. The standard deviation, often abbreviated SD, is mathematically the square root of the variance. The standard deviation and variance both measure dispersion, but because the standard deviation is measured in the same units as the original measure and the variance is measured in squared units, the standard deviation is usually more directly interpretable and meaningful.

standard error
The spread of the averages around the average of averages in a sampling distribution.

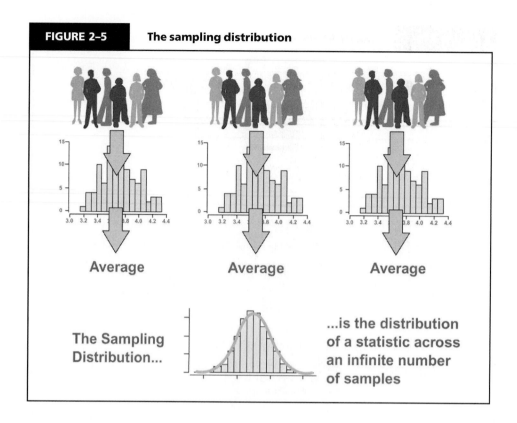

FIGURE 2–5   **The sampling distribution**

separate in your minds from standard deviations. Getting confused? Go get a cup of coffee and come back in 10 minutes . . .. Okay, let's try once more . . .). A *standard deviation* is the spread of the scores around the average in a *single sample*. The standard error is the spread of the averages around the average of averages in a *sampling distribution*. Got it?

2-3b Sampling Error

sampling error
The error in measurement associated with sampling.

In sampling, the standard error is called **sampling error**. Sampling error gives you some idea of the precision of your statistical estimate. A low sampling error means that you had relatively less variability or range in the sampling distribution. But here I go again; you never actually see the sampling distribution! So how do you calculate sampling error? You base your calculation *on the standard deviation of your sample*: the greater the sample's standard deviation, the greater the standard error (and the sampling error). The standard error is also related to the sample size: the greater your sample size, the *smaller* the standard error. Why? Because the greater the sample size, the closer your sample is to the actual population itself. If you take a sample that consists of the entire population, you actually have no sampling error because you don't have a sample; you have the entire population (that is, a census). In that case, the mean you estimate is the parameter.

2-3c The 68, 95, 99 Percent Rule

You've probably heard this one before, but it's so important that it's always worth repeating. There is a general rule that applies whenever you have a normal or bell-shaped distribution. Start with the average—the center of the distribution. If you go up and down (that is, left and right) one standard unit, you will include approximately 68 percent of the cases in the distribution (68 percent of the area under the curve). If you go up and down two standard units, you will include approximately 95 percent of the cases. If you go plus or minus three standard units, you will include 99 percent of the cases.

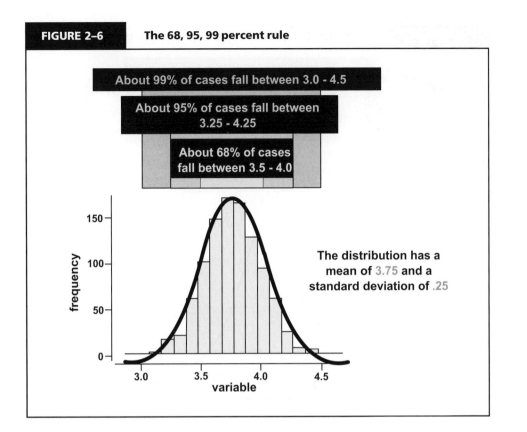

FIGURE 2–6   The 68, 95, 99 percent rule

About 99% of cases fall between 3.0 - 4.5

About 95% of cases fall between 3.25 - 4.25

About 68% of cases fall between 3.5 - 4.0

The distribution has a mean of 3.75 and a standard deviation of .25

Notice that I didn't specify in the previous few sentences whether I was talking about standard *deviation* units or standard *error* units. That's because the same rule holds for both types of distributions (the raw data and sampling distributions). For instance, in Figure 2–6, the mean of the distribution is 3.75 and the standard unit is .25. (If this were a distribution of raw data, we would be talking in standard-deviation units. If it were a sampling distribution, we'd be talking in standard-error units.) If you go up and down one standard unit from the mean, you would be going up and down .25 from the mean of 3.75. Within this range—3.5 to 4.0—you would expect to see approximately 68 percent of the cases. This section is marked in red on Figure 2–6. I leave it to you to figure out the other ranges. What does this all mean, you ask. If you are dealing with raw data and you know the mean and standard deviation of a sample, you can *predict* the intervals within which 68, 95, and 99 percent of your cases would be expected to fall. We call these intervals the—guess what—68, 95, and 99 percent confidence intervals.

Now, here's where everything should come together in one great aha! experience if you've been following along. If you have a *sampling distribution*, you should be able to predict the 68, 95, and 99 percent confidence intervals for where the population parameter should be; and isn't that why you sampled in the first place? So that you could predict where the population is on that variable? There's only one hitch. You don't actually have the sampling distribution. (I know this is the third time I've said this.) However, you do have the distribution for the sample itself, and from that distribution, you can estimate the standard error (the sampling error) because it is based on the standard deviation and you have that. Of course, you don't actually know the population parameter value; you're trying to find that out, but you can use your best estimate for that—the sample statistic. Now, if you have the mean of the sampling distribution (or set it to the mean from your sample) and you have an estimate of the standard error, which you calculate that from your sample, you have the two key ingredients that you need for your sampling distribution to estimate confidence intervals for the population parameter.

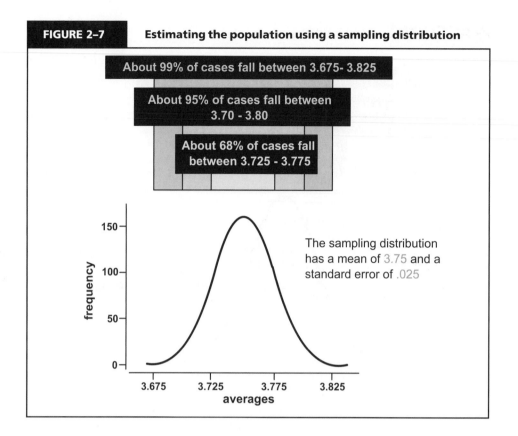

FIGURE 2–7   **Estimating the population using a sampling distribution**

About 99% of cases fall between 3.675- 3.825

About 95% of cases fall between 3.70 - 3.80

About 68% of cases fall between 3.725 - 3.775

The sampling distribution has a mean of 3.75 and a standard error of .025

frequency (y-axis: 0, 50, 100, 150)

averages (x-axis: 3.675, 3.725, 3.775, 3.825)

Perhaps an example will help. Let's assume you did a study and drew a single sample from the population. Furthermore, let's assume that the average for the sample was 3.75 and the standard deviation was .25. This is the raw data distribution depicted in Figure 2–7. What would the sampling distribution be in this case? Well, you don't actually construct it (because you would need to take an infinite number of samples) but you *can* estimate it. For starters, you must assume that the mean of the sampling distribution is the mean of the sample, which is 3.75. Then, you calculate the standard error. To do this, use the standard deviation for your sample and the sample size (in this case $N = 100$), which gives you a standard error of .025 (just trust me on this). Now you have everything you need to estimate a confidence interval for the population parameter. You would estimate that the probability is 68 percent that the true parameter value falls between 3.725 and 3.775 (3.75 plus and minus .025); that the 95 percent confidence interval is 3.700 to 3.800; and that you can say with 99 percent confidence that the population value is between 3.675 and 3.825. Using your sample, you have just estimated the average for your population (that is, the mean of the sample which is 3.75) and you have given odds that the actual population mean falls within certain ranges.

2-4 Probability Sampling

probability sampling
Method of sampling that utilizes some form of random selection.

A **probability sampling** method is any method of sampling that utilizes some form of random selection. To have a random selection method, you must set up some process or procedure that ensures that the different units in your population have equal probabilities of being chosen. Humans have long practiced various forms of random selection, such as picking a name out of a hat, or choosing the short straw. These days, we tend to use computers as the mechanism for generating random numbers as the basis for random selection.

2-4a Some Definitions

Before I can explain the various probability methods, I have to define the following basic terms:

- N is the number of cases in the sampling frame.
- n is the number of cases in the sample.
- $_NC_n$ is the number of combinations (subsets) of n from N.
- $f = n/N$ is the sampling fraction.

That's it. Now that you understand those terms, I can define the different probability sampling methods.

2-4b Simple Random Sampling

The simplest form of random sampling is called **simple random sampling**. Pretty tricky, huh? Here's the quick description of simple random sampling:

- **Objective:** To select n units out of N such that each $_NC_n$ has an equal chance of being selected.
- **Procedure:** Use a table of random numbers, a computer random-number generator, or a mechanical device to select the sample.

Let's see if I can make this somewhat stilted description a little more real. How do you select a simple random sample? Let's assume that you are doing some research with a small service agency to assess clients' views of quality of service over the past year. First, you have to get the sampling frame organized. To accomplish this, you go through agency records to identify every client over the past 12 months. If you're lucky, the agency has accurate computerized records and can quickly produce such a list (Figure 2–8). Then, you have to draw the *sample* and decide on the number of clients you would like to have in the final sample. For the sake of the example, let's say you want to select 100 clients to survey and that there were 1000 clients over the past 12 months. Then, the sampling fraction is $f = n/N = 100/1000 = .10$, or 10 percent. To draw the sample, you have several options. You could print the list of 1000 clients, tear them into separate strips, put the strips in a hat, mix them up, close your eyes, and pull out the first 100. This mechanical procedure would be tedious and the quality of the sample would depend on how thoroughly you mixed up the paper

simple random sampling
A method of sampling that involves drawing a sample from a population so that every possible sample has an equal probability of being selected.

FIGURE 2–8   **Simple random sampling**

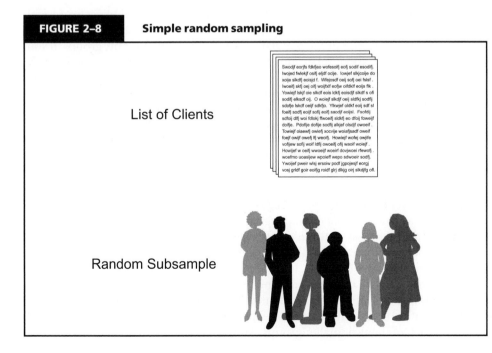

List of Clients

Random Subsample

strips and how randomly you reached into the hat. Perhaps a better procedure would be to use the kind of ball machine that is popular with many of the state lotteries. You would need three sets of balls numbered 0 to 9, one set for each of the digits from 000 to 999. (If you select 000 you call that 1000.) Number the list of names from 1 to 1000 and then use the ball machine to select the three digits that selects each person. The obvious disadvantage here is that you need to get the ball machines. (Where do they make those things, anyway? Is there a ball machine industry?)

Neither of these mechanical procedures is feasible and, with the development of inexpensive computers, there is a much easier way. Here's a simple procedure that's especially useful if you have the names of the clients already on the computer. Many computer programs can generate a series of random numbers. Let's assume you copy and paste the list of client names into a column in an Excel spreadsheet. Then, in the column right next to it paste the function = RAND(), which is Excel's way of putting a random number between 0 and 1 in the cells. Then, sort both columns—the list of names and the random number—by the random numbers. This rearranges the list in random order from the lowest to the highest random number. Then, all you have to do is take the first hundred names in this sorted list. Pretty simple. You could probably accomplish the whole thing in under a minute.

Simple random sampling is easy to accomplish and explain to others. Because simple random sampling is a fair way to select a sample, it is reasonable to generalize the results from the sample back to the population. Simple random sampling is not the most statistically efficient method of sampling and you may—just because of the luck of the draw—not get a good representation of subgroups in a population. To deal with these issues, you have to turn to other sampling methods.

2-4c Stratified Random Sampling

stratified random sampling
A method of sampling that involves dividing your population into homogeneous subgroups and then taking a simple random sample in each subgroup.

Stratified random sampling, also sometimes called *proportional* or *quota* random sampling, involves dividing your population into homogeneous subgroups and then taking a simple random sample in each subgroup. The following restates this in more formal terms:

> **Objective:** Divide the population into nonoverlapping groups *(strata)* N_1, N_2, N_3, … N_i, such that $N_1 + N_2 + N_3 + \ldots + N_i = N$. Then do a simple random sample of $f = n/N$ in each strata.

You might prefer stratified sampling over simple random sampling for several reasons. First, it ensures that you will be able to represent not only the overall population but also key subgroups of the population, especially small minority groups. If you want to be able to talk about subgroups, this may be the only way to ensure effectively you'll be able to do so. If the subgroup is extremely small, you can use different sampling fractions *(f)* within the different strata to randomly oversample the small group. (Although you'll then have to weight the within-group estimates using the sampling fraction whenever you want overall population estimates.) When you use the same sampling fraction within strata you are conducting *proportionate* stratified random sampling. Using different sampling fractions in the strata is called *disproportionate* stratified random sampling. Second, stratified random sampling has more statistical precision than simple random sampling if the strata or groups are homogeneous. If they are, you should expect the variability within groups to be lower than the variability for the population as a whole. Stratified sampling capitalizes on that fact.

For example, let's say that the population of clients for your agency can be divided as shown in Figure 2–9 into three groups: Caucasian, African American, and Hispanic American. Furthermore, let's assume that both the African Americans and Hispanic Americans are relatively small minorities of the clientele (10 percent and 5 percent, respectively). If you just did a simple random sample of $n = 100$ with a sampling fraction of 10 percent, you would expect by chance alone to get 10 and 5 persons from each of the two smaller groups. And, by chance, you could get even fewer

| FIGURE 2–9 | **Stratified random sampling** |

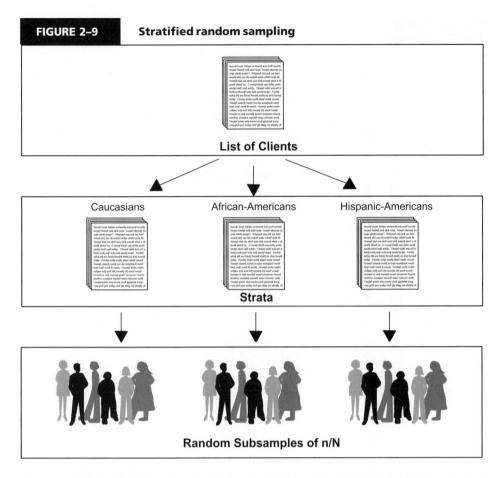

List of Clients

Caucasians   African-Americans   Hispanic-Americans

Strata

Random Subsamples of n/N

than that! If you stratify, you can do better. First, you would determine how many people you want to have in each group. Let's say you still want to take a sample of 100 from the population of 1000 clients over the past year; but suppose you think that to say anything about subgroups, you will need at least 25 cases in each group. So, you sample 50 Caucasians, 25 African Americans, and 25 Hispanic Americans. You know that 10 percent of the population, or 100 clients, are African American. If you randomly sample 25 of these, you have a within-stratum sampling fraction of $25/100 = 25\%$. Similarly, you know that 5 percent, or 50 clients, are Hispanic American. So your within-stratum sampling fraction will be $25/50 = 50\%$. Finally, by subtraction you know there are 850 Caucasian clients. Your within-stratum sampling fraction for them is $50/850 =$ about 5.88%. Because the groups are more homogeneous within group than across the population as a whole, you can expect greater statistical precision (less variance), and, because you stratified, you know you will have enough cases from each group to make meaningful subgroup inferences.

2-4d Systematic Random Sampling

Systematic random sampling is a sampling method where you determine randomly where you want to start selecting in the sampling frame and then follow a rule to select every xth element in the sampling frame list (where the ordering of the list is assumed to be random). To achieve a systematic random sample, follow these steps:

1. Number the units in the population from 1 to N.
2. Decide on the n (sample size) that you want or need.
3. Calculate $k = N/n =$ the interval size.
4. Randomly select an integer between 1 and k.
5. Take every kth unit.

systematic random sampling
A sampling method in which you determine randomly where you want to start selecting in the sampling frame and then follow a rule to select every xth element the sampling frame list (where the ordering of the list is assumed to be random).

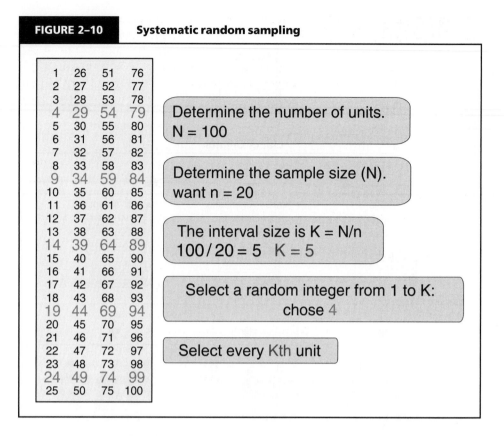

FIGURE 2–10   **Systematic random sampling**

Determine the number of units.
N = 100

Determine the sample size (N).
want n = 20

The interval size is K = N/n
100 / 20 = 5   K = 5

Select a random integer from 1 to K:
chose 4

Select every Kth unit

All of this will be much clearer with an example. Let's assume, as shown in Figure 2–10, that you have a population that only has $N = 100$ people in it and that you want to take a sample of $n = 20$. To use systematic sampling, the population must be listed in a random order. The sampling fraction would be $f = 20/100 = 20\%$. In this case, the interval size, k, is equal to $N/n = 100/20 = 5$. Now, select a random integer from 1 to 5. In this example, imagine that you chose 4. Now, to select the sample, start with the 4th unit in the list and take every kth unit (every 5th, because $k = 5$). You would be sampling units 4, 9, 14, 19, and so on, to 100 and you would wind up with 20 units in your sample. For this to work, it is essential that the units in the population be randomly ordered, at least with respect to the characteristics you are measuring. Why would you ever want to use systematic random sampling? For one thing, it is fairly easy to do. You only have to select a single random number to start things off.

It may also be more precise than simple random sampling. Finally, in some situations there is simply no easier way to do random sampling. For instance, I once had to do a study that involved sampling a collection of books in the library. Once selected, I would have to go to the shelf, locate the book, and record when it last circulated. I knew that I had a fairly good sampling frame in the form of the shelf list (which is a card catalog where the entries are arranged in the order they occur on the shelf). To do a simple random sample, I could have estimated the total number of books and generated random numbers to draw the sample; but how would I find book #74,329 easily if that is the number I selected? I couldn't very well count the cards until I came to 74,329! Stratifying wouldn't solve that problem either. For instance, I could have stratified by card catalog drawer and drawn a simple random sample within each drawer. But I'd still be stuck counting cards. Instead, I did a systematic random sample. I estimated the number of books in the entire collection. Let's imagine it was 100,000. I decided that I wanted to take a sample of 1000 for a sampling fraction of $1000/100,000 = 1\%$. To get the sampling interval k, I divided $N/n = 100,000/100 = 1000$. Then I selected a random integer between 1 and 1000. Let's say I got 257. Next I did a little side study to determine how thick a thousand cards are in the card catalog (taking into account the varying ages of the cards).

Let's say that on average I found that two cards that were separated by 1000 cards were about 2.75 inches apart in the catalog drawer. That information gave me everything I needed to draw the sample. I counted to the 257th by hand and recorded the book information. Then, I took a compass. (Remember those from your high-school math class? They're the funny little metal instruments with a sharp pin on one end and a pencil on the other that you used to draw circles in geometry class.) Then I set the compass at 2.75", stuck the pin end in at the 257th card and pointed with the pencil end to the next card (approximately 1000 books away). In this way, I approximated selecting the 257th, 1257th, 2257th, and so on. I was able to accomplish the entire selection procedure in very little time using this systematic random sampling approach. I'd probably still be there counting cards if I'd tried another random sampling method. (Okay, so I have no life. I got compensated nicely, I don't mind saying, for coming up with this scheme.)

2-4e Cluster (Area) Random Sampling

The problem with random sampling methods when you have to sample a population that's dispersed across a wide geographic region is that you will have to cover a lot of ground geographically to get to each of the units you sampled. Imagine taking a simple random sample of all the residents of New York State to conduct personal interviews. By the luck of the draw, you will wind up with respondents who come from all over the state. Your interviewers are going to have a lot of traveling to do. It is precisely to address this problem that **cluster or area random sampling** was invented.

In cluster sampling, you follow these steps:

1. Divide population into clusters (usually along geographic boundaries).
2. Randomly sample clusters.
3. Measure *all* units within sampled clusters.

For instance, Figure 2–11 shows a map of the counties in New York State. Let's say that you have to do a survey of town governments that requires you to go to the towns personally to interview key town officials. If you do a simple random sample of towns statewide, your sample is likely to come from all over the state and you will have to be prepared to cover the entire state geographically. Instead, you can do a cluster sampling of counties, let's say five counties in this example (shaded in the figure). Once these are selected, you go to *every* town government in the five county areas. Clearly this strategy will help you economize on mileage. Instead of having to travel all over the state, you can concentrate exclusively within the counties you selected. Cluster or area sampling is useful in situations like this, and is done primarily for efficiency of administration.

2-4f Multi-Stage Sampling

The four methods covered so far—simple, stratified, systematic, and cluster—are the simplest random sampling strategies. In most real applied social research, you would use sampling methods that are considerably more complex than these simple variations. The most important principle here is that you can combine these simple methods in a variety of useful ways to help you address your sampling needs in the most efficient and effective manner possible. Combining sampling methods is called **multistage sampling**.

For example, consider the idea of sampling New York State residents for face-to-face interviews. Clearly you would want to do some type of *cluster sampling* as the first stage of the process. You might sample townships or census tracts throughout the state. In cluster sampling, you would then measure everyone in the clusters you selected. Even if you are sampling census tracts, you may not be able to measure *everyone* who is in the census tract. So, you might set up a systematic random sampling

cluster or area random sampling
A sampling method that involves dividing the population into groups called *clusters*, randomly selecting clusters, and then sampling each element in the selected clusters. This method is useful when sampling a population that is spread across a wide geographic area.

multistage sampling
The combining of several sampling techniques to create a more efficient or effective sample than the use of any one sampling type can achieve on its own.

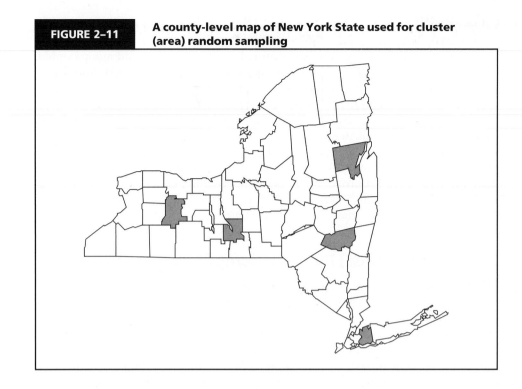

FIGURE 2–11   A county-level map of New York State used for cluster (area) random sampling

process within the clusters. In this case, you would have a two-stage sampling process with stratified samples within cluster samples. Alternatively, consider the problem of sampling students in grade schools. You might begin with a national sample of school districts stratified by economics and educational level. Within selected districts, you might do a simple random sample of schools; within schools, you might do a simple random sample of classes or grades; and, within classes, you might even do a simple random sample of students. In this case, you have three or four stages in the sampling process and you use both stratified and simple random sampling. By combining different sampling methods, you can achieve a rich variety of probabilistic sampling methods to fit a wide range of social research contexts.

2-5 Nonprobability Sampling

nonprobability sampling
Sampling that does not involve random selection.

The difference between nonprobability and probability sampling is that **nonprobability sampling** does not involve random selection and probability sampling does. Does that mean that nonprobability samples aren't representative of the population? Not necessarily; but it does mean nonprobability samples cannot depend upon the rationale of probability theory. At least with a probabilistic sample, you know the odds or probability that you have represented the population well. You can estimate confidence intervals for the statistic. With nonprobability samples, you may or may not represent the population well, and it will often be hard for you to know how well you've done so. In general, researchers prefer probabilistic or random sampling methods over nonprobabilistic ones and consider them to be more accurate and rigorous. However, in some circumstances in applied social research, it is not feasible, practical, or theoretically sensible to use random sampling. In the following paragraphs, I will present a variety of nonprobabilistic sampling alternatives to the probabilistic methods described earlier.

Nonprobability sampling methods are divided into two broad types: *accidental or purposive.* Most sampling methods are purposive in nature because the sampling problem is usually approached with a specific plan in mind. The most important distinctions among these types of sampling methods are between the different types of purposive sampling approaches.

2-5a Accidental, Haphazard, or Convenience Sampling

One of the most common methods of sampling goes under the various titles listed here: *accidental, haphazard,* or *convenience.* I would include in this category the traditional person-on-the-street interviews conducted frequently by television news programs to get a quick (although nonrepresentative) reading of public opinion. I would also argue that the typical use of college students in much psychological research is primarily a matter of convenience. (You don't really believe that psychologists use college students because they think they're representative of the population at large, do you?) In clinical practice, you might use clients available to you as your sample. In many research contexts, you sample by asking for volunteers. Clearly, the problem with all these types of samples is that you have no evidence that they are representative of the populations you're interested in generalizing to, and in many cases, you would suspect that they are not.

2-5b Purposive Sampling

In purposive sampling, you sample with a *purpose* in mind. Usually you would be seeking one or more specific predefined groups. For instance, have you ever run into people in a mall or on the street carrying clipboards and stopping various people and asking to interview them? Most likely, they are conducting a purposive sample (and most likely they are engaged in market research). They might be looking for Caucasian females between 30 and 40 years old. They size up the people passing by and stop people who look to be in that category and ask whether they will participate. One of the first things they're likely to do is verify that the respondent does in fact meet the criteria for being in the sample. Purposive sampling can be useful in situations where you need to reach a targeted sample quickly and where sampling for proportionality is not the primary concern. With a purposive sample, you are likely to get the opinions of your target population, but you are also likely to overweight subgroups in your population that are more readily accessible.

All of the methods that follow can be considered subcategories of purposive sampling methods. You might sample for specific groups or types of people as in modal instance, expert, or quota sampling. You might sample for diversity as in **heterogeneity sampling**, or you might capitalize on informal social networks to identify specific respondents who are hard to locate otherwise, as in **snowball sampling**. In all of these methods, you know what you want—you are sampling with a purpose.

heterogeneity sampling
Sampling for diversity or variety.

Modal Instance Sampling In statistics, the *mode* is the most frequently occurring value in a distribution. In sampling, when you do a **modal instance sample**, you are sampling the most frequent case, or the typical case. Many informal public opinion polls, for instance, interview a typical voter. This sampling approach has a number of problems. First, how do you know what the typical or modal case is? You could say that the modal voter is a person of average age, educational level, and income in the population, but, it's not clear that using the averages of these is the fairest (consider the skewed distribution of income, for instance). In addition, how do you know that those three variables—age, education, income—are the ones most relevant for classifying the typical voter? What if religion or ethnicity is an important determinant of voting decisions? Clearly, modal instance sampling is only sensible for informal sampling contexts.

snowball sampling
A sampling method in which you sample participants based upon referral from prior participants.

modal instance sampling
Sampling for the most typical case.

Expert Sampling **Expert sampling** involves the assembling of a sample of persons with known or demonstrable experience and expertise in some area. Often, you convene such a sample under the auspices of a panel of experts. There are actually two reasons you might do expert sampling. First, it is the best way to elicit the views of persons who have specific expertise. In this case, expert sampling is

expert sampling
A sample of people with known or demonstrable experience and expertise in some area.

essentially just a specific subcase of purposive sampling. The other reason you might use expert sampling is to provide evidence for the validity of another sampling approach you've chosen. For instance, let's say you do modal instance sampling and are concerned that the criteria you used for defining the modal instance is subject to criticism. You might convene an expert panel consisting of persons with acknowledged experience and insight into that field or topic and ask them to examine your modal definitions and comment on their appropriateness and validity. The advantage of doing this is that you aren't out on your own trying to defend your decisions; you have some acknowledged experts to back you. The disadvantage is that even the experts can be, and often are, wrong.

Quota Sampling

quota sampling
Any sampling method in which you sample until you achieve a specific number of sampled units for each subgroup of a population.

In **quota sampling**, you select people nonrandomly according to some fixed quota. The two types of quota sampling are proportional and nonproportional. In **proportional quota sampling**, you want to represent the major characteristics of the population by sampling a proportional amount of each. For instance, if you know the population has 40 percent women and 60 percent men and that you want a total sample size of 100, you should continue sampling until you get those percentages and then stop. So, if you already have the 40 women for your sample, but not the 60 men, you would continue to sample men but even if legitimate women respondents come along, you would not sample them because you have already met your quota. The problem here (as in much purposive sampling) is that you have to decide the specific characteristics on which you will base the quota. Will it be by gender, age, education, race, religion, and so on?

proportional quota sampling
A sampling method in which you sample until you achieve a specific number of sampled units for each subgroup of a population, where the proportions in each group are the same.

nonproportional quota sampling
A sampling method in which you sample until you achieve a specific number of sampled units for each subgroup of a population, where the proportions in each group are not the same.

Nonproportional quota sampling is less restrictive. In this method, you specify the minimum number of sampled units you want in each category. Here, you're not concerned with having numbers that match the proportions in the population. Instead, you simply want to have enough to ensure that you will be able to talk about even small groups in the population. This method is the nonprobabilistic analogue of stratified random sampling in that it is typically used to ensure that smaller groups are adequately represented in your sample.

Heterogeneity Sampling

You sample for heterogeneity when you want to include all opinions or views, and you aren't concerned about representing these views proportionately. Another term for this is sampling for *diversity*. In many brainstorming or nominal group processes (including concept mapping), you would use some form of heterogeneity sampling because your primary interest is in getting a broad spectrum of ideas, not identifying the average or modal instance ones. In effect, what you would like to be sampling is not people, but ideas. You imagine that there is a universe of all possible ideas relevant to some topic and that you want to sample this population, not the population of people who have the ideas. Clearly, to get all of the ideas, and especially the outlier or unusual ones, you have to include a broad and diverse range of participants. Heterogeneity sampling is, in this sense, almost the opposite of modal instance sampling.

Snowball Sampling

In snowball sampling, you begin by identifying people who meet the criteria for inclusion in your study. You then ask them to recommend others they know who also meet the criteria. Although this method would hardly lead to representative samples, at times it may be the best method available. Snowball sampling is especially useful when you are trying to reach populations that are inaccessible or hard to find. For instance, if you are studying the homeless, you are not likely to be able to find good lists of homeless people within a specific geographical area. However, if you go to that area and identify one or two, you may find that they know who the other homeless people in their vicinity are and how you can find them.

Summary

So, that's the basics of sampling methods. Quite a few options, aren't there? How about a table to summarize the choices and give you some idea of when they might be appropriate. Table 2–1 shows each sampling method, when it might best be used, and the major advantages and disadvantages of each.

TABLE 2–1   **Summary of sampling methods**

Probability Sampling Method	Use	Advantages	Disadvantages
Simple random sampling	Anytime	Simple to implement; easy to explain to nontechnical audiences	Requires a sample list (sampling frame) to select from
Stratified random sampling	When concerned about underrepresenting smaller subgroups	Allows you to oversample minority groups to ensure enough for subgroup analyses	Requires a sample list (sampling frame) from which to select
Systematic random sampling	When you want to sample every kth element in an ordered set	Does not require that you count through all of the elements in the list to find the ones randomly selected	If the order of elements is nonrandom, there could be systematic bias
Cluster (area) random sampling	When organizing geographically makes sense	Is more efficient than other methods when sampling across a geographically dispersed area	Is usually not used alone; is coupled with other methods in a multistage approach
Multistage random sampling	Anytime	Combines sophistication with efficiency	Can be complex and difficult to explain to nontechnical audiences
Non-probability Sampling Methods			
Accidental, haphazard, or convenience nonprobability sampling	Anytime	Is very easy to do; almost like not sampling at all	Has very weak external validity; is likely to be biased
Modal instance purposive nonprobability sampling	When you want to measure only a typical respondent	Is easily understood by nontechnical audiences	Results limited to only the modal case; has little external validity
Modal purposive nonprobability sampling	As an adjunct to other sampling strategies	Experts can provide opinions to support research conclusions	Is likely to be biased; has limited external validity
Quota purposive nonprobability sampling	When you want to represent subgroups	Allows for oversampling smaller subgroups	Is likely to be more biased than stratified random sampling; often depends on who comes along when
Heterogeneity purposive nonprobability sampling	When you want to sample for diversity or variety	Is easy to implement and explain; is useful when you're interested in sampling for variety rather than representativeness	Won't represent population views proportionately
Snowball purposive nonprobability sampling	With hard-to-reach populations	Can be used when there is no sampling frame	Has low external validity

Sampling is a critical component in virtually all social research. While I've presented a wide variety of sampling methods in this chapter, it's important that you keep them in perspective. The key is not which sampling method you use. The key is external validity—how valid the inferences from your sample are. You can have the best sampling method in the world and it won't guarantee that your generalizations are valid (although it does help!). Alternatively, you can use a relatively weak nonprobability sampling method and find that it is perfectly useful for your context. Ultimately whether your generalizations from your study to other persons, places, or times are valid is a judgment. Your critics, readers, friends, supporters, funders, and so on, will judge the quality of your generalizations, and they may not even agree with each other in their judgment. What might be convincing to one person or group may fail with another. Your job as a social researcher is to create a sampling strategy that is appropriate to the context and will ensure that your generalizations are as convincing as possible to as many audiences as is feasible.

Login to the Online Edition of your text at www.atomicdog.com to find additional resources located in the Study Guide at the end of each chapter.

Observation and Measurement

CHAPTER 3

The Theory of Measurement

Measurement is the process of observing and recording the observations that are collected as part of a research effort. There are two major issues that will be considered here.

First, you have to understand the fundamental ideas or theory involved in measuring. In this chapter, I focus on how we think about and assess quality of measurement. In the section on construct validity, I present the theory of what constitutes a good measure. In the section on reliability of measurement, I consider the consistency or dependability of measurement, including consideration of true score theory and a variety of reliability estimators. In the section on levels of measurement, I explain the meaning of the four major levels of measurement: **nominal**, **ordinal**, **interval**, and **ratio**.

3-1 Construct Validity

In the first chapter of this book, you were introduced to an idea about ideas. When researchers think about what to study, they go through a process of defining the concepts they are interested in and the relationships that might exist between various concepts. The method of concept mapping was introduced as one way to go from an abstract notion about something to a more specific conceptualization of the idea. Once the concept has been defined and differentiated from other concepts, it can be formally studied as a construct. The steps involved in moving toward a concrete representation of the construct and the issues involved in determining how well that process has been conducted are the subject of this chapter. The most important characteristic that a measure of a construct can have is **validity**.

Construct validity refers to the degree to which inferences can legitimately be made from the **operationalizations** in your study to the theoretical constructs on which those operationalizations are based. Whoa! Can you believe that the term *operationalization* has eight syllables? That's a mouthful. What does it mean here? An operationalization is your translation of an idea or construct into something real and concrete. Let's say you have an idea for a treatment or program you would like to create. The operationalization is the program or treatment itself, as it exists after you create it. The construct validity issue is the degree to which the actual (operationalized) program reflects the ideal (the program as you conceptualized or envisioned it). Imagine that you want to measure the construct of self-esteem. You have an idea of what self-esteem means. You construct a ten-item paper-and-pencil instrument to measure self-esteem. The instrument is the operationalization; it's the translation of the idea of self-esteem into something concrete, into specific operations. The construct validity question here would be how well the ten-item instrument (the operationalization) reflects the idea you had of self-esteem. Well, I'll cover this in more detail later, but I didn't want to start the chapter with an eight-syllable word that will confuse you at the outset.

---

validity
The best available approximation of the truth of a given proposition, inference, or conclusion.

construct validity
The degree to which inferences can legitimately be made from the operationalizations in your study to the theoretical constructs on which those operationalizations are based.

operationalization
The act of translating a construct into its manifestation—for example, translating the idea of your treatment or program into the actual program, or translating the idea of what you want to measure into the real measure. The result is also referred to as an *operationalization*; that is, you might describe your actual program as an *operationalized program*.

Like **external validity** (see the discussion in Chapter 2) construct validity is related to generalizing. However, whereas external validity involves generalizing from your study context to other people, places, or times, construct validity involves generalizing from your program or measures to the *concept or idea* of your program or measures. You might think of construct validity as a labeling issue. When you implement a program that you call a Head Start program, is your label an accurate one? When you measure what you term *self-esteem* is that what you were really measuring?

I would like to address two major issues here. The first is the more straightforward one. I'll discuss several ways of thinking about the idea of construct validity, and several metaphors that might provide you with a foundation in the richness of this idea. Then, I'll discuss the major construct validity threats, the kinds of arguments your critics are likely to raise when you make a claim that your program or measure is valid.

In this text, as in most research methods texts, construct validity is presented in the section on measurement; it is typically presented as one of many different types of validity (for example, **face validity**, **predictive validity**, or **concurrent validity**) that you might want to be sure your measures have. I don't see it that way at all. I see construct validity as the overarching quality of measurement with all of the other measurement validity labels falling beneath it. I don't see construct validity as limited only to measurement. As I've already implied, I think it is as much a part of the independent variable—the program or treatment—as it is the dependent variable. So, I'll try to make some sense of the various measurement validity types in this chapter and try to move you to think instead of the validity of *any* operationalization as falling within the general category of construct validity, with a variety of subcategories and subtypes.

This view of validity has much in common with the perspective developed by Samuel Messick, who had a very influential career in test development and validation at the Educational Testing Service. Messick (1995) thought of validity as a unified idea with many facets, including the theories that dictate what the structure of constructs should look like and the social consequences of test scores. We will return to consideration of facets of construct validity, but first let's look at some history to see how these ideas evolved in the real world.

During World War II, the U.S. government involved hundreds (and perhaps thousands) of psychologists and psychology graduate students in the development of an array of measures that were relevant to the war effort. They needed personality screening tests for prospective fighter pilots, personnel measures that would enable sensible assignment of people to job skills, psychophysical measures to test reaction times, and so on. After the war, these psychologists needed to find gainful employment outside of the military, and it's not surprising that many of them moved into testing and measurement in a civilian context. During the early 1950s, the American Psychological Association became increasingly concerned with the quality or validity of all of the new measures that were being generated and decided to convene an effort to set standards for psychological measures. The first formal articulation of the idea of construct validity came from this effort and was couched under the somewhat grandiose term of the nomological network (see Section 3-1e, The Nomological Network). The nomological network provided a theoretical basis for the idea of construct validity, but it didn't provide practicing researchers with a way to actually establish whether their measures had construct validity. In 1959, an attempt was made to develop a concrete, practical method for assessing construct validity using what is called a *multitrait-multimethod matrix*, or MTMM for short (see Section 3-1f, The Multitrait-Multimethod Matrix). To argue that your measures had construct validity under the MTMM approach, you had to demonstrate that there was *both convergent* and discriminant validity in your measures. You demonstrated construct validity when you showed that measures that are theoretically supposed to be highly

external validity
The degree to which the conclusions in your study would hold for other persons in other places and at other times.

face validity
A type of validity that assures that "on its face" the operationalization seems like a good translation of the construct.

predictive validity
A type of construct validity based on the idea that your measure is able to predict what it theoretically should be able to predict.

concurrent validity
An operationalization's ability to distinguish between groups that it should theoretically be able to distinguish between.

interrelated are, in practice, highly interrelated. You showed discriminant validity when you demonstrated that measures that shouldn't be related to each other in fact were not.

While the MTMM did provide a methodology for assessing construct validity, it was a difficult one to implement well, especially in applied social research contexts and, in fact, has seldom been formally attempted. When the thinking about construct validity that underlies both the nomological network and the MTMM is examined carefully, one of the key themes that can be identified is in the idea of pattern. When you claim that your programs or measures have construct validity, you are essentially claiming that you, as a researcher, understand how your constructs or theories of the programs and measures operate in theory, and you are claiming that you can provide evidence that they behave in practice the way you think they should, that they follow the expected pattern.

The researcher essentially has a theory about how the programs and measures relate to each other (and other theoretical terms), a *theoretical pattern* if you will. The researcher provides evidence through observation that the programs or measures actually behave that way in reality, an *observed pattern*. When you claim construct validity, you're essentially claiming that your observed pattern—how things operate in reality—corresponds with your theoretical pattern—how you think the world works. I call this process **pattern matching**, and I believe that it is the heart of construct validity. It is clearly an underlying theme in both the nomological network and the MTMM ideas. In addition, I think that, as researchers, we can develop concrete and feasible methods that enable practicing researchers to assess pattern matches to assess the construct validity of their research. Section 3-1g, Pattern Matching for Construct Validity, lays out my idea of how you might use this approach to assess construct validity.

pattern matching
The degree of correspondence between two patterns. For instance, you might look at a pattern match of a theoretical expectation pattern with an observed pattern to see if you are getting the outcomes you expect or if your measures intercorrelate the way you would theoretically predict they would.

3-1a Measurement Validity Types

There's an awful lot of confusion in the methodological literature that stems from the wide variety of labels used to describe the validity of measures. I want to make two cases here. First, it's dumb to limit our scope only to the validity of measures. I really want to talk about the validity of any operationalization. That is, any time you translate a concept or construct into a functioning and operating reality (*the operationalization*), you need to be concerned about how well you performed the translation. This issue is as relevant when talking about treatments or programs as it is when talking about measures. (In fact, come to think of it, you could also think of sampling in this way. The population of interest in your study is the construct and the sample is your operationalization. If you think of it this way, you are essentially talking about the construct validity of the sampling and construct validity merges with the idea of external validity as discussed in Chapter 2. The construct validity question, "How well does my sample represent the idea of the population?" merges with the external validity question, "How well can I generalize from my sample to the population?") Second, I want to use the term *construct validity* to refer to the general case of translating any construct into an operationalization. Let's use all of the other typical measurement-related validity terms to reflect different ways you can demonstrate different aspects of construct validity.

With all that in mind, following is a list of the validity types that are typically mentioned in texts and research papers when talking about the quality of measurement and how I would organize and categorize them.

Construct Validity

- **Translation validity**
  - Face validity
  - Content validity

- **Criterion-related validity**
  - Predictive validity
  - Concurrent validity
  - Convergent validity
  - Discriminant validity

I have to warn you here that I made this list up. I've never heard of **translation validity** before, but I needed a good name to summarize what both face and **content validity** are getting at, and that one seemed sensible. (See how easy it is to be a methodologist?) All of the other labels are commonly known, but the way I've organized them is different than I've seen elsewhere.

Let's see if I can make some sense out of this list. First, as mentioned previously, I would like to use the term *construct validity* to be the overarching category. Construct validity is the approximate truth of the conclusion that your operationalization accurately reflects its construct. All of the other validity types essentially address some aspect of this general issue (which is why I've subsumed them under the general category of construct validity). Second, I make a distinction between two broad types: translation validity and criterion-related validity. That's because I think these correspond to the two major ways you can ensure and assess the validity of an operationalization.

In translation validity, you focus on whether the operationalization is a good reflection of the construct. This approach is definitional in nature; it assumes you have a good, detailed definition of the construct and that you can check the operationalization against it. In **criterion-related validity**, you examine whether the operationalization behaves the way it should given your theory of the construct. This type of validity is a more relational approach to construct validity. It assumes that your operationalization should function in predictable ways in relation to other operationalizations based on your theory of the construct. (If all this seems a bit dense, hang in there until you've gone through the following discussion and then come back and reread this paragraph.) Let's go through the specific validity types.

Translation Validity In essence, both of the translation validity types (face and content validity) attempt to assess the degree to which you accurately *translated* your construct into the operationalization, and hence the choice of name. Let's look at the two types of translation validity.

Face Validity. In face validity, you look at the operationalization and see whether *on its face* it seems like a good translation of the construct. This is probably the weakest way to try to demonstrate construct validity. For instance, you might look at a measure of math ability, read through the questions, and decide it seems like this is a good measure of math ability (the label *math ability* seems appropriate for this measure). Or, you might observe a teenage pregnancy-prevention program and conclude that it is indeed a teenage pregnancy-prevention program. Of course, if this is all you do to assess face validity, it would clearly be weak evidence because it is essentially a subjective judgment call. (Note that just because it is weak evidence doesn't mean that it is wrong. You need to rely on your subjective judgment throughout the research process. It's just that this form of judgment won't be especially convincing to others.) You can improve the quality of a face-validity assessment considerably by making it more systematic. For instance, if you are trying to assess the face validity of a math-ability measure, it would be more convincing if you sent the test to a carefully selected sample of experts on math-ability testing and they all reported back with the judgment that your measure appears to be a good measure of math ability.

Content Validity. In content validity, you essentially check the operationalization against the relevant content domain for the construct. This approach assumes

translation validity
A type of construct validity related to how well you translated the idea of your measure into its operationalization.

content validity
A check of the operationalization against the relevant content domain for the construct.

criterion-related validity
The validation of a measure based on its relationship to another independent measure as predicted by your theory of how the measures should behave.

that you have a good detailed description of the content domain, something that's not always true. For instance, you might lay out all of the criteria that should be met in a program that claims to be a teenage pregnancy-prevention program. You would probably include in this domain specification the definition of the target group, criteria for deciding whether the program is preventive in nature (as opposed to treatment-oriented), and criteria that spell out the content that should be included such as basic information on pregnancy, the use of abstinence, birth control methods, and so on. Then, armed with your criteria, you create a type of checklist when examining your program. Only programs that meet the checklist criteria can legitimately be defined as teenage pregnancy-prevention programs. This all sounds fairly straightforward, and for many operationalizations it will be. However, for other constructs (such as self-esteem or intelligence), it will not be easy to decide which criteria constitute the content domain.

Criterion-Related Validity In criterion-related validity, you check the performance of your operationalization against some criterion. How is this different from translation validity? In translation validity, the question is, How well did you translate the idea of the construct into its manifestation? No other measure comes into play. In criterion-related validity, you usually make a prediction about how the operationalization will *perform in relation to some other measure* based on your theory of the construct. The differences among the criterion-related validity types is in the criteria they use as the standard for judgment.

For example, think again about measuring self-esteem. For content validity, you would try to describe all the things that self-esteem is in your mind and translate that into a measure. You might say that self-esteem involves how good you feel about yourself, that it includes things like your self-confidence and the degree to which you think positively about yourself. You could translate these notions into specific questions, a translation validity approach. On the other hand, you might reasonably expect that people with high self-esteem, as you construe it, would tend to act in certain ways. You might expect that you could distinguish them from people with low self-esteem. For instance, you might argue that high self-esteem people will volunteer for a task that requires self-confidence (such as speaking in public). Notice that in this case, you validate your self-esteem measure by demonstrating that it is correlated with some other independent indicator (raising hands to volunteer) that you theoretically expect high self-esteem people to evidence. This is the essential idea of criterion-related validity: validating a measure based on its relationship to another independent measure.

Predictive Validity. In predictive validity, you assess the operationalization's ability to predict something it should theoretically be able to predict. For instance, you might theorize that a measure of math ability should be able to predict how well a person will do in an engineering-based profession. You could give your measure to experienced engineers and see whether there is a high correlation between scores on the measure and their salaries as engineers. A high correlation would provide evidence for predictive validity; it would show that your measure can correctly predict something that you theoretically think it should be able to predict.

Concurrent Validity. In concurrent validity, you assess the operationalization's ability to distinguish between groups that it should theoretically be able to distinguish between. For example, if you come up with a way of assessing manic-depression, your measure should be able to distinguish between people who are diagnosed manic-depressive and those diagnosed paranoid schizophrenic. If you want to assess the concurrent validity of a new measure of empowerment, you might give the measure to both migrant farm workers and to the farm owners, theorizing that your measure should show that the farm owners are higher in empowerment. As in any discriminating test, the results are more powerful if you are able to show that you can discriminate between two similar groups.

Convergent Validity. In **convergent validity**, you examine the degree to which the operationalization is similar to (converges on) other operationalizations to which it theoretically should be similar. For instance, to show the convergent validity of a Head Start program, you might gather evidence that shows that the program is similar to other Head Start programs. To show the convergent validity of a test of arithmetic skills, you might correlate the scores on your test with scores on other tests that purport to measure basic math ability, where high correlations would be evidence of convergent validity.

Discriminant Validity. In discriminant validity, you examine the degree to which the operationalization is not similar to (diverges from) other operationalizations that it theoretically should be not be similar to. For instance, to show the discriminant validity of a Head Start program, you might gather evidence that shows that the program is *not* similar to other early childhood programs that don't label themselves as Head Start programs. To show the discriminant validity of a test of arithmetic skills, you might correlate the scores on your test with scores on tests of verbal ability, where *low* correlations would be evidence of discriminant validity.

3-1b Idea of Construct Validity

Construct validity refers to the degree to which inferences can legitimately be made from the operationalizations in your study to the theoretical constructs on which those operationalizations were based. (I know I've said this before, but it never hurts to repeat something, especially when it sounds complicated.) I find that it helps me when thinking about construct validity to make a distinction between two broad territories that I call the *land of theory* and the *land of observation* as illustrated in Figure 3–1. The land of theory is what goes on inside your mind, and your attempt to explain or articulate this to others. It is all of the ideas, theories, hunches, and **hypotheses** you have about the world. It includes the idea or construct of the outcomes or measures you believe you are trying to affect. The land of observation consists of what you see happening in the world around you and the public manifestations of that world. In the land of observation, you find your actual program or treatment, and your actual measures or observational procedures. Presumably, you have constructed the land of observation based on your theories. You developed the program to reflect the kind of program you had in mind. You created the measures to get at what you wanted to get at.

Construct validity is an assessment of how well your actual programs or measures reflect your ideas or theories, how well the bottom of Figure 3–1 reflects the

convergent validity
The degree to which the operationalization is similar to (converges on) other operationalizations to which it should be theoretically similar.

hypothesis
A model in which two mutually exclusive hypotheses that together exhaust all possible outcomes are tested, such that if one hypothesis is accepted, the second must therefore be rejected.

FIGURE 3–1   **The idea of construct validity**

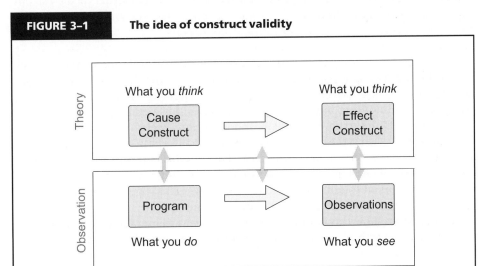

top. Why is this important? Because when you think about the world or talk about it with others (land of theory), you are using words that represent concepts. If you tell parents that a special type of math tutoring will help their child do better in math, you are communicating at the level of concepts or constructs. You aren't describing in operational detail the specific things that the tutor will do with their child. You aren't describing the specific questions that will be on the math test on which their child will excel. You are talking in general terms, using constructs. If you based your recommendation on research that showed that the special type of tutoring improved children's math scores, you would want to be sure that the type of tutoring you are referring to is the same as what that study implemented and that the type of outcome you're saying should occur was the type the study measured. Otherwise, you would be mislabeling or misrepresenting the research. In this sense, construct validity can be viewed as a *truth in labeling* issue.

The truth in labeling aspect of validity is reminiscent of what Messick (1995) was writing about when describing the *consequential* facet of validity. In addition to focusing on the relative success of a translation of a construct to a measure as many other validity theorists have done, Messick asked us to consider what happens to individuals or groups as a result of a testing process in terms of the effect on people who took the test. Therefore, his model of validity added a kind of ethical dimension because it takes into account the fact that sometimes the consequences of a testing process can be positive, as when a person succeeds or a program gets better, or negative, which is particularly troublesome when invalidity in a test creates systematic bias in scoring or unfairness in application of results.

Definitionalist versus Relationalist Views There really are two broad ways of looking at the idea of construct validity. I'll call the first the *definitionalist* perspective because it essentially holds that the way to ensure construct validity is to define the construct so precisely that you can operationalize it in a straightforward manner. In a definitionalist view, either you have operationalized the construct correctly or you haven't; it's either/or type of thinking. Either this program is a "Type A Tutoring Program" or it isn't. Either you're measuring self-esteem or you aren't.

The other perspective I'd call *relationalist*. To a relationalist, things are not either/or or black and white; concepts are more or less related to each other. The meaning of terms or constructs differs relatively, not absolutely. The program in your study might be a "Type A Tutoring Program" in some ways, while in others it is not. It might be more that type of program than another program. Your measure might be capturing some of the construct of self-esteem, but it may not capture all of it. There may be another measure that is closer to the construct of self-esteem than yours is. Relationalism suggests that meaning changes gradually. It rejects the idea that you can rely on operational definitions as the basis for construct definition.

To get a clearer idea of this distinction, you might think about how the law approaches the construct of truth. Most of you have heard the standard oath that witnesses in a U.S. court are expected to swear. They are to tell "the truth, the whole truth and nothing but the truth." What does this mean? If witnesses had to swear only to tell the truth, they might choose to interpret that to mean that they should make sure what they say is true. However, that wouldn't guarantee that they would tell *everything* they knew to be true. They might leave out some important things and still tell the truth. They just wouldn't be telling everything. On the other hand, they are asked to tell "nothing but the truth." This suggests that you can say simply that Statement X is true and Statement Y is not true.

Now, let's see how this oath translates into a measurement and construct validity context. For instance, you might want your measure to reflect the construct, the whole construct, and nothing but the construct. What does this mean? Let's assume, as shown in Figure 3–2, that you have five distinct constructs that are all conceptually related to each other: self-esteem, self-worth, self-disclosure,

| FIGURE 3–2 | Distinguishing the construct of self-esteem from other similar constructs |

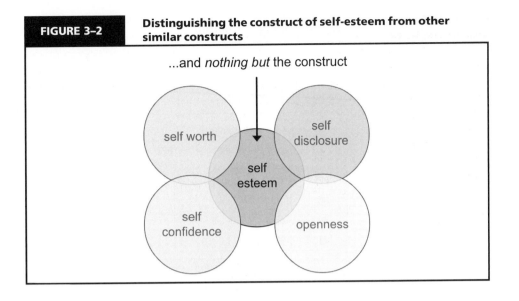

self-confidence, and openness. Most people would say that these concepts are similar, although they can be distinguished from each other. If you were trying to develop a measure of self-esteem, what would it mean to measure self-esteem, all of self-esteem, and nothing but self-esteem? If the concept of self-esteem overlaps with the others, how could you possibly measure all of it (that would presumably include the part that overlaps with others) *and* nothing but it? You couldn't! If you believe that meaning is relational in nature—that some concepts are closer in meaning than others—the legal model discussed here does not work well as a model for construct validity.

In fact, you will see that most social research methodologists have (whether they've thought about it or not) rejected the definitionalist perspective in favor of a relationalist one. To establish construct validity from a relationalist perspective you have to meet the following conditions:

- You have to set the construct you want to operationalize for example, self-esteem) within a *semantic net* (or net of meaning). This means that you have to tell what your construct is more or less similar to in meaning.
- You need to be able to provide direct evidence that you *control* the operationalization of the construct and that your operationalizations look like what they should theoretically look like. If you are trying to measure self-esteem, you have to be able to explain why you operationalized the questions the way you did. If all your questions are addition problems, how can you argue that your measure reflects self-esteem and not adding ability?
- You have to provide evidence that your data supports your theoretical view of the relations among constructs. If you believe that self-esteem is closer in meaning to self-worth than it is to anxiety, you should be able to show that measures of self-esteem are more highly correlated with measures of self-worth than with ones of anxiety.

3-1c Convergent and Discriminant Validity

Convergent and discriminant validity are both considered subcategories or subtypes of construct validity. The important thing to recognize is that they work together; if you can demonstrate that you have evidence for both convergent and discriminant validity, you have by definition demonstrated that you have evidence for construct validity. However, neither one alone is sufficient for establishing construct validity.

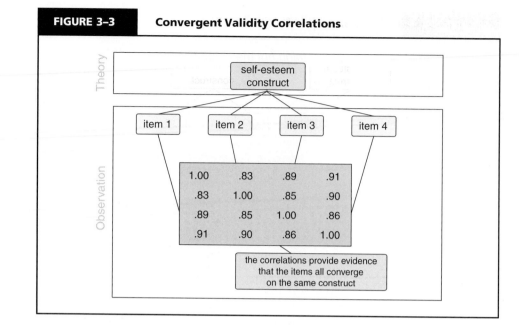

FIGURE 3–3 **Convergent Validity Correlations**

I find it easiest to think about convergent and discriminant validity as two interlocking propositions. In simple words, I would describe what they are doing as follows:

- Measures of constructs that theoretically *should* be related to each other are, in fact, observed to be related to each other (that is, you should be able to show a correspondence or *convergence* between similar constructs).
- Measures of constructs that theoretically should *not* be related to each other are, in fact, observed not to be related to each other (that is, you should be able to *discriminate* between dissimilar constructs).

To estimate the degree to which any two measures are related to each other you would typically use the correlation coefficient discussed in Chapter 12. That is, you look at the patterns of intercorrelations among the measures. Correlations between theoretically similar measures should be "high," whereas correlations between theoretically dissimilar measures should be "low."

The main problem that I have with this convergent-discriminant idea has to do with my use of the quotations around the terms *high* and *low* in the previous sentence. The problem is simple: how high do correlations need to be to provide evidence for convergence and how low do they need to be to provide evidence for discrimination? The answer is that nobody knows! In general, convergent correlations should be as high as possible and discriminant ones should be as low as possible, but there is no hard and fast rule. Well, let's not let that stop us. One thing you can assume to be true is that the convergent correlations should always be higher than the discriminant ones. At least that helps a bit.

Before we get too deep into the idea of convergence and discrimination, let's take a look at each one using a simple example.

Convergent Validity To establish convergent validity, you need to show that measures that should be related are in reality related. In Figure 3–3, you see four measures (each is an item on a scale) that all purport to reflect the construct of self-esteem. For instance, Item 1 might be the statement, "I feel good about myself," rated using a 1 to 5 scale. You theorize that all four items reflect the idea of self-esteem (which is why I labeled the top part of the figure Theory). On the bottom part of the figure (Observation), you see the intercorrelations of the four scale items. This might be based on giving your scale out to a sample of respondents. You

| FIGURE 3–4 | **Discriminant validity correlations** |

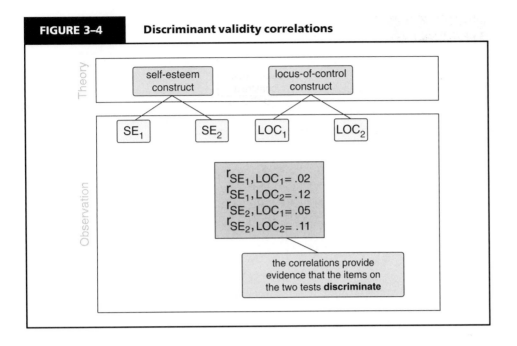

should readily see that the item intercorrelations for all item pairings are extremely high. (Remember that correlations range from −1.00 to +1.00.) The correlations provide support for your theory that all four items are related to the same construct.

Notice, however, that whereas the high intercorrelations demonstrate the four items are probably related to the same construct, that doesn't automatically mean that the construct is self-esteem. Maybe there's some other construct to which all four items are related (more about this later). However, at least, you can assume from the pattern of correlations that the four items are converging on the same thing, whatever it might be called.

Discriminant Validity To establish **discriminant validity**, you need to show that measures that should not be related are in reality not related. In Figure 3–4, you again see four measures (each is an item on a scale). Here, however, two of the items are thought to reflect the construct of self-esteem, whereas the other two are thought to reflect locus of control. The top part of the figure shows the theoretically expected relationships among the four items. If you have discriminant validity, the relationship between measures from different constructs should be low. (Again, nobody knows how low low should be, but I'll deal with that later.) There are four correlations between measures that reflect different constructs, and these are shown on the bottom of the figure (Observation). You should see immediately that these four cross-construct correlations are low (near zero) and certainly much lower than the convergent correlations in Figure 3–3.

As I mentioned previously, just because there is evidence that the two sets of two measures seem to be unrelated to different constructs (because their intercorrelations are so low) doesn't mean that the constructs they're related to are self-esteem and locus of control. However, the correlations do provide evidence that the two sets of measures are discriminated from each other.

discriminant validity
The degree to which concepts that should not be related theoretically are, in fact, not interrelated in reality.

Putting It All Together Okay, so where does this leave us? I've shown how to provide evidence for convergent and discriminant validity separately; but as I said at the outset, to argue for construct validity, you really need to be able to show that both of these types of validity are supported. Given the previous discussions of convergent and discriminant validity, you should be able to see that you could put both

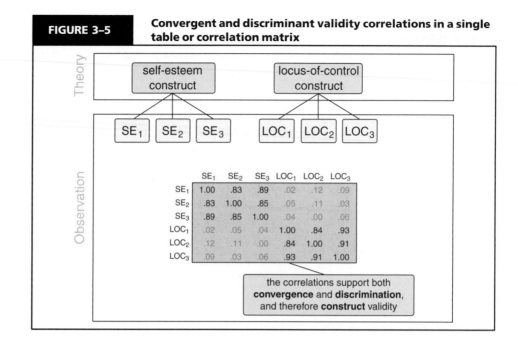

FIGURE 3–5 Convergent and discriminant validity correlations in a single table or correlation matrix

principles together into a single analysis to examine both at the same time. This is illustrated in Figure 3–5.

Figure 3–5 shows six measures: three that are theoretically related to the construct of self-esteem and three that are thought to be related to locus of control. The top part of the figure shows this theoretical arrangement. The bottom of the figure shows what a correlation matrix based on a pilot sample might show. To understand this table, first you need to be able to identify the convergent correlations and the discriminant ones. The two sets or blocks of convergent coefficients appear in a darker font: one 3×3 block for the self-esteem intercorrelations in the upper left of the table, and one 3×3 block for the locus-of-control correlations in the lower right. In addition, two 3×3 blocks of discriminant coefficients appear in a lighter-shaded font, although if you're really sharp you'll recognize that they are the same values in mirror image. (Do you know why? You might want to read up on correlations in Chapter 12.)

How do you make sense of the correlations' patterns? Remember that I said previously that there are no firm rules for how high or low the correlations need to be to provide evidence for either type of validity but that the convergent correlations should always be higher than the discriminant ones. Take a good look at the table and you will see that in this example all convergent correlations are always higher than any of the discriminant ones. I would conclude from this that the correlation matrix provides evidence for both convergent and discriminant validity, all in one table!

It's true the pattern supports discriminant and convergent validity, but does it show that the three self-esteem measures actually measure self-esteem or that the three locus-of-control measures actually measure locus of control? Of course not. That would be much too easy.

So, what good is this analysis? It does show that, as you predicted, the three self-esteem measures seem to reflect the same construct (whatever that might be). The three locus-of-control measures also seem to reflect the same construct (again, whatever that is), and the two sets of measures seem to reflect two different constructs (whatever they are). That's not bad for one simple analysis.

Okay, so how do you get to the really interesting question? How do you show that your measures are actually measuring self-esteem or locus of control? I hate to disappoint you, but there is no simple answer to that. (I bet you knew that was coming.) You can do several things to address this question. First, you can use other ways to address construct validity to help provide further evidence that you're measuring what you say you're measuring. For instance, you might use a face validity or content validity approach to demonstrate that the measures reflect the constructs you say they are. (See the discussion of types of construct validity in this chapter for more information.)

One of the most powerful approaches is to include even more constructs and measures. The more complex your theoretical model (if you find confirmation of the correct pattern in the correlations), the more evidence you are providing that you know what you're talking about (theoretically speaking). Of course, it's also harder to get all the correlations to give you the exact right pattern as you add more measures. In many studies, you simply don't have the luxury of adding more and more measures because it's too costly or demanding. Despite the impracticality, if you can afford to do it, adding more constructs and measures enhances your ability to assess construct validity using approaches like the MTMM and the nomological network described later in this chapter.

Perhaps the most interesting approach to getting at construct validity involves the idea of pattern matching. Instead of viewing convergent and discriminant validity as differences of kind, pattern matching views them as differences in degree. Because of this, pattern matching seems a more reasonable idea when compared with the MTMM and the nomological network, and helps you avoid the problem of how high or low correlations need to be to say that you've established convergence or discrimination.

3-1d The Nomological Network

The nomological network (Figure 3–6) is an idea that was developed by Lee Cronbach and Paul Meehl in 1955 as part of the American Psychological Association's efforts to develop standards for psychological testing. The term *nomological* is derived from Greek and means lawful, so the nomological network can be thought

FIGURE 3–6   **The nomological network**

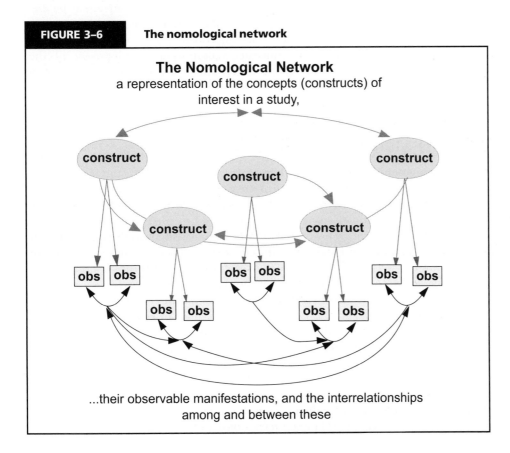

The Nomological Network
a representation of the concepts (constructs) of
interest in a study,

...their observable manifestations, and the interrelationships
among and between these

of as the lawful network. The nomological network was Cronbach and Meehl's view of construct validity. In short, to provide evidence that your measure has construct validity, Cronbach and Meehl argued that you had to develop a nomological network for your measure. This network would include the theoretical framework for what you are trying to measure, an empirical framework for how you are going to measure it, and specification of the linkages among and between these two frameworks.

According to Cronbach and Meehl, the nomological network is founded on the following principles that guide the researcher trying to establish construct validity:

- "Scientifically, to make clear what something is or means, so that laws can be set forth in which that something occurs.
- The laws in a nomological network may relate to:

  - Observable properties or quantities to each other
  - Different theoretical constructs to each other
  - Theoretical constructs to observables

- At least some of the laws in the network must involve observables.
- Learning more about a theoretical construct is a matter of elaborating the nomological network in which it occurs or of increasing the definiteness of its components.
- The basic rule for adding a new construct or relation to a theory is that it must generate laws (nomologicals) confirmed by observation or reduce the number of nomologicals required to predict some observables.
- Operations which are qualitatively different overlap or measure the same thing."

What Cronbach and Meehl were trying to do with this idea is to link the conceptual/theoretical realm with the observable one because this is the central concern of construct validity. Although the nomological network idea may be useful as a philosophical foundation for construct validity, it does not provide a practical and usable methodology for actually assessing construct validity. The next phase in the evolution of the idea of construct validity—the development of the MTMM—moved us a bit further toward a methodological approach to construct validity.

3-1e The Multitrait-Multimethod Matrix

multitrait-multimethod (MTMM) matrix
A matrix of correlations arranged to facilitate the assessment of construct validity. The MTMM assumes that you have measured each construct (trait) with different methods in a fully crossed design (traits by methods).

The **multitrait-multimethod matrix** (hereafter labeled **MTMM**) is an approach to assessing the construct validity of a set of measures in a study. It was developed in 1959 by Campbell and Fiske in part as an attempt to provide a practical methodology that researchers could actually use (as opposed to the nomological network idea, which was theoretically useful but did not include a methodology). Along with the MTMM, Campbell and Fiske introduced two new types of validity: convergent and discriminant—as subcategories of construct validity. To recap, convergent validity is the degree to which concepts that should be related theoretically are interrelated in reality. Discriminant validity is the degree to which concepts that should *not* be related theoretically are, in fact, *not* interrelated in reality. You can assess both convergent and discriminant validity using the MTMM. To be able to claim that your measures have construct validity, you have to demonstrate both convergence and discrimination.

The MTMM (Figure 3–7) is simply a matrix or table of correlations arranged to facilitate the assessment of construct validity. The MTMM assumes that you measure each of several concepts (called *traits* by Campbell and Fiske) by each of several methods (such as a paper-and-pencil test, a direct observation, or a performance

FIGURE 3–7   **The MTMM matrix**

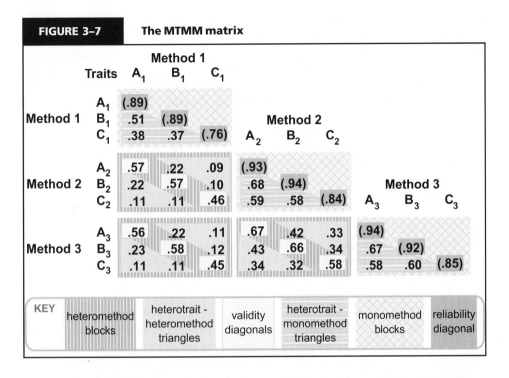

measure). The MTMM is a restrictive methodology; ideally, you should measure *each* concept by *each* method.

To construct an MTMM, you need to arrange the correlation matrix by methods within concepts. Figure 3–7 shows an MTMM for three concepts (traits 1, 2, and 3), each of which measured with three different methods (A, B, and C). Note that you lay the matrix out in blocks by *method*. Essentially, the MTMM is just a correlation matrix between your measures, with one exception: instead of 1's along the diagonal (as in the typical correlation matrix) you substitute an estimate of the reliability of each measure as the diagonal (see Section 3-2, Reliability).

Before you can interpret an MTMM, you must understand how to identify the different parts of the matrix. First, you should note that the matrix consists of nothing but correlations. It is a square, symmetric matrix, so you need to look at only half of it. Figure 3–7 shows the lower triangle. Second, these correlations can be grouped into three kinds of shapes: diagonals, triangles, and blocks. The specific shapes are as follows:

- *The reliability diagonal (monotrait-monomethod)*. These are estimates of the reliability of each measure in the matrix. You can estimate reliabilities in different ways (for example, test-retest or internal consistency). There are as many correlations in the reliability diagonal as there are measures; in this example, there are nine measures and nine reliabilities. The first reliability in the example is the correlation of Trait A, Method 1 with Trait A, Method 1. (Hereafter, I'll abbreviate this relationship A1-A1). Notice that this is essentially the correlation of the measure with itself. In fact, such a correlation would always be perfect ($r = 1.0$). Instead, you substitute an estimate of reliability. You could also consider these values to be monotrait-monomethod correlations.

- *The validity diagonals (monotrait-heteromethod)*. These are correlations between measures of the same trait measured using different methods. Since the MTMM is organized into method blocks, there is one validity diagonal in each method block. For example, look at the A1-A2 correlation of .57 in Figure 3–7. This is the correlation between two measures of the same trait (A) measured with two different measures (1 and 2). Because the two measures are of the same trait or concept, you would expect them to be strongly correlated. You could also consider these values to be monotrait-heteromethod correlations.

- *The heterotrait-monomethod triangles.* These are the correlations among measures that share the same method of measurement, for instance, A1-B1 = .51 in the upper left heterotrait-monomethod triangle in Figure 3–7. Note that what these correlations share is method, not trait or concept. If these correlations are high, it is because measuring different things with the same method results in correlated measures. Or, in more straightforward terms, you have a strong methods factor.
- *Heterotrait-heteromethod triangles.* These are correlations that differ in both trait and method. For instance, A1-B2 is .22 in the example in Figure 3–7. Generally, because these correlations share neither trait nor method you expect them to be the lowest in the matrix.
- *The monomethod blocks.* These consist of all of the correlations that share the same method of measurement. There are as many blocks as there are methods of measurement.
- *The heteromethod blocks.* These consist of all correlations that do *not* share the same methods. There are $[K(K-1)]/2$ such blocks, where $K =$ the number of methods. In the example in Figure 3–7, there are three methods, so there are $[3(3-1)]/2 = [3(2)]/2 = 6/2 = 3$ such blocks.

Principles of Interpretation Now that you can identify the different parts of the MTMM, you can begin to understand the rules for interpreting it. You should realize that MTMM interpretation requires the researcher to use judgment. Even though some of the principles might be violated in a specific MTMM, you might still wind up concluding that you have fairly strong construct validity. In other words, you won't necessarily get *perfect* adherence to these principles in applied research settings, even when you do have evidence to support construct validity. To me, interpreting an MTMM is a lot like a physician's reading of an x-ray. A practiced eye can often spot things that the neophyte misses! A researcher who is experienced with MTMM can use it to identify weaknesses in measurement as well as to assess construct validity.

To help make the principles more concrete, let's make the example a bit more realistic. Imagine that you are going to conduct a study of sixth-grade students and you want to measure three traits or concepts: Self-Esteem (SE), Self-Disclosure (SD), and Locus of Control (LC). Furthermore, you want to measure each of these traits three different ways: a Paper-and-Pencil (P&P) measure, a Teacher rating, and a Parent rating. The results are arrayed in the MTMM as shown in Figure 3–8. As the principles are presented, try to identify the appropriate coefficients in the MTMM and make a judgment yourself about the strength of construct validity claims.

FIGURE 3–8		An example of an MTMM matrix								
		P&P			**Teacher**			**Parent**		
	Traits	SE_1	SD_1	LC_1	SE_2	SD_2	LC_2	SE_3	SD_3	LC_3
P&P	SE_1	(.89)								
	SD_1	.51	(.89)							
	LC_1	.38	.37	(.76)						
Teacher	SE_2	.57	.22	.09	(.93)					
	SD_2	.22	.57	.10	.68	(.94)				
	LC_2	.11	.11	.46	.59	.58	(.84)			
Parent	SE_3	.56	.22	.11	.67	.42	.33	(.94)		
	SD_3	.23	.58	.12	.43	.66	.34	.67	(.92)	
	LC_3	.11	.11	.45	.34	.32	.58	.58	.60	(.85)

The following list contains the basic principles or rules for the MTMM. You use these rules to determine the strength of the construct validity:

- Coefficients in the reliability diagonal should consistently be the highest in the matrix. That is, a trait should be more highly correlated with itself than with anything else! This rule is uniformly true in the example in Figure 3–8.
- Coefficients in the validity diagonals should be significantly different from zero and high enough to warrant further investigation. This rule is essentially evidence of convergent validity. All of the correlations in Figure 3–8 meet this criterion.
- A validity coefficient should be higher than the values in its column and row in the same heterotrait-heteromethod triangle. In other words, (SE P&P) − (SE Teacher) should be greater than (SE P&P) − (SD Teacher), (SE P&P) − (LC Teacher), (SE Teacher) − (SD P&P), and (SE Teacher) − (LC P&P). This is true in all cases in Figure 3–8.
- A validity coefficient should be higher than all coefficients in the heterotrait-monomethod triangles. This rule essentially emphasizes that trait factors should be stronger than methods factors. Note that this is *not* true in all cases in the example in Figure 3–8. For instance, the (LC P&P) − (LC Teacher) correlation of .46 is less than (SE Teacher) − (SD Teacher), (SE Teacher) − (LC Teacher), and (SD Teacher) − (LC Teacher)—evidence that there might be a methods factor, especially on the Teacher observation method.
- The same *pattern* of trait interrelationship should be seen in all triangles. The example in Figure 3–8 clearly meets this criterion. Notice that in all triangles the SE-SD relationship is approximately twice as large as the relationships that involve LC.

Advantages and Disadvantages of MTMM

The MTMM idea provided an operational methodology for assessing construct validity. In the one matrix, it was possible to examine both convergent and discriminant validity simultaneously. By including methods on an equal footing with traits, Campbell and Fiske stressed the importance of looking for the effects of how we measure in addition to what we measure. In addition, MTMM provided a rigorous framework for assessing construct validity.

Despite these advantages, MTMM has received little use since its introduction in 1959 for several reasons. First, in its purest form, MTMM requires a fully crossed measurement design; each of several traits is measured by each of several methods. Although Campbell and Fiske explicitly recognized that one could have an incomplete design, they stressed the importance of multiple replication of the same trait across methods. In some applied research contexts, it just isn't possible to measure all traits with all desired methods. (For example, what would you use to obtain multiple observations of weight?) In most applied social research, it isn't feasible to make methods an explicit part of the research design. Second, the judgmental nature of the MTMM may have worked against its wider adoption (although it should actually be perceived as a strength). Many researchers wanted a test for construct validity that would result in a single statistical coefficient that could be tested—the equivalent of a reliability coefficient. It was impossible with MTMM to quantify the *degree* of construct validity in a study. Finally, the judgmental nature of MTMM meant that different researchers could legitimately arrive at different conclusions.

A Modified MTMM —Leaving Out the Methods Factor

What if we try to obtain some of the benefits of the MTMM while minimizing some of the disadvantages that have limited its use? One of the major limiting aspects of the MTMM is the requirement that each construct be measured with multiple methods, a requirement that is just not practical in most applied social research. What if we eliminate that requirement? In this case, the MTMM becomes equivalent to a

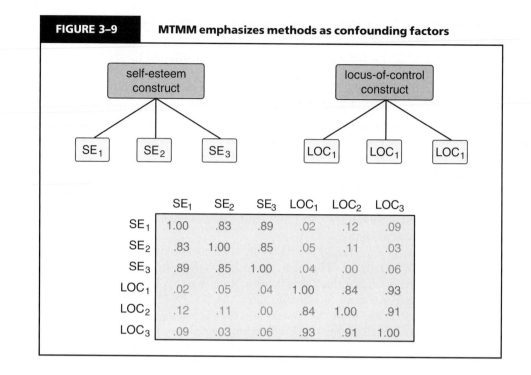

FIGURE 3–9 **MTMM emphasizes methods as confounding factors**

multitrait matrix and would look like the matrix shown earlier in Figure 3–5 when describing convergent and discriminant validity.

The important thing to notice about the matrix in Figure 3–5 is that *it does not include a methods factor* as a true MTMM would. The matrix does examine both convergent and discriminant validity (just like the MTMM) but it explicitly looks at only construct intrarelationships and interrelationships. That is, it doesn't look at methods relationships like a full MTMM does.

You can see in Figure 3–9 that the MTMM idea really had two major themes. The first is the idea of looking simultaneously at the pattern of convergence and discrimination. This idea is similar in purpose to the notions implicit in the nomological network described earlier; you are looking at the *pattern* of interrelationships based on your theory of the nomological net. The second idea in MTMM is the emphasis on methods as a potential confounding factor.

Although methods may confound the results, they won't necessarily do so in any given study; and, perhaps it is too much to ask of any single methodology that it simultaneously be able to assess construct validity and address the potential for methods factors in measurement. Perhaps if you split the two agendas, you will find that the feasibility of examining convergent and discriminant validity is greater; but what do you do about methods factors? One way to deal with them is to replicate research projects, rather than try to incorporate a methods test into a single research study. Thus, if you find a particular outcome in a study using several measures, you might see whether that same outcome is obtained when you replicate the study using *different methods of measurement* for the same constructs. The methods issue is considered more as an issue of generalizability (across measurement methods) rather than one of construct validity.

When viewed without the methods component, the idea of a MTMM is a much more realistic and practical approach for assessing convergent and discriminant validity, and hence construct validity. You will see that when you move away from the explicit consideration of methods and when you begin to see convergence and discrimination as differences of degree, you essentially have the foundation for the pattern matching approach to assessing construct validity as discussed in the following section.

3-1f Pattern Matching for Construct Validity

The idea of using pattern matching as a rubric for assessing construct validity is an area in which I have tried to make a contribution (Trochim, 1985, 1989), although my work was clearly foreshadowed, especially in much of Donald T. Campbell's writings on the MTMM. Here, I'll try to explain what I mean by pattern matching with respect to construct validity.

The Theory of Pattern Matching A pattern is any arrangement of objects or entities. The term *arrangement* is used here to indicate that a pattern is by definition nonrandom and at least potentially describable. All theories imply some pattern, but theories and patterns are not the same thing. In general, a theory postulates structural relationships between key constructs. The theory can be used as the basis for generating patterns of predictions. For instance, $E = MC^2$ can be considered a theoretical formulation. A pattern of expectations can be developed from this formula by generating predicted values for one of these variables given fixed values of the others. Not all theories are stated in mathematical form, especially in applied social research, but all theories provide information that enables the generation of patterns of predictions.

Pattern matching always involves an attempt to link two patterns where one is a theoretical pattern and the other is an observed or operational one. The top part of Figure 3–10 shows the realm of theory. The theory might originate from a formal tradition of theorizing, might be the investigator's ideas or hunches, or might arise from some combination of these. The conceptualization task involves the translation of these ideas into a specifiable theoretical pattern indicated by the top shape in the figure. The bottom part of the figure indicates the realm of observation. This is broadly meant to include direct observation in the form of impressions, field notes, and the like, as well as more formal objective measures. The collection or organization of relevant operationalizations (relevant to the theoretical pattern) is termed the *observational pattern* and is indicated by the lower shape in the figure.

FIGURE 3–10   **The idea of pattern matching**

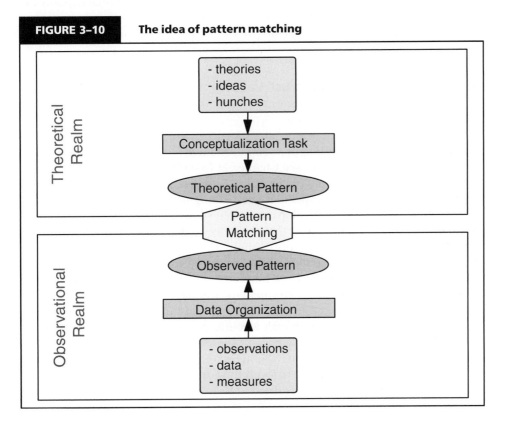

The inferential task involves the attempt to relate, link, or match these two patterns as indicated by the double arrows in the center of the figure. To the extent that the patterns match, one can conclude that the theory and any other alternative theories that predict the same observed pattern may be plausible explanations for it.

It is important to demonstrate that no plausible alternative theories can account for the observed pattern and this task is made much easier when the theoretical pattern of interest is a unique one. In effect, a more complex theoretical pattern is like a unique fingerprint that one is seeking in the observed pattern. With more complex theoretical patterns, it is usually more difficult to construe sensible alternative patterns that would also predict the same result. To the extent that theoretical and observed patterns do not match, the theory may be incorrect or poorly formulated, the observations may be inappropriate or inaccurate, or some combination of both states may exist.

All research employs pattern-matching principles, although this is seldom done consciously. In the traditional two-group experimental context (see Chapter 9), for instance, the typical theoretical outcome pattern is the hypothesis that there will be a significant difference between treated and untreated groups. The observed outcome pattern might consist of the averages for the two groups on one or more measures. The pattern match is accomplished by a test of significance such as the *t*-test or ANOVA. In survey research, pattern matching forms the basis of generalizations across different concepts or population subgroups. (This is covered in Chapter 4.) In qualitative research pattern matching lies at the heart of any attempt to conduct thematic analyses. (This is discussed in Chapter 6.)

Although current research methods can be described in pattern-matching terms, the idea of pattern matching implies more and suggests how one might improve on these current methods. Specifically, pattern matching implies that *more complex patterns, if matched, yield greater validity for the theory.* Pattern matching does not differ fundamentally from traditional hypothesis testing and model building approaches. A theoretical pattern is a hypothesis about what is expected in the data. The observed pattern consists of the data used to examine the theoretical model. The major differences between pattern matching and more traditional hypothesis-testing approaches are that pattern matching encourages the use of more complex or detailed hypotheses and treats the observations from a multivariate rather than a univariate perspective.

Pattern Matching and Construct Validity Although pattern matching can be used to address a variety of questions in social research, the emphasis here is on its use in assessing construct validity.

Figure 3-11 shows the pattern-matching structure for an example involving five measurement constructs: arithmetic, algebra, geometry, spelling, and reading. This example uses concept mapping (see Chapter 2) to develop the theoretical pattern among these constructs. In concept mapping, you generate a large set of potential arithmetic, algebra, geometry, spelling, and reading questions. You sort them into piles of similar questions and develop a map that shows each question in relation to the others. On the map, questions that are more similar are closer to each other; those that are less similar are more distant. From the map, you can find the straight-line distances between all pair of points (all questions). This mapping is the matrix of interpoint distances. You might use the questions from the map when constructing your measurement instrument, or you might sample from these questions. On the observed side, you have one or more test instruments that contain a number of questions about arithmetic, algebra, geometry, spelling, and reading. You analyze the data and construct a matrix of interitem correlations.

What you want to do is compare the matrix of interpoint distances from your concept map (the theoretical pattern) with the correlation matrix of the questions (the observed pattern). How do you achieve this? Let's assume that you had 100 prospective questions on your concept map, 20 for each construct. Correspondingly, you

FIGURE 3–11   A pattern-matching example

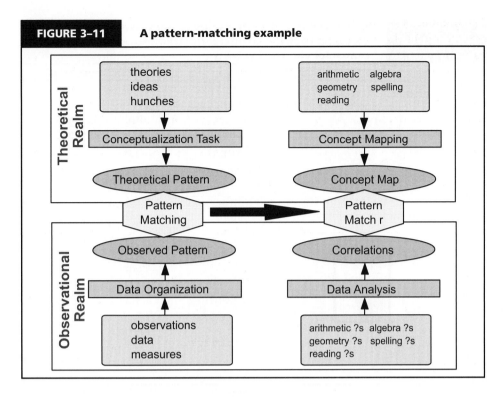

have 100 questions on your measurement instrument, 20 in each area. Thus, both matrices are 100 × 100 in size. Because both matrices are symmetric, you actually have $[N(N-1)]/2 = [100(99)]/2 = 9900/2 = 4950$ unique pairs (excluding the diagonal). If you string out the values in each matrix, you can construct a vector or column of 4950 numbers for each matrix. The first number is the value comparing pair $(1,2)$; the next is $(1,3)$, and so on, to $(N-1,N)$ or $(99,100)$. This procedure is illustrated in Figure 3–12. Now, you can compute the overall correlation between these two columns, which is the correlation between the theoretical and observed patterns (the pattern matching correlation). In this example, let's assume it is $-.93$. Why would it be a *negative* correlation? Because you are correlating *distances* on the map with the *similarities* in the correlations and you expect that *greater* distance on the map should be associated with *lower* correlation and *less* distance with *greater* correlation.

The pattern matching correlation is the overall estimate of the degree of construct validity in this example because it estimates the degree to which the operational measures reflect your theoretical expectations.

Advantages and Disadvantages of Pattern Matching   The pattern-matching approach to construct validity has several disadvantages. The most obvious is that pattern matching requires that you specify your theory of the constructs rather precisely. This is typically not done in applied social research, at least not to the level of specificity implied here; but perhaps it *should* be done. Perhaps the more restrictive assumption in pattern matching is that you are able to structure the theoretical and observed patterns the same way so that you can directly correlate them. This method requires you to quantify both patterns and, ultimately, describe them in matrices that have the same dimensions. In most research as it is currently done, it is relatively easy to construct a matrix of the interitem correlations from the data. However, researchers seldom currently use methods like concept mapping to estimate theoretical patterns that can be linked with the observed ones. Again, perhaps this ought to be done more frequently.

The pattern-matching approach has a number of advantages, especially relative to the MTMM. First, it is more *general* and *flexible* than MTMM. It does not require

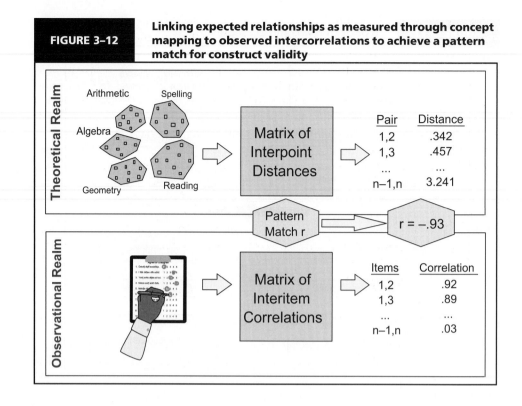

FIGURE 3–12   **Linking expected relationships as measured through concept mapping to observed intercorrelations to achieve a pattern match for construct validity**

that you measure each construct with multiple methods. Second, it treats convergence and discrimination as a *continuum*. Concepts are more or less similar and so their interrelations would be more or less convergent or discriminant, which moves the convergent/discriminant distinction away from the simplistic dichotomous categorical notion to one that is more suitably post-positivist and continuous in nature. Third, the pattern-matching approach does make it possible to estimate the overall construct validity for a set of measures in a specific context—it is the correlation of the theoretical expectations with the observed relationships. Notice that you don't estimate construct validity for a single measure because construct validity, like discrimination, is always a relative metric. Just as you can ask only whether you have distinguished something if there is something to distinguish it from, you can assess construct validity only in terms of a theoretical semantic or nomological net, the conceptual context within which it resides. The pattern-matching correlation tells you, for your particular study, whether there is a demonstrable relationship between how you theoretically expect your measures to interrelate and how they interrelate in practice. Finally, because pattern matching requires a more specific theoretical pattern than you typically articulate, it *requires* you to specify what you think about the constructs. That's got to be a good thing.

Social research has long been criticized for conceptual sloppiness, for repackaging old constructs in new terminology and failing to develop an evolution of research around key theoretical constructs. Perhaps the emphasis on theory articulation in pattern matching will encourage researchers to be more careful about the conceptual underpinnings of their empirical work, and, after all, isn't that what construct validity is all about?

3-1g Structural Equation Modeling

Like pattern matching, structural equation modeling (SEM) is a method that allows researchers to compare the theoretical with the actual, that is, models based on unobserved ideas with models based on data from observed measurements. In fact, we might even describe it as a very good and general way to do MTMM analysis, pattern-matching analysis, or practically any sort of problem that involves an assessment of construct validity. It is a method that is flexible enough to fit specific construct validity questions, whether having to do with the structural validity of a single measure or of an entire system of related constructs as in MTMM analysis. In a sense, we could say that the mathematics and technology needed to examine a model like the one Cronbach and Meehl proposed in their 1955 article (for example, the nomological network in Figure 3–6) have caught up with the theory a mere 50 years later! As software to conduct SEM studies has improved, these kinds of studies have become common in the social science literature. Graphic user interfaces (GUIs) make it possible to draw the model like the one in Figure 3–6 as you would on paper, and then submit the model for testing based on the data you have collected to represent the constructs. With SEM, we can now estimate the overall goodness of fit of the theory to the data as well as study component relationships within the model. As a final note, we would do well to be mindful that construct validation is a "never-ending procedure" (Fiske, 2002, p. 175), even with the sophistication of SEM computer programs that can solve a large and complex set of equations simultaneously. Just as methods of evaluating aspects of validity will evolve, so will theories that generate the constructs we seek to understand.

3-1h Threats to Construct Validity

Before I launch into a discussion of the most common threats to construct validity, take a moment to recall what a threat to validity is. In a research study, you are likely to reach a conclusion that your program was a good operationalization of what you wanted and that your measures reflected what you wanted them to reflect. Would you be correct? How will you be criticized if you make these types of claims? How might you strengthen your claims? The kinds of questions and issues your critics will raise are what I mean by threats to construct validity.

I take the list of threats from the discussion in Cook and Campbell (1979). Although I love their discussion, I do find some of their terminology less than straightforward; much of what I'll do here is try to explain this stuff in terms that the rest of us might hope to understand. One way we can sort the threats to validity is into two major categories: those resulting implicitly from the study design and those arising from the behavior or participants.

Design Threats to Validity

Inadequate Preoperational Explication of Constructs. This section title isn't nearly as ponderous as it sounds. Here, *preoperational* means before translating constructs into measures or treatments, and *explication* means explanation; in other words, *you didn't do a good enough job of defining (operationally) what you mean by the construct.* How is this a threat? Imagine that your program consisted of a new type of approach to rehabilitation. A critic comes along and claims that, in fact, your program is neither *new* nor a true *rehabilitation* program. You are being accused of doing a poor job of thinking through your constructs. Here are some possible solutions:

- Think through your concepts better.
- Use methods (for example, concept mapping) to articulate your concepts.
- Get experts to critique your operationalizations.

Mono-Operation Bias. **Mono-operation bias** pertains to the independent variable, cause, program, or treatment in your study: it does not pertain to measures or outcomes (see mono-method bias in the following section). *If you use only a single version of a program in a single place at a single point in time, you may not be capturing the full breadth of the concept of the program.* Every operationalization is flawed relative to the construct on which it is based. If you conclude that your program reflects the construct of the program, your critics are likely to argue that the results of your

mono-operation bias
A threat to construct validity that occurs when you rely on only a single implementation of your independent variable, cause, program, or treatment in your study.

study reflect only the peculiar version of the program that you implemented, and not the actual construct you had in mind. Solution: try to implement multiple versions of your program.

Mono-Method Bias.
Mono-method bias refers to your measures or observations, not to your programs or causes. *Otherwise, it's essentially the same issue as mono-operation bias. With only a single version of a self-esteem measure, you can't provide much evidence that you're really measuring self-esteem.* Your critics will suggest that you aren't measuring self-esteem, that you're measuring only part of it, for instance. Solution: try to implement multiple measures of key constructs and try to demonstrate (perhaps through a pilot or side study) that the measures you use behave as you theoretically expect them to behave.

Interaction of Different Treatments.
In the real world, you cannot control or even know about all of the possible experiences that participants might have had that could possibly interact with the things your study has included. For example, let's say you give a new program designed to encourage high-risk teenage girls to go to school and not become pregnant. The results of your study show that the girls in your treatment group have higher school attendance and lower birth rates. You're feeling pretty good about your program until your critics point out that the targeted at-risk treatment group in your study is also likely to be involved simultaneously in several other programs designed to have similar effects. Can you really claim that the program effect is a consequence of your program? The real program that the girls received may actually be the *combination* of the separate programs in which they participated. What can you do about this threat? One approach is to try to isolate the effects of your program from the effects of any other treatments. You could do this by creating a research design that uses a control group (This is discussed in detail in Chapter 7.) In this case, you might randomly assign some high-risk girls to receive your program and some to a no-program control group. Even if girls in both groups receive some other treatment or program, the only systematic difference between the groups is your program. If you observe differences between them on outcome measures, the differences must be due to the program. By using a control group that makes your program the only thing that differentiates the two groups, you control for the potential confound of multiple treatments.

Interaction of Testing and Treatment.
Does testing or measurement itself make the groups more sensitive or receptive to the treatment? If it does, the testing is in effect a part of the treatment; it's inseparable from the effect of the treatment. This is a labeling issue (and, hence, a concern of construct validity) because you want to use the label *program* to refer to the program alone, but in fact it includes the testing. As in the previous threat, one way to control for this is through research design. If you are worried that a pretest makes your program participants more sensitive or receptive to the treatment, randomly assign your program participants into two groups, one of which gets the pretest and the other not. If there are differences on outcomes between these groups, you have evidence that there is an effect of the testing. If not, the testing doesn't matter. In fact, there is a research design known as the Solomon four-group design that was created explicitly to control for this. (This is discussed in Section 9-6a, The Solomon Four-Group Design.)

Restricted Generalizability across Constructs.
This is what I like to refer to as the unintended consequences threat to construct validity. You do a study and conclude that Treatment X is effective. In fact, Treatment X does cause a reduction in symptoms, but what you failed to anticipate was the drastic negative consequences of the side effects of the treatment. When you say that Treatment X is effective, you have defined *effective* in regard to only the directly targeted symptom. But, in fact, significant unintended consequences might affect constructs you did not measure and

cannot generalize to. This threat should remind you that you have to be careful about whether your observed effects (Treatment X is effective) would generalize to other potential outcomes. How can you deal with this threat? The critical issue here is to try to anticipate the unintended and measure any potential outcomes. For instance, the drug Viagra was not originally developed to help erectile dysfunction. It was created as a drug for hypertension. When that didn't pan out, it was tried as an anti-angina medicine. (The chemists had reason to think a drug designed for hypertension might work on angina.) It was only a chance observation, when the drug was being tested in Wales and men were reporting penile erections, that led the pharmaceutical company to investigate that potential outcome. This is an example of an unintended positive outcome (although there is more recent evidence on Viagra to suggest that the initial enthusiasm needs to be tempered by the potential for its own unanticipated negative side effects).

Confounding Constructs and Levels of Constructs. *This issue has to do with the decisions you make about how frequently or how intensely your study participants are exposed to the independent variable (the program, treatment, or intervention).* Imagine a study to test the effect of a new drug treatment for cancer. A fixed dose of the drug is given to a randomly assigned treatment group and a placebo to the other group. No treatment effects are detected, or perhaps the observed result is true only for a certain dosage level. Slight increases or decreases of the dosage may radically change the results. In this context, it is not fair for you to use the label for the drug as a description for your treatment because you looked only at a narrow range of dose. Like the other construct validity threats, this threat is essentially a labeling issue; your label is not a good description for what you implemented. What can you do about it? If you find a treatment effect at a specific dosage, be sure to conduct subsequent studies that explore the range of effective doses. Note that, although I use the term *dose* here, you shouldn't limit the idea to medical studies. If you find an educational program effective at a particular dose—say 1 hour of tutoring a week—conduct subsequent studies to see if dose responses change as you increase or decrease from there. Similarly, if you don't find an effect with an initial dose, don't automatically give up. It may be that at a higher dose will achieve the desired outcome.

The Social Threats to Construct Validity. The remaining major threats to construct validity can be distinguished from the ones I discussed previously because they all stem from the social and human nature of the research endeavor. I cover these in the following sections.

Hypothesis Guessing. *Most people don't just participate passively in a research project. They guess at what the real purpose of the study is.* Therefore, they are likely to base their behavior on what they guess, not just on your treatment. In an educational study conducted in a classroom, students might guess that the key dependent variable has to do with class participation levels. If they increase their participation not because of your program but because they think that's what you're studying, you cannot label the outcome as an effect of the program. It is this labeling issue that makes this a construct validity threat. This is a difficult threat to eliminate. In some studies, researchers try to hide the real purpose of the study, but this may be unethical depending on the circumstances. In some instances, they eliminate the need for participants to guess by telling them the real purpose (although who's to say that participants will believe them). If this is a potentially serious threat, you may think about trying to control for it explicitly through your research design. For instance, you might have multiple program groups and give each one slightly different explanations about the nature of the study even though they all get exactly the same treatment or program. If they perform differently, it may be evidence that they were guessing differently and that this was influencing the results.

Evaluation Apprehension. Many people are anxious about being evaluated. Some are even phobic about testing and measurement situations. If their apprehension makes them perform poorly (and not your program conditions), you certainly can't label that as a treatment effect. Another form of evaluation apprehension concerns the human tendency to want to look good or look smart and so on. If, in their desire to look good, participants perform better (and not as a result of your program), you would be wrong to label this as a treatment effect. In both cases, the apprehension becomes confounded with the treatment itself and you have to be careful about how you label the outcomes. Researchers take a variety of steps to reduce apprehension. In any testing or measurement situation, it is probably a good idea to give participants some time to get comfortable and adjusted to their surroundings. You might ask a few warm-up questions knowing that you are not going to use the answers and trying to encourage the participant to get comfortable responding. (I guess this would be the social research equivalent to the mid-stream urine sample!) In many research projects, people misunderstand what you are measuring. If it is appropriate, you may want to tell them that there are no right or wrong answers and that they aren't being judged or evaluated based on what they say or do.

Experimenter Expectancies.   These days, where we engage in lots of nonlaboratory applied social research, we generally don't use the term *experimenter* to describe the person in charge of the research. So, let's relabel this threat *researcher expectancies. The researcher can bias the results of a study in countless ways, both consciously or subconsciously.* Sometimes the researcher can communicate what the desired outcome for a study might be (and the participants' desire to look good leads them to react that way). For instance, the researcher might look pleased when participants give a desired answer. If researcher feedback causes the response, it would be wrong to label the response a treatment effect. As in many of the previous threats, probably the most effective way to address this threat is to control for it through your research design. For instance, if resources allow, you can have multiple experimenters who differ in their characteristics. Or, you can address the threat through measurement; you can measure expectations prior to the study and use this information in that analysis to attempt to adjust for expectations.

3-2 Reliability

reliability
The degree to which a measure is consistent or dependable; the degree to which it would give you the same result over and over again, assuming the underlying phenomenon is not changing.

Reliability has to do with the quality of measurement. In its everyday sense, reliability is the consistency or repeatability of your measures. Before I can define reliability precisely, I have to lay the groundwork. First, you have to learn about the foundation of reliability, the true score theory of measurement. Along with that, you need to understand the different types of measurement error because errors in measures play a key role in degrading reliability. With this foundation, you can consider the basic theory of reliability, including a precise definition of reliability. There you will find out that you cannot calculate reliability—you can only estimate it. Because of this, there are a variety of different types of reliability and multiple ways to estimate reliability for each type. In the end, it's important to integrate the idea of reliability with the other major criteria for the quality of measurement—validity—and develop an understanding of the relationships between reliability and validity in measurement.

3-2a True Score Theory

true score theory
A theory that maintains that every measurement is an additive composite of two components: the true ability of the respondent and random error.

True score theory is a theory about measurement. Like all theories, you need to recognize that it is not proved; it is postulated as a model of how the world operates. Like many powerful models, true score theory is a simple one. Essentially, true score theory maintains that every measurement is an additive composite of two

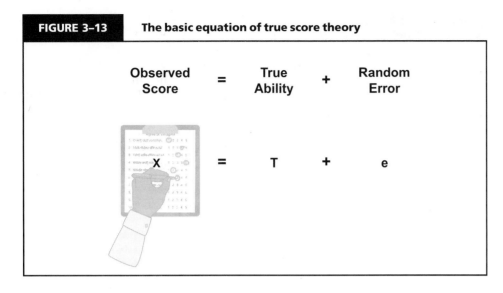

FIGURE 3–13   **The basic equation of true score theory**

components: true ability (or the true level) of the respondent on that measure and random error. This is illustrated in Figure 3–13. You observe the measurement: a score on the test, the total for a self-esteem instrument, or the scale value for a person's weight. You don't observe what's on the right side of the equation. (Only God knows what those values are.) You assume that there are only the two components to the right side of the equal sign in the equation.

The simple equation of $X = T + e_X$ has a parallel equation at the level of the variance or variability of a measure. That is, across a set of scores, you can assume

$$\mathrm{var}(X) = \mathrm{var}(T) + \mathrm{var}(e_X)$$

In more human terms, this means that the variability of your measure is the sum of the variability due to true score and the variability due to random error. This will have important implications when we consider some of the more advanced models for adjusting for errors in measurement later in Section 14-4a, Nonequivalent Groups Analysis.

Why is true score theory important? For one thing, it is a simple yet powerful model for measurement. It is a reminder that most measurement has an error component. Second, true score theory is the foundation of reliability theory, which will be discussed later in this chapter. A measure that has no random error (is all true score) is perfectly reliable; a measure that has no true score (is all random error) has zero reliability. Third, true score theory can be used in computer simulations as the basis for generating observed scores with certain known properties.

You should know that the true score model is not the only measurement model available. Measurement theorists continue to come up with more and more complex models that they think represent reality even better. However, these models are complicated enough that they lie outside the boundaries of this book. In any event, true score theory should give you an idea of why measurement models are important at all and how they can be used as the basis for defining key research ideas.

3-2b Measurement Error

True score theory is a good simple model for measurement, but it may not always be an accurate reflection of reality. In particular, it assumes that any observation is composed of the true value plus some random error value; but is that reasonable? What if all error is not random? Isn't it possible that some errors are systematic, that they hold across most or all of the members of a group? One way to deal with this notion is to revise the simple true score model by dividing the error component

FIGURE 3–14	Random and systematic errors in measurement

$$X = T + e$$
$$X = T + e_r + e_s$$

FIGURE 3–15	Random error adds variability to a distribution but does not affect central tendency (the average)

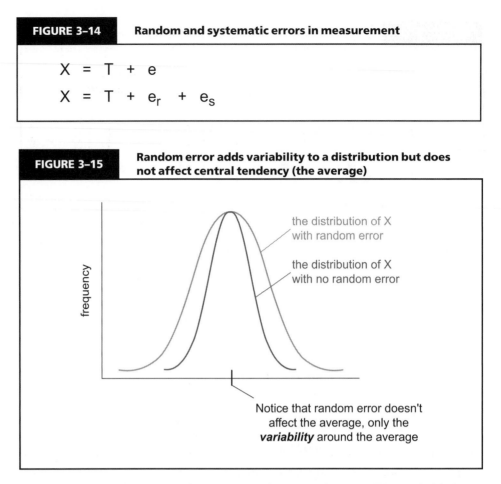

the distribution of X with random error

the distribution of X with no random error

frequency

Notice that random error doesn't affect the average, only the *variability* around the average

into two subcomponents, random error and systematic error. Figure 3–14 shows these two components of measurement error, what the difference between them is, and how they affect research.

What Is Random Error? Random error is caused by any factors that randomly affect measurement of the variable across the sample. For instance, people's moods can inflate or deflate their performance on any occasion. In a particular testing, some children may be in a good mood and others may be depressed. If mood affects the children's performance on the measure, it might artificially inflate the observed scores for some children and artificially deflate them for others. The important thing about random error is that it does not have any consistent effects across the entire sample. Instead, it pushes observed scores up or down randomly. This means that if you could see all the random errors in a distribution they would have to sum to 0. There would be as many negative errors as positive ones. (Of course, you can't see the random errors because all you see is the observed score *X*. God can see the random errors, but she's not telling us what they are!) The important property of random error is that it adds variability to the data but does not affect average performance for the group (Figure 3–15). Because of this, random error is sometimes considered *noise*.

What Is Systematic Error? Systematic error is caused by any factors that systematically affect measurement of the variable across the sample. For instance, if there is loud traffic going by just outside of a classroom where students are taking a test, this noise is liable to affect all of the children's scores—in this case, systematically lowering them. Unlike random error, systematic errors tend to be either positive or negative consistently; because of this, systematic error is sometimes considered to be *bias* in measurement (Figure 3–16).

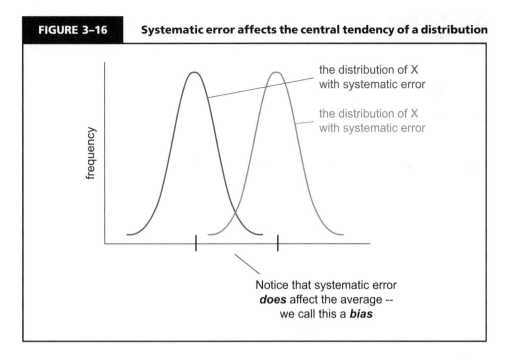

FIGURE 3–16   **Systematic error affects the central tendency of a distribution**

the distribution of X
with systematic error

the distribution of X
with systematic error

frequency

Notice that systematic error
does affect the average --
we call this a ***bias***

Reducing Measurement Error So, how can you reduce measurement errors, random or systematic? One thing you can do is to pilot test your instruments to get feedback from your respondents regarding how easy or hard the measure was and information about how the testing environment affected their performance. Second, if you are gathering measures using people to collect the data (as interviewers or observers), you should make sure you train them thoroughly so that they aren't inadvertently introducing error. Third, when you collect the data for your study you should double-check the data thoroughly. All data entry for computer analysis should be double-punched and verified. This means that you enter the data twice, the second time having your data-entry machine check that you are typing the exact same data you typed the first time. Fourth, you can use statistical procedures to adjust for measurement error. These range from rather simple formulas you can apply directly to your data to complex modeling procedures for modeling the error and its effects. Finally, one of the best things you can do to deal with measurement errors, especially systematic errors, is to use multiple measures of the same construct. Especially if the different measures don't share the same systematic errors, you will be able to *triangulate* across the multiple measures and get a more accurate sense of what's happening.

3-2c Theory of Reliability

What is *reliability?* We hear the term used a lot in research contexts, but what does it really mean? If you think about how we use the word *reliable* in everyday language, you might get a hint. For instance, we often speak about a machine as reliable: "I have a reliable car." Or, news people talk about a "usually reliable source." In both cases, the word *reliable* usually means dependable or trustworthy. In research, the term *reliable* also means dependable in a general sense, but that's not a precise enough definition. What does it mean to have a dependable measure or observation in a research context? The reason dependable is not a good enough description is that it can be confused too easily with the idea of a valid measure (see Section 3-1, Construct Validity). Certainly, when researchers speak of a dependable measure, we mean one that is both reliable and valid. So we have to be a little more precise when we try to define reliability.

| FIGURE 3–17 | Reliability and true score theory |

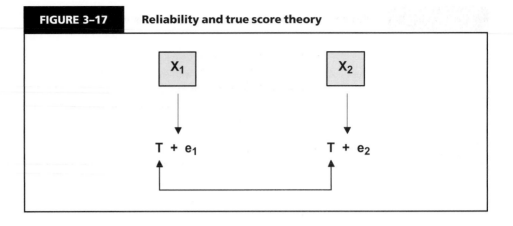

In research, the term *reliability* means repeatability or consistency. A measure is considered reliable if it would give you the same result over and over again (assuming that what you are measuring isn't changing).

Let's explore in more detail what it means to say that a measure is repeatable or consistent. I'll begin by defining a measure that I'll arbitrarily label X. It might be a person's score on a math achievement test or a measure of severity of illness. It is the value (numerical or otherwise) that you observe in your study. Now, to see how repeatable or consistent an observation is, you can measure it twice. You use subscripts to indicate the first and second observation of the same measure as shown in Figure 3–17. If you assume that what you're measuring doesn't change between the time of the first and second observation, you can begin to understand how you get at reliability. Although you observe a single score for what you're measuring, you usually think of that score as consisting of two parts: the true score or actual level for the person on that measure and the error in measuring it (see Section 3-2a, True Score Theory).

It's important to keep in mind that you observe the X score; you never actually see the true (T) or error (e) scores. For instance, a student may get a score of 85 on a math achievement test. That's the score you observe, an X of 85. However, the reality might be that the student is actually better at math than that score indicates. Let's say the student's true math ability is 89 ($T = 89$). That means that the error for that student is −4. What does this mean? Well, while the student's true math ability may be 89, he or she may have had a bad day, may not have had breakfast, may have had an argument with someone, or may have been distracted while taking the test. Factors like these can contribute to errors in measurement that make the students' observed abilities appear lower than their true or actual abilities.

Okay, back to reliability. If your measure, X, is reliable, you should find that if you measure or observe it twice on the same persons, the scores should be pretty much the same, result each time you measure in time. Why would they be the same? If you look at Figure 3–17, you should see that the only thing that the two observations have in common is their true scores, T. How do you know that? Because the error scores (e_1 and e_2) have different subscripts indicating that they are different values. (You are likely to have different errors on different occasions.) However, the true score symbol (T) is (by definition in this example) the same for both observations. What does this mean? The two observed scores, X_1 and X_2, are related only to the degree that the observations share a true score. You should remember that the error score is assumed to be random (see Section 3-2a, True Score Theory). Sometimes errors will lead you to perform better on a test than your true ability (you had a good day guessing!) while other times they will lead you to score worse. The true score—your true ability on that measure—would be the same on both observations (assuming, of course, that your true ability didn't change between the two measurement occasions).

FIGURE 3–18   Reliability can be expressed as a simple ratio

$$\frac{\text{true level on the measure}}{\text{the entire measure}}$$

FIGURE 3–19   The reliability ratio can be expressed in terms of variances

$$\frac{\text{the variance of the true score}}{\text{the variance of the measure}}$$

FIGURE 3–20   The reliability ratio expressed in terms of variances in abbreviated form

$$\frac{\text{var}(T)}{\text{var}(X)}$$

With this in mind, I can now define reliability more precisely. Reliability is a ratio or fraction. In layperson terms, you might define this ratio as shown in Figure 3–18.

You might think of reliability as the proportion of truth in your measure. Now, it makes no sense to speak of the reliability of a measure for an individual; reliability is a characteristic of a measure that's taken across individuals. So, to get closer to a more formal definition, I'll restate the definition of reliability in terms of a set of observations. The easiest way to do this is to speak of the variance of the scores. Remember that the variance is a measure of the spread or distribution of a set of scores. So, I can now state the definition as shown in Figure 3–19.

I might put this into slightly more technical terms by using the abbreviated name for the variance and our variable names (Figure 3–20).

We're getting to the critical part now. If you look at the equation in Figure 3–20, you should recognize that you can easily determine or calculate the bottom part of the reliability ratio; it's just the variance of the set of observed scores. (You remember how to calculate the variance, don't you? It's the sum of the squared deviations of the scores from their mean, divided by the number of scores. If you're still not sure, see Chapter 12.) So how do you calculate the variance of the true scores? You can't see the true scores. (You only see X!) Only God knows the true score for a specific observation. Therefore, if you can't calculate the variance of the true scores, you can't compute the ratio, which means *you can't compute reliability!* Everybody got that? Here's the bottom line:

You can't compute reliability because you can't calculate the variance of the true scores!

Great. So where does that leave you? If you can't compute reliability, perhaps the best you can do is to estimate it. Maybe you can get an estimate of the variability of the true scores. How do you do that? Remember your two observations, X_1 and X_2? You assume (using true score theory described earlier in this chapter) that these two observations would be related to each other to the degree that they share true scores. So, let's calculate the correlation between X_1 and X_2. Figure 3–21 shows a simple formula for the correlation.

FIGURE 3–21	The formula for estimating reliability

$$\frac{covariance(X_1, X_2)}{sd(X_1) * sd(X_2)}$$

standard deviation
The spread or variability of the scores around their average in a *single sample*. The standard deviation, often abbreviated sd, is mathematically the square root of the variance. The standard deviation and variance both measure dispersion, but because the standard deviation is measured in the same units as the original measure and the variance is measured in squared units, the standard deviation is usually more directly interpretable and meaningful.

In Figure 3–21, the *sd* stands for the **standard deviation** (which is the square root of the variance). If you look carefully at this equation, you can see that the covariance, which simply measures the shared variance between measures, must be an indicator of the variability of the true scores because the true scores in X_1 and X_2 are the only things the two observations share! So, the top part is essentially an estimate of *var(T)* in this context. In addition, since the bottom part of the equation multiplies the standard deviation of one observation with the standard deviation of the same measure at another time, you would expect that these two values would be the same (it is the same measure we're taking) and that this is essentially the same thing as squaring the standard deviation for either observation. However, the square of the standard deviation is the same thing as the variance of the measure. So, the bottom part of the equation becomes the variance of the measure (or *var[X]*). If you read this paragraph carefully, you should see that the correlation between two observations of the same measure *is* an estimate of reliability. Got that? I've just shown that a simple and straightforward way to estimate the reliability of a measure is to compute the correlation of the measure administered twice!

It's time to reach some conclusions. You know from this discussion that you cannot calculate reliability because you cannot measure the true score component of an observation. You also know that you can estimate the true score component as the covariance between two observations of the same measure. With that in mind, you can estimate the reliability as the correlation between two observations of the same measure. It turns out that there are several ways to estimate this reliability correlation. These are discussed in Section 3-2d, Types of Reliability.

There's only one other issue I want to address here. How big is an estimate of reliability? To figure this out, let's go back to the equation given earlier (Figure 3–22).

Remember, because $X = T + e$, you can substitute in the bottom of the ratio as shown in Figure 3–23.

With this slight change, you can easily determine the range of a reliability estimate. If a measure is *perfectly* reliable, there is no error in measurement; everything you observe is true score. Therefore, for a perfectly reliable measure, var(*e*) is zero and the equation would reduce to the equation shown in Figure 3–24.

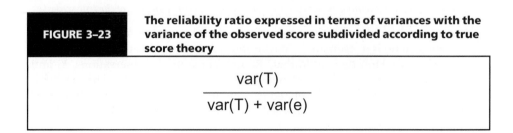

FIGURE 3–22	The reliability ratio expressed in terms of variances in abbreviated form

$$\frac{var(T)}{var(X)}$$

FIGURE 3–23	The reliability ratio expressed in terms of variances with the variance of the observed score subdivided according to true score theory

$$\frac{var(T)}{var(T) + var(e)}$$

FIGURE 3–24	**When there is no error in measurement, you have perfect reliability and the reliability estimate is 1.0**

$$\frac{\text{var}(T)}{\text{var}(T)}$$

FIGURE 3–25	**When there is only error in measurement, you have no reliability and the reliability estimate is 0**

$$\frac{0}{\text{var}(e)}$$

Therefore, reliability = 1. Now, if you have a perfectly unreliable measure, there is no true score; the measure is entirely error. In this case, the equation would reduce to the equation shown in Figure 3–25.

Therefore, the reliability = 0. From this you know that reliability will always range between 0 and 1.

The value of a reliability estimate tells you the proportion of variability in the measure attributable to the true score. A reliability of .5 means that about half of the variance of the observed score is attributable to truth and half is attributable to error. A reliability of .8 means the variability is about 80% true ability and 20% error, and so on.

3-2d Types of Reliability

You learned in Section 3-2c, Theory of Reliability, that it's not possible to calculate reliability exactly. Instead, you have to estimate reliability, and this is always an imperfect endeavor. Here, I want to introduce the major reliability estimators and talk about their strengths and weaknesses.

There are four general classes of reliability estimates, each of which estimates reliability in a different way:

- **Inter-rater or inter-observer reliability** is used to assess the degree to which different raters/observers give consistent estimates of the same phenomenon.
- **Test-retest reliability** is used to assess the consistency of a measure from one time to another.
- **Parallel-forms reliability** is used to assess the consistency of the results of two tests constructed in the same way from the same content domain.
- **Internal consistency reliability** is used to assess the consistency of results across items within a test.

I'll discuss each of these in turn.

Inter-Rater or Inter-Observer Reliability Whenever you use humans as a part of your measurement procedure, you have to worry about whether the results you get are reliable or consistent. People are notorious for their inconsistency. We are easily distractible. We get tired of doing repetitive tasks. We daydream. We misinterpret.

So how do you determine whether two observers are being consistent in their observations? You probably should establish inter-rater reliability outside of the context of the measurement in your study. After all, if you use data from your study to establish reliability, and you find that reliability is low, you're kind of stuck. Probably it's best to do this as a side study or pilot study. If your study continues for a

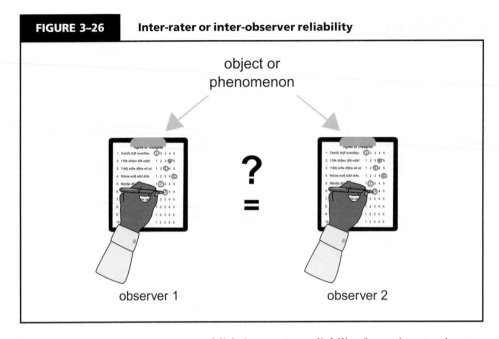

FIGURE 3–26   **Inter-rater or inter-observer reliability**

long time, you may want to reestablish inter-rater reliability from time to time to ensure that your raters aren't changing.

There are two major ways to actually estimate inter-rater reliability. If your measurement consists of categories—the raters are checking off which category each observation falls in—you can calculate the percent of agreement between the raters. For instance, let's say you had 100 observations that were being rated by two raters. For each observation, the rater could check one of three categories. Imagine that on 86 of the 100 observations the raters checked the same category. In this case, the percentage of agreement would be 86%. Okay, it's a crude measure, but it does give an idea of how much agreement exists, and it works no matter how many categories are used for each observation.

The other major way to estimate inter-rater reliability is appropriate when the measure is a continuous one. In such a case, all you need to do is calculate the correlation between the ratings of the two observers. For instance, they might be rating the overall level of activity in a classroom on a 1 to 7 scale. You could have them give their rating at regular time intervals (every 30 seconds). The correlation between these ratings would give you an estimate of the reliability or consistency between the raters (Figure 3–26).

You might think of this type of reliability as calibrating the observers. There are other things you could do to encourage reliability between observers, even if you don't estimate it. For instance, I used to work in a psychiatric unit where every morning a nurse had to do a ten-item rating of each patient on the unit. Of course, we couldn't count on the same nurse being present every day, so we had to find a way to ensure that all the nurses would give comparable ratings. The way we did it was to hold weekly calibration meetings where we would have all of the nurses' ratings for several patients and discuss why they chose the specific values they did. If there were disagreements, the nurses would discuss them and attempt to come up with rules for deciding when they would give a 3 or a 4 for a rating on a specific item. Although this was not an estimate of reliability, it probably went a long way toward improving the reliability between raters.

Test-Retest Reliability You estimate test-retest reliability when you administer the same test to the same (or a similar) sample on two different occasions (Figure 3–27). This approach assumes that there is no substantial change in the construct being measured between the two occasions. The amount of time allowed between measures is critical. You know that if you measure the same thing twice,

| FIGURE 3–27 | Test-retest reliability |

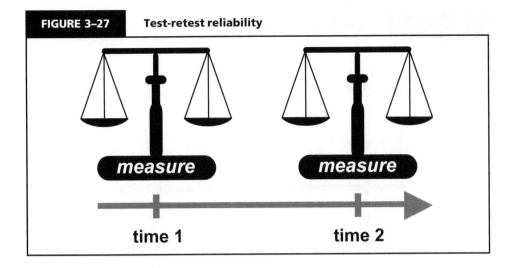

the correlation between the two observations will depend in part on how much time elapses between the two measurement occasions. The shorter the time gap, the higher the correlation; the longer the time gap, the lower the correlation because the two observations are related over time; the closer in time you get, the more similar the factors that contribute to error. Since this correlation is the test-retest estimate of reliability, you can obtain considerably different estimates depending on the interval.

Parallel-Forms Reliability In parallel-forms reliability, you first have to create two parallel forms. One way to accomplish this is to start with a large set of questions that address the same construct and then randomly divide the questions into two sets. You administer both instruments to the same sample of people. The correlation between the two parallel forms is the estimate of reliability. One major problem with this approach is that you have to be able to generate lots of items that reflect the same construct, which is often no easy feat. Furthermore, this approach makes the assumption that the randomly divided halves are parallel or equivalent. Even by chance, this will sometimes not be the case. The parallel-forms approach is similar to the split-half reliability described later. The major difference is that parallel forms are constructed so that the two forms can be used independently of each other and considered equivalent measures. For instance, you might be concerned about a testing threat to internal validity. If you use Form A for the pretest and Form B for the posttest, you minimize that problem. It would even be better if you randomly assign individuals to receive Form A or B on the pretest and then switch them on the posttest. With split-half reliability, you have an instrument to use as a single-measurement instrument and develop randomly split halves only for purposes of estimating reliability (Figure 3–28).

Internal-Consistency Reliability In internal-consistency reliability estimation, you use your single measurement instrument administered to a group of people on one occasion to estimate reliability. In effect, you judge the reliability of the instrument by estimating how well the items that reflect the same construct yield similar results. You are looking at how consistent the results are for different items for the same construct within the measure. There are a wide variety of internal-consistency measures you can use.

Average Interitem Correlation. The average interitem correlation uses all of the items on your instrument that are designed to measure the same construct. You first compute the correlation between each pair of items, as illustrated Figure 3–29. For example, if you have six items, you will have fifteen different item pairings

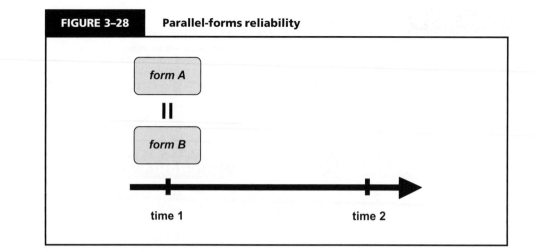

FIGURE 3–28   **Parallel-forms reliability**

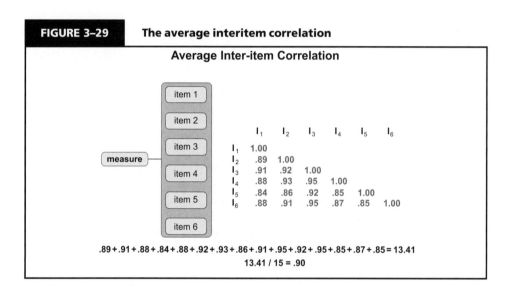

FIGURE 3–29   **The average interitem correlation**

(fifteen correlations). The average interitem correlation is simply the average or mean of all these correlations. In the example, you find an average interitem correlation of .90 with the individual correlations ranging from .84 to .95.

Average Item-Total Correlation. This approach also uses the interitem correlations. In addition, you compute a total score for the six items and use that as a seventh variable in the analysis. Figure 3–30 shows the six item-to-total correlations at the bottom of the correlation matrix. They range from .82 to .88 in this sample analysis, with the average of these at .85.

Split-Half Reliability. In split-half reliability, you randomly divide all items that purport to measure the same construct into two sets. You administer the entire instrument to a sample of people and calculate the total score for each randomly divided half. The split-half reliability estimate, as shown in Figure 3–31, is simply the correlation between these two total scores. In the example, it is .87.

  If you think about this in practice, it might occur to you that (1) basically we are pretending we have two equivalent tests, both half as long as the "real" test, and (2) not all tests are the same length. So you might reasonably wonder about the relationship of test length to reliability. In general, longer tests are more reliable, so the split-half procedures systematically underestimate the reliability of a test. A formula has been developed to help us estimate the reliability of the full test based

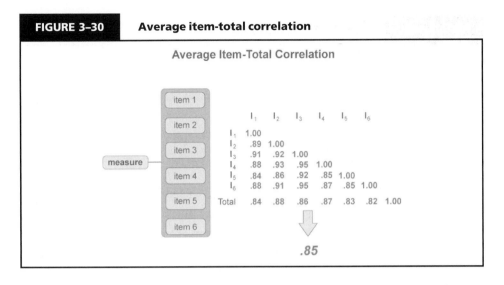

FIGURE 3–30   **Average item-total correlation**

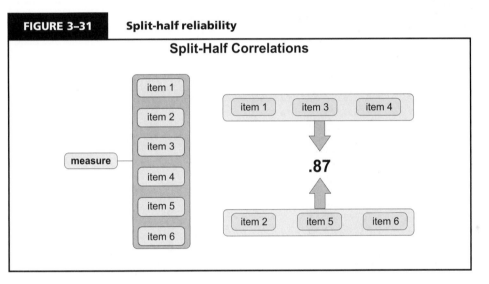

FIGURE 3–31   **Split-half reliability**

on the split-half estimate. This formula is called the *Spearman-Brown formula* and is shown in Figure 3–32.

Cronbach's Alpha (α). Imagine that you compute one split-half reliability and then randomly divide the items into another set of split halves and recompute, and keep doing this until you have computed all possible split-half estimates of reliability. **Cronbach's alpha** is mathematically equivalent to the average of all possible split-half estimates (although that's not how it's typically computed). Notice that when I say you compute all possible split-half estimates, I don't mean that each time you measure a new sample! That would take forever. Instead, you calculate all split-half estimates from the same sample. Because you measured your entire sample on each of the six items, all you have to do is have the computer analysis do the random subsets of items and compute the resulting correlations. Figure 3–33 shows several of the split-half estimates for our six-item example and lists them as SH with a subscript. Keep in mind that although Cronbach's alpha is equivalent to the average of all possible split-half correlations, you would never actually calculate it that way. Some clever mathematician (Cronbach, I presume!) figured out a way to get the mathematical equivalent a lot more quickly.

Comparison of Reliability Estimators. Each of the reliability estimators has certain advantages and disadvantages. Inter-rater reliability is one of the best ways

Cronbach's alpha
One specific method of estimating the reliability of a measure. Although not calculated in this manner, Cronbach's alpha can be thought of as analogous to the average of all possible split-half correlations.

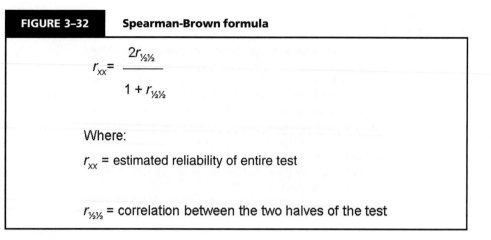

FIGURE 3–32   **Spearman-Brown formula**

$$r_{xx} = \frac{2r_{\frac{1}{2}\frac{1}{2}}}{1 + r_{\frac{1}{2}\frac{1}{2}}}$$

Where:

r_{xx} = estimated reliability of entire test

$r_{\frac{1}{2}\frac{1}{2}}$ = correlation between the two halves of the test

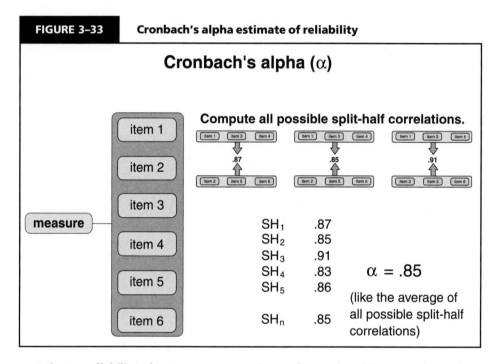

FIGURE 3–33   **Cronbach's alpha estimate of reliability**

Cronbach's alpha (α)

Compute all possible split-half correlations.

	item 1	item 3	item 4

.87

| | item 2 | item 5 | item 6 |

| | item 1 | item 3 | item 4 |

.85

| | item 2 | item 5 | item 6 |

| | item 1 | item 3 | item 4 |

.91

| | item 2 | item 5 | item 6 |

measure — item 1, item 2, item 3, item 4, item 5, item 6

SH_1 .87
SH_2 .85
SH_3 .91
SH_4 .83
SH_5 .86

SH_n .85

$\alpha = .85$

(like the average of all possible split-half correlations)

to estimate reliability when your measure is an observation. However, it requires multiple raters or observers. As an alternative, you could look at the correlation of ratings of the same single observer repeated on two different occasions. For example, let's say you collected videotapes of child-mother interactions and had a rater code the videos for how often the mother smiled at the child. To establish inter-rater reliability, you could take a sample of videos and have two raters code them independently. To estimate test-retest reliability, you could have a single rater code the same videos on two different occasions. You might use the inter-rater approach especially if you were interested in using a team of raters and you wanted to establish that they yielded consistent results. If you get a suitably high inter-rater reliability, you could then justify allowing them to work independently on coding different videos. You might use the test-retest approach when you have only a single rater and don't want to train any others. On the other hand, in some studies it is reasonable to do both to help establish the reliability of the raters or observers.

You use the parallel-forms estimator only in situations where you intend to use the two forms as alternate measures of the same thing. Both the parallel forms and all of the internal consistency estimators have one major constraint: you have to have lots of items designed to measure the same construct. This is relatively easy to achieve in certain contexts like achievement testing. (It's easy, for instance, to construct many similar addition problems for a math test.) However, for more complex or subjective constructs, this can be a real challenge. With lots of items, Cronbach's alpha tends to be the most frequently used estimate of internal consistency.

The test-retest estimator is especially feasible in most experimental and quasi-experimental designs that use a no-treatment control group. In these designs, you always have a control group that is measured on two occasions (pretest and posttest). The main problem with this approach is that you don't have any information about reliability until you collect the posttest and, if the reliability estimate is low, you're pretty much sunk.

Each of the reliability estimators gives a different value for reliability. In general, the test-retest and inter-rater reliability estimates will be lower in value than the parallel-forms and internal-consistency estimates because they involve measuring at different times or with different raters. Since reliability estimates are often used in statistical analyses of quasi-experimental designs (see Section 10-1, The Nonequivalent-Groups Design), the fact that different estimates can differ considerably makes the analysis even more complex.

3-2e Reliability and Validity

We often think of reliability and validity as separate ideas but, in fact, they're related to each other. Here, I want to show you two ways you can think about their relationship.

One of my favorite metaphors for the relationship between reliability and validity is that of the target. Think of the center of the target as the concept you are trying to measure. Imagine that for each person you are measuring, you are taking a shot at the target. If you measure the concept perfectly for a person, you are hitting the center of the target. If you don't, you are missing the center. The more you are off for that person, the further you are from the center (Figure 3–34).

Figure 3–34 shows four possible situations. In the first one, you are hitting the target consistently, but you are missing the center of the target. That is, you are consistently and systematically measuring the wrong value for all respondents. This measure is reliable, but not valid. (It's consistent but wrong.) The second shows hits that are randomly spread across the target. You seldom hit the center of the target but, on average, you are getting the right answer for the group (but not very well for individuals). In this case, you get a valid group estimate, but you are inconsistent. Here, you can clearly see that reliability is directly related to the variability of your measure. The third scenario shows a case where your hits are spread across the target and you are consistently missing the center. Your measure in this case is neither reliable nor valid. Finally, the figure shows the RobinHood scenario; you consistently hit the center of the target. Your measure is both reliable and valid. (I bet you never thought of Robin Hood in those terms before.)

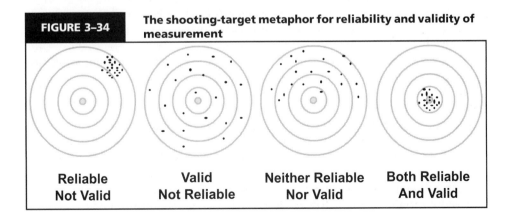

| **FIGURE 3–34** | **The shooting-target metaphor for reliability and validity of measurement** |

Reliable Not Valid   **Valid Not Reliable**   **Neither Reliable Nor Valid**   **Both Reliable And Valid**

FIGURE 3–35	Comparison of reliability and validity of measurement

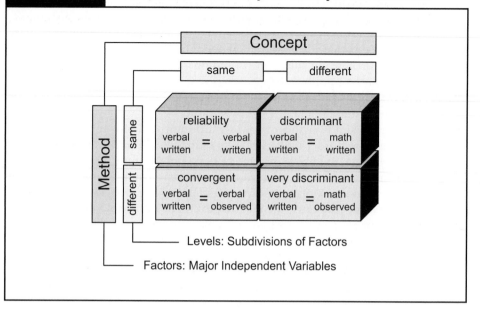

Another way to think about the relationship between reliability and validity is shown in Figure 3–35, which contains a 2 × 2 table. The columns of the table indicate whether you are trying to measure the same or different concepts. The rows show whether you are using the same or different methods of measurement. Imagine that you have two concepts you would like to measure: student verbal and math ability. Furthermore, imagine that you can measure each of these in two ways. First, you can use a written, paper-and-pencil examination (much like the SAT or GRE examinations). Second, you can ask the students' classroom teachers to give you a rating of the students' ability based on their own classroom observation.

The first cell on the upper left shows the comparison of the verbal written test score with the verbal written test score; but how can you compare the same measure with itself? You could do this by estimating the reliability of the written test through a test-retest correlation, parallel forms, or an internal consistency measure (see Section 3-2d, Types of Reliability). What you are estimating in this cell is the reliability of the measure.

The cell on the lower left shows a comparison of the verbal written measure with the verbal teacher observation rating. Because you are trying to measure the same concept, you are looking at convergent validity (see Section 3-1a, Measurement Validity Types).

The cell on the upper left shows the comparison of the verbal written examination with the math written examination. Here, you are comparing two different concepts (verbal versus math) and so you would expect the relationship to be lower than a comparison of the same concept with itself (verbal versus verbal or math versus math). Thus, you are trying to discriminate between two concepts and this could be labeled discriminant validity.

Finally, you have the cell on the lower right. Here, you are comparing the verbal written examination with the math teacher observation rating. Like the cell on the upper right, you are also trying to compare two different concepts (verbal versus math), so this is also a discriminant validity estimate. However, here you are also trying to compare two different methods of measurement (written examination versus teacher observation rating). So, I'll call this very discriminant to indicate that you would expect the relationship in this cell to be even lower than in the one above it.

The four cells incorporate the different values that you examine in the MTMM approach to estimating construct validity described earlier in this chapter. When you look at reliability and validity in this way, you see that, rather than being distinct, they actually form a continuum. On one end is the situation where the concepts and methods of measurement are the same (reliability) and on the other is the situation where both concepts and methods of measurement are different (very discriminant validity).

3-3 Levels of Measurement

The *level of measurement* refers to the relationship among the values that are assigned to the attributes for a variable. What does that mean? Begin with the idea of the variable, for example party affiliation (Figure 3–36). That variable has a number of attributes. Let's assume that in this particular election context, the only relevant attributes are republican, democrat, and independent. For purposes of analyzing the results of this variable, we arbitrarily assign the values 1, 2, and 3 to the three attributes. The *level of measurement* describes the relationship among these three values. In this case, the numbers function as shorter placeholders for the lengthier text terms. Don't assume that higher values mean more of something or lower numbers signify less. Don't assume the value of 2 means that democrats are twice something that republicans are or that republicans are in first place or have the highest priority just because they have the value of 1. In this case, the level of measurement can be described as nominal.

3-3a Why Is Level of Measurement Important?

First, knowing the level of measurement helps you decide how to interpret the data from that variable. When you know that a measure is nominal (like the one just described), you know that the numerical values are short codes for the longer names. Second, knowing the level of measurement helps you decide what statistical analysis is appropriate on the values that were assigned. If a measure is nominal, you know that you would never average the data values or do a *t*-test on the data.

There are typically four levels of measurement that are defined (Figure 3–37):

- *Nominal.* In nominal measurement the numerical values simply name the attribute uniquely. No ordering of the cases is implied. For example, jersey numbers in basketball are measures at the nominal level. A player with number 30 is not more of anything than a player with number 15, and is certainly not twice whatever number 15 is.

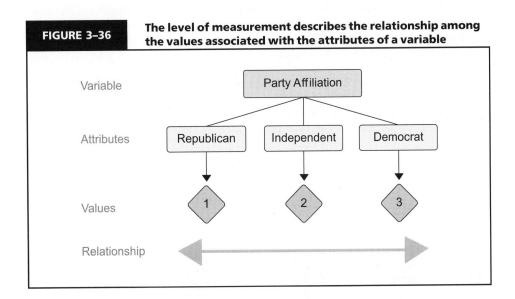

| FIGURE 3–36 | The level of measurement describes the relationship among the values associated with the attributes of a variable |

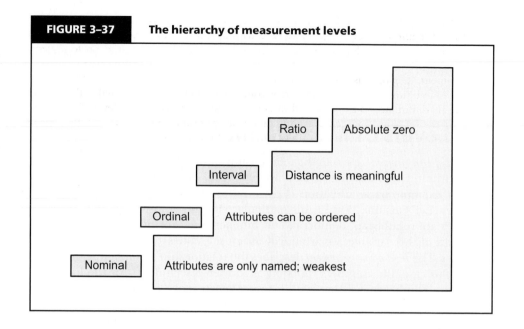

FIGURE 3–37   **The hierarchy of measurement levels**

- *Ordinal.* In ordinal measurement the attributes can be rank-ordered. Here, distances between attributes do not have any meaning. For example, on a survey you might code Educational Attainment as 0 = less than H.S.; 1 = some H.S.; 2 = H.S. degree, 3 = some college, 4 = college degree; 5 = post college. In this measure, higher numbers mean *more* education. Is distance from 0 to 1 the same as 3 to 4? Of course not. The interval between values is not interpretable in an ordinal measure.
- *Interval.* In interval measurement the distance between attributes *does* have meaning. For example, when we measure temperature (in Fahrenheit), the distance from 30 to 40 is same as distance from 70 to 80. The interval between values is interpretable. Because of this, it makes sense to compute an average of an interval variable, where it doesn't make sense to do so for ordinal scales. Note, however, that in interval measurement ratios don't make any sense; 80 degrees is not twice as hot as 40 degrees (although the attribute value is twice as large).
- *Ratio.* In ratio measurement there is always a meaningful absolute zero that is meaningful. This means that you can construct a meaningful fraction (or ratio) with a ratio variable. Weight is a ratio variable. In applied social research most *count* variables are ratio, for example, the number of clients in the past 6 months. Why? Because you can have zero clients and because it is meaningful to say, "We had twice as many clients in the past 6 months as we did in the previous 6 months."

It's important to recognize that there is a hierarchy implied in the level of measurement idea. At lower levels of measurement, assumptions tend to be less restrictive and data analyses tend to be less sensitive. At each level up the hierarchy, the current level includes all of the qualities of the one below it and adds something new. In general, it is desirable to have a higher level of measurement (such as interval or ratio) rather than a lower one (such as nominal or ordinal).

Summary

This chapter laid the foundation for the idea of measurement. Three broad topics were considered. First, *construct validity* refers to the degree to which you are measuring what you intended to measure. Construct validity is divided into translation validity (the degree to which you translated the construct well) and criterion-related validity (the degree to which your measure relates to or predicts other criteria as theoretically predicted). There is a long tradition of methods that attempt to assess construct validity that goes back to the original articulation of the nomological network, through the MTMM matrix and on to pattern-matching approaches. Second, *reliability* refers to the consistency or dependability of your measurement. Reliability is based on true score theory, which holds that any observation can be divided into two—a true score and error component. Reliability is defined as the ratio of the true score variance to the observed variance in a measure. Third, the level of a measure describes the relationship implicit among that measure's values and determines the type of statistical manipulations that are sensible. With these three ideas—construct validity, reliability, and level of measurement—as a foundation, you can now move on to some of the more practical and useful aspects of measurement in the next few chapters.

Login to the Online Edition of your text at www.atomicdog.com to find additional resources located in the Study Guide at the end of each chapter.

Survey research (Fowler, 2001) is one of the most important areas of measurement in applied social research. In this chapter, I'll begin at the most specific level: how to construct the questions for a survey. I'll discuss a number of issues, including the different types of questions, decisions about question content, decisions about question wording, decisions about response format, and question placement and sequence in your instrument. I'll turn next to some of the special issues involved when there is an interviewer collecting the responses. I'll then move to a broader view and examine the different types of surveys that are possible. These are roughly divided into two general categories: questionnaires and interviews. Next, I'll explain how you select the survey method that's best for your situation. Finally, I'll consider some of the advantages and disadvantages of each type of survey method.

4-1 Constructing the Survey

Constructing a survey instrument is an art in itself. You must make numerous small decisions—about content, wording, format, and placement—that can have important consequences for your entire study. Although there's no one perfect way to accomplish this job, I do have advice to offer that might increase your chances of developing a better final product.

Three primary issues are involved in writing a question:

- Determining the question content, scope, and purpose
- Choosing the response format that you use for collecting information from the respondent
- Figuring out how to word the question to get at the issue of interest

After you have your questions written, there is also the issue of how best to place them in your survey.

You'll see that although many aspects of survey construction are just common sense, if you are not careful, you can make critical errors that have dramatic effects on your results. It cannot be emphasized enough that pilot testing of questions and surveys will always pay off in identification of problems with wording, omissions, typos, and various surprising responses to items that you had been thinking were just right.

4-1a Types of Questions

Survey questions can be divided into two broad types: *structured* and *unstructured*. From an instrument design point of view, the structured questions pose the greater

---

FIGURE 4–1	Dichotomous response formats for a survey question

Do you believe that the death penalty is ever justified?

_____Yes

_____No

Please enter your gender:

☐ Male   ☐ Female

---

difficulties (see Section 4-1c, Response Format). From a content perspective, it may actually be more difficult to write good unstructured questions. Here, I'll discuss the variety of structured questions you can consider for your survey. (I discuss unstructured questioning more in Section 4-2, Interviews.)

Dichotomous Response Formats When a question has two possible responses, it has a dichotomous response format. Surveys often use **dichotomous questions** that ask for a Yes/No, True/False, or Agree/Disagree response (Figure 4–1). There are a variety of ways to lay these questions out on a questionnaire.

dichotomous question
A question with two possible responses.

Questions Based on Level of Measurement We can also classify questions in terms of the level of measurement used in the question's **response format**. (The idea of level of measurement is covered in Chapter 3.) For instance, you might measure occupation using a **nominal response format** as in Figure 4–2. In a nominal response format, the number next to each response has no meaning except as a placeholder for that response; the choices in the example are a 2 for a lawyer and a 1 for a truck driver. From the numbering system used, you can't infer that a lawyer is twice something that a truck driver is. The primary reason you might number responses in this manner is to speed data entry. The person entering the data from this survey would need to enter only a short number rather than a longer category name like "truck driver."

When you ask respondents to rank order their preferences, you are using an **ordinal response format**. For example, in Figure 4–3, the respondent is asked to rate candidate preferences.

In this example, you want the respondent to put a 1, 2, 3, or 4 next to the candidate, where 1 is the respondent's first choice. Note that this could get confusing. The respondents might check their candidate instead of entering a number, or assign higher numbers to candidates they prefer more instead of understanding that you want rank ordering where a higher number means a lower rank. Notice in

response format
A response format that has a number beside each choice where the number has no meaning except as a placeholder for that response.

nominal response format
A response format that has a number beside each choice where the number has no meaning except as a placeholder for that response.

ordinal response format
A response format in which respondents are asked to rank the possible answers in order of preference.

FIGURE 4–2	A nominal-level response format for a survey question

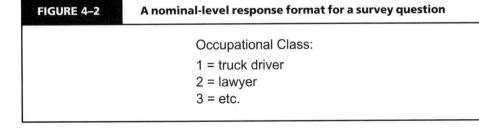

Occupational Class:
1 = truck driver
2 = lawyer
3 = etc.

| **FIGURE 4–3** | **An ordinal-level response format for a survey question** |

Rank the candidates in order of
preference from best to worst...

___Bob Dole

___Bill Clinton

___Newt Gingrich

___Al Gore

---

interval-level response format
A response measured on an interval level, where the size of the interval between potential response values is meaningful. Most 1 to 5 rating responses can be considered interval level.

Likert response format
An interval-level response format that uses a 5-point integer scale. For instance, a 1 to 5 rating would be considered a Likert response format.

semantic differential
A scaling method in which an object is assessed by the respondent on a set of bipolar adjective pairs.

response scale
A sequential numerical response format, such as a 1-to-5 rating format.

filter or contingency question
A question you ask the respondents to determine whether they are qualified or experienced enough to answer a subsequent one.

the example that I stated the prompt (question) explicitly, so the respondent knows I want a number from 1 to 4.

You can also construct survey questions using an **interval-level response format**. One of the most common of these types is the traditional 1 to 5 rating (or 1 to 7, or 1 to 9, and so on). This is sometimes referred to as a *Likert scale*. However, as you will see in Chapter 5, a Likert scale is much more than this response format alone, so it's probably better to call the 1 to 5 rating a **Likert response format**. In Figure 4–4, you see how you might ask an opinion question using a 1 to 5 bipolar scale. (It's called *bipolar* because there is a neutral point, and the two ends of the scale are at opposite positions of the opinion.)

An interval response format is used with an approach called the **semantic differential**, as shown in Figure 4–5. Here, an item is assessed by the respondent on a set of bipolar adjective pairs (in this example, a 5-point rating **response scale** is used).

Finally, another type of interval response format occurs when you use a cumulative or Guttman scale to collect responses. Here, the respondents check each item with which they agree. The items themselves are constructed so that they are cumulative; if you agree with one item, you probably agree with all of the ones above it in the list (Figure 4–6). Each item also has a scale score that is not shown with the item. A respondent's score is the highest scale score of an item with which he or she agreed.

Filter or Contingency Questions   Sometimes, you have to ask the respondents one question to determine whether they are qualified or experienced enough to answer a subsequent one. This requires using a **filter or contingency question**. For instance, you may want to ask one question if the respondent has ever smoked marijuana and a different question if he or she has not. In this case, you would have to construct a filter question to determine first whether the respondent has ever smoked marijuana (Figure 4–7).

| **FIGURE 4–4** | **An interval-level response format for a survey question** |

The death penalty is justifiable under some circumstances.

1	2	3	4	5
strongly disagree	disagree	neutral	agree	strongly agree

FIGURE 4–5   A semantic differential response format for a survey question

Please state your opinions on national health insurance on the scale below

	very much	some-what	neither	some-what	very much	
interesting	☐	☐	☐	☐	☐	boring
simple	☐	☐	☐	☐	☐	complex
uncaring	☐	☐	☐	☐	☐	caring
useful	☐	☐	☐	☐	☐	useless

FIGURE 4–6   A cumulative response format for a survey question

Please check each statement that you agree with:
___Are you willing to permit immigrants to live in your country?
___Are you willing to permit immigrants to live in your community?
___Are you willing to permit immigrants to live in your neighborhood?
___Would you be willing to have an immigrant live next door to you?
___Would you let your child marry an immigrant?

FIGURE 4–7   A filter or contingency question

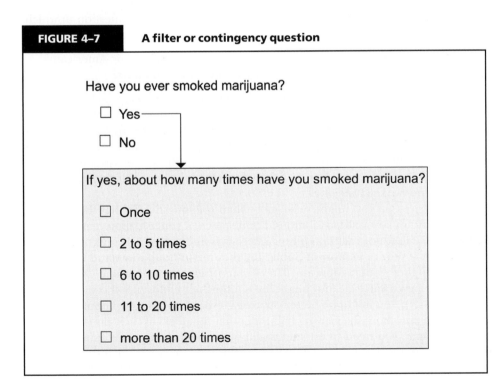

Have you ever smoked marijuana?
☐ Yes
☐ No

If yes, about how many times have you smoked marijuana?

☐ Once

☐ 2 to 5 times

☐ 6 to 10 times

☐ 11 to 20 times

☐ more than 20 times

Filter questions can be complex. Sometimes, you have to have multiple filter questions to direct your respondents to the correct subsequent questions. You should keep the following conventions in mind when using filters:

- *Try to avoid having more than three levels (two jumps) for any question.* Too many jumps will confuse respondents and may discourage them from continuing with the survey.
- *If there are only two levels, use graphics to jump (for example an arrow and box).* The example in Figure 4–7 shows how you can make effective use of an arrow and box to help direct the respondent to the correct subsequent question.
- *If possible, jump to a new page.* If you can't fit the response to a filter on a single page, it's probably best to be able to say something like, *If YES, please turn to page 4*, rather than *If YES, please go to Question 38*, because the respondent will generally have an easier time finding a page than a specific question. One of the advantages of Web-based or other electronically formatted surveys is that branching questions can be programmed to make the transition from one item to another very simple for the respondent because the branched item automatically appears where and when it should.

4-1b Question Content

For each question in your survey, you should ask yourself how well it addresses the content you are trying to get at. The following sections cover some content-related questions you can ask about your survey questions.

Is the Question Necessary and Useful? Examine each question to determine whether you need to ask it at all and whether you need to ask it at the level of detail you currently have, as in the following examples:

- Do you need the age of each child or just the number of children younger than 16?
- Do you need to ask income or can you estimate?

Are Several Questions Needed? Sometimes, we develop a question in which we try to ask about too many things at once, as in the following examples:

- What are your feelings toward African-Americans and Hispanic-Americans?
- What do you think of proposed changes in benefits and hours?

It's hard—often impossible—for respondents to answer such questions because they have conflicting opinions. They may feel very differently about African-Americans and Hispanic-Americans, or about changes in benefits versus changes in hours. You can often spot these kinds of problem questions by looking for the conjunction *and* in your question. We refer to this classic question-writing problem as the *double-barreled question*. You should think about splitting each of the questions into two separate ones.

Another reason you might need more than one question is that the question you ask does not cover all possibilities. For instance, if you ask about earnings, the respondent might not mention all income (such as dividends or gifts). If you ask respondents if they're in favor of public TV, they might not understand that you're asking about their general opinion. They may not be in favor of public TV for themselves (they never watch it), but might favor it for their children (who watch *Sesame Street* regularly). You might be better off asking two questions: one about their own viewing and one about the viewing habits of other members of their households.

Sometimes, you need to ask additional questions because your question does not provide you with enough context to interpret the answer. For instance, if you ask about attitudes toward Catholics, can you interpret this without finding out about your respondents' attitudes toward religion in general or other religious groups?

At times, you need to ask additional questions because your question does not determine the intensity of the respondent's attitude or belief. For example, if respondents say they support public TV, you probably should also ask whether they ever watch it or if they would be willing to have their tax dollars spent on it. It's one thing for respondents to tell you they support something, but the intensity of that response is greater if they are willing to back their sentiment of support with their behavior.

Do Respondents Have the Needed Information? Look at each question in your survey to see whether the respondent is likely to have the necessary information to be able to answer the question. For example, let's say you want to ask the following question:

> Do you think Dean Rusk acted correctly during the Bay of Pigs crisis?

The respondents won't be able to answer this question if they have no idea who Dean Rusk was or what the Bay of Pigs crisis was. In surveys of television viewing, you cannot expect the respondent to answer questions about shows they have never watched. You should ask a filter question first (such as, Have you ever watched the show *ER?*) before asking for opinions about it.

Does the Question Need to Be More Specific? Sometimes, researchers ask their questions too generally and the information they obtain is difficult to interpret. For example, let's say you want to find out the respondent's opinions about a specific book. You could ask the following question:

> How well did you like the book?

and offer some scale ranging from "Not at All" to "Extremely Well," but what would the response mean? What does it mean to say you liked a book extremely well? Instead, you might ask questions designed to be more specific:

> Did you recommend the book to others?

or

> Did you look for other books by that author?

Is the Question Sufficiently General? You can err in the other direction as well by being too specific. For instance, if you ask people to list the television programs they liked best in the past week, you could get a different answer than if you asked them which show they've enjoyed most over the past year. Perhaps a show they don't usually like had a great episode in the past week, or their favorite show was preempted by another program.

Is the Question Biased or Loaded? One danger in question writing is that your own biases and blind spots may affect the wording (see Section 4-1d, Question Wording). For instance, you might generally be in favor of tax cuts. If you ask the question,

> What do you see as the benefits of a tax cut?

you're asking about only one side of the issue. You might get a different picture of the respondents' positions if you also asked about the disadvantages of tax cuts. The same thing could occur if you are in favor of public welfare and you ask

> What do you see as the disadvantages of eliminating welfare?

without also asking about the potential benefits.

Will the Respondent Answer Truthfully? For each question on your survey, ask yourself whether respondents will have any difficulty answering the question truthfully. If there is some reason why they may not, consider rewording the question. For instance, some people are sensitive about answering questions about their exact age or income. In this case, you might give them **response brackets** to choose from (such as between 30 and 40 years old, or between $50,000 and $100,000 annual income). Sometimes, even bracketed responses won't be enough. Some people do not like to share how much money they give to charitable causes. (They may be afraid of opening themselves up to even more solicitations.) No matter how you word the question, they would not be likely to tell you their contribution rate. Sometimes, you can work around such problems by posing the question in terms of a *hypothetical projective respondent* (a little bit like a projective test). For example, they might respond if you ask how much money "people you know" typically give in a year to charitable causes. Finally, you can sometimes dispense with asking a question at all if you can obtain the answer unobtrusively. (This is covered in Chapter 6.) If you are interested in finding out which magazines the respondents read, you might instead tell them you are collecting magazines for a recycling drive and ask if they have any old ones to donate. Of course, you have to consider the ethical implications of such deception!

4-1c Response Format

The response format is how you collect the answer from the respondent. Some people use the term *response scale*, but you will see in Chapter 5 that the term *scales* has a very specific meaning that we shouldn't confuse with the way you collect the data. Let's start with a simple distinction between what I call **structured response formats** and **unstructured response formats**.

Structured Response Formats Structured response formats help the respondent respond more easily and help the researcher accumulate and summarize responses more efficiently, but they can also constrain the respondent and limit the researcher's ability to understand what the respondent really means. There are many different structured response formats, each with their own strengths and weaknesses. We'll review the major ones here.

Fill-in-the-Blank. One of the simplest response formats is a blank line that can be used to collect data for a number of different response types. For instance, asking your gender as shown in Figure 4–8 is one of the simplest fill-in-the-blank formats.

Blanks are also used for checking responses in dichotomous questions, as illustrated in Figure 4–9.

Here, the respondent would probably put a checkmark or an *X* next to the response. This is also an example of a *dichotomous* response because it has only two possible values. Other common dichotomous responses are True/False and Yes/No. Another common use of a fill-in-the-blank response format is in a preference ranking, as described earlier in Figure 4–3, where respondents entered their rank

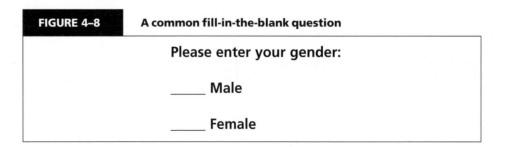

| FIGURE 4–8 | A common fill-in-the-blank question |

Please enter your gender:

_____ **Male**

_____ **Female**

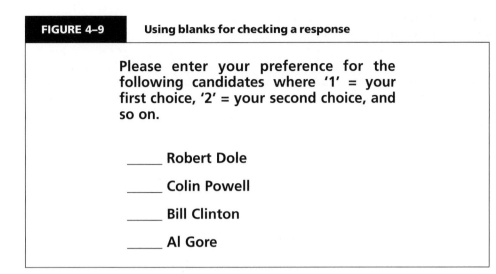

FIGURE 4–9   **Using blanks for checking a response**

> Please enter your preference for the following candidates where '1' = your first choice, '2' = your second choice, and so on.
>
> _____ Robert Dole
>
> _____ Colin Powell
>
> _____ Bill Clinton
>
> _____ Al Gore

preferences for four candidates into the blank line in front of each category. Notice that, in this case, you expect the respondent to place a number on every blank, whereas in the previous example, you expect the respondent to choose only one.

And there's always the classic fill-in-the-blank test item (Figure 4–10).

Check the Answer.   The respondent places a check next to the response(s). The simplest form would be the example given previously in Figure 4–9, which asks the respondents to indicate their gender. Sometimes, you supply a box that the person can fill in with an *X*, which is sort of a variation on the checkmark. Figure 4–11 shows a check-box format.

Notice that in this example, it is possible to check more than one response. By convention, you usually use the check-mark format when you want to allow the respondent to select multiple items.

This type of question is sometimes referred to as a **multioption variable**. You have to be careful when you analyze data from a multioption variable. Because the respondent can select any of the options, you have to treat this type of variable in your analysis as though each option is a separate variable. For instance, for each option you would normally enter into a computer either a 0 if the respondent did not check it or a 1 if the respondent did check it. For the previous example, if the respondent had only a printer and CD-ROM drive, you would enter the sequence 1, 1, 0, 0, 0 in five separate variables. There is an important reason why you should code this variable as either 0 or 1 when you enter the data. If you do, and you want to determine what percentage of your **sample** has a printer, all you have to do is compute the average of the 0's and 1's for the printer variable. For instance, if you have 10 respondents and only 3 have a printer, the average would be 3/10 =.30, or 30%, which is the percentage who checked that item.

The previous example is also a good example of a checklist item. When you use a checklist, you want to be sure that you ask the following questions:

- Are all of the alternatives covered?
- Is the list of reasonable length (not too long)?

multioption variable
A question format in which the respondent can pick multiple variables from a list.

sample
The actual units you select to participate in your study.

FIGURE 4–10   **A fill-in-the-blank test item**

> Name: _____

FIGURE 4–11   The check-box format

Please check if you have the following item on the computer you use most:

❑   modem

❑   printer

❑   CD-ROM drive

❑   joystick

❑   scanner

- Is the wording impartial?
- Is the form of the response easy, uniform?

Sometimes, you may not be sure that you have covered all of the possible responses in a checklist. If that is the case, you should probably allow the respondent to write in any other options that apply.

Circle the Answer. Sometimes, respondents are asked to circle an item to indicate their response. Usually, you are asking them to circle a number. For instance, you might have the example shown in Figure 4–12.

If respondents are answering questions on a computer, it's not feasible to have them circle a response. In this case, you would most likely use an option button, as shown in Figure 4–13. With an option button, only one option at a time can be checked. The rule of thumb is that you ask people to circle an item or click a button when you want them to be able to select only one of the options. In contrast to the multioption variable, this type of item is referred to as a **single-option variable;** even though the respondents have multiple choices, they can select only one of them. You would analyze this as a single variable that can take the integer values from 1 to 5.

single-option variable
A question response list from which the respondent can check only one response.

FIGURE 4–12   A circle-the-answer response format

Capital punishment is the best way to deal with convicted murderers.

| 1 | ② | 3 | 4 | 5 |
| Strongly Disagree | Disagree | Neutral | Agree | Strongly Agree |

FIGURE 4–13   An option button response format on the Web.

Capital punishment is the best way to deal with convicted murderers.

| ○ | ○ | ○ | ○ | ○ |
| Strongly Disagree | Disagree | Neutral | Agree | Strongly Agree |

| **FIGURE 4–14** | **The unstructured response format** |

Please add any other comments:

_____

_____

_____

Unstructured Response Formats A wide variety of structured response formats exist; however, there are relatively few unstructured ones. What is an unstructured response format? Generally, it is written text. If the respondent (or interviewer) writes down text as the response, you have an unstructured response format. These can vary from short comment boxes to the transcript of an interview.

In almost every short questionnaire, there's usually one or more short text field questions. One of the most frequent is shown in Figure 4–14.

Actually, there's really not much more to text-based response formats of this type than writing the prompt and allowing enough space for a reasonable response.

Transcripts are an entirely different matter. In those cases, the transcriber has to decide whether to transcribe every word or record only major ideas, thoughts, quotes, and so on. In detailed transcriptions, you may also need to distinguish different speakers (such as the interviewer and respondent) and have a standard convention for indicating comments about what's going on in the interview, including nonconversational events that take place and thoughts of the interviewer.

4-1d Question Wording

One of the major difficulties in writing good survey questions is getting the wording right. Even slight wording differences can confuse the respondent or lead to incorrect interpretations of the question. Here, I outline some questions you can ask about how you worded each of your survey questions.

Can the Question be Misunderstood? The survey author always has to be on the lookout for questions that could be misunderstood or confusing. For instance, if you ask a person for his or her nationality, it might not be clear what you want. (Do you want someone from Indonesia to say _Indonesian, Asian,_ or _Pacific Islander?_) Or, if you ask for marital status, do you want people to say simply that they are either married or not married? Or do you want more detail (like divorced, widow/widower, and so on)?

Some terms are too vague to be useful. For instance, if you ask a question about the mass media, what do you mean? The newspapers? Radio? Television?

Here's one of my favorites. Let's say you want to know the following:

What kind of headache remedy do you use?

Do you want to know what brand name medicine respondents take? Do you want to know about home remedies? Are you asking whether they prefer a pill, capsule, or caplet?

What Assumptions Does the Question Make? Sometimes, you don't stop to consider how a question will appear from the respondent's point of view. You don't think about the assumptions behind the questions. For instance, if you ask what social class someone's in, you assume that they know what social class is and that they think of themselves as being in one. In this case, you may need to use a filter question first to determine whether either of these assumptions is true.

- For historical demographics, follow chronological order.
- Ask about one topic at a time.
- When switching topics, use a transition.
- Reduce response set (the tendency of the respondent to just keep checking the same response).
- For filter or contingency questions, make a flowchart.

4-1f The Golden Rule

You are imposing in the life of your respondents. You are asking for their time, their attention, their trust, and often, for their personal information. Therefore, you should always keep in mind the golden rule of survey research (and, I hope, for the rest of your life as well!):

> Do unto your respondents as you would have them do unto you!

To put this in more practical terms, you should keep the following in mind:

- Thank the respondent at the beginning for allowing you to conduct your study.
- Keep your survey as short as possible—include only what is absolutely necessary.
- Be sensitive to the needs of the respondent.
- Be alert for any sign that the respondent is uncomfortable.
- Thank the respondent at the end for participating.
- Assure the respondent that you will send a copy of the final results—and make sure you do.

4-2 Interviews

Interviews (McCracken, 1988) are among the most challenging and rewarding forms of measurement. They require a personal sensitivity and adaptability as well as the ability to stay within the bounds of the designed protocol. Here, I describe the preparation you typically need to do for an interview study and the process of conducting the interview itself. Keep in mind that the distinction between an interview and a questionnaire is not always clear-cut. Interviewers typically use a type of questionnaire instrument as the script for conducting the interview. It often has both structured and unstructured questions on it. This type of interview questionnaire would also have instructions for the interviewer that are not seen by the respondent and may include space for the interviewer to record any observations about the progress and process of the interview. These features would not be present in a mailed questionnaire.

4-2a The Role of the Interviewer

The interviewer is really the jack-of-all-trades in survey research. The interviewer's role is complex and multifaceted. It includes the following tasks:

- *Locate and enlist cooperation of respondents.* The interviewer has to find the respondent. In door-to-door surveys, this means being able to locate specific addresses. Often, the interviewer has to work at the least desirable times (like immediately after dinner or on weekends) because that's when respondents are most readily available.
- *Motivate respondents to do a good job.* If the interviewer does not take the work seriously, why would the respondent? The interviewer has to be motivated and has to be able to communicate that motivation to the respondent. Often, this means that the interviewer has to be convinced of the importance of the research.

- *Clarify any confusion/concerns.* Interviewers have to be able to think on their feet. Respondents may raise objections or concerns that were not anticipated. The interviewer has to be able to respond candidly and informatively.
- *Observe quality of responses.* Whether the interview is personal or over the phone, the interviewer is in the best position to judge the quality of the information that is being recorded. Even a verbatim transcript will not adequately convey how seriously the respondent took the task, or any gestures or body language that was observed.
- *Conduct a good interview.* Last, and certainly not least, the interviewer has to conduct a good interview! Every interview has a life of its own. Some respondents are motivated and attentive; others are distracted or disinterested. The interviewer also has good or bad days. Assuring a consistently high-quality interview is a challenge that requires constant effort.

4-2b Training the Interviewers

One of the most important aspects of any interview study is the training of the interviewers themselves. In many ways, the interviewers are your measures, and the quality of the results is totally in their hands. Even in small studies involving only a single researcher-interviewer, it is important to organize in detail and rehearse the interviewing process before beginning the formal study.

Here are some of the major topics that you should consider during interviewer training:

- *Describe the entire study.* Interviewers need to know more than simply how to conduct the interview itself. They should learn about the background for the study, previous work that has been done, ethical safeguards and procedures, and why the study is important.
- *State who is the sponsor of research.* Interviewers need to know whom they are working for. They—and their respondents—have a right to know not only what agency or company is conducting the research but also who is paying for the research.
- *Teach enough about survey research.* Although you seldom have the time to teach a full course on survey-research methods, the interviewers need to know enough that they respect the survey method and are motivated. Sometimes, it may not be apparent why a question or set of questions was asked in a particular way. The interviewers will need to understand the rationale behind the way you constructed the instrument.
- *Explain the sampling logic and process.* Naive interviewers may not understand why sampling is so important. They may wonder why you go through the difficulty of selecting the sample so carefully. You will have to explain that sampling is the basis for the conclusions that will be reached and for the degree to which your study will be useful.
- *Explain interviewer bias.* Interviewers need to know the many ways they can inadvertently bias the results. They also need to understand why it is important that they not bias the study. This is especially a problem when you are investigating political or moral issues on which people have strongly held convictions. Although the interviewers may think they are doing good for society by slanting results in favor of what they believe, they need to recognize that doing so could jeopardize the entire study in the eyes of others.
- *Walk through the interview.* When you first introduce the interview, it's a good idea to walk through the entire protocol so that the interviewers can get an idea of the various parts or phases and how they interrelate.
- *Explain respondent selection procedures, including the following:*
  - *Reading maps:* It's astonishing how many adults don't know how to follow directions on a map. In personal interviews, interviewers may need to locate respondents spread over a wide geographic area. They often have to

people who have limited access or none at all. These issues have been labeled "non-observation errors" (Groves, 1989) due to the fact that many households do not have computer access and that access is much less likely among the disabled, poor, and minority populations. Internet users tend to be younger and better educated (Fricker, Galesic, Tourangeau, & Yan, 2005). If you do not know how many people have received a survey via a listserv, how do you calculate your response rate? And how do you know whether the kind of person you were targeting actually completed the survey? Given these complications, you may consider the possibility of conducting dual-media surveys, where you make the survey available through multiple channels (for example, e-survey and mail survey) and allow respondents to select their preferred method of response.

Interviews Interviews are a far more personal form of research than questionnaires. In the personal interview, the interviewer works directly with the respondent. In contrast to mail surveys, the interviewer has the opportunity to probe or ask follow-up questions, and interviews are generally easier for the respondent, especially if you are seeking opinions or impressions. Interviews can be time-consuming, and they are resource intensive. The interviewer is considered a part of the measurement instrument, and interviewers have to be well trained to respond to any possible situation.

An increasingly important type of interview is the group interview or focus group. In a **focus group**, the interviewer is essentially a facilitator of the group discussion. Small groups of five to ten people are asked to discuss one or more focus questions. The facilitator strives to ensure that each person has an opportunity to give an opinion. Focus groups enable deeper consideration of complex issues than many other survey methods. When people hear the points others make, it often will trigger ideas or responses they wouldn't have thought of by themselves (much like in brainstorming). But you always have to be concerned about how respondents in a group might be constrained from saying what they believe because others are present.

Almost everyone is familiar with the **telephone interview**. Telephone interviews enable a researcher to gather information rapidly. Most of the major public opinion polls that are reported are based on telephone interviews. Like personal interviews, they allow for some personal contact between the interviewer and the respondent. They also allow the interviewer to ask follow-up questions. But they have some major disadvantages: many people don't have publicly listed telephone numbers, some don't have telephones, people often don't like the intrusion of a call to their homes, and telephone interviews have to be relatively short or people will feel imposed upon.

4-3b Selecting the Survey Method

Selecting the type of survey you are going to use is one of the most critical decisions in many social research contexts. A few simple rules will help you make the decision; you have to use your judgment to balance the advantages and disadvantages of different survey types. Here, all I want to do is give you a number of questions you might ask to guide your decision.

Population Issues The first set of considerations has to do with the population and its accessibility.

- *Can the population units be identified?* For some populations, you have a complete listing of the units to be sampled. For others, such a list is difficult or impossible to compile. For instance, there are complete listings of registered voters or persons with active drivers' licenses, but no one keeps a complete list of homeless people. If you are doing a study that requires input from homeless persons, it's likely that you'll need to go and find the respondents personally.

focus group
A qualitative measurement method where input on one or more focus topics is collected from participants in a small-group setting where the discussion is structured and guided by a facilitator.

telephone interview
A personal interview that is conducted over the telephone.

In such contexts, you can pretty much rule out the idea of mail surveys or telephone interviews.

- *Is the population literate?* Questionnaires require that your respondents read. Although this might seem initially like a reasonable assumption for most adult populations, recent research suggests that the instance of adult illiteracy is alarmingly high. Even if your respondents can read to some degree, your questionnaire might contain difficult or technical vocabulary. Clearly, you would expect some populations to be illiterate. Young children would not be good targets for questionnaires.

- *Are there language issues?* We live in a multilingual world. Virtually every society has members who speak a language other than the predominant language. Some countries (like Canada) are officially multilingual, and our increasingly global economy requires us to do research that spans countries and language groups. Can you produce multiple versions of your questionnaire? For mail instruments, can you know in advance which language your respondent speaks, or do you need to send multiple translations of your instrument? Can you be confident that important connotations in your instrument are not culturally specific? Could some of the important nuances get lost in the process of translating your questions?

- *Will the population cooperate?* People who do research on illegal immigration have a difficult methodological problem. They often need to speak with illegal immigrants or people who may be able to identify others who are. Why would those respondents cooperate? Although the researcher may mean no harm, the respondents are at considerable risk legally if information they divulge should get into the hands of the authorities. The same can be said for any target group that is engaging in illegal or unpopular activities.

- *What are the geographic restrictions?* Is your population of interest dispersed over too broad a geographic range for you to study feasibly with a personal interview? It may be possible for you to send a mail instrument to a nationwide sample. You may be able to conduct phone interviews with them, but it will almost certainly be less feasible to do research that requires interviewers to visit directly with respondents if they are widely dispersed.

Sampling Issues The *sample* is the actual group you will have to contact in some way. When doing survey research, you need to consider several important sampling issues.

- *What data is available?* What information do you have about your sample? Do you have current addresses? Current phone numbers? Are your contact lists up to date?

- *Can respondents be found?* Can your respondents be located? Some people are very busy. Some travel a lot. Some work the night shift. Even if you have an accurate phone, address, or email address, you may not be able to locate or make contact with your sample.

- *Who is the respondent?* Who is the respondent in your study? Let's say you draw a sample of households in a small city. A household is not a respondent. Do you want to interview a specific individual? Do you want to talk only to the head of household (how is that person defined)? Are you willing to talk to any member of the household? Do you decide that you will speak to the first adult member of the household who opens the door? What if that person is unwilling to be interviewed but someone else in the house is willing? How do you deal with multifamily households? Similar problems arise when you sample groups, agencies, or companies. Can you survey any member of the organization? Or do you want to speak only to the director of human resources? What if the person you would like to interview is unwilling or unable to participate? Do you use another member of the organization?

- *Can all members of the population be sampled?* If you have an incomplete list of the population (sampling frame), you may not be able to sample every member of the population. Lists of various groups are extremely hard to keep up to date. People move or change their names. Even though they are on your sampling frame listing, you may not be able to get to them. It's also possible they are not even on the list.

- *Are response rates likely to be a problem?* Even if you are able to solve all of the other population and sampling problems, you still have to deal with the issue of response rates. Some members of your sample will simply refuse to respond. Others have the best of intentions but can't seem to find the time to send in your questionnaire by the due date. Still others misplace the instrument or forget about the appointment for an interview. Low response rates are among the most difficult of problems in survey research. They can ruin an otherwise well-designed survey effort.

Question Issues Sometimes, the nature of what you want to ask respondents determines the type of survey you select.

- *What types of questions can you ask?* Are you going to be asking personal questions? Are you going to need to get lots of detail in the responses? Can you anticipate the most frequent or important types of responses and develop reasonable closed-ended questions?
- *How complex will the questions be?* Sometimes, you are dealing with a complex subject or topic. The questions you want to ask are going to have multiple parts. You may need to branch to subquestions.
- *Will filter questions be needed?* A filter question may be needed to determine whether the respondent is qualified to answer your question(s) of interest. For instance, you wouldn't want to ask for respondents' opinions about a specific computer program without first screening to find out whether they have any experience with the program. Sometimes, you have to filter on several variables (for example, age, gender, and experience). The more complicated the filtering, the less likely it is that you can rely on paper-and-pencil instruments without confusing the respondent.
- *Can question sequence be controlled?* Is your survey one in which you can construct a reasonable sequence of questions in advance? Or are you doing an initial exploratory study in which you may need to ask follow-up questions that you can't easily anticipate?
- *Will lengthy questions be asked?* If your subject matter is complicated, you may need to give the respondent some detailed background for a question. Can you reasonably expect your respondent to sit still long enough in a phone interview to listen to your question?
- *Will long response scales be used?* If you are asking people about the different computer equipment they use, you may have to have a lengthy response list (CD-ROM drive, floppy drive, mouse, touch pad, modem, network connection, external speakers, and so on). Clearly, it may be difficult to ask about each of these in a short phone interview.

Content Issues The content of your study can also pose challenges for the different survey types you might use.

- *Can the respondents be expected to know about the issue?* If respondents do not keep up with the news (for example, by reading the newspaper, watching television news, or talking with others), they may not even know of the news issue you want to ask them about. Or, if you want to do a study of family finances and you are talking to the spouse who doesn't pay the bills on a regular basis, he or she may not have the information to answer your questions.
- *Will the respondent need to consult records?* Even if the respondents understand what you're asking about, you may need to allow them to consult their records to get an accurate answer. For instance, if you ask them how much money they

spent on food in the past month, they may need to look up their personal check and credit card records. In this case, you don't want to be involved in an interview where they would have to go look things up while they keep you waiting (and they wouldn't be comfortable with that).

Bias Issues People come to the research endeavor with their own sets of biases and prejudices. Sometimes, these biases will be less of a problem with certain types of survey approaches.

- *Can social desirability be avoided?* Respondents generally want to look good in the eyes of others. None of us likes to look as if we don't know an answer. We don't want to say anything that would be embarrassing. If you ask people about information that may put them in this kind of position, they may not tell you the truth, or they may spin the response so that it makes them look better. This may be more of a problem in a face-to face interview situation or a phone interview.
- *Can interviewer distortion and subversion be controlled?* Interviewers may distort an interview as well. They may not ask difficult questions or ones that make them uncomfortable. They may not listen carefully to respondents on topics for which they have strong opinions. They may make the judgment that they already know what the respondent would say to a question based on their prior responses, even though that may not be true.
- *Can false respondents be avoided?* With mail surveys, it may be difficult to know who actually responded. Did the head of household complete the survey or someone else? Did the chief executive officer actually give the responses or instead pass the task off to a subordinate? Are the people you're speaking with on the phone actually who they say they are? At least with personal interviews, you have a reasonable chance of knowing to whom you are speaking. In mail surveys or phone interviews, this may not be the case.

Administrative Issues Last, but certainly not least, you have to consider the feasibility of the survey method for your study.

- *Costs.* Cost is often the major determining factor in selecting survey type. You might prefer to do personal interviews but can't justify the high cost of training and paying for the interviewers. You may prefer to send out an extensive mailing but can't afford the postage to do so.
- *Facilities.* Do you have the facilities (or access to them) to process and manage your study? In telephone interviews, do you have well-equipped phone surveying facilities? For focus groups, do you have a comfortable and accessible room to host the group? Do you have the equipment needed to record and transcribe responses?
- *Time.* Some types of surveys take longer than others. Do you need responses immediately (as in an overnight public opinion poll)? Have you budgeted enough time for your study to send out mail surveys and follow-up reminders and to get the responses back by mail? Have you allowed for enough time to get enough personal interviews to justify that approach?
- *Personnel.* Different types of surveys make different demands of personnel. Interviews require well-trained and motivated interviewers. Group-administered surveys require people who are trained in group facilitation. Some studies may be in a technical area that requires some degree of expertise in the interviewer.

Clearly, there are lots of issues to consider when you are selecting which type of survey to use in your study, and there is no clear and easy way to make this decision in many contexts because it might be that no single approach is clearly the best. You may have to make trade-offs and weigh the advantages and disadvantages discussed in the next section. There is judgment involved. Two expert researchers

TABLE 4–1	Advantages and Disadvantages of Different Survey Methods

| | Questionnaire | | | | Interview | | |
Issue	Group	Mail	Email/Web	Drop-Off	Personal	Phone	Focus Group
Are visual presentations possible?	Yes	Yes	Yes	Yes	Yes	No	Yes
Are long response categories possible?	Yes	Yes	???	Yes	???	No	???
Is privacy a feature?	No	Yes	Yes	No	Yes	???	No
Is the method adaptable on the spot?	No	No	No	No	Yes	Yes	Yes
Are longer open-ended questions feasible?	No	No	No	No	Yes	Yes	Yes
Are reading and writing needed?	???	Yes	Yes	Yes	No	No	No
Can you judge quality of response?	Yes	No	No	???	Yes	???	Yes
Are high response rates likely?	Yes	No	No	Yes	Yes	No	Yes
Can you explain study in person?	Yes	No	No	Yes	Yes	???	Yes
Is it low cost?	Yes	Yes	Yes	No	No	No	No
Are staff and facilities needs low?	Yes	Yes	Yes	No	No	No	No
Does it give access to dispersed samples?	No	Yes	Yes	No	No	No	No
Does respondent have time to formulate answers?	No	Yes	Yes	Yes	No	No	No
Is there personal contact?	Yes	No	No	Yes	Yes	No	Yes
Is a long survey feasible?	No	No	No	No	Yes	No	No
Is there quick turnaround?	No	Yes	Yes	No	No	Yes	???

might, for the same problem or issue, select entirely different survey methods, but if you select a method that isn't appropriate or doesn't fit the context, you can doom a study before you even begin designing the instruments or questions themselves.

4-3c Advantages and Disadvantages of Survey Methods

It's hard to compare the advantages and disadvantages of the major different survey types. Even though each type has some general advantages and disadvantages, there are exceptions to almost every rule. Table 4–1 shows my general assessment.

Summary

A lot of territory was covered in this chapter. You've learned about the different types of surveys—questionnaires and interviews—and how to choose between them. You learned how to construct a questionnaire and address issues of question content, response formats, and question wording and placement. You learned how to train interviewers and the basic steps involved in conducting an interview. Based on this chapter, you should feel pretty confident taking a crack at developing your own survey. The next chapter introduces you to several types of quantitative measurements—scales and indexes—where you attempt to represent a construct with a specific score or value.

Login to the Online Edition of your text at www.atomicdog.com to find additional resources located in the Study Guide at the end of each chapter.

CHAPTER 5

Scales and Indexes

In this chapter, I discuss the two most common approaches for creating quantitative measures of a construct: scaling and indexes. The terms *scale* and *index* are difficult to distinguish, and there are conflicting views in social research about how they should be defined and distinguished. Indexes typically combine different variables into a single score. Often, the variables combined are very different types of constructs and may even be measured in very different ways. So, an index tends to be a composite of differing elements. I consider the basic process in constructing an index and assessing its quality. Scaling evolved from the need to measure abstract or subjective constructs that may seem to be unmeasurable, such as attitudes and beliefs. I discuss general issues in scaling, including the distinction between a scale and a response format. I also explain the difference between multidimensional and unidimensional scaling. Finally, I look in depth at three types of unidimensional scales: Thurstone, Likert, and Guttman. From these discussions, you should learn not only how to use indexes and scales but also when each type is most appropriate.

5-1 Indexes

index
A quantitative score that measures a construct of interest by applying a formula or a set of rules that combines relevant data.

An **index** is a quantitative score constructed by applying a set of rules to combine two or more variables to reflect a more general construct. So, what does this mean? First, an index is a score, a numerical value, that purportedly measures something. Second, an index is a composite. It puts different variables together. Often, these variables are very different kinds of things and may even be measured in different ways and on different scales. Third, the variables are put together using a rule or set of rules. Sometimes, the rule is as simple as just adding up or averaging the scores of each variable to get a total index score. Sometimes, the rule is actually a formula or set of procedures for describing how the variables are combined. Finally, we usually construct an index because we want to measure something that none of the individual components alone does a good job of measuring. An index score is typically trying to get at something that cuts across the variables that are combined, that is more general than its composite parts.

5-1a Some Common Indexes

You are probably already familiar with several famous indexes. One of the best known is the consumer price index (CPI), which is collected every month by the Bureau of Labor Statistics of the U.S. Department of Labor (U.S. Department of Labor, 2004). Each month, the CPI index is reported and is considered to be a reflection of generally how much consumers have to pay for things. To construct this single score each month, government analysts identified eight major categories of spending for the typical consumer: food and beverages, housing, apparel, transportation, medical care, recreation, education and communication, and other goods and services. They then break down these eight areas into more than 200 specific categories. For each of these, they sample from the many items that reflect each category. For example, to represent the "apple" category that is in the "food and beverages" area, they might sample a "particular plastic bag of golden delicious apples, U.S. extra fancy grade, weighing 4.4 pounds" (U.S. Department of Labor, 2004). Each month, people call all over the country to get the current price for more than 80,000 items. Through a rather complicated weighting scheme that takes into account things like the location and the probability that the item will be purchased, these prices are combined. That is, there is a series of formulas and rules that are used each month to combine the prices into an index score. Actually, they compute thousands of different CPI scores each month to reflect different groups of consumers and different locations, although one of these is typically reported in the news as the CPI. The CPI is considered an index of consumer costs and, therefore, is a general economic indicator. It illustrates one of the most important reasons for creating an index—to track a phenomenon and its ups and downs over time.

A second well-known type of index is the socioeconomic status index (SES). Unlike the CPI, SES almost always involves the combination of several very different types of variables. Traditionally, SES is a combination of three constructs: income, education, and occupation. Income would typically be measured in dollars. Education might be measured in years or degree achieved. And occupation typically would be classified into categories or levels by status. Then, these very different elements would need to be combined to get the SES score. In one of the early classic studies in this area (Duncan, 1981), the researchers used the degree to which education and income predicted occupation as the basis for constructing the index score. This SES measure is now typically referred to as the *Duncan socioeconomic index* (SEI). For this index, an SEI score has been created for each of hundreds of occupations. The score is a weighted combination of "occupational education" (the percentage of people in that occupation who had 1 year or more of college education) and "occupational income" (the percentage of people in the occupation who earned more than a specific annual income). With the SEI, all you need to know is the occupation of a person, and you can look up the SEI score that presumably reflects the status of the occupation as related to both education and income. Almost from its inception, the measurement of socioeconomic status has been controversial, and different researchers attempt to accomplish it in a variety of ways (Hauser & Warren, 1996; Stevens & Cho, 1985).

5-1b Constructing an Index

Several steps are typically followed in constructing an index. I'll go over them briefly here, but you should know that, in practice, each one of these steps is considerably more complex than I'm able to convey in this brief description. Each step can involve sophisticated methods and considerable effort, when accomplished well. Here are the basic steps:

1. *Conceptualize the index.* It probably won't surprise you that the first thing you need to decide is what you would like the index to measure. This may seem like a simple issue at first. However, for almost anything you would like to measure with an index, different people might reasonably disagree about what it means. What is socioeconomic status? Does it include income, education, and occupation? If you measure education and occupation, won't that be highly related to income? If so, do you need a separate component that reflects income or will just the two components be sufficient? If you were trying to measure a construct like "quality of life," what components would you need to include to capture the construct? Even with a well-established measure such as the CPI, researchers worry about defining basic terms like "consumption by whom" and "prices of what"? To begin composing an index, you need first to identify the construct you are trying to reflect in the index and describe the variables that are components of the construct. There are a wide variety of ways to accomplish this step. You can make it up using your own hunches and intuitions (a surprisingly large amount of social

research happens this way). You can review the literature and use current theory as a guide. You can engage experts or key stakeholders in formal processes for conceptualizing, using approaches like brainstorming, concept mapping, or interviewing to identify what the key concept you are trying to measure means to different people. Think about several conceptual issues at this stage. What is the purpose of the index? How will it be used and by whom? Is this a one-time or short-term measure, or one that you would like to use over a long period?

2. *Operationalize and measure the components.* It is one thing to say that you would like to measure education and occupation as major components of socioeconomic status. It is quite another to figure out how to measure each one. If you are trying to measure education as it relates to status, do you simply count the number of years in school? If two people spend the same number of years in college majoring in very different subjects, should they get the same numerical value on educational status? Or should we give more "points" for someone majoring in one field than another. Should all bachelor's degrees be counted the same? If you are trying to look at occupation as it relates to status, how do you even classify occupations? How do you decide the numerical value for each occupation as it relates to status? Over time, do occupations change in status? Are new occupations created? (There weren't any Web programmers before the Internet!) If so, how do you accommodate this in an index that tries to measure changes in status over years or decades? What is the unit for which you are measuring? Are you measuring educational levels of individuals? Or are you looking at some other unit like the community or an organization? For example, if you want to measure the educational level of a community and you know the number of years a representative sample of community members went to school, it may be reasonable simply to average the number of years for the community estimate. But if you have a coding only by level of education (for example, 1 = grade school, 2 = some high school, 3 = some college, 4 = associates degree, 5 = bachelor's degree, etc.), you cannot average these values. In this case, you may need to calculate the proportion of the community that achieved a particular level (for example, the proportion of high school graduates) as an estimate of the community educational level. In any event, you need to figure out how you will measure each component of an index before you can move on to calculating the composite index score.

3. *Develop the rules for calculating the index score.* Once you have the components that you think make up the construct of interest, you need to figure out how to combine these component scores to create a single index score. There are many complications here. In the simplest case, you might be able to combine the component scores just by adding or averaging them. In essence, this is what the CPI does. This can be done for the CPI because each consumer item is measured in the same way—its price. But what if each component is measured in entirely different ways? In SES measures, you can't measure income the same way you measure education. So, you're not likely to be able to add or average the scores for income and education in any straightforward way. Even if the components are measured in a similar manner, what if you think different components should be given different emphasis in measuring the construct. For example, what if you believe that income should be considered more important than education when trying to measure socioeconomic status? How much more important? You can do several things when combining the components of an index. It helps if you can develop a model of the index that shows the index score, each of the components, and how you think theoretically these are related. You then need to develop precise rules for how to combine the components in the model. Sometimes, these rules can be stated as a set of procedures that you follow to compute the index, almost like a recipe. In other cases, the rules are essentially a formula or set of formulas (a simple average of several components is essentially a formula).

4. *Are you giving each component equal weight or you are constructing a weighted index score?* A **weighted index** is one where you combine different components of the

weighted index
A quantitative score that measures a construct of interest by applying a formula or a set of rules that combines relevant data where the data components are weighted differently.

index in different amounts or with different emphasis. You're almost certainly familiar with a weighted index because most of you have probably had a teacher that at one time or another used a weighting scheme to come up with your grade for a class. For example, imagine that your teacher measures you on three characteristics: test scores, class participation, and a class project. For the sake of argument (and this is no simple matter in itself), let's assume that you are scored on each of those on a 0 to 100 scale. If you score perfectly on all your tests, you get a 100 on the test score; if your project is perfect, you get 100 on the project score. One way to get a total index score for your course performance would be to average these three components. But what if you (or, more to the point, your professor) believe that these components should not receive equal weight? For instance, maybe participation should be weighted only half as much as the test or project component. You might reason that it doesn't matter how much you participate as long as you can do well on the tests and project. To construct this index score, you would need a formula that weights the test and project components twice as high as the participation. Here's one:

$$\text{Performance} = [(2 \times \text{Test}) + (2 \times \text{Project}) + (1 \times \text{Participation})]/5$$

Why divide by 5? I want the final index score to be on a scale of 1 to 100. Notice that the idea of weighting in index construction can get rather confusing (so what's new?). For example, your professor could have measured both your test and project performance on a 1 to 40 scale (where best performance gets a 40) and your attendance on a 1 to 20 scale. Then, to construct your index score, you might simply add the three component scores! It looks like this is not a weighted index, and technically, it isn't because you're simply adding the scores. But the truth is that you built the weighting into the measurement of each component.

5. *Validate the index score.* Once you have constructed the index, you will need to validate it. This is essentially accomplished in the same way any measure is validated (see Section 3-1, Construct Validity). If the index score is going to be used over time, it is especially important to do periodic validation studies because it's quite possible that the components or how they relate to the index score have changed in important ways over time. For instance, the classification of occupations today differs in important ways from classifications used in 1950. And the selection of consumer goods continually changes over time. Consequently, indexes like the CPI and SES have to be recalibrated or adjusted periodically if they are to be valid reflections of the construct of interest.

Indexes are essential in social research. They range from formal, complex, sophisticated national indexes that track phenomena over years or decades to simple measures developed for use in a single study (or to compute your grade for a course!).

5-2 Scaling

Scaling is the branch of measurement that involves the construction of a measure based on associating qualitative judgments about a construct with quantitative metric units. Like an index, a scale is typically designed to yield a single numerical score that represents the construct of interest. In many ways, scaling remains one of the most mysterious and misunderstood aspects of social research measurement. It attempts to do one of the most difficult of research tasks—measure abstract concepts.

Most people don't understand what scaling is. The basic idea of scaling is described in Section 5-2a, General Issues in Scaling. The discussion includes the important distinction between a scale and a response format. Scales are generally divided into two broad categories: unidimensional and multidimensional. The unidimensional scaling methods were developed in the first half of the twentieth

scaling
The branch of measurement that involves the construction of an instrument that associates qualitative constructs with quantitative metric units.

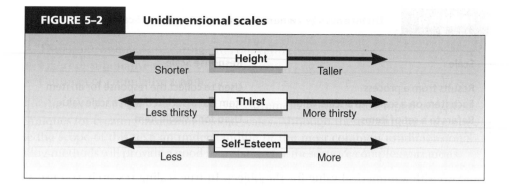

weight are unidimensional, but what about a concept like self-esteem? If you think you can measure a person's self-esteem well with a single ruler that goes from low to high, you probably have a unidimensional construct.

What would a two-dimensional concept be? Many models of intelligence or achievement postulate two major dimensions: mathematical and verbal ability. In this type of two-dimensional model, a person can be said to possess two types of achievement, as illustrated in Figure 5–3. Some people will be high in verbal skills and lower in math. For others, it will be the reverse. If a concept is truly two-dimensional, it is not possible to depict a person's level on it by using only a single number line. In other words, to describe achievement, you would need to locate a person as a point in two-dimensional (*x, y*) space, as shown in Figure 5–3.

Okay, let's push this one step further: How about a three-dimensional concept? Psychologists who study the idea of meaning theorized that the meaning of a term could be well described in three dimensions. Put in other terms, any objects can be distinguished or differentiated from each other along three dimensions. They labeled these three dimensions activity, evaluation, and potency. They called this general theory of meaning the **semantic differential**. Their theory essentially states that you can rate any object along those three dimensions. For instance, think of the idea of ballet. If you like the ballet, you would probably rate it high on activity, favorable on evaluation, and powerful on potency. On the other hand, think about the concept of a book like a novel. You might rate it low on activity (it's passive), favorable on evaluation (assuming you like it), and about average on potency. Now, think of the idea of going to the dentist. Most people would rate it low on activity (it's a passive activity), unfavorable on evaluation, and powerless on potency. (Few routine activities make you feel as powerless!) The theorists who came up with the idea of the semantic differential thought that the meaning of any concepts could be described well by rating the concept on these three dimensions. In other words, to describe the meaning of an object, you have to locate it as a dot somewhere within the cube (three-dimensional space), as shown in Figure 5–4.

semantic differential
A scaling method in which the respondent assesses an object on a set of bipolar adjective pairs.

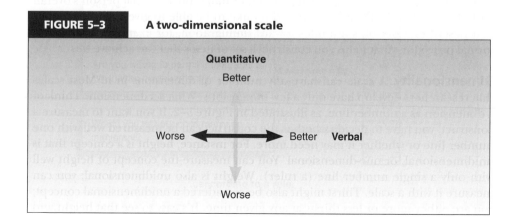

FIGURE 5–4   **A three-dimensional scale**

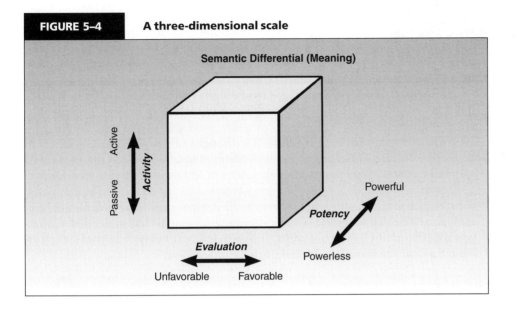

Unidimensional Versus Multidimensional What are the advantages of using a unidimensional model? Unidimensional concepts are generally easier to understand. You have either more or less of it, and that's all. You're either taller or shorter, heavier or lighter. It's also important to understand what a unidimensional scale is as a foundation for comprehending the more complex multidimensional concepts. But the best reason to use unidimensional scaling is that you believe the concept you are measuring is unidimensional in reality. As you've seen, many familiar concepts (height, weight, temperature) are actually unidimensional. However, if the concept you are studying is, in fact, multidimensional in nature, a unidimensional scale or number line won't describe it well. If you try to measure academic achievement on a single dimension, you would place every person on a single line, ranging from low to high achievers. How would you score someone who is a high math achiever and terrible verbally, or vice versa? A unidimensional scale can't capture that more general type of achievement; you would need at least two unidimensional scales.

There are three major types of unidimensional scaling methods. They are similar in that they each measure the concept of interest on a number line. However, they differ considerably in how they arrive at scale values for different items. The three methods are Thurstone, or equal-appearing interval scaling; Likert, or summative scaling; and Guttman, or cumulative scaling. Each of these approaches is described in the following sections.

5-2b Thurstone Scaling

Thurstone was one of the first and most productive scaling theorists. He actually invented three different methods for developing a unidimensional scale, which can be considered different ways to do **Thurstone scaling**: the *method of equal-appearing intervals*, the *method of successive intervals*, and the *method of paired comparisons*. The three methods differed in how the scale values for items were constructed, but in all three cases, respondents rated the resulting scale the same way. To illustrate Thurstone's (1925) approach, I'll show you the easiest method of the three to implement: the method of equal-appearing intervals.

Developing the focus. The method of equal-appearing intervals starts like almost every other scaling method—with a large set of statements to which people respond. Oops! I did it again! You can't start with the set of statements; you have

Thurstone scaling
The process of developing a scale in which the scale items have interval-level numerical values where the final score is the average scale value of all items with which the respondent agreed.

to first define the focus for the scale you're trying to develop. Let this be a warning to all of you: Methodologists like me often start our descriptions with the first objective, methodological step (in this case, developing a set of statements) and forget to mention critical foundational issues like the development of the focus for a project. So, let's try this again....

The method of equal-appearing intervals starts like almost every other scaling method—with the development of the focus for the scaling project. Because this is a unidimensional scaling method, you have to be able to assume that the concept you are trying to scale is reasonably thought of as one-dimensional. The description of this concept should be as clear as possible so that the person(s) who will create the statements has a clear idea of what you are trying to measure. I like to state the focus for a scaling project in the form of an open-ended statement to give to the people who will create the draft or candidate statements. You want to be sure that everyone who is generating statements has some idea of what you are after in this focus command. You especially want to be sure that technical language and acronyms are spelled out and understood.

Generating potential scale items. In this phase, you're ready to create statements. Who should create the statements for a scale? That depends. You might have experts who know something about the phenomenon you are studying. Because the people affected are likely to be expert about what they're experiencing, you might sample them to generate statements. For instance, if you are trying to create a scale for quality of life for people who have a certain type of health condition, you might want to ask them to create potential items. Finally, you can make up the items. Obviously, each of these approaches has advantages and disadvantages, so in many situations, you may want to use some or all of them.

You want a large set of candidate statements—usually, as many as 80 to 100—because you are going to select your final scale items from this pool. You also want to be sure that all of the statements are worded similarly—that they don't differ in grammar or structure. For instance, you might want them each to be worded as a statement with which respondents agree or disagree. You don't want some of them to be statements, while others are questions.

Rating the scale items. So, now you have a set of items or statements. The next step is to have a group of people called *judges* rate each statement on a 1 to 11 scale in terms of how much each statement indicates a *favorable* attitude toward the construct of interest. Pay close attention here! You *don't* want the judges to tell you what their attitudes on the statements are, or whether they would agree with the statements. You want them to rate the favorableness of each statement in terms of the construct you are trying to measure, where 1 = extremely unfavorable attitude toward the construct and 11 = extremely favorable attitude towards the construct. One easy way to actually accomplish this is to type each statement on a separate index card and have each judge rate them by sorting them into 11 piles, as shown in Figure 5–5. Who should the judges be? As with generating the items, there is no simple answer. Generally, you want to have people who are "experts"

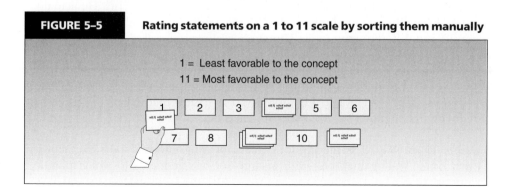

| FIGURE 5–5 | Rating statements on a 1 to 11 scale by sorting them manually |

1 = Least favorable to the concept
11 = Most favorable to the concept

FIGURE 5–6   **Histogram for a scale statement.**

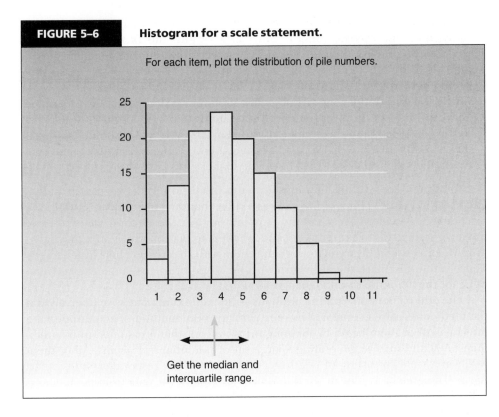

For each item, plot the distribution of pile numbers.

Get the median and
interquartile range.

on the construct of interest do this. But there are many kinds of expertise, ranging from academically trained and credentialed experts to the people who are most directly experienced with the phenomenon.

Computing scale score values for each item. The next step is to analyze the rating data. For each item or statement, you need to compute the median and the interquartile range. The *median* is the value above and below which 50 percent of the ratings fall. The first quartile (Q1) is the value below which 25 percent of the cases fall and above which 75 percent of the cases fall—in other words, the 25th percentile. The median is the 50th percentile. The third quartile, Q3, is the 75th percentile. The interquartile range is the difference between third and first quartile, or Q3–Q1. Figure 5–6 shows a histogram for a single item and indicates the median and interquartile range.

You can compute these values easily with any introductory statistics program or with most spreadsheet programs. To facilitate the final selection of items for your scale, you might want to sort the table of medians and interquartile ranges in ascending order by median and, within that, in descending order by interquartile range.

Selecting the final scale items. Now you have to select the final statements for your scale. You should select statements that are at equal intervals across the range of medians. Ideally, one statement would be selected for each of the 11 median values. Within each value, you should try to select the statement that has the smallest interquartile range (the statement with the least amount of variability across judges). You don't want the statistical analysis to be the only deciding factor here. Look over *the candidate statements at each level, and select the statement that makes the most* sense. If you find that the best statistical choice is a confusing statement, select the next best choice.

Administering the scale. You now have a scale—a yardstick you can use for measuring the construct of interest. Each of your final scale items has a scale score—the median value. And the item scores should range across the spectrum of potential attitudes or beliefs on this construct (because you selected items throughout the median range). You can now give the final set of items to respondents and ask them to agree or disagree with each statement. To get an individual's final scale score, average only the scale scores of all the items that person agreed with. When you average the scale items for the statements with which the respondent agreed, you get an average score that has to range between 1 and 11. If they agreed with scale items that were low in favorableness to the construct, then the average of the items they agreed to should be low. If they agreed with items that your judges had said were highly favorable to the construct, then their final score will be on the higher end of the scale.

You should see a couple of things from this discussion. First, you use the judges to create your scale. Think of the scale as a ruler that ranges from 1 to 11 with one scale item or statement at each of the 11 points on the ruler. Second, when you give the set of scale items to a respondent and ask them to tell you which ones they agree with, you are essentially trying to measure them with that ruler. Their scale score—where you would mark the individual on your 11-point ruler—is the average item value for the items the respondent agreed with.

The other Thurstone scaling methods—the method of successive intervals and the method of paired comparisons—are similar to the method of equal-appearing intervals. All of them begin by focusing on a concept that is assumed to be unidimensional and involve generating a large set of potential scale items. All of them result in a scale consisting of relatively few items that the respondent rates on an Agree/Disagree basis. The major differences are in how the data from the judges is collected. For instance, the method of paired comparisons requires each judge to make a judgment about each pair of statements. With lots of statements, this can become time-consuming.

5-2c Likert Scaling

Likert scaling

The process of developing a scale in which the ratings of the items are summed to get the final scale score. Ratings are usually done using a 1 to 5 Disagree-to-Agree response format Likert scales are also sometimes called summated scales.

Like Thurstone or Guttman scaling, **Likert scaling** (Murphy & Likert, 1938) is a unidimensional scaling method. Here, I'll explain the basic steps in developing a Likert or summative scale. You may remember learning the term *Likert scale* in Chapter 4. A Likert scale is a type of response scale and is different from Likert scaling (see the discussion in Section 5-2a, General Issues in Scaling, and Table 5–1 for the differences between response scales and scaling).

Defining the focus. As in all scaling methods, the first step is to define what it is you are trying to measure. Because this is a unidimensional scaling method, it is assumed that the concept you want to measure is one-dimensional in nature. You might operationalize the definition as an instruction to the people who are going to create or generate the initial set of candidate items for your scale.

Generating the items. Next, you have to create the set of potential scale items. These should be items that can be rated on a 1 to 5 or 1 to 7 disagree-agree response scale. Sometimes, you can create the items by yourself based on your intimate understanding of the subject matter. More often than not, though, it's helpful to engage a number of people in the item creation step. For instance, you might use some form of brainstorming to create the items. It's desirable to have as large a set of potential items as possible at this stage; about 80 to 100 would be best.

Rating the items. The next step is to have a group of judges rate the items. Usually, you would use a 1 to 5 rating scale where:

1 = Strongly unfavorable to the concept
2 = Somewhat unfavorable to the concept
3 = Undecided
4 = Somewhat favorable to the concept
5 = Strongly favorable to the concept

Notice that, as in other scaling methods, the judges are not telling you what they believe; they are judging how favorable each item is with respect to the construct of interest.

Who should the judges be? As in any scaling method, that's not an easy question to answer. Some argue that experts familiar with the process should be used. Others suggest that you should use a random sample of the same types of people who are ultimately your respondents of interest for the scale. There are advantages and disadvantages to each.

Selecting the items. The next step is to compute the intercorrelations between all pairs of items, based on the ratings of the judges. In making judgments about which items to retain for the final scale, there are several analyses you can perform:

- Throw out any items that have a low correlation with the total (summed) score across all items. In most statistics packages, it is relatively easy to compute this type of item-total correlation. First, you create a new variable that is the sum of all of the individual items for each respondent. Then, you include this variable in the correlation-matrix computation. (If you include it as the last variable in the list, the resulting item-total correlations will all be the last line of the correlation matrix and will be easy to spot.) How low should the correlation be for you to throw out the item? There is no fixed rule here; you might eliminate all items that have a correlation with the total score less than .6, for example. (The idea of correlation is covered in Section 12-3d, Correlation.)
- For each item, get the average rating for the top quarter of judges and the bottom quarter. Then, do a *t*-test of the differences between the mean value for the item for the top and bottom quarter judges. (An in-depth discussion of *t*-tests appears in Chapter 12.) Higher *t*-values mean that there is a greater difference between the highest and lowest judges. In more practical terms, items with higher *t*-values are better discriminators, so you want to keep these items. In the end, you will have to use your judgment about which items are most sensibly retained. You want a relatively small number of items on your final scale (from 10 to 15), and you want them to have high item-total correlations and high discrimination (that is, high *t*-values).

Administering the scale. You're now ready to use your Likert scale. Each respondent is asked to rate each item on some response scale. For instance, respondents could rate each item on a 1 to 5 response scale where:

1 = Strongly disagree
2 = Disagree
3 = Undecided
4 = Agree
5 = Strongly agree

There are a variety of possible response scales (1 to 7, 1 to 9, 0 to 4). All of these odd-numbered scales have a middle value, which is often labeled *neutral or undecided*. It is also possible to use a forced-choice response scale with an even number of responses and no middle neutral or undecided choice. In this situation, respondents are forced to decide whether they lean more toward the "agree" or "disagree" end of the scale for each item.

The final score for the respondent on the scale is the sum of his or her ratings for all of the items. (This is why this is sometimes called a *summated scale.*) On some scales, you will have items that are reversed in meaning from the overall direction of the scale. These are called *reversal items.* You will need to reverse the response value for each of these items before summing for the total. That is, if the respondent gave a 1, you make it a 5; if a respondent gave a 2, you make it a 4; 3 = 3; 4 = 2; and 5 = 1. Researchers disagree about whether you should have a "neutral" or

TABLE 5–2		The Employment Self-Esteem Likert Scale		
Strongly disagree	Somewhat disagree	Somewhat agree	Strongly agree	1. I feel good about my work on the job.
Strongly disagree	Somewhat disagree	Somewhat agree	Strongly agree	2. On the whole, I get along well with others at work.
Strongly disagree	Somewhat disagree	Somewhat agree	Strongly agree	3. I am proud of my ability to cope with difficulties at work.
Strongly disagree	Somewhat disagree	Somewhat agree	Strongly agree	4. When I feel uncomfortable at work, I know how to handle it.
Strongly disagree	Somewhat disagree	Somewhat agree	Strongly agree	5. I can tell that other people at work are glad to have me there.
Strongly disagree	Somewhat disagree	Somewhat agree	Strongly agree	6. I know I'll be able to cope with work for as long as I want.
Strongly disagree	Somewhat disagree	Somewhat agree	Strongly agree	7. I am proud of my relationship with my supervisor at work.
Strongly disagree	Somewhat disagree	Somewhat agree	Strongly agree	8. I am confident that I can handle my job without constant assistance.
Strongly disagree	Somewhat disagree	Somewhat agree	Strongly agree	9. I feel like I make a useful contribution at work.
Strongly disagree	Somewhat disagree	Somewhat agree	Strongly agree	10. I can tell that my coworkers respect me.

"undecided" point on the scale (an odd number of responses) or whether the response scale should be a "forced choice" one with no neutral point and an even number of responses (as in a 1 to 4 scale).

Table 5–2 shows an example of a hypothetical ten-item Likert scale that attempts to estimate the level of self-esteem (Rosenberg, 1965) a person has on the job. Notice that this instrument has no center or neutral point in the response scale; the respondent has to declare whether he or she is in agreement or disagreement with the item.

5-2d Guttman Scaling

Guttman scaling
The process of developing a scale in which the items are assigned scale values that allow them to be placed in a cumulative ordering with respect to the construct being scaled.

Guttman scaling (Guttman, 1950) is also sometimes known as *cumulative scaling* or *scalogram analysis*. In Chapter 4, I introduced the term *Guttman scale* in Section 4-1a, Types of Questions. A Guttman scale is a type of response scale and is different from Guttman scaling (see the discussion in 5-2a, General Issues in Scaling, and Table 5–1 for the differences between response scales and scaling). The purpose of Guttman scaling is to establish a one-dimensional continuum for a concept you want to measure. What does that mean? Essentially, you would like a set of items or statements so that a respondent who agrees with any specific question in the list will also agree with al previous questions. Put more formally, you would like to be able to predict item responses perfectly knowing only the total score for the respondent. For example, imagine a ten-item cumulative scale. If the respondent scores a 4, it should mean that he or she agreed with the first four statements. If the respondent scores an 8, it should mean he or she agreed with the first eight. The object is to find a set of items that perfectly matches this pattern. In practice, you would seldom expect to find this cumulative patern perfectly. So, you use scalogram analysis to examine how closely a set of items corresponds with this idea of cumulativeness. Here, I'll explain how you develop a Guttman scale.

Define the focus. As in all of the scaling methods, you begin by defining the focus for your scale. Let's imagine that you want to develop a cumulative scale that measures U.S. citizen attitudes toward immigration. You would want to be sure to specify in your definition whether you are talking about any type of immigration (legal and illegal) from anywhere (Europe, Asia, Latin and South America, Africa).

Develop the items. Next, as in all scaling methods, you would develop a large set of items that reflect the concept. You might do this yourself, or you might engage a knowledgeable group to help. Of course, as with all scaling methods, you would want to come up with many more statements (about 80 to 100 is desirable) than you will ultimately need.

Rate the items. Next, you would want to have a group of judges rate the statements or items in terms of how favorable they are to the concept of interest. They would give a *Yes* if the item is favorable toward the construct and a *No* if it is not. Notice that you are not asking the judges whether they personally agree with the statement. Instead, you're asking them to make a judgment about how the statement is related to the construct of interest.

Develop the cumulative scale. The key to Guttman scaling is in the analysis. You construct a matrix or table that shows the responses of all the judges on all of the items. You then sort this matrix so that judges who agree with more statements are listed at the top and those who agree with fewer are at the bottom. For judges with the same number of agreements, sort the statements from left to right from those that most agreed to, to those that fewest agreed to. You might get a table something like the one in Figure 5–7. Notice that the scale is nearly cumulative when you read from left to right across the columns (items). Specifically, a person who agreed with item 7 always agreed with item 2. Someone who agreed with item 5 always agreed with items 7 and 2. The matrix shows that the cumulativeness of the scale is not perfect, however. While, in general, a person agreeing with item 3 tended to also agree with 5, 7, and 2, there are several exceptions to that rule.

Although you can examine the matrix if there are only a few items in it, if there are many items, you need to use a data analysis called *scalogram analysis* to determine the subsets of items from the pool that best approximate the

---

FIGURE 5–7   **Developing a cumulative scale with guttman scaling**

When sorted by row and column, it will show whether there is a cumulative scale.

Respondent	Item 2	Item 7	Item 5	Item 3	Item 8	Item ...
7	Y	Y	Y	Y	Y	Y
15	Y	Y	Y	–	Ⓨ	–
3	Y	Y	Y	Y	–	–
29	Y	Y	Y	Y	–	–
19	Y	Y	Y	–	–	–
32	Y	Y	–	Ⓨ	–	–
41	Y	Y	–	–	–	–
6	Y	Y	–	–	–	–
14	Y	–	–	Ⓨ	–	–
33	–	–	–	–	–	–

Exceptions

cumulative property. Then, you review these items and select your final scale elements. There are several statistical techniques for examining the table to find a cumulative scale. Because there is seldom a perfectly cumulative scale, you usually have to test how good it is. These statistics also estimate a scale score value for each item. This scale score is used in the final calculation of a respondent's score.

Administering the scale. After you've selected the final scale items, it's relatively simple to administer the scale. You simply present the items and ask respondents to check items with which they agree.

Each scale item has a scale value associated with it (obtained from the scalogram analysis). To compute a respondent's scale score, you simply sum the scale values of every item the respondent agrees with. In this example, the final value should be an indication of the respondent's view on the construct of interest.

5-3 Indexes and Scales

At this point, you should have a much clearer sense of how indexes and scales are similar to and different from each other. One clear commonality is that both an index and a scale yield a single numerical score or value that is designed to reflect the construct of interest.

But there are lots of ways in which scales and indexes are different. Indexes very often are used to combine component scores that differ greatly from one another and are measured in different ways, like income, occupation, and education in SES. Scales typically involve rating a set of similar items on the same response scale, as in the 1 to 5 Likert response format. Indexes often combine numerical values that are counts or are more objectively observable (like prices). Scales very often are constructed to get at more subjective and judgmental constructs like attitudes or beliefs.

Needless to say, there's considerable disagreement among researchers about whether and how indexes and scales can be defined and distinguished. Some researchers argue that a scale is a particular type or subset of an index. Others argue that they are very different things altogether. Some maintain that a unique feature of scaling is the sophistication of the methodology used to select the items; others contend that good index development can get as sophisticated and advanced as any scaling procedure. And so it goes. However we define them, it should be clear to you that both indexes and scales are essential tools in social research.

Summary

A lot of territory was covered in this chapter. We began by learning about indexes. We briefly looked at two of the most famous indexes: the consumer price index (CPI) and socioeconomic status (SES). I then went through the basic steps for how to construct an index score. Next, I showed you what a scale is and described the basic univariate scale types: Thurstone, Likert, and Guttman. You saw that scales can be used as stand-alone instruments, but they can also be integrated into a larger survey. Based on this chapter, you should have a feel for what would be involved in creating and using either an index or scale. The next chapter introduces you to several very different forms of measurement—qualitative and unobtrusive—that aren't geared to generating a single score like an index or scale does, but that are at least as important for social research.

Login to the Online Edition of your text at www.atomicdog.com to find additional resources located in the Study Guide at the end of each chapter.

Qualitative and Unobtrusive Measures

case study
coding
content analysis
data audit
direct observation
exception dictionary
external validity
field research
hypothesis
indirect measure
mixed methods research
participant observation

qualitative measures
qualitative data
quantitative
reliability
sample
sampling
secondary analysis
true score theory
unitizing
unobtrusive measures
unstructured interviewing
validity

mixed methods research
Any research that uses multiple research methods to take advantage of the unique advantages that each method offers. For instance, a study that combines case study interviews with an experimental design can be considered mixed methods.

Mixed Methods Research One of the most important areas in applied social research these days is called **mixed methods research**. In mixed methods research, we simultaneously conduct both qualitative and quantitative research to achieve the advantages of each and mitigate their weaknesses. There are several different ways to accomplish the mixing of methods. These tend to differ in how and at what stage of the research you bring the quantitative and qualitative traditions together. For instance, you can conduct qualitative and quantitative substudies as though they are independent of each other on separate parallel tracks where you bring together the results of each at the end in a synthesis or summary. Or you can mix quantitative and qualitative data collection methods throughout, analyzing the results together and examining the similarities and contrasts. Or you can integrate the qualitative and quantitative approaches into a new synthetic method, such as when we combine qualitative brainstorming and quantitative rating approaches into a single method. Or you can integrate the paradigmatic perspectives of qualitative and quantitative traditions at all stages of a research project, repeatedly and dynamically using each to question and improve the results of the other.

Quantitative research excels at summarizing large amounts of data and reaching generalizations based on statistical estimations. Qualitative research excels at telling the story from the participant's viewpoint, providing the rich, descriptive detail that sets quantitative results into their human context. We are only beginning to learn about how we can best integrate these great traditions of qualitative and quantitative research, and many of today's social research students will spend much of their careers exploring this idea.

6-1b Qualitative and Quantitative Data

It may seem odd that I would argue that there is little difference between qualitative and quantitative data. After all, qualitative data typically consists of words, whereas quantitative data consists of numbers. Aren't these fundamentally different? I don't think so, for the following reasons:

- All qualitative data can be coded quantitatively.
- All quantitative data is based on qualitative judgment.

I'll consider each of these reasons in turn.

coding
The process of categorizing qualitative data.

All Qualitative Data Can Be Coded Quantitatively What I mean here is simple. Anything that is qualitative can be assigned meaningful numerical values. These values can then be manipulated numerically or quantitatively to help you achieve greater insight into the meaning of the data so you can examine specific hypotheses. Consider an example. Many surveys have one or more short, open-ended questions that ask the respondent to supply text responses. The most familiar instance is probably the sentence that is often tacked onto a short survey: "Please add any additional comments." The immediate responses are text-based and qualitative, but you can always (and usually will) perform some type of simple classification of the text responses. You might sort the responses into simple categories, for example. Often, you'll give each category a short label that represents the theme in the response. What you don't often recognize is that even the simple act of categorizing can be viewed as a quantitative one. For instance, let's say that you develop five themes that the respondents express in their open-ended responses. Assume that you have ten respondents. You could easily set up a simple **coding** table like the one in Table 6–1 to represent the coding of the ten responses into the five themes.

This is a simple qualitative thematic coding analysis. But you can represent exactly the same information quantitatively as in Table 6–2.

Notice that this is exactly the same data. The first table (Table 6–1) would probably be called a qualitative coding, while the second (Table 6–2) is clearly quantitative. The quantitative coding gives you additional useful information and makes it

TABLE 6–1	Coding of Qualitative Data into Five Themes for Ten Respondents				
Person	Theme 1	Theme 2	Theme 3	Theme 4	Theme 5
1	✓	✓		✓	
2	✓		✓		
3	✓	✓		✓	
4		✓		✓	
5		✓		✓	✓
6	✓	✓			✓
7			✓	✓	✓
8		✓		✓	
9			✓		✓
10				✓	✓

TABLE 6–2	Quantitative Coding of the Data in Table 6–1					
Person	Theme 1	Theme 2	Theme 3	Theme 4	Theme 5	Totals
1	1	1	0	1	0	3
2	1	0	1	0	0	2
3	1	1	0	1	0	3
4	0	1	0	1	0	2
5	0	1	0	1	1	3
6	1	1	0	0	1	3
7	0	0	1	1	1	3
8	0	1	0	1	0	2
9	0	0	1	0	1	2
10	0	0	0	1	1	2

possible to do analyses that you couldn't do with the qualitative coding. For instance, simply by adding down the columns in Table 6–2, you can say that Theme 4 was the most frequently mentioned, and by adding across the rows, you can say that all respondents touched on two or three of the five themes.

The point is that the line between qualitative and quantitative is less distinct than we sometimes imagine. All qualitative data can be quantitatively coded in an almost infinite variety of ways. This doesn't detract from the qualitative information. You can still do any judgmental syntheses or analyses you want, but recognizing the similarities between qualitative and quantitative information opens up new possibilities for interpretation that might otherwise go unutilized. Now to the other side of the coin. . . .

All Quantitative Data Is Based on Qualitative Judgment Numbers in and of themselves can't be interpreted without understanding the assumptions that underlie them. Take, for example, a simple 1 to 5 rating variable, shown in Figure 6–1.

Here, the respondent answered 2 = Disagree. What does this mean? How do you interpret the value 2 here? You can't really understand this quantitative value unless you dig into some of the judgments and assumptions that underlie it:

- Did the respondent understand the term *capital punishment*?
- Did the respondent understand that 2 means that he or she is disagreeing with the statement?

FIGURE 6–1	A rating illustrates that quantitative data is based on qualitative judgments

Capital punishment is the best way to deal with convicted murderers.

1	②	3	4	5
Strongly disagree	Disagree	Neutral	Agree	Strongly agree

- Does the respondent have any idea about alternatives to capital punishment (otherwise, how can he or she judge what's best)?
- Did the respondent read carefully enough to determine that the statement was limited only to convicted murderers (for instance, rapists were not included)?
- Does the respondent care, or was he or she just circling anything arbitrarily?
- How was this question presented in the context of the survey (for example, did the questions immediately before this one bias the response in any way)?
- Was the respondent mentally alert (especially if this is late in a long survey or the respondent had other things going on earlier in the day)?
- What was the setting for the survey (lighting, noise, and other distractions)?
- Was the survey anonymous? Was it confidential?
- In the respondent's mind, is the difference between a 1 and a 2 the same as between a 2 and a 3 (meaning, is this an interval scale)?

I could go on and on, but my point should be clear. All numerical information involves numerous judgments about what the number means. Quantitative and qualitative data are, at some level, virtually inseparable. Neither exists in a vacuum; neither can be considered totally apart from the other. To ask which is better or more valid or has greater verisimilitude or whatever ignores the intimate connection between them. To do the highest quality research, you need to incorporate both the qualitative and quantitative approaches.

6-1c Qualitative Data

Qualitative data is extremely varied in nature. It includes virtually any information that can be captured that is not numerical in nature (Miles & Huberman, 1994). Here are some of the major categories or types of qualitative data:

- *In-depth interviews.* These include both individual interviews (one-on-one) as well as group interviews (including focus groups). The data can be recorded in numerous ways, including stenography, audio recording, video recording, and written notes. In-depth interviews differ from **direct observation** primarily in the nature of the interaction. In interviews, it is assumed that there is a questioner and one or more interviewees. The purpose of the interview is to probe the ideas of the interviewees about the phenomenon of interest.
- *Direct observation.* I use the term *direct observation* broadly here. It differs from interviewing in that the observer does not actively query the respondent. It can include everything from field research, where one lives in another context or culture for a period of time, to photographs that illustrate some aspect of the phenomenon. The data can be recorded in many of the same ways as interviews (stenography, audio, and video) and through pictures (photos or drawings). (For example, courtroom drawings of witnesses are a form of direct observation.)
- *Written documents.* Usually, this refers to existing documents (as opposed to transcripts of interviews conducted for the research). It can include newspapers, magazines, books, websites, memos, transcripts of conversations, annual reports, and so on. Usually, written documents are analyzed with some form of content analysis (see Section 6-2b, Content Analysis).

direct observation
The process of observing a phenomenon to gather information about it. This process is distinguished from participant observation in that a direct observer does not typically try to become a participant in the context and does strive to be as unobtrusive as possible so as not to bias the observations.

6-1d Qualitative Measures and Observations

A variety of methods are common in qualitative measurement. In fact, the methods are limited primarily by the imagination of the researcher. Here, I discuss a few of the more common methods.

Participant Observation One of the most common methods for qualitative data collection—**participant observation**—is also one of the most demanding. It requires that the researcher become a participant in the culture or context being observed. The literature on participant observation discusses how to enter the context, the role of the researcher as a participant, the collection and storage of field notes, and the analysis of field data. Participant observation often requires months or years of intensive work because the researcher needs to become accepted as a natural part of the culture to ensure that the observations are of the natural phenomenon.

participant observation
A method of qualitative observation in which the researcher becomes a participant in the culture or context being observed.

Direct Observation Direct observation is distinguished from participant observation in a number of ways. First, a direct observer doesn't typically try to become a participant in the context. However, the direct observer does strive to be as unobtrusive as possible so as not to bias the observations. Second, direct observation suggests a more detached perspective. The researcher is watching, rather than both watching and taking part. Consequently, technology can be a useful part of direct observation. For instance, you can videotape the phenomenon or observe from behind one-way mirrors. Third, direct observation tends to be more structured than participant observation. The researcher is observing certain sampled situations or people, rather than trying to become immersed in the entire context. Finally, direct observation tends not to take as long as participant observation. For instance, one might observe mother-child interactions under specific circumstances in a laboratory setting, looking especially for the nonverbal cues being used.

Unstructured Interviewing **Unstructured interviewing** involves direct interaction between the researcher and a respondent or group. It differs from traditional structured interviewing in several important ways. First, although the researcher may have some initial guiding questions or core concepts to ask about, there is no formal structured instrument or protocol. Second, the interviewer is free to move the conversation in any direction of interest that may come up. Consequently, unstructured interviewing is particularly useful for exploring a topic broadly. However, there is a price for this lack of structure. Because each interview tends to be unique with no predetermined set of questions asked of all respondents, it is usually more difficult to analyze unstructured interview data, especially when synthesizing across respondents.

unstructured interviewing
An interviewing method that uses no predetermined interview protocol or survey and in which the interview questions emerge and evolve as the interview proceeds.

Unstructured interviewing may very well be the most common form of data collection of all. You could say it is the method being used whenever anyone asks someone else a question! It is especially useful when conducting site visits or casual focus groups designed to explore a context or situation.

Case Studies A **case study** is an intensive study of a specific individual or specific context. For instance, Freud developed case studies of several individuals as the basis for the theory of psychoanalysis, and Piaget did case studies of children to study developmental phases. Case studies are extensively used in business, law, and policy analysis, with the level of analysis varying from a particular individual to the history of an organization or an event. There is no single way to conduct a case study, and a combination of methods (such as unstructured interviewing and direct observation) is often used. We include case studies in our discussion of qualitative research strategies, but quantitative approaches to studying cases are quite possible and

case study
An intensive study of a specific individual or specific context.

becoming more common with new technology. For example, sometimes researchers provide participants with electronic data collection devices (sometimes called *ambulatory data loggers*) to capture a stream of live events in the natural context. This kind of data can be examined using many kinds of graphic and time series analyses.

Sometimes qualitative case studies can become a form of intervention as well as evaluation. An interesting recent example of this is the Most Significant Change (MSC) technique (Dart & Davies, 2003). The MSC approach generates stories directly from program participants by asking them to describe the most significant change they have experienced or observed in a given period as a result of the program. This form of case study is well suited to understanding change processes as they unfold, but as Dart and Davies pointed out, it can also be used to summarize change at the conclusion of a program and may include both quantitative and qualitative indicators.

Focus Groups Focus groups have become extremely popular in marketing and other kinds of social research because they enable researchers to obtain detailed information about attitudes, opinions, and preferences of selected groups of participants. These methods can be used to generate as many ideas on a topic as possible and to achieve consensus in a group. Sometimes a focus group can be effectively used as a first stage in development of a survey through the identification of potential items relevant to a topic or population. Careful planning of a focus group includes the following considerations:

- What will the specific focus be? It is wise to keep the number of focus questions limited to about five to seven.
- Who will participate? Generally speaking, seven to twelve participants per group will be optimal, but the number of groups you conduct will depend on how much diversity you want to include your sample.
- How will you record the observations? (Audiotaping and videotaping, transcripts, and detailed note taking can be used solely or in combination.)
- How will you analyze the data? There are several approaches to focus group analysis, but perhaps the main consideration is to have a written plan prior to conducting your groups.

It is also very important to carefully think about the ethics of inviting people to discuss topics in a focus group format, especially if the topic is a sensitive one and if your participants are in some way considered vulnerable or have ongoing relationships with one another.

6-1e The Quality of Qualitative Research

Some qualitative researchers reject the framework of validity that is commonly accepted in more quantitative research in the social sciences. They reject the idea that there is a single reality that exists separate from our perceptions. In their view, each of us sees a different reality because we see it from a different perspective and through different experiences. They don't think research can be judged using the criteria of validity. Research is less about getting at the truth than it is about reaching meaningful conclusions, deeper understanding, and useful results. These qualitative researchers argue for different standards of judging the quality of qualitative research.

For instance, Guba and Lincoln (1981) proposed four criteria for judging the soundness of qualitative research and explicitly offered these as an alternative to the four criteria often used in the quantitative tradition (Cook & Campbell, 1979). They thought that their four criteria better reflected the underlying assumptions involved in much qualitative research. Their proposed criteria and the analogous quantitative criteria are listed in Table 6–3.

TABLE 6–3	Criteria for Judging Research Quality from a More Qualitative Perspective

Traditional Criteria for Judging Quantitative Research	Alternative Criteria for Judging Qualitative Research
Internal validity	Credibility
External validity	Transferability
Reliability	Dependability
Objectivity	Confirmability

Credibility The **credibility** criteria involve establishing that the results of qualitative research are credible or believable from the perspective of the participant in the research. Since from this perspective the purpose of qualitative research is to describe or understand the phenomena of interest from the participants' eyes, the participants are the only ones who can legitimately judge the credibility of the results.

Transferability **Transferability** refers to the degree to which the results of qualitative research can be generalized or transferred to other contexts or settings. From a qualitative perspective, transferability is primarily the responsibility of the one doing the generalizing. The qualitative researcher can enhance transferability by doing a thorough job of describing the research context and the assumptions that were central to the research. The person who wishes to transfer the results to a different context is then responsible for making the judgment of how sensible the transfer is.

Dependability The traditional quantitative view of *reliability* is based on the assumption of replicability or repeatability (see Section 3-2, Reliability). Essentially, it is concerned with whether you would obtain the same results if you could observe the same thing twice. However, you can't actually measure the same thing twice; by definition, if you are measuring twice, you are measuring two different things. This thinking goes back at least to the ancient Greek Democritus, who argued that we can never step into the same river twice because the river is constantly changing. To estimate reliability, quantitative researchers construct various hypothetical notions (for example, true score theory as described in (see Section 3-2a) to try to get around this fact.

The idea of **dependability**, on the other hand, emphasizes the need for the researcher to account for the ever-changing context within which research occurs. The researcher is responsible for describing the changes that occur in the setting and how these changes might affect the conclusions that are reached. Reliability emphasizes the researcher's responsibility to develop measures that, in the absence of any real change, would yield consistent results. Dependability emphasizes the researcher's responsibility to describe the ever-changing research context.

Confirmability Qualitative research tends to assume that each researcher brings a unique perspective to the study. **Confirmability** refers to the degree to which others can confirm or corroborate the results. There are a number of strategies for enhancing confirmability. The researcher can actively search for and describe negative instances that contradict prior observations. After the study, a researcher can conduct a **data audit** that examines the data collection and analysis procedures and makes judgments about the potential for bias or distortion.

credibility
Establishing that the results of qualitative research are believable from the perspective of the participant in the research.

transferability
The degree to which the results of qualitative research can be generalized or transferred to other contexts or settings.

dependability
In qualitative research, the degree to which the research adequately describes the continuously changing context and its effects on conclusions.

confirmability
The degree to which others can confirm or corroborate the results in qualitative research.

data audit
A systematic assessment of data and data collection procedures conducted to establish and document the credibility of data collection processes and potential inaccuracies in the data.

6-2c Secondary Analysis of Data

Secondary analysis, like content analysis, makes use of already existing data sources. However, *secondary analysis* typically refers to the reanalysis of quantitative data, rather than text.

In our modern world, an unbelievable mass of data is routinely collected by governments, businesses, schools, and other organizations. Much of this information is stored in electronic databases that can be accessed and analyzed. In addition, many research projects store raw data in electronic form in computer archives so that others can also analyze the data. Examples of data available for secondary analysis include:

- Census Bureau data
- Crime records
- Standardized testing data
- Economic data
- Consumer data

Secondary analysis often involves combining information from multiple databases to examine research questions. For example, you might join crime data with census information to assess patterns in criminal behavior by geographic location and group.

Secondary analysis has several advantages. First, it is efficient. It makes use of data that was already collected by someone else. It is the research equivalent of recycling. Second, it often allows you to extend the scope of your study considerably. In many small research projects, it is impossible to consider taking a national sample because of the costs involved. Many archived databases are already national in scope, and by using them, you can leverage a relatively small budget into a much broader study than if you collected the data yourself.

However, secondary analysis is not without difficulties. Frequently, it is no trivial matter to access and link data from large complex databases. Often, you have to make assumptions about which data to combine and which variables are appropriately aggregated into indexes (see Chapter 5). Perhaps more important, when you use data collected by others, you often don't know what problems occurred in the original data collection. Large, well-financed national studies are usually documented thoroughly, but even detailed documentation of procedures is often no substitute for direct experience collecting data.

One of the most important and least utilized purposes of secondary analysis is to replicate prior research findings. In any original data analysis, there is the potential for errors. In addition, data analysts tend to approach the analysis from their own perspective, using the analytic tools with which they are familiar. In most research, the data is analyzed only once by the original research team. It seems an awful waste. Data that might have taken months or years to collect is examined only once in a relatively brief way and from one analyst's perspective. In social research, we generally do a terrible job of documenting and archiving the data from individual studies and making it available in electronic form for others to reanalyze, and we tend to give little professional credit to studies that are reanalyzed. Nevertheless, in the hard sciences, the tradition of replicability of results is a critical one, and we in the applied social sciences could benefit by directing more of our efforts to secondary analysis of existing data.

Summary

This chapter began by comparing qualitative and quantitative data. I made the point that each type of data has its strengths and weaknesses, and that they are often best when used together. Qualitative data can always be quantified, and quantitative data is always based on qualitative assumptions.

Qualitative data can be collected through a variety of methods, including in-depth interviews, direct observation, and written documents. Standards for judging the quality of qualitative data include credibility, transferability, dependability, and confirmability.

Unobtrusive measures are ways of collecting data that don't require researcher interaction with the population of interest. Indirect measures require the researcher to set up conditions so that those being studied are unaware that they are being studied. Content analysis involves the systematic assessment of existing texts and, because it does not require original data collection, is typically considered unobtrusive. Similarly, by definition, the secondary analysis of existing data makes use of information that was previously collected and, as such, does not intrude on respondents.

Login to the Online Edition of your text at www.atomicdog.com to find additional resources located in the Study Guide at the end of each chapter.

PART 4

Design and Structure

CHAPTER 7

Design

KEY TERMS

causal
causal relationship
compensatory equalization of treatment
compensatory program
compensatory rivalry
construct validity
control group
covariation of the cause and effect
design
diffusion or imitation of treatment
external validity
history threat
instrumentation threat
internal validity
maturation threat
mortality threat
multiple-group threat
null case
plausible alternative explanation
posttest-only nonexperimental design
posttest-only randomized experiment

pre-post nonequivalent groups quasi-experiment
quasi-experimental designs
random selection
regression artifact
regression threat
regression to the mean
resentful demoralization
samples
selection bias
selection threat
selection-history threat
selection-instrumentation
selection-maturation threat
selection-mortality
selection-regression
selection-testing threat
single-group threats
social interaction threats
social threats to internal validity
temporal precedence
testing threat
variable

Design

design
The design of a study is the specification of how the research question will be answered. A research design should specify how the selection of participants, method of assignment, and choice of measures and time frame work together to accomplish the study objectives.

Research **design** provides the glue that holds the research project together. A design is used to structure the research, to show how all of the major parts of the research project—the samples or groups, measures, treatments or programs, and methods of assignment—work together to address the central research questions. In this chapter, after a brief introduction to research design, I'll show you how to classify the major types of designs. You'll see that a major distinction is between the experimental designs that use random assignment to groups or programs and the quasi-experimental designs that don't use random assignment. (People often confuse random selection with the idea of random assignment. You should make sure that you understand the distinction between random selection and random assignment as described in Chapter 9.) Understanding the relationships among designs is important when you need to make design choices, which involves thinking about the strengths and weaknesses of different designs.

7-1 Internal Validity

internal validity
The approximate truth of inferences regarding cause-effect or causal relationships.

Internal validity is the approximate truth about inferences regarding cause-effect or causal relationships. Thus, internal validity is relevant only in studies that try to establish a causal relationship. It's not relevant in most observational or descriptive studies, for instance. However, for studies that assess the effects of social programs or interventions, internal validity is perhaps the primary consideration. In such contexts, you want to be able to conclude that your program or treatment made a difference—it improved test scores or reduced symptoms, as shown in Figure 7–1. However, there may be reasons, other than your program, that explain why test scores improve or symptoms are reduced. The key question of internal validity is whether observed changes can be attributed to your program or intervention (the cause) and not to other possible causes (sometimes described as alternative explanations for the outcome).

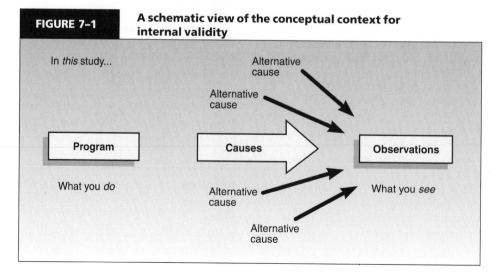

FIGURE 7–1   **A schematic view of the conceptual context for internal validity**

In *this* study...

Alternative cause

Alternative cause

Program

What you *do*

Causes

Alternative cause

Observations

What you *see*

Alternative cause

One of the things that's most difficult to grasp about internal validity is that it is relevant only to the specific study in question. That is, you can think of internal validity as a zero-generalizability concern. All that internal validity means is that you have evidence that what you did in the study (for example, the program) caused what you observed (the outcome) to happen. It doesn't tell you whether what you did for the program was what you wanted to do or whether what you observed was what you wanted to observe; those are construct validity concerns (see Chapter 3). It is possible to have internal validity in a study and not have construct validity. For instance, imagine a study in which you are looking at the effects of a new computerized tutoring program on math performance in first-grade students. Imagine that the tutoring is unique in that it has a heavy computer-game component and you think that will really improve math performance. Finally, imagine that you were wrong. (Hard, isn't it?) It turns out that math performance did improve and that it was because of something you did, but it had nothing to do with the computer program. What caused the improvement was the individual attention that the adult tutor gave to the child; the computer program didn't make any difference. This study would have internal validity because something you did affected something that you observed. (You did cause *something* to happen.) The study would not have construct validity because the label "computer-math program" does not accurately describe the actual cause. A more accurate label might be "personal adult attention."

Since the key issue in internal validity is the **causal** one, I'll begin by discussing the conditions that need to be met to establish a **causal relationship** in a research project. Then I'll discuss the different threats to internal validity—the kinds of criticisms your critics will raise when you try to conclude that your program caused the outcome. For convenience, I divide the threats to validity into three categories. The first involves the **single-group threats**—criticisms that apply when you are studying only a single group that receives your program. The second consists of the **multiple-group threats**—criticisms that are likely to be raised when you have several groups in your study (such as a program and a comparison group). Finally, I'll discuss what I call the **social threats to internal validity**—threats that arise because social research is conducted in real-world human contexts where people will react to not only what affects them but also what is happening to others around them.

7-1a Establishing Cause and Effect

How do you establish a cause-effect (causal) relationship? What criteria do you have to meet? Generally, you must meet three criteria before you can say that you have evidence for a causal relationship:

- Temporal precedence
- Covariation of the cause and effect
- No plausible alternative explanations

Temporal Precedence To establish **temporal precedence**, you have to show that your cause happened *before* your effect. Sounds easy, huh? Of course, my cause has to happen before the effect. Did you ever hear of an effect happening before its cause? Before you get lost in the logic here, consider a classic example from economics: does inflation cause unemployment? It certainly seems plausible that as inflation increases, more employers find that to meet costs they have to lay off employees. So it seems that inflation could, at least partially, be a cause for unemployment. However, both inflation and employment rates are occurring together on an ongoing basis. Is it possible that fluctuations in employment can affect inflation? If employment in the workforce increases (lower unemployment), there is likely to be more demand for goods, which would tend to drive up the prices (that

causal
Pertaining to a cause-effect relationship.

causal relationship
A cause effect relationship. For example, when you evaluate whether your treatment or program causes an outcome to occur, you are examining a causal relationship.

single-group threats
A threat to internal validity that occurs in a study that uses only a single program or treatment group and no comparison or control.

multiple-group threat
An internal validity threat that occurs in studies that use multiple groups—for instance, a program and a comparison group.

social threats to internal validity
Threats to internal validity that arise because social research is conducted in real-world human contexts where people will react to not only what affects them, but also to what is happening to others around them.

temporal precedence
Establishing that the hypothesized cause occurs earlier in time than the effect.

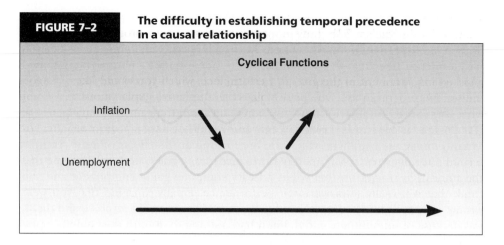

FIGURE 7–2 **The difficulty in establishing temporal precedence in a causal relationship**

is, inflate them), at least until supply can catch up. So which is the cause and which the effect, inflation or unemployment? It turns out that this kind of cyclical situation involves ongoing processes that interact and that both may cause and, in turn, be affected by the other (Figure 7–2). It is hard to establish a causal relationship in this situation.

Covariation of the Cause and Effect

covariation of the cause and effect
A criterion for establishing a causal relationship that holds that the cause and effect must be related or co-vary.

Covariation of the Cause and Effect What does this mean? Before you can show that you have a causal relationship you have to show that you have some type of relationship. For instance, consider the syllogism:

$$\text{If } X \text{ then } Y$$
$$\text{If not } X \text{ then not } Y.$$

If you observe that whenever X is present, Y is also present, and whenever X is absent, Y is too, you have demonstrated that there is a relationship between X and Y. I don't know about you, but sometimes I find it's not easy to think about X's and Y's. Let's put this same syllogism in program evaluation terms:

$$\text{If program then outcome}$$
$$\text{If not program then not outcome.}$$

Or, in colloquial terms: whenever you give the program, you observe the outcome, but when you don't give the program, you don't observe the outcome. This provides evidence that the program and outcome are related. Notice, however, that this syllogism doesn't provide evidence that the program caused the outcome; perhaps some other factor present with the program caused the outcome rather than the program. The relationships described so far are simple binary relationships. Sometimes you want to know whether different amounts of the program lead to different amounts of the outcome—a continuous relationship:

$$\text{If more of the program then more of the outcome}$$
$$\text{If less of the program then less of the outcome.}$$

third-variable or missing variable problem
In a two-variable cause-effect relationship, when the effect can be explained by a third variable other than the cause.

plausible alternative explanation
Any other cause that can bring about an effect that is different from your hypothesized or manipulated cause.

No Plausible Alternative Explanations Just because you show there's a relationship doesn't mean it's a causal one. It's possible that some other variable or factor is causing the outcome. This is sometimes referred to as the **third-variable or missing-variable problem**, and it's at the heart of the internal-validity issue. What are some of the possible **plausible alternative explanations?** Later in this chapter, when I discuss the threats to internal validity (see Sections 7-1b through 7-1d), you'll see that each threat describes a type of alternative explanation.

To argue that you have demonstrated internal validity—that you have shown there's a causal relationship—you have to rule out the plausible alternative explanations. How do you do that? One of the major ways is with your research design.

Let's consider a simple single-group threat to internal validity, a history threat which we'll define in Section 7-1b. Let's assume you measure your program group before you begin the program (to establish a baseline), you give the group the program, and then you measure the member's performance afterward in a posttest. You see a marked improvement in the group's performance, which you would like to infer is caused by your program. One of the plausible alternative explanations is that you have a history threat; it's not your program that caused the gain but some other specific historical event. For instance, your antismoking campaign did not cause the reduction in smoking; but rather the Surgeon General's latest report was issued between the time you gave your pretest and posttest. How do you rule this out with your research design? One of the simplest ways would be to incorporate the use of a **control group**—a group, comparable to your program group, that didn't receive the program. However, the group did experience the Surgeon General's latest report. If you find that it didn't show a reduction in smoking even though it experienced the same Surgeon General's report, you have effectively ruled out the Surgeon General's report as a plausible alternative explanation, in this example a history threat.

In most applied social research that involves evaluating programs, temporal precedence is not a difficult criterion to meet because you administer the program before you measure effects. Establishing covariation is relatively simple because you have some control over the program and can set things up so you have some people who get it and some who don't (if X and if not X). Typically, the most difficult criterion to meet is the third—ruling out alternative explanations for the observed effect. That is why research design is such an important issue and why it is intimately linked to the idea of internal validity.

control group
A group, comparable to the program group, that did not receive the program.

7-1b Single-Group Threats

What is meant by a *single-group threat*? Let's consider two single-group designs and then consider the threats that are most relevant with respect to internal validity. The top design in Figure 7–3 shows a posttest-only single-group design. Here, a group of people receives your program and afterward is given a posttest. In the bottom part of the figure, you see a pretest-posttest, single-group design. In this case,

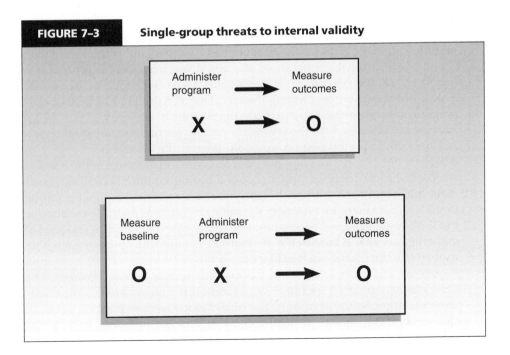

| **FIGURE 7–3** | **Single-group threats to internal validity** |

Administer program → Measure outcomes

X → O

Measure baseline | Administer program → Measure outcomes

O | X → O

the participants receive a pretest or baseline measure, the program or treatment, and then a posttest.

To help make this a bit more concrete, let's imagine that you are studying the effects of a compensatory education program in mathematics for first-grade students on a measure of math performance, such as a standardized math-achievement test. In the post-only design, you would give the first graders the program and then give a math-achievement posttest. You might choose not to give them a baseline measure because you have reason to believe they have no prior knowledge of the math skills you are teaching. It wouldn't make sense to pretest them if you expect them all to get a score of zero. In the pre-post design, you are not willing to assume that your group members have no prior knowledge. You measure the baseline to determine where the students start out in math achievement. You might hypothesize that the change or gain from pretest to posttest is due to your special math-tutoring program. This is a **compensatory program** because it is given only to students who are identified as potentially low in math ability on the basis of some screening mechanism.

With either of these scenarios in mind, consider what would happen if you observe a certain level of posttest math achievement or a change or gain from pretest to posttest. You want to conclude that the observed outcome is due to your math program. How could you be wrong? Here are some of the threats to internal validity that your critics might raise, some of the plausible alternative explanations for your observed effect:

- *History threat*. It's not your math program that caused the outcome; it's something else, some historical event that occurred. For instance, lots of first graders watch the public TV program *Sesame Street*, and every *Sesame Street* show presents some elementary math concepts. Perhaps these shows caused the outcome and not your math program. That's a **history threat**.
- *Maturation threat*. The children would have had the exact same outcome even if they had never had your special math-training program. All you are doing is measuring normal maturation or growth in the understanding that occurs as part of growing up; your math program has no effect. How is this maturation explanation different from a history threat? In general, if a specific event or chain of events could cause the outcome, it is a history threat, whereas a **maturation threat** consists of all the events that naturally occur in your life that could cause the outcome (without being specific as to which ones are the active causal agents).
- *Testing threat*. This threat occurs only in the pre-post design. What if taking the pretest made some of the children more aware of that kind of math problem; it primed them for the program so that when you began the math training, they were ready for it in a way that they wouldn't have been without the pretest. This is what is meant by a **testing threat**; taking the pretest, not getting your program affects how participants do on the posttest.
- *Instrumentation threat*. Like the testing threat, the **instrumentation threat** operates only in the pretest-posttest situation. What if the change from pretest to posttest is due not to your math program but rather to a change in the test that was used? In many schools, when repeated testing is administered, the exact same test is not used (in part because teachers are worried about a testing threat); rather, alternative forms of the same tests are given out. These alternative forms were designed to be equivalent in the types of questions and level of difficulty, but what if they aren't? Perhaps part or all of any pre-post gain is attributable to the change in instrument, not to your program. Instrumentation threats are especially likely when the instrument is a human observer. The observers may get tired over time or bored with the observations. Conversely, they might get better at making the observations as they practice more. In either event, the change in instrumentation, not the program, leads to the outcome.

---

compensatory program
A program given to only those who need it on the basis of some screening mechanism.

history threat
A threat to internal validity that occurs when some historical event affects your study outcome. hypothesis A specific statement of prediction.

maturation threat
A threat to validity that is a result of natural maturation that occurs between pre- and postmeasurement.

testing threat
A threat to internal validity that occurs when taking the pretest affects how participants do on the posttest.

instrumentation threat
A threat to internal validity that arises when the instruments (or observers) used on the posttest and the pretest differ.

- *Mortality threat.* Mortality doesn't mean that people in your study are dying (although if they are, it would be considered a **mortality threat**). Mortality is used metaphorically here. It means that people are dying with respect to your study. Usually, it means that they are dropping out of the study. What's wrong with that? Let's assume that in your compensatory math-tutoring program you have a nontrivial drop-out rate between pretest and posttest. Assume also that the kids who are dropping out had the low pretest math-achievement test scores. If you look at the average gain from pretest to posttest using all of the scores available to you on each occasion, you would include these low-pretest subsequent dropouts in the pretest and not in the posttest. You'd be dropping out the potential low scorers from the posttest, or you'd be artificially inflating the posttest average over what it would have been if no students had dropped out. You won't necessarily solve this problem by comparing pre-post averages for only those kids who stayed in the study. This subsample would certainly not be representative even of the original entire sample. Furthermore, you know that because of regression threats (see the following section) these students may appear to actually do worse on the posttest, simply as an artifact of the nonrandom dropout or mortality in your study. When mortality is a threat, the researcher can often gauge the degree of the threat by comparing the drop-out group against the non–drop-out group on pretest measures. If there are no major differences, it may be more reasonable to assume that mortality was happening across the entire sample and is not biasing results greatly. However, if the pretest differences are large, you must be concerned about the potential biasing effects of mortality.

- *Regression threat.* A **regression threat**, also known as a **regression artifact** or **regression to the mean**, is a statistical phenomenon that occurs whenever you have a nonrandom sample from a population and two measures that are imperfectly correlated. Okay, I know that's gibberish. Let me try again. Assume that your two measures are a pretest and posttest. You can certainly bet these aren't perfectly correlated with each other. Furthermore, assume that your sample consists of low pretest scorers. The regression threat means that the pretest average for the group in your study will appear to increase or improve (relative to the overall population) even if you don't do anything to them—even if you never give them a treatment. Regression is a confusing threat to understand at first. I like to think about it as the *you can only go up (or down) from here* phenomenon. If you include in your program only the kids who constituted the lowest ten percent of the class on the pretest, what are the chances that they would constitute exactly the lowest ten percent on the post-test? Not likely. Most of them would score low on the posttest, but they aren't likely to be exactly the lowest ten percent twice. For instance, maybe a few kids made a few lucky guesses and scored at the eleventh percentile on the pretest; they might not be so lucky on the posttest. Now if you choose the lowest ten percent on the pretest, they can't get any lower than being the lowest; they can only go up from there, relative to the larger population from which they were selected. This purely statistical phenomenon is what we mean by a regression threat. You can see a more detailed discussion of why regression threats occur and how to estimate them in the following section on regression to the mean.

How do you deal with these single-group threats to internal validity? Although you can rule out threats in several ways, one of the most common approaches to ruling those discussed previously is through your research design. For instance, instead of doing a single-group study, you could incorporate a control group. In this scenario, you would have two groups: one receives your program and the other one doesn't. In fact, the only difference between these groups should be the program. If that's true, the control group would experience all the same history and

mortality threat
A threat to validity that occurs because a significant number of participants drop out.

regression threat
A statistical phenomenon that causes a group's average performance on one measure to regress toward or appear closer to the mean of that measure than anticipated or predicted. Regression occurs whenever you have a nonrandom sample from a population and two measures that are imperfectly correlated. A regression threat will bias your estimate of the group's posttest performance and can lead to incorrect causal inferences.

regression artifact
See regression threat.

regression to the mean
See regression threat.

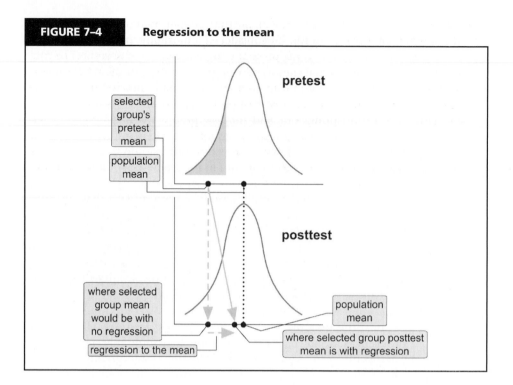

FIGURE 7–4   **Regression to the mean**

maturation threats, have the same testing and instrumentation issues, and have similar rates of mortality and regression to the mean. In other words, a good control group is one of the most effective ways to rule out the single-group threats to internal validity. Of course, when you add a control group, you no longer have a single-group design, and you still have to deal with two major types of threats to internal validity: the multiple-group threats to internal validity and the social threats to internal validity (see the respective sections later in this chapter).

Regression to the Mean   A regression threat, also known as a *regression artifact* or *regression to the mean*, is a statistical phenomenon that occurs whenever you have a nonrandom sample from a population and two measures that are imperfectly correlated.

Figure 7–4 shows the regression to the mean phenomenon. The top part of the figure shows the pretest distribution for a population. Pretest scores are distributed normally; the frequency distribution looks like a bell-shaped curve. Assume that the sample for your study was selected exclusively from the low pretest scorers. You can see on the top part of the figure where their pretest mean is; clearly, it is considerably below the population average. What would you predict the posttest to look like? First, assume that your program or treatment doesn't work at all (the **null case**). A naive assumption would be that your sample would score as badly on the posttest as on the pretest; but they don't! The bottom of the figure shows where the sample's posttest mean would have been without regression and where it actually is. In actuality, the sample's posttest mean wound up closer to the posttest population mean than the pretest mean was to the pretest population mean. In other words, the sample's mean appears to *regress toward the mean* of the population from pretest to posttest.

Why Does Regression to the Mean Happen?   To see why regression to the mean happens, consider a concrete case. In your study, you select the lowest 10 percent of the population based on pretest scores. What are the chances that on the posttest that exact group will once again constitute the lowest 10 percent of the population? Slim to none. Most of them will probably be in the lowest ten percent on the posttest, but if even only a few are not, the group's mean will have to be

null case
The case where the null hypothesis appears to be correct. In a two group design, for example, the null case is the finding that there is no difference between the two groups.

proportionally closer to the population's posttest than it was to the pretest. The same thing is true on the other end. If you select as your sample the highest 10 percent pretest scorers, they aren't likely to be the highest ten percent on the posttest (even though most of them may be in the top 10 percent). If even a few score below the top 10 percent on the posttest, the group's posttest mean will have to be proportionally closer to the population posttest mean than to its pretest mean.

Regression to the mean can be very hard to grasp. It even causes experienced researchers difficulty in its more advanced variations. To help you understand what regression to the mean is, and how it can be described, I've listed a few statements you should memorize about the regression to the mean phenomenon (and I provide a short explanation for each):

- *Regression to the mean is a statistical phenomenon.* Regression to the mean occurs for two reasons. First, it results because you asymmetrically sampled from the population. If you randomly sample from the population, you would observe (subject to random error) that the population and your sample have the same pretest average. Because a random sample is already at the population mean on the pretest, it is impossible for it to regress toward the mean of the population any more.

- *Regression to the mean is a group phenomena.* You cannot tell which way an individual's score will move based on the regression to the mean phenomenon. Even though the group's average will move toward the population's, some individuals in the group are likely to move in the other direction.

- *Regression to the mean happens between any two variables.* Here's a common research mistake. You run a program and don't find any overall group effect. So, you decide to look at those who did best on the posttest (your success stories) and see how much they gained over the pretest. You are selecting a group that is extremely high on the posttest. The group members are unlikely to be the best on the pretest as well (although many of them will be). So, the group's pretest mean *has* to be closer to the population mean than its posttest one. You describe this nice gain and are almost ready to write up your results when someone suggests you look at your failure cases (the people who scored worst on your posttest). When you check on how they scored on the pretest, you find that they weren't the worst scorers there. If they had been the worst scorers both times, you would have simply said that your program didn't have any effect on them. But now it looks worse than that; it looks like your program actually made them worse relative to the population! What will you do? How will you ever get your grant renewed? Or your paper published? Or, heaven help you, how will you ever get tenured?

  What you have to realize is that the pattern of results I just described happens every time you measure two measures. It happens forward in time (from pretest to posttest). It happens backward in time (from posttest to pretest). It happens across measures collected at the same time (height and weight)! It will happen even if you don't give your program or treatment.

- *Regression to the mean is a relative phenomenon.* Regression to the mean has nothing to do with overall maturational trends. Notice in Figure 7–4 that I didn't bother labeling the *x*-axis in either the pretest or posttest distribution. It could be that everyone in the population gains 20 points (on average) between the pretest and the posttest. But regression to the mean would still be operating, even in that case. That is, the low scorers would, on average, gain more than the population gain of 20 points (and thus their mean would be closer to the population's).

- *You can have regression up or down.* If your sample consists of below-population-mean scorers, the regression to the mean will make it appear that they move *up* on the other measure. However, if your sample consists of high scorers, the mean will appear to move *down* relative to the population. (Note that even if the mean increases, the group could lose ground to the population. So, if a high-pretest-scoring sample gains 5 points on the posttest while the overall sample gains 15, you could suspect regression to the mean as an alternative explanation [to our program] for that relatively low change.)

- *The more extreme the sample group, the greater the regression to the mean.* If your sample differs from the population by only a little bit on the first measure, there won't be much regression to the mean because there isn't much room for regression; the group is already near the population mean. So, if you have a sample, even a nonrandom one, that is a good subsample of the population, regression to the mean will be inconsequential (although it will be present). However, if your sample is extreme relative to the population (for example, the lowest or highest 10 percent), the group's mean is further from the population's and has more room to regress.

- *The less correlated the two variables, the greater the regression to the mean.* The other major factor that affects the amount of regression to the mean is the correlation between the two variables. If the two variables are *perfectly* correlated, the highest scorer on one is the highest on the other, next highest on one is next highest on the other, and so on. No regression to the mean occurs. However, this is unlikely to ever happen in practice. Measurement theory demonstrates that there is no such thing as perfect measurement; all measurement is assumed (under the true score model, as discussed in Chapter 3) to have some random error in measurement. It is only when the measure has no random error—is perfectly reliable—that you can expect it to correlate perfectly. Since that doesn't happen in the real world, you have to assume that measures have some degree of unreliability, that relationships between measures will not be perfect, and that there will appear to be regression to the mean between these two measures, given asymmetrically sampled subgroups.

The Formula for the Percent of Regression to the Mean You can estimate exactly the percent of regression to the mean in any given situation with the following formula:

$$P_{rm} = 100(1 - r)$$

where:

P_{rm} = the percent of regression to the mean
   r = the correlation between the two measures

Consider the following four cases:

- If $r = 1$, there is no (0%) regression to the mean.
- If $r = .5$, there is 50% regression to the mean.
- If $r = .2$, there is 80% regression to the mean.
- If $r = 0$, there is 100% regression to the mean.

In the first case, the two variables are perfectly correlated and there is no regression to the mean. With a correlation of .5, the sampled group moves *50 percent* of the distance from the no-regression point to the mean of the population. If the correlation is a small .20, the sample will regress 80 percent of the distance. If no correlation exists between the measures, the sample regresses all the way back to the population mean! It's worth thinking about what this last case means. With zero correlation, knowing a score on one measure gives you absolutely no information about the likely score for that person on the other measure. In that case, your best guess for how any person would perform on the second measure will be the mean of that second measure.

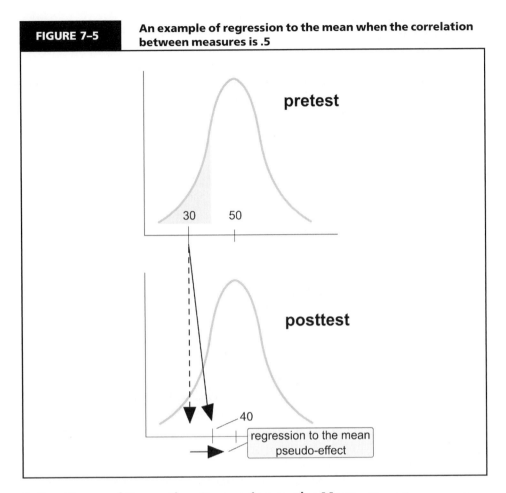

FIGURE 7–5 **An example of regression to the mean when the correlation between measures is .5**

pretest

30 50

posttest

40

regression to the mean
pseudo-effect

Estimating and Correcting Regression to the Mean Given the percentage formula, for any given situation you can estimate the regression to the mean. All you need to know is the mean of the sample on the first measure, the population mean on both measures, and the correlation between measures. Consider a simple example as shown in Figure 7–5. Here, assume that the pretest population mean is 50 and that you selected a low-pretest scoring sample that has a mean of 30. To begin with, also assume that you do not give any program or treatment (the null case) and that the population is not changing over time on the characteristic being measured (steady-state). Given this, you would predict that the population mean would be 50 and that the sample would get a posttest score of 30 *if there was no regression to the mean*. Now, assume that the correlation is .50 between the pretest and posttest for the population. Given the formula, you would expect the sampled group to regress 50 percent of the distance from the no-regression point to the population mean, or 50 percent of the way from 30 to 50. In this case, you would observe a score of 40 for the sampled group, which would constitute a 10-point pseudo-effect or regression artifact.

Now, relax some of the initial assumptions. For instance, as illustrated in Figure 7–6, assume that between the pretest and posttest the population gained 15 points on average (and that this gain was uniform across the entire distribution; that is, the variance of the population stayed the same across the two measurement occasions). In this case, a sample that had a pretest mean of 30 would be expected to reach a posttest mean of 45 (30 + 15) if there is no regression to the mean ($r = 1$). But here, the correlation between pretest and posttest is .5, so you would expect to see regression to the mean that covers 50 percent of the distance from the mean of 45 to the population posttest mean of 65. That is, you would observe a posttest average of 55 for your sample, again a pseudo-effect of 10 points.

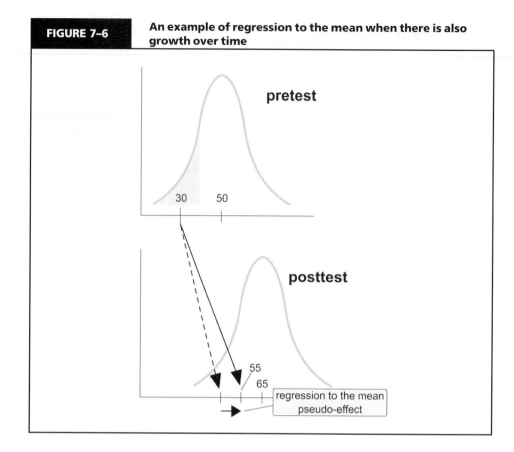

FIGURE 7–6 An example of regression to the mean when there is also growth over time

Regression to the mean is one of the trickiest threats to validity. It is subtle in its effects, and even excellent researchers sometimes fail to catch a potential regression artifact. You might want to learn more about the regression to the mean phenomenon. One good way to do that would be to simulate the phenomenon. If you already understand the basic idea of simulation, you can do a manual (dice rolling) simulation of regression artifacts or a computerized simulation of regression artifacts.

7-1c Multiple-Group Threats

A multiple-group design typically involves at least two groups and before-after measurements. Most often, one group receives the program or treatment while the other does not and constitutes the control or comparison group. However, sometimes one group gets the program and the other gets either the standard program or another program you would like to compare. In this case, you would be comparing two programs for their relative outcomes. Typically, you would construct a multiple-group design so that you could compare the groups directly. In such designs, the key internal validity issue is the degree to which the groups are comparable before the study. If they are comparable and the only difference between them is the program, posttest differences can be attributed to the program; but that's a big *if*. If the groups aren't comparable to begin with, you won't know how much of the outcome to attribute to your program or to the initial differences between groups.

There really is only one multiple-group threat to internal validity: that the groups were not comparable before the study. This threat is called a **selection bias** or **selection threat**. A selection threat is *any* factor other than the program that leads to posttest differences between groups. Whenever you suspect that outcomes differ between groups not because of your program but because of prior group differences, you are suspecting a selection bias. Although the term *selection bias* is used as the general category for all prior differences, when you know specifically what

selection bias
Any factor other than the program that leads to posttest differences between groups.

selection threat
See selection bias.

the group difference is, you usually hyphenate it with the selection term. The multiple-group selection threats directly parallel the single-group threats. For instance, whereas history is a single-group threat, selection-history is its multiple-group analogue.

As with the single-group threats to internal validity, I'll provide simple examples involving a new compensatory mathematics-tutoring program for first graders. The design is a pretest-posttest design that divides the first graders into two groups: one receiving the new tutoring program and the other not receiving it. Here are the major multiple-group threats to internal validity for this case:

- *Selection-history threat.* A **selection-history threat** is any other event that occurs between pretest and posttest that the groups experience differently. Because this is a selection threat, the groups differ in some way. Because it's a history threat, the way the groups differ is with respect to their reactions to history events. For example, what if the television-viewing habits of the children in one group differ from those of the children in the other group? Perhaps the program-group children watch *Sesame Street* more frequently than those in the control group do. Since *Sesame Street* is a children's show that presents simple mathematical concepts in interesting ways, it may be that a higher average posttest math score for the program group doesn't indicate the effect of your math tutoring; it's really an effect of the two groups experiencing a relevant event differentially—in this case *Sesame Street*—between the pretest and posttest.

selection-history threat
A threat to internal validity that results from any other event that occurs between pretest and posttest that the groups experience differently.

- *Selection-maturation threat.* A **selection-maturation threat** results from differential rates of normal growth between pretest and posttest for the groups. In this case, the two groups are different in their rates of maturation with respect to math concepts. It's important to distinguish between history and maturation threats. In general, *history* refers to a discrete event or series of events, whereas *maturation* implies the normal, ongoing developmental process that takes place. In any case, if the groups are maturing at different rates with respect to the outcome, you cannot assume that posttest differences are due to your program; they may be selection-maturation effects.

selection-maturation threat
A threat to internal validity that arises from any differential rates of normal growth between pretest and posttest for the groups.

- *Selection-testing threat.* A **selection-testing threat** occurs when a *differential* effect of taking the pretest exists between groups on the posttest. Perhaps the test primed the children in each group differently or they may have learned differentially from the pretest. In these cases, an observed posttest difference can't be attributed to the program. It could be the result of selection-testing.

selection-testing threat
A threat to internal validity that occurs when a differential effect of taking the pretest exists between groups on the posttest.

- *Selection-instrumentation threat.* **Selection-instrumentation** refers to any differential change in the test used for each group from pretest to posttest. In other words, the test changes differently for the two groups. Perhaps the test consists of observers, who rate the class performance of the children. What if the program group observers, for example, become better at doing the observations while, over time, the comparison group observers become fatigued and bored. Differences on the posttest could easily be due to this differential instrumentation—selection-instrumentation—and not to the program.

selection-instrumentation
A threat to internal validity that results from differential changes in the test used for each group from pretest to posttest.

- *Selection-mortality threat.* **Selection-mortality** arises when there is differential nonrandom dropout between pretest and posttest. In our example, different types of children might drop out of each group, or more may drop out of one than the other. Posttest differences might then be due to the different types of dropouts—the selection-mortality—and not to the program.

selection-mortality
A threat to internal validity that arises when there is differential nonrandom dropout between pretest and posttest.

- *Selection-regression threat.* Finally, **selection-regression** occurs when there are different rates of regression to the mean in the two groups. This might happen if one group is more extreme on the pretest than the other. In the context of our example, it may be that the program group is getting a disproportionate number of children with low math ability because teachers think they need the math tutoring more (and the teachers don't understand the need for comparable program and comparison groups). Because the tutoring group has

selection-regression
A threat to internal validity that occurs when there are different rates of regression to the mean in the two groups.

the lower scorers, its mean regresses a greater distance toward the overall population mean and its group members appear to gain more than their comparison-group counterparts. This is not a real program gain; it's a selection-regression artifact.

When you move from a single group to a multiple group study, what do you gain from the rather significant investment in a second group? If the second group is a control group and is comparable to the program group, you can rule out the single-group threats to internal validity because those threats will all be reflected in the comparison group and cannot explain why posttest group differences would occur. But the key is that the groups must be comparable. How can you possibly hope to create two groups that are truly comparable? The best way to do that is to randomly assign persons in your sample into the two groups—you conduct a randomized or true experiment (see the discussion of experimental designs in Chapter 9).

However, in many applied research settings you can't randomly assign, either because of logistical or ethical factors. In those cases, you typically try to assign two groups nonrandomly so that they are as equivalent as you can make them. You might, for instance, have one classroom of first graders assigned to the math-tutoring program and the other class assigned to the comparison group. In this case, you would hope the two are equivalent, and you may even have reasons to believe that they are. Nonetheless, they may not be equivalent, and because you did not use a procedure like random assignment to at least ensure that they are probabilistically equivalent, you have to take extra care to look for preexisting differences and adjust for them in the analysis. If you measure the groups on a pretest, you can examine whether they appear to be similar on key measures before the study begins and make some judgment about the plausibility that a selection bias exists. There are also ways to adjust statistically for preexisting differences between groups if they are present, although these procedures are notoriously assumption-laden and fairly complex. Research designs that look like randomized or true experiments (they have multiple groups and pre-post measurement) but use nonrandom assignment to choose the groups are called *quasi-experimental designs* (see the discussion of quasi-experimental designs in Chapter 10).

Even if you move to a multiple-group design and have confidence that your groups are comparable, you cannot assume that you have strong internal validity. A number of social threats to internal validity arise from the human interaction in applied social research and you will need to address them.

7-1d Social Interaction Threats

Applied social research is a human activity. The results of such research are affected by the human interactions involved. The **social interaction threats** to internal validity refer to the social pressures in the research context that can lead to posttest differences not directly caused by the treatment itself. Most of these threats occur because the various groups (for example, program and comparison), or key people involved in carrying out the research (such as managers, administrators, teachers, and principals), are aware of each other's existence and of the role they play in the research project or are in contact with one another. Many of these threats can be minimized by *isolating the two groups from each other*, but this leads to other problems. For example, it's hard to randomly assign and then isolate; this is likely to reduce generalizability or **external validity** (see external validity in Chapter 2). Here are the major social interaction threats to internal validity:

- *Diffusion or imitation of treatment.* **Diffusion or imitation of treatment** occurs when a comparison group learns about the program either directly or indirectly from program group participants. In a school context, children from different groups within the same school might share experiences during lunch

social interaction threats
Threats to internal validity that arise because social research is conducted in real-world human contexts where people react to not only what affects them, but also to what is happening to others around them.

external validity
The degree to which the conclusions in your study would hold for other persons in other places and at other times.

diffusion or imitation of treatment
A social threat to internal validity that occurs because a comparison group learns about the program either directly or indirectly from program group participants.

hour. Or, comparison group students, seeing what the program group is getting, might set up their own experience to try to imitate that of the program group. In either case, if the diffusion or imitation affects the posttest performance of the comparison group, it can jeopardize your ability to assess whether your program is causing the outcome. Notice that this threat to validity tends to equalize the outcomes between groups, minimizing the chance of seeing a program effect even if there is one.

- *Compensatory rivalry*. In the **compensatory rivalry** case, the comparison group knows what the program group is getting and develops a competitive attitude with the program group. The students in the comparison group might see the special math-tutoring program the other group is getting and feel jealous. This could lead them to compete with the program group "just to show" how well they can do. Sometimes, in contexts like these, the participants are even encouraged by well-meaning teachers or administrators to compete with one another. (Although this might make educational sense as a motivation for the students in both groups to work harder, it works against the ability of researchers to see the effects of their program.) If the rivalry between groups affects posttest performance, it could make it more difficult to detect the effects of the program. As with diffusion and imitation, this threat generally equalizes the posttest performance across groups, increasing the chance that you won't see a program effect, even if the program is effective.

compensatory rivalry A social threat to internal validity that occurs when one group knows the program another group is getting and, because of that, develops a competitive attitude with the other group.	

- *Resentful demoralization*. **Resentful demoralization** is almost the opposite of compensatory rivalry. Here, students in the comparison group know what the program group is getting and instead of developing a rivalry, the group members become discouraged or angry and give up (sometimes referred to informally as the *screw-you effect*). Or, if the program group is assigned to an especially difficult or uncomfortable condition, they can rebel in the form of resentful demoralization. Unlike the previous two threats, this one is likely to exaggerate posttest differences between groups, making your program look even more effective than it actually is.

resentful demoralization A social threat to internal validity that occurs when the comparison group knows what the program group is getting and becomes discouraged or angry and gives up.

- *Compensatory equalization of treatment*. **Compensatory equalization of treatment** is the only threat of the four that primarily involves the people who help manage the research context rather than the participants themselves. When program and comparison-group participants are aware of one another's conditions, they might wish they were in the other group (depending on the perceived desirability of the program, it could work either way). In our education example, they or their parents or teachers might pressure the administrators to have them reassigned to the other group. The administrators may begin to feel that the allocation of goods to the groups is not fair and may compensate one group for the perceived advantage of the other. If the special math-tutoring program were being done with state-of-the-art computers, you can bet that the parents of the children assigned to the traditional noncomputerized comparison group will pressure the principal to equalize the situation. Perhaps the principal will give the comparison group some other good or grant access to the computers for other subjects. If these compensating programs equalize the groups on posttest performance, they will tend to work against your detecting an effective program even when it does work. For instance, a compensatory program might improve the self-esteem of the comparison group and eliminate your chances of discovering whether the math program would cause changes in self-esteem relative to traditional math training.

compensatory equalization of treatment A social threat to internal validity that occurs when the control group is given a program or treatment (usually, by a well-meaning third party) designed to make up for or "compensate" for the treatment the program group gets.

As long as people engage in applied social research, you have to deal with the realities of human interaction and its effect on the research process. The threats described here can often be minimized by constructing multiple groups that are unaware of each other (for example, a program group from one school and a comparison group from another) or by training administrators in the importance of preserving group membership and not instituting equalizing programs. However, researchers will never be able to eliminate entirely the possibility that human interactions are making it more difficult to assess cause-effect relationships.

7-2 Introduction to Design

Research design can be thought of as the *structure* of research; the research design tells you how all the elements in a research project fit together. Researchers often use notational systems to describe a design, which enables them to summarize a complex design structure efficiently. A design includes the following elements:

- *Observations or measures.* These are symbolized by an *O* in design notation. An *O* can refer to a single measure (a measure of body weight), a single instrument with multiple items (a ten-item, self-esteem scale), a complex multipart instrument (a survey), or a whole battery of tests or measures given out on one occasion. If you need to distinguish among specific measures, you can use subscripts with the *O*, as in O_1, O_2, and so on.

- *Treatments or programs.* These are symbolized with an *X* in design notation. The *X* can refer to a simple intervention (such as a one-time surgical technique) or to a complex hodgepodge program (such as an employment-training program). Usually, a no-treatment control or comparison group has no symbol for the treatment. (Although some researchers use *X+* and *X–* to indicate the treatment and control, respectively.) As with observations, you can use subscripts to distinguish different programs or program variations.

- *Groups.* Each group in a design is given its own line in the design structure. For instance, if the design notation has three lines, the design contains three groups.

- *Assignment to group.* Assignment to group is designated by a letter at the beginning of each line (or group) that describes how the group was assigned. The major types of assignment are:

      R = random assignment
      N = nonequivalent groups
      C = assignment by cutoff

   Don't worry at this point if you don't know what some of these are; each of these assignment strategies characterizes a different type of design and will be described later when discussing that design type.

- *Time.* Time moves from left to right. Elements that are listed on the left occur before elements that are listed on the right.

It's always easier to explain design notation through examples than it is to describe it in words. Figure 7–7 shows the design notation for a pretest-posttest (or before-after) treatment versus comparison-group randomized experimental design. Let's go through each of the parts of the design. There are two lines in the notation, so you should realize that the study has two groups. There are four *O*s in the notation: two on each line and two for each group. When the *O*s are stacked vertically on top of each other, it means they are collected at the same time. In the notation, the two *O*s taken before (to the left of) the treatment are the pretest. The two *O*s taken after the treatment is given are the posttest. The *R* at the beginning of each line signifies that the two groups are randomly assigned (making it an experimental design as described in Chapter 9).

The design is a treatment-versus-comparison-group one, because the top line (treatment group) has an *X*, whereas the bottom line (control group) does not. You should be able to see why many of my students call this type of notation the tic-tac-toe method of design notation; there are lots of *X*s and *O*s! Sometimes you have to use more than simply the *O*s or *X*s. Figure 7–8 shows the identical research

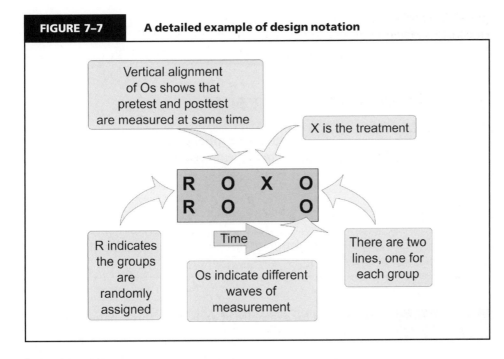

FIGURE 7–7   A detailed example of design notation

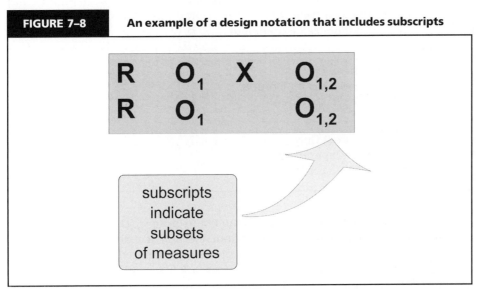

FIGURE 7–8   An example of a design notation that includes subscripts

design with some subscripting of the *O*s. What does this mean? Because all of the *O*s have a subscript of 1, some measure or set of measures was collected for both groups on both occasions. But the design also has two *O*s with a subscript of 2, both taken at the posttest. This means that some measure or set of measures was collected *only* at the posttest.

With this simple set of rules for describing a research design in notational form, you can concisely explain even complex design structures. In addition, using a notation helps show common design substructures across different designs that you might not recognize as easily without the notation.

7-3 Types of Designs

What are the different major types of research designs? You can classify designs into a simple threefold classification by asking some key questions as shown in Figure 7–9.

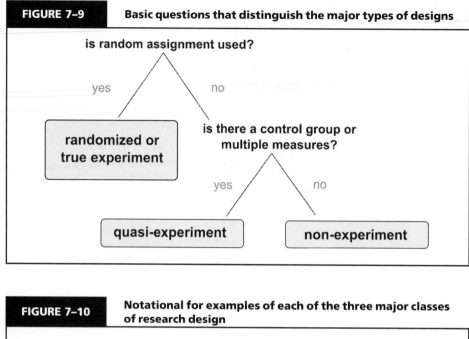

| FIGURE 7–9 | Basic questions that distinguish the major types of designs |

is random assignment used?

yes / no

randomized or true experiment

is there a control group or multiple measures?

yes / no

quasi-experiment   **non-experiment**

| FIGURE 7–10 | Notational for examples of each of the three major classes of research design |

Posttest Only Randomized Experiment	R X O R O
Pretest-Posttest Nonequivalent Groups Quasi-Experiment	N O X O N O O
Posttest Only Non-Experiment	X O

First, does the design use random assignment to groups? (Don't forget that random *assignment* is not the same thing as random selection of a sample from a population!) If random assignment is used, the design is a randomized experiment or *true* experiment. If random assignment is not used, ask a second question: Does the design use *either* multiple groups or multiple waves of measurement? If the answer is yes, label it a quasi-experimental design. If not, call it a nonexperimental design.

This threefold classification is especially useful for describing the design with respect to internal validity. A randomized experiment generally is the strongest of the three designs when your interest is in establishing a cause-effect relationship. A nonexperiment is generally the weakest in this respect. I have to hasten to add here that I don't mean that a nonexperiment is the weakest of the three designs *overall*, but only with respect to internal validity or causal assessment. In fact, the simplest form of nonexperiment is a one-shot survey design that consists of nothing but a single observation *O*. This is probably one of the most common forms of research and, for some research questions—especially descriptive ones—is clearly a strong design. When I say that the nonexperiment is the weakest with respect to internal validity, all I mean is that it isn't a particularly good method for assessing the cause-effect relationships that you think might exist between a program and its outcomes.

To illustrate the different types of designs, consider one of each in design notation as shown in Figure 7–10. The first design is a **posttest-only randomized experiment**. You can tell it's a randomized experiment because it has an *R* at the

posttest-only randomized experiment
An experiment in which the groups are randomly assigned and receive only a posttest.

beginning of each line, indicating random assignment. The second design is a **pre-post nonequivalent groups quasi-experiment**. You know it's not a randomized experiment because random assignment wasn't used. You also know it's not a non-experiment because both multiple groups and multiple waves of measurement exist. That means it must be a quasi-experiment. You add the label *nonequivalent* because in this design you do not explicitly control the assignment and the groups may be nonequivalent or not similar to each other (see nonequivalent group designs, Chapter 11). Finally, you see a **posttest-only nonexperimental design**. You might use this design if you want to study the effects of a natural disaster like a flood or tornado and you want to do so by interviewing survivors. Notice that in this design, you don't have a comparison group (for example, you didn't interview in a town down the road that didn't have the tornado to see what differences the tornado caused) and you don't have multiple waves of measurement (a pre-tornado level of how people in the ravaged town were doing before the disaster). Does it make sense to do the nonexperimental study? Of course! You could gain valuable information by well-conducted post-disaster interviews. However, you may have a hard time establishing which of the things you observed are due to the disaster rather than to other factors like the peculiarities of the town or pre-disaster characteristics.

pre-post nonequivalent groups quasi-experiment
A research design in which groups receive both a pre- and posttest, and group assignment is not randomized, and therefore, the groups may be nonequivalent, making it a quasi-experiment.

posttest-only nonexperimental design
A research design in which only a posttest is given. It is referred to as nonexperimental because no control group exists.

Summary

Research design helps you put together all of the disparate pieces of your research project: the participants or sample, the measures, and the data analysis. This chapter showed that research design is intimately connected with the topic of internal validity because the type of research design you construct determines whether you can address causal questions, such as whether your treatment or program made a difference on outcome measures. There are three major types of problems—threats to validity—that occur when trying to ensure internal validity. Single-group threats occur when you have only a single program group in your study. Researchers typically try to avoid single-group threats by using a comparison group, but this leads to multiple-group threats or selection threats when the groups are not comparable. Since all social research involves human interaction, you must also be concerned about social threats to internal validity that can make your groups perform differently but are unrelated to the treatment or program. Research designs can get somewhat complicated. To keep them straight and describe them succinctly researchers use design notation that describes the design in abstract form.

Login to the Online Edition of your text at www.atomicdog.com to find additional resources located in the Study Guide at the end of each chapter.

Qualitative and Mixed Methods Designs

KEY TERMS

ethnography
feasibility
field research
grounded theory

mixed methods
phenomenology
rigor
relevance

mixed m
Any rese
methods
advantag
instance
interviev
can be c

relevar
In qua
which
butior
goodr
goals

rigor
In qu
the m
the d
probl

feasil
In qu
the d
part
to ha
impl

CHAPTER 8

Qualitative and Mixed Methods Designs

mixed methods
Any research that uses multiple research methods to take advantage of the unique advantages that each method offers. For instance, a study that combines case study interviews with an experimental design can be considered mixed methods.

relevance
In qualitative research, the degree to which a study may make a practical contribution to a substantive area as well as the goodness of fit of methods to the study goals in all aspects of the design.

rigor
In qualitative research, the soundness of the methods chosen and degree to which the design has accounted for potential problems in any stage of the research.

feasibility
In qualitative research, the "doability" of the design—the degree to which each part of the study is realistic and appears to have a high probability of success in implementation.

Qualitative methods have been growing in scope and sophistication, but designing a qualitative study presents special challenges. Many of the philosophical and practical issues are still actively discussed, providing an ongoing stimulus to critical thinking about the nature of research and the criteria that make it "good." As a student, you can look at this situation from an idealistic perspective and be grateful that you are not merely being forced to memorize a set of procedures but being trained to be thoughtful, creative, and responsible in designing your study. I've noticed that students who think of themselves as practical but not particularly mathematical may tend toward qualitative research to avoid statistics. This attitude should be checked at the door, along with any notion that a qualitative design is easier or necessarily more meaningful. Here I'll introduce qualitative and **mixed methods** design with some comments on justification (why you would consider this kind of design), and then provide a brief overview of some of the traditions and alternatives.

The main reasons that a researcher might consider doing a qualitative study is when the state of knowledge in an area is quite limited; when constructs are not well understood, defined, or measured; or when prior research has apparently hit a dead end. Thus, it is impossible to plan a study with the same level of detail and probability (both literally and figuratively) as a typical quantitative study. The major justification for doing the qualitative study *might* in fact be the prospect of an eventual quantitative study of the problem. In addition, qualitative research is emergent; that is, it is well suited to situations in which preconceived notions are purposely limited and where the intent of the researcher is a more gradual process of discovery as the study unfolds. It allows for flexibility in procedures as circumstances during data collection change. All of these characteristics make the research design process challenging, especially when it comes to obtaining study approval or funding from quantitatively oriented faculty or review panels.

This does not mean that there is little to define the qualitative research design process except the absence of statistics. Morse (2003), who has served on or consulted with grant agency panels in several countries, provided some guidance by elaborating on Guba's (1981) criteria for evaluating qualitative research: **relevance**, **rigor**, and **feasibility**. Relevance refers to the potential impact of a study in the topic area. Will it potentially make a difference? The rigor of the proposed study can be assessed by asking whether the methods proposed are both appropriate and strong relative to the problem that is to be studied. Last, but not least, a judgment of feasibility can be made to indicate whether all practical aspects of the proposal are in order. Morse recommended a broad assessment of feasibility, including the qualifications of the investigator, access to the study population (including any potential ethical complications), and the overall likelihood that the study can be completed as proposed. All three dimensions can be translated into critical questions that can be considered with regard to all aspects of any qualitative study proposal, from topic to analysis to dissemination. It would be wise for a study designer to try to think like a study reviewer, and Morse has provided a helpful guide.

Elliot Eisner is a well known educational researcher who has contributed much to better understanding and use of qualitative research methods (1991). One of his contributions is elaboration of six features that "make a study qualitative". These features are presented in Table 8–1.

TABLE 8–1	**Eisner's Six Features of a Qualitative Study**

1) The study is *field focused*.
2) The study employs the *self as an instrument*.
3) The study has an *interpretive character*.
4) The study *makes use of expressive language and the presence of voice in text*.
5) The study *pays attention to particulars*.
6) The study is believable because of its *coherence, insight and instrumental utility*.

The field focus of qualitative research refers to the emphasis on naturalistic settings, documents, conversations and other phenomena represented life as it is experienced. This of course contrasts with the experimental lab situation in which control is highly valued.

When we think of using ourselves as a measurement instrument, we are utilizing our senses and our sensibility. That is, the researcher is open to subjective experience as seen, heard and felt, but also as processed through all that makes us individual humans through our personal history.

Interpretation occurs at two levels, according to Eisner. First, there is the level of explanation, or accounting for how something seems to happen in a particular context. The second aspect of interpretation is related to understanding the apparent meaning of the experience for those being observed. How does a person seem to feel, think, behave in a given set of circumstances? The goal is to go beyond surface characterization to something called "thick description". Thick description means that the story is told in detail, communicating the essence of what it is like for the participants.

The use of expressive language and the presence of voice is a particularly distinctive feature of qualitative research reports in contrast to quantitative studies. As Eisner said, in a qualitative study it is clear that the story is being told by a person and not a machine; an empathic person with emotions that the reader can understand and relate to just as the writer has felt them when in the research setting.

Paying attention to particulars refers to the level of analysis, and the extent that the study attempts to relate particulars to other levels. For example, a case study might be a complete report on very individual characteristics of the case, with no interest in generalizing to other cases. In contrast, when we derive a sample from a population in a quantitative study, the usual intent is to generalize to the population.

Judgments about the value of a qualitative study are a summary, integrative kind of judgment based on characteristics such as coherence, insight, and instrumental utility. It is the weight of combined evidence rationally assessed, rather than a summary statistical indicator such as an effect size or probability value.

One of the reasons that qualitative research is sometimes not regarded as seriously as quantitative is the misconception that analysis of qualitative data is unsystematic and superficial. This notion is as mistaken as the idea that because procedures may be adapted to changing circumstances in the course of a study, that the analysis can be invented on the fly after the data is collected. A well-planned qualitative study includes an integrated approach to design and analysis. Constas (1992) provided some helpful guidance on this issue by highlighting the importance of making procedures public rather than private, and therefore explicit and replicable. You should know what you are going to do with your data before you collect it, practice your procedures, and write them down in advance. In Chapter 13, you'll become familiar with some of the possibilities for analysis. Here I'll focus on considerations in making decisions about the design of the study.

In addition to a critical perspective like that of a review panel member, a study designer should review the research paths previously established in qualitative methodology traditions. A qualitative tradition is a general way of thinking about conducting qualitative research. It describes, either explicitly or implicitly, the purpose of the qualitative research, the role of the researcher(s), the stages of research, and the method of data analysis. The term *tradition* may make you think that we must be talking about "old stuff," but perhaps as with music, there are roots in the traditions that continue to produce lively new branches. Here, four of the major qualitative traditions are introduced: ethnography, phenomenology, field research, and grounded theory.

8-1 Ethnography

ethnography
Study of a culture using qualitative field research.

The ethnographic approach to qualitative research comes largely from the field of anthropology. The emphasis in **ethnography** is on studying a phenomenon in the context of its culture. Originally, the idea of a culture was tied to the notion of ethnicity and geographic location, but it has been broadened to include virtually any group or organization.

Ethnography is an extremely broad area with a great variety of practitioners and methods. However, the most common ethnographic approach is participant observation as a part of **field research**. The ethnographer becomes immersed in the culture as an active participant and records extensive field notes. As in **grounded theory**, there is no preset limiting of what will be observed and no obvious ending point in an ethnographic study.

field research
A research method in which the researcher goes into the field to observe the phenomenon in its natural state.

grounded theory
An iterative qualitative approach that includes initial generative questions, gathering qualitative data, identifying theoretical concepts, verifying emerging concepts in data, reconsidering theoretical concepts, and so on, until a detailed theory that is grounded in observation is achieved.

One example of a researcher who has made extensive and very productive use of ethnographic methods is Professor Myra Bluebond-Langner of Rutgers University. Since the 1970s, she has been studying the experiences of children with life-threatening illness as well as the experiences of their families (2000). Bluebond-Langner used ethnography to capture the complexity of the life circumstances of children and families in this situation. She documented the effects of physical, psychological, environmental, ethical, legal, cultural, and other variables by recording and studying the lived experience of the people in their own words. Her current work involves a prospective study of how children make decisions when cure for disease is not likely. The design of the study is longitudinal (over 2 years) and includes participant observation and collection of transcripts of formal and informal conversations involving approximately 80 children, their relatives and health care providers.*

8-2 Phenomenology

phenomenology
A philosophical perspective as well as an approach to qualitative methodology that focuses on people's subjective experiences and interpretations of the world.

The **phenomenology** tradition emphasizes the study of how the phenomenon is experienced by respondents or research participants. It has a long history in several social research disciplines, including psychology, sociology, and social work. Phenomenology is a school of thought that focuses on people's subjective experiences and interpretations of the world. That is, the phenomenologist wants to understand how the world appears to others.

For some researchers, the phenomenological approach is more philosophy than methodology. In an attempt to maintain the essence of the study of subjective lived experience, but also meet criteria for scientific investigation, Giorgi and Giorgi (2003) developed a more systematic and specific set of procedures for phenomenological studies. Their model is represented in Figure 8–1.

One of the key features of the model is the emphasis on maintaining the meaning of the original verbalizations of the participants throughout the steps in the study. As with the previously cited work by Bluebond-Langner, the phenomenologi-

---

*Downloaded from http://children.camden.rutgers.edu/ResearchProjects/Bluebond_MDM.htm; accessed August, 2006

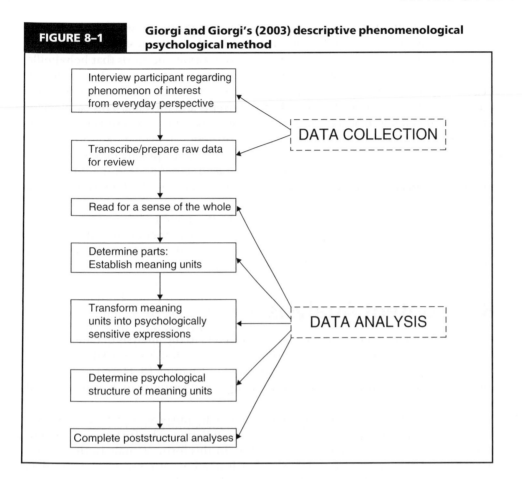

FIGURE 8–1   Giorgi and Giorgi's (2003) descriptive phenomenological psychological method

cal method may be particularly valuable in the study of topics in which trust with participants may be especially important and not easily obtained. In addition, as the Giorgis' study of homophobia illustrates, the method is also well suited to inquiry into topics that are relatively new, complex, and sensitive.

8-3 Field Research

Field research can also be considered either a broad tradition of qualitative research or a method of gathering qualitative data. The essential idea is that the researcher goes into the field to observe the phenomenon in its natural state or "in situ" (on site). As such, it is probably most related to the method of participant observation. The field researcher typically takes extensive field notes that are subsequently coded and analyzed for major themes. The series of studies conducted by Michelle Fine and her colleagues in women's prisons, described in Section 8-5, Mixed Methods, represent an excellent example of field research. Among the striking aspects of this work is the inclusion of prison inmates (who were also students in the program being studies) as collaborators and co-authors.

8-4 Grounded Theory

Grounded theory is a qualitative research tradition that was originally developed by Glaser and Strauss (1967). The self-defined purpose of grounded theory is to develop theory about phenomena of interest, but Glaser and Strauss are not talking about abstract theorizing. Instead, the theory needs to be grounded or rooted in observations—hence, the term.

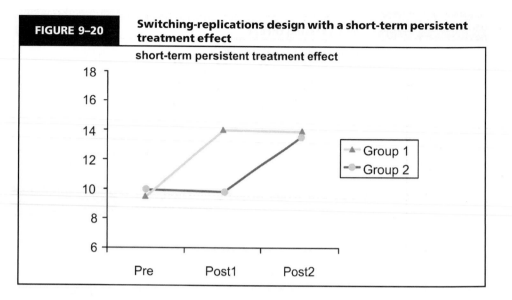

FIGURE 9–20   **Switching-replications design with a short-term persistent treatment effect**

short-term persistent treatment effect

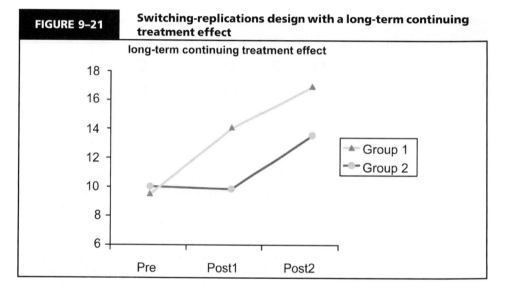

FIGURE 9–21   **Switching-replications design with a long-term continuing treatment effect**

long-term continuing treatment effect

improve even after the formal program period because they continue to apply the skills and improve in them.

I said earlier that both the Solomon four-group and the switching-replications designs addressed specific threats to internal validity. It's obvious that the Solomon design addressed a testing threat. But what does the switching-replications design address? Remember that in randomized experiments, especially when the groups are aware of each other, there is the potential for social threats to internal validity; compensatory rivalry, compensatory equalization, and resentful demoralization are all likely to be present in educational contexts where programs are given to some students and not to others. The switching-replications design helps mitigate these threats because it ensures that everyone will eventually get the program. In addition, it allocates who gets the program first in the fairest possible manner, through the lottery of random assignment.

Summary

This chapter introduced experimental designs. The basic idea of a randomized experiment was presented along with consideration of how it addresses internal validity, the key concepts of probabilistic equivalence, and the distinction between random selection and random assignment. Experimental designs can be classified as signal enhancers or noise reducers. Factorial designs were presented as signal enhancers that emphasize studying different combinations of treatment (signal) features. Two types of noise-reducing strategies—randomized blocks and covariance designs—were presented along with descriptions of how each acts to reduce noise in the data. Finally, two hybrid experimental designs—the Solomon four-groups and switching-replications designs—were presented to illustrate the versatility of experimental designs and the ability to tailor designs that address specific threats to internal validity.

Login to the Online Edition of your text at www.atomicdog.com to find additional resources located in the Study Guide at the end of each chapter.

CHAPTER 10

Quasi-Experimental Design

KEY TERMS

construct validity
control group
double-pretest design
internal validity
nonequivalent dependent variables
   (NEDV) design
nonequivalent-groups design
   (NEGD)
null case
pattern-matching
pattern-matching NEDV design
proxy-pretest design
quantitative
quasi-experimental design
random assignment
regression-discontinuity (RD)

regression line
regression point displacement (RPD)
regression to the mean
selection bias
selection-history threat
selection instrumentation
selection-maturation threat
selection mortality
separate pre-post samples
selection regression
selection testing
selection threat
statistics
switching-replications design
threats to internal validity

quasi-experimental design
Research designs that have several of the key features of randomized experimental designs, such as pre-post measurement and treatment-control group comparisons, but lack random assignment to a treatment group.

internal validity
The approximate truth of inferences regarding cause-effect or causal relationships.

A **quasi-experimental design** is one that looks a bit like an experimental design but lacks the key ingredient—random assignment. My mentor, Don Campbell, often referred to these designs as "queasy" experiments because they give experimental purists a queasy feeling. With respect to **internal validity**, they often appear to be inferior to randomized experiments. However, there is something compelling about these designs; taken as a group, they are more frequently implemented than their randomized cousins.

I'm not going to try to cover the quasi-experimental designs comprehensively. Instead, I'll present two of the classic quasi-experimental designs in some detail. Probably the most commonly used quasi-experimental design (and it may be the most commonly used of all designs) is the nonequivalent-groups design (NEGD). In its simplest form, it requires a pretest and posttest for a treated and comparison group. It's identical to the Analysis of Covariance (ANCOVA) randomized experimental design (see Chapter 9), except that the groups are not created through random assignment. You will see that the lack of random assignment and the potential nonequivalence between the groups complicates the statistical analysis of the nonequivalent groups design (as covered in the discussion of analysis in Chapter 12).

The second design I'll focus on is the regression-discontinuity design. I'm not including it just because I did my dissertation on it and wrote a book about it (although those were certainly factors weighing in its favor). I include it because I believe it is an important (and often misunderstood) alternative to randomized experiments because its distinguishing characteristic—assignment to treatment using a cutoff score on a pretreatment variable—allows you to assign to the program those who need or deserve it most. At first glance, the regression-discontinuity design strikes most people as biased because of regression to the mean (discussed in Chapter 7). After all, you're assigning low scorers to one group and high scorers to the other. In the discussion of the statistical analysis of the regression discontinuity design (see Chapter 12), I'll show you why this isn't the case.

Finally, I'll briefly present an assortment of other quasi-experiments that have specific applicability or noteworthy features, including the proxy-pretest design, double-pretest design, nonequivalent dependent-variables design, pattern-matching design, and the regression point displacement design.

10-1 The Nonequivalent-Groups Design

nonequivalent-groups design (NEGD)
A pre-post two-group quasi-experimental design structured like a pretest-posttest randomized experiment, but lacking random assignment to group.

The **nonequivalent-groups design (NEGD)** is probably the most frequently used design in social research. Why? Because it is one of the most intuitively sensible designs around. If you want to study the effects of your program, you probably recognize the need to have a group of people receive the program. That's your program group, and, you probably see that it would be sensible to measure that group before and after the program so you can see how much the program improved or

| FIGURE 10–1 | Notation for the nonequivalent-groups design (NEGD) |

$$N \quad O \quad X \quad O$$
$$N \quad O \qquad \quad O$$

changed them. That's the pre-post measurement. Once you understand the basic problem of internal validity (see Chapter 7), you will readily admit that it would be nice to have a comparable group that differs from your program group in only one respect—it doesn't get the program. That's your **control group**. Put all of these elements together and you have the basic NEGD. Although the design is intuitively straightforward, it is not without its difficulties or challenges. The major challenge stems from the term *nonequivalent* in its title. If your comparison group is really similar to the program group in all respects—except for receiving the program—this design is an excellent one. But how do you ensure that the groups are equivalent? And, what do you do if they are not? That's the central challenge for this design and I'll take some time here to address this issue.

control group
A group, comparable to the program group, that did not receive the program.

10-1a The Basic Design

The NEGD is structured like a pretest-posttest randomized experiment, but it lacks the key feature of the randomized designs—**random assignment**. The design notation for the basic NEGD is shown in Figure 10–1.

In the NEGD, you most often use intact groups that you think are similar as the treatment and control groups. In education, you might pick two comparable classrooms or schools. In community-based research, you might use similar communities. You try to select groups that are as similar as possible so that you can fairly compare the treated one with the comparison one; but you can never be sure the groups are comparable. Put another way, it's unlikely that the two groups would be as similar as they would if you assigned them through a random lottery. Because it's often likely that the groups are not equivalent, this design was named the *nonequivalent-groups design* to remind us of that. The design notation (see Figure 10–1) uses the letter *N* to indicate that the groups are nonequivalent.

So, what does the term *nonequivalent* mean? In one sense, it means that assignment to group was not random. In other words, the researcher did not control the assignment to groups through the mechanism of random assignment. As a result, the groups may be different prior to the study. That is, the NEGD is especially susceptible to the internal validity threat of selection (see Chapter 7). Any previous differences between the groups may affect the outcome of the study. Under the worst circumstances, this can lead you to conclude that your program didn't make a difference, when in fact it did, or that it did make a difference, when in fact it didn't.

random assignment
Process of assigning your sample into two or more subgroups by chance. Procedures for random assignment can vary from flipping a coin to using a table of random numbers to using the random number capability built into a computer.

10-1b The Bivariate Distribution

Let's begin our exploration of the NEGD by looking at some hypothetical results. Figure 10–2a shows a bivariate distribution in the simple pre-post, two-group study. The *treated cases* are indicated with *X*s and the *comparison cases* are indicated with *O*s. A couple of things should be obvious from the graph. To begin, you don't even need **statistics** to see that there is a whopping treatment effect. (Although statistics would help you estimate the size of that effect more precisely.) The program cases (*X*s) consistently score better on the posttest than the comparison cases (*O*s) do. If positive scores on the posttest are better, you can conclude that the program improved things. Second, in the NEGD the biggest threat to internal validity is

statistics
The process of estimating various features from data, often using probability theory.

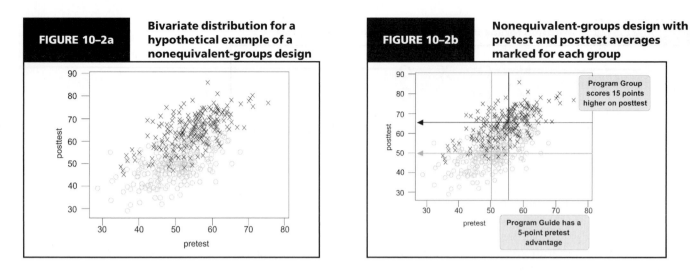

FIGURE 10–2a — Bivariate distribution for a hypothetical example of a nonequivalent-groups design

FIGURE 10–2b — Nonequivalent-groups design with pretest and posttest averages marked for each group

selection bias
Any factor other than the program that leads to posttest differences between groups.

selection threat
Any factor other than the program that leads to post test differences between groups

selection-maturation threat
A threat to internal validity that arises from any differential rates of normal growth between pretest and posttest for the groups.

selection—that the groups differed before the program. Does that appear to be the case here? Although it may be harder to see, the program group does appear to be a little further to the right on average. This suggests that program group participants did have an initial advantage on the pretest and that the positive results may be due in whole or in part to this initial difference.

You can see the initial difference, the **selection bias**, when you look at the graph in Figure 10–2b. It shows that the program group scored about 5 points higher than the comparison group on the pretest. The comparison group had a pretest average of about 50, whereas the program group averaged about 55. It also shows that the program group scored about 15 points higher than the comparison group on the posttest. That is, the comparison group posttest score was again about 55, whereas this time the program group scored around 65. These observations suggest that there is a potential **selection threat,** although the initial 5-point difference doesn't explain why you observe a 15-point difference on the posttest. It may be that there is still a legitimate treatment effect here, even given the initial advantage of the program group.

Possible Outcome 1[1] Let's take a look at several different possible outcomes from a NEGD to see how they might be interpreted. The important point here is that each of these outcomes has a different storyline. Some are more susceptible to threats to internal validity than others. Before you read each of the descriptions, take a good look at the associated graph and try to figure out how you would explain the results. If you were a critic, what kinds of problems would you be looking for? Then, read the synopsis and see if it agrees with your perception.

Sometimes it's useful to look at the means for the two groups. Figure 10–3 shows the means for the distribution in with the pre-post means of the program group joined with a line beginning and ending with triangles and the pre-post means of the comparison group joined with a line beginning and ending with squares. This first outcome shows the situation in the two bivariate plots. Here, you can see much more clearly both the original pretest difference of 5 points and the larger 15-point posttest difference.

How might you interpret these results? To begin, you need to recall that with the NEGD you are usually most concerned about selection threats. Which selection threats might be operating here? The key to understanding this outcome is that the comparison group did not change between the pretest and the posttest. Therefore, it would be hard to argue that that the outcome is due to a **selection-maturation threat**. Why? Remember that a selection-maturation threat means that the groups

[1]The discussion of the five possible outcomes is based on the discussion in Cook, T.D. and Campbell, D.T. (1979). *Quasi-Experimentation: Design & Analysis Issues for Field Settings.* Houghton Mifflin, Boston, pp. 103–112.

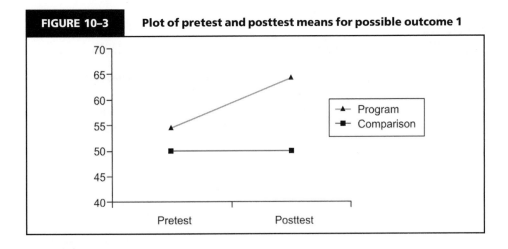

| FIGURE 10–3 | Plot of pretest and posttest means for possible outcome 1 |

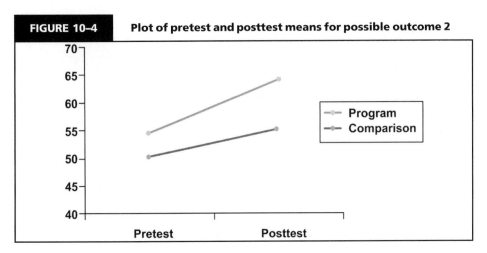

| FIGURE 10–4 | Plot of pretest and posttest means for possible outcome 2 |

are maturing at different rates and that this creates the illusion of a program effect when there is not one. However, because the comparison group didn't mature (change) at all, it's hard to argue that differential maturation produced the outcome. What could have produced the outcome? A **selection-history threat** certainly seems plausible. Perhaps some event occurred (other than the program) that the program group reacted to and the comparison group didn't. Maybe a local event occurred for the program group but not for the comparison group. Notice how much more likely it is that outcome pattern 1 is caused by such a history threat than by a maturation difference. What about the possibility of **selection regression?** This one actually works a lot like the selection-maturation threat. If the jump in the program group is due to **regression to the mean**, it would have to be because the program group was below the overall population pretest average and consequently regressed upwards on the posttest. However, if that's true, it should be even more the case for the comparison group who started with an even lower pretest average. The fact that it doesn't appear to regress at all helps rule out the possibility that outcome 1 is the result of regression to the mean.

Possible Outcome 2 The second hypothetical outcome (see Figure 10–4) presents a different picture. Here, both the program and comparison groups gain from pre to post, with the program group gaining at a slightly faster rate. This is almost the definition of a selection-maturation threat. The fact that the two groups differed to begin with suggests that they may already be maturing at different rates. The posttest scores don't do anything to help rule out that possibility. This outcome might also arise from a selection-history threat. If the two groups, because of

selection-history threat
A threat to internal validity that results from any other event that occurs between pretest and posttest that the groups experience differently.

selection regression
A threat to internal validity that occurs when there are different rates of regression to the mean in the two groups.

regression to the mean
See regression threat.

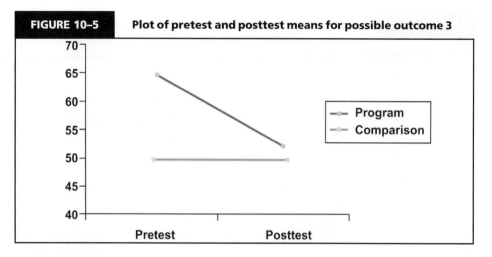

FIGURE 10–5   Plot of pretest and posttest means for possible outcome 3

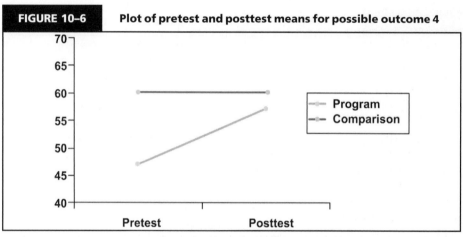

FIGURE 10–6   Plot of pretest and posttest means for possible outcome 4

selection testing
A threat to internal validity that occurs when a differential effect of taking the pretest exists between groups on the posttest.

selection instrumentation
A threat to internal validity that results from differential changes in the test used for each group from pretest to posttest.

selection mortality
A threat to internal validity that arises when there is differential nonrandom dropout between groups during the test.

their initial differences, react differently to some historical event, you might obtain the outcome pattern shown. Both **selection testing** and **selection instrumentation** are also possibilities, depending on the nature of the measures used. This pattern could indicate a **selection-mortality** problem if there are more low-scoring program cases that drop out between testings. What about selection-regression? It doesn't seem likely, for much the same reasoning as for outcome 1. If there were an upward regression to the mean from pre to post, you would expect that regression to be greater for the comparison group because it has the lower pretest score.

Possible Outcome 3 This third possible outcome (see Figure 10–5) cries out selection-regression! Or, at least it would if it could cry out. The regression scenario is that the program group was selected so that it was extremely high (relative to the population) on the pretest. The fact that the group scored lower, approaching the comparison group on the posttest, may simply be due to its regressing toward the population mean. You might observe an outcome like this when you study the effects of giving a scholarship or an award for academic performance. You give the award because students did well (in this case, on the pretest). When you observe the group's posttest performance, relative to an average group of students, it appears to perform worse. Pure regression! Notice how this outcome doesn't suggest a selection-maturation threat. What kind of maturation process would have to occur for the highly advantaged program group to decline while a comparison group evidences no change?

Possible Outcome 4 The fourth possible outcome also suggests a selection-regression threat (Figure 10–6). Here, the program group is disadvantaged to

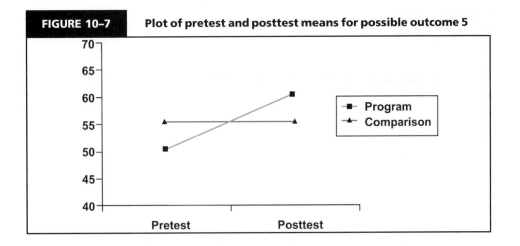

FIGURE 10–7   Plot of pretest and posttest means for possible outcome 5

begin with. The fact that it appears to pull closer to the comparison group on the posttest may be due to regression. This outcome pattern may be suspected in studies of compensatory programs—programs designed to help address some problem or deficiency. For instance, compensatory education programs are designed to help children who are doing poorly in some subject. They are likely to have lower pretest performance than more average comparison children. Consequently, they are likely to regress to the mean in a pattern similar to the one shown in outcome 4.

Possible Outcome 5   This last hypothetical outcome (Figure 10–7) is sometimes referred to as a *crossover pattern*. Here, the comparison group doesn't appear to change from pre to post; but the program group does, starting out lower than the comparison group and ending up above it. This is the clearest pattern of evidence for the effectiveness of the program of all five of the hypothetical outcomes. It's hard to come up with a threat to internal validity that would be plausible here. Certainly, there is no evidence for selection maturation here unless you postulate that the two groups are involved in maturational processes that tend to start and stop and just coincidentally you caught the program group maturing while the comparison group had gone dormant. However, if that were the case, why did the program group actually cross over the comparison group? Why didn't it approach the comparison group and stop maturing? How likely is this outcome as a description of normal maturation? Not very. Similarly, this isn't a selection-regression result. Regression might explain why a low-scoring program group approaches the comparison group posttest score (as in outcome 4), but it doesn't explain why it crosses over.

Although this fifth outcome is the strongest evidence for a program effect, you can't very well construct your study expecting to find this kind of pattern. It would be a little bit like giving your program to the toughest cases and seeing whether you can improve them so much that they not only become like average cases but actually outperform them. That's an awfully big expectation with which to saddle any program. Typically, you wouldn't want to subject your program to that kind of expectation. If you do happen to find that kind of result, you really have a program effect that beats the odds.

10-2 The Regression-Discontinuity Design

What a terrible name! In everyday language, both parts of the term *regression-discontinuity* have primarily negative connotations. To most people *regression* implies a reversion backward or a return to some earlier, more primitive state, whereas *discontinuity* suggests an unnatural jump or shift in what might otherwise be a smoother, more continuous process. To a research methodologist, however, the

regression-discontinuity (RD)
A pretest-posttest program-comparison group quasi-experimental design in which a cutoff criterion on the preprogram measure is the method of assignment to group.

term *regression-discontinuity* carries no such negative meaning. Instead, the **regression-discontinuity (RD)** design is seen as a useful method for determining whether a program or treatment is effective.

The label *RD design* actually refers to a set of design variations. In its simplest most traditional form, the RD design is a pretest-posttest program-comparison group strategy. The unique characteristic that sets RD designs apart from other pre-post group designs is the method by which research participants are assigned to conditions. In RD designs, participants are assigned to program or comparison groups solely on the basis of a cutoff score on a pre-program measure. Thus, the RD design is distinguished from randomized experiments (or randomized clinical trials) and from other quasi-experimental strategies by its unique method of assignment. This cutoff criterion implies the major advantage of RD designs; they are appropriate when you want to target a program or treatment to those who most need or deserve it. Thus, unlike its randomized or quasi-experimental alternatives, the RD design does not require you to assign potentially needy individuals to a no-program comparison group to evaluate the effectiveness of a program.

The RD design has not been used frequently in social research. The most common implementation has been in compensatory education evaluation where school children who obtain scores that fall below some predetermined cutoff value on an achievement test are assigned to remedial training designed to improve their performance. The low frequency of use may be attributable to several factors. Certainly, the design is a relative latecomer. Its first major field tests did not occur until the mid-1970s, when it was incorporated into the nationwide evaluation system for compensatory education programs funded under Title I of the Elementary and Secondary Education Act (ESEA) of 1965. In many situations, the design has not been used because one or more key criteria were absent. For instance, RD designs force administrators to assign participants to conditions solely on the basis of quantitative indicators, thereby often unpalatably restricting the degree to which judgment, discretion, or favoritism can be used. Perhaps the most telling reason for the lack of wider adoption of the RD design is that at first glance the design doesn't seem to make sense. In most research, you want to have comparison groups that are equivalent to program groups on pre-program indicators so that post-program differences can be attributed to the program itself. However, because of the cutoff criterion in RD designs, program and comparison groups are deliberately and maximally different on pre-program characteristics, an apparently insensible anomaly. An understanding of how the design actually works depends on at least a conceptual familiarity with regression analysis, thereby making the strategy a difficult one to convey to nonstatistical audiences.

Despite its lack of use, the RD design has great potential for evaluation and social research. From a methodological point of view, inferences drawn from a well-implemented RD design are comparable in internal validity to conclusions from randomized experiments. Thus, the RD design is a strong competitor to randomized designs when causal hypotheses are being investigated. From an ethical perspective, RD designs are compatible with the goal of getting the program to those most in need. It is not necessary to deny the program from potentially deserving recipients simply for the sake of a scientific test. From an administrative viewpoint, the RD design is often directly usable with existing measurement efforts, such as the regularly collected statistical information typical of most management-information systems. The advantages of the RD design warrant greater educational efforts on the part of the methodological community to encourage its use where appropriate.

10-2a The Basic RD Design

The basic RD design is a pretest-posttest two-group design. The term *pretest-posttest* implies that the same measure (or perhaps alternative forms of the same measure)

FIGURE 10–8	Notation for the regression-discontinuity (RD) design

$$C \quad O \quad X \quad O$$
$$C \quad O \quad \quad O$$

is administered before and after some program or treatment. (In fact, the RD design does not require that the pre and post measures be the same.) The term *pretest* implies that the same measure is given twice, whereas the term *pre-program* measure implies more broadly that before and after measures may be the same or different. It is assumed that a cutoff value on the pretest or pre-program measure is being used to assign persons or other units to the program. Two-group versions of the RD design might imply either that some treatment or program is being contrasted with a no-program condition or that two alternative programs are being compared. The description of the basic design as a two-group design implies that a single pretest-cutoff score is used to assign participants to either the program, or comparison group. The term *participants* refers to the units assigned. In many cases, participants are individuals, but they could be any definable units such as hospital wards, hospitals, counties, and so on. The term *program* is used in this discussion of the RD design to refer to any program, treatment, or manipulation whose effects you want to examine. In notational form, the basic RD design might be depicted as shown Figure 10–8:

- *C* indicates that groups are assigned by means of a cutoff score.
- An *O* stands for the administration of a measure to a group.
- An *X* depicts the implementation of a program.
- Each group is described on a single line (for example, program group on top and control group on the bottom).

To make this initial presentation more concrete, imagine a hypothetical study examining the effect of a new treatment protocol for inpatients with a particular diagnosis. For simplicity, assume that you want to try the new protocol on patients who are considered most ill and that for each patient you have a continuous quantitative indicator of health that is a composite rating that takes values from 1 to 100, where high scores indicate greater health. Furthermore, assume that a pretest cutoff score of 50 was (more or less arbitrarily) chosen as the assignment criterion or that all who score lower than 50 on the pretest will be given the new treatment protocol, whereas those who score 50 or higher will be given the standard treatment.

It is useful to begin by considering what the data might look like if you did not administer the treatment protocol but instead measured all participants only at two points in time. Figure 10–9a shows the hypothetical bivariate distribution for this situation. Each item on the figure indicates a single person's pretest and posttest scores. The blue *X*s to the left of the cutoff show the program cases. They are more severely ill on both the pretest and posttest. The green circles show the comparison group that is comparatively healthy on both measures. The vertical line at the pretest score of 50 indicates the cutoff point. (In Figure 10–9a, the assumption is that no treatment has been given.) The solid line through the bivariate distribution is the linear **regression line**. The distribution depicts a strong positive relationship between the pretest and posttest; in general, the more healthy a person is at the pretest, the more healthy he or she is on the posttest, and the more severely ill a person is at the pretest, the more ill that person is on the posttest.

Consider what the outcome might look like if the new treatment protocol is administered and has a positive effect (Figure 10–9b). For simplicity, assume that

regression line
A line that describes the relationship between two or more variables.

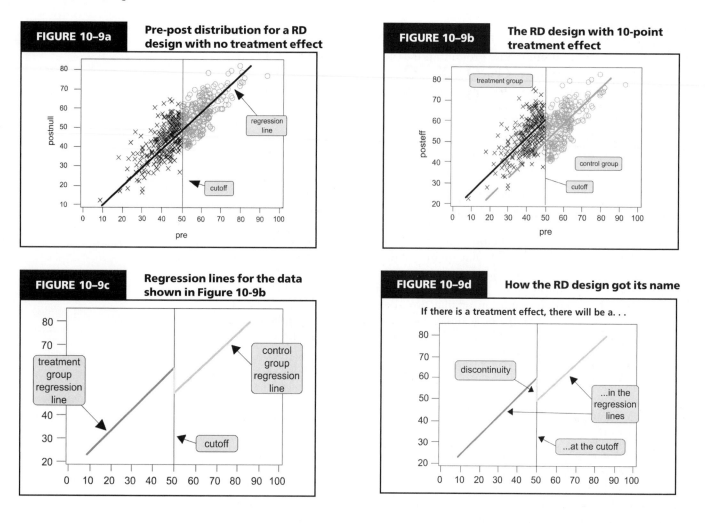

FIGURE 10–9a — Pre-post distribution for a RD design with no treatment effect

FIGURE 10–9b — The RD design with 10-point treatment effect

FIGURE 10–9c — Regression lines for the data shown in Figure 10-9b

FIGURE 10–9d — How the RD design got its name

the treatment had a constant effect that raised each treated person's health score by 10 points.

Figure 10–9b is identical to Figure 10–9a except that all points to the left of the cutoff (that is, the treatment group) have been raised by 10 points on the posttest. The dashed line in Figure 10–9b shows what you would expect the treated group's regression line to look like if the program had no effect (as was the case in Figure 10–9a).

It is sometimes difficult to see the forest for the trees in these types of bivariate plots. So, let's remove the individual data points and look only at the regression lines. The plot of regression lines for the treatment effect case of Figure 10–9b is shown in Figure 10–9c.

On the basis of Figure 10–9c, you can now see how the RD design got its name; a program effect is suggested when you observe a *jump* or *discontinuity* in the regression lines at the cutoff point. This is illustrated in Figure 10–9d.

The Logic of the RD Design The previous discussion indicates what the key feature of the RD design is: *assignment based on a cutoff value on a pre-program measure.* The cutoff rule for the simple two-group case is essentially as follows:

- All persons on one side of the cutoff are assigned to one group.
- All persons on the other side of the cutoff are assigned to the other group.

The choice of cutoff value is usually based on one of two factors. It can be made solely on the basis of the program resources that are available. For instance, if a program can handle only 25 persons and 70 people apply, you can choose a cutoff point that distinguishes the 25 most needy persons from the rest. Alternatively, you can choose the cutoff on substantive grounds. If the pre-program assignment measure is an indication of severity of illness measured on a 1 to 7 scale and physicians or other experts believe that all patients scoring 5 or more are critical and fit well the criteria defined for program participants, you might use a cutoff value of 5.

To interpret the results of an RD design, you must know the nature of the assignment variable and the outcome measure, as well as who received the program. Without this information, no distinct outcome pattern directly indicates whether an effect is positive or negative.

To illustrate this, consider a new hypothetical example of an RD design. Assume that a hospital administrator would like to improve the quality of patient care through the institution of an intensive quality-of-care (QOC) training program for staff. Because of financial constraints, the program is too costly to implement for all employees and so instead it will be administered to the entire staff from specifically targeted units or wards that seem most in need of improving quality of care. Two general measures of quality of care are available. The first is an aggregate rating of quality of care based on observation and rating by an administrative staff member and will be labeled here the QOC rating. The second is the ratio of the number of recorded patient complaints relative to the number of patients in the unit over a fixed period of time and will be termed here the *Complaint Ratio*. In this scenario, the administrator could use either the QOC rating or Complaint Ratio as the basis for assigning units to receive the training. Similarly, the effects of the training could be measured on either variable. Figures 10–10a through 10–10d show four outcomes of alternative RD implementations possible under this scenario.

Only the regression lines are shown in Figures 10–10a through 10–10d. It is worth noting that even though all four outcomes have the same pattern of regression lines, they imply very different results. In Figure 10–10a and Figure 10–10b, hospital units were assigned to training because they scored below some cutoff score on the QOC rating. In Figure 10–10c and Figure 10–10d, units received training because they scored above the cutoff score value on the Complaint Ratio measure. In each graph, the dashed line indicates the regression line you would expect to find for the training group if the training had no effect. This dashed line represents the no-discontinuity projection of the comparison-group regression line into the region of the program group pretest scores.

You can clearly see that even though the outcome regression lines are the same in all four groups, you would interpret the four graphs differently. Figure 10–10a depicts a positive effect because training raised the program group's regression line on the QOC rating over what would have been expected. Figure 10–10b, however, shows a negative effect because the program raised training group scores on the Complaint Ratio. indicating increased complaint rates. Figure 10–10c shows a positive effect because the regression line was lowered on the Complaint Ratio relative to what you would have expected. Finally, Figure 10–10d shows a negative effect where the training resulted in lower QOC ratings than you would expect otherwise. The point here is a simple one. A discontinuity in regression lines indicates a program effect in the RD design, but the discontinuity alone is not sufficient to tell you whether the effect is positive or negative. To make this determination, you need to know who received the program and how to interpret the direction of scale values on the outcome measures.

The Role of the Comparison Group in RD Designs With this introductory discussion of the design in mind, you can now see what constitutes the benchmark for comparison in the RD design. In experimental or other quasi-experimental designs, you either assume or try to provide evidence that the program and comparison groups are equivalent prior to the program so that post-program differences can be attributed to the manipulation. The RD design involves no such assumption.

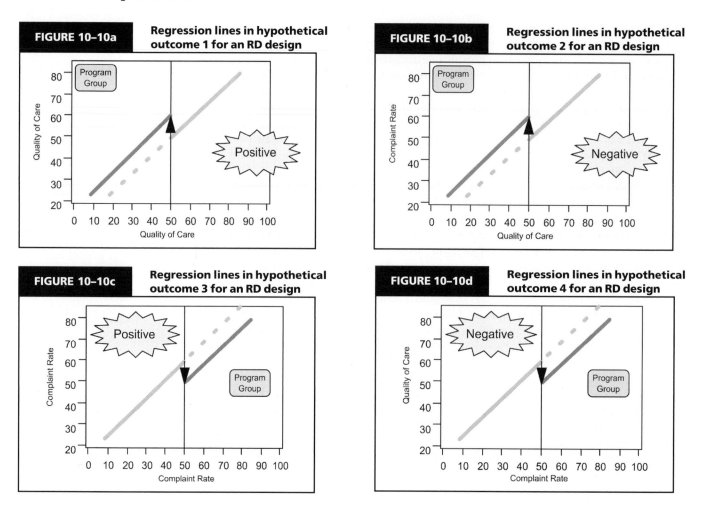

FIGURE 10–10a Regression lines in hypothetical outcome 1 for an RD design

FIGURE 10–10b Regression lines in hypothetical outcome 2 for an RD design

FIGURE 10–10c Regression lines in hypothetical outcome 3 for an RD design

FIGURE 10–10d Regression lines in hypothetical outcome 4 for an RD design

Instead, with RD designs you assume that in the absence of the program the pre-post relationship would be equivalent for the two groups. Thus, the strength of the RD design is dependent on two major factors. The first is the assumption that there is no spurious discontinuity in the pre-post relationship that happens to coincide with the cutoff point. The second factor concerns the degree to which you can know and correctly model the pre-post relationship and constitutes the major problem in the statistical analysis of the RD design, which will be discussed in Chapter 12.

The Internal Validity of the RD Design

Internal validity refers to whether one can infer that the treatment or program being investigated caused a change in outcome indicators. Internal validity is not concerned with your ability to generalize but rather focuses on whether a causal relationship can be demonstrated for the immediate research context. Research designs that address causal questions are often compared on their relative ability to yield internally valid results.

In most causal-hypothesis tests, the central inferential question is whether any observed outcome differences between groups are attributable to the program or instead to some other factor. To argue for the internal validity of an inference, the analyst must attempt to demonstrate that the program—and not some plausible alternative explanation—is responsible for the effect. In the literature on internal validity, these plausible alternative explanations or factors are often termed **threats to internal validity** (as described in Chapter 7–1). Many threats can be ruled out by including a control group. Assuming that the control group is equivalent to the program group prior to the study, the control group pre-post gain shows you what

threats to internal validity
Any factor that can lead you to reach an incorrect conclusion about whether there is a causal relationship in your study.

would have happened in the program group if it had not had the program. A different rate of gain in the program group provides evidence for the relative effect of the program itself. Thus, randomized-experimental designs are considered strong in internal validity because they give you confidence in the probabilistic, pre-program equivalence between groups that results from random assignment and helps ensure that the control group provides a legitimate reflection of all nonprogram factors that might affect outcomes.

RD designs contain several selection threats to internal validity because of the deliberate pre-program differences between groups. (These are discussed in Chapter 7.) These threats might, at first glance, appear to be a problem. For instance, a selection-maturation threat implies that different rates of maturation between groups explain outcome differences. For the sake of argument, let's consider a pre-post distribution with a linear relationship having a slope equal to two units. This implies that on average, a person with a given pretest score will have a posttest score two times higher. Clearly there is maturation in this situation; that is, people are getting consistently higher scores over time. If a person has a pretest score of 10 units, you would predict a posttest score of 20 for an absolute gain of 10. However, if a person has a pretest score of 50, you would predict a posttest score of 100 for an absolute gain of 50. Thus, the second person naturally gains or matures more in absolute units, although the rate of gain relative to the pretest score is constant. Along these lines, in the RD design, you expect that all participants may mature and that in absolute terms this maturation might be different for the two groups on average. Nevertheless, a program effect in the RD design is not indicated by a difference between the posttest averages of the groups, but rather by a change in the pre-post relationship at the cutoff point. In this example, although you might expect different absolute levels of maturation, a single, continuous regression line with a slope equal to 2 describes these different maturational rates perfectly. More to the point, for selection-maturation to be a threat to internal validity in RD designs, it must induce a discontinuity in the pre-post relationship that happens to coincide with the cutoff point—an unlikely scenario in most studies.

Another selection threat to internal validity that might intuitively seem likely in the RD design concerns the possibility of differential regression to the mean or a selection-regression threat (as described in Chapter 7–1b). The phenomenon of regression to the mean arises when you asymmetrically sample groups from a distribution. On any subsequent measure, the obtained sample group mean will be closer to the population mean for that measure (in standardized units) than the sample mean from the original distribution is to its population mean. In RD designs, you deliberately create asymmetric samples through the cutoff assignment and consequently expect regression towards the mean in both groups. In general, you should expect the low-scoring pretest group to evidence a relative gain on the posttest and the high-scoring pretest group to show a relative loss. As with selection-maturation, even though you expect to see differential regression to the mean, it poses no problem for the internal validity of the RD design. Regression to the mean does not result in a discontinuity in the bivariate relationship coincidental with the cutoff point. In fact, the regression to the mean that occurs is continuous across the range of the pretest scores and is described by the regression line itself. (After all, the term *regression* was originally coined by Galton to refer to the fact that a regression line describes regression to the mean.)

Although the RD design might initially seem susceptible to selection biases, it is not. The previous discussion demonstrates that only factors that would naturally induce a discontinuity in the pre-post relationship could be considered threats to the internal validity of inferences from the RD design. In principle then, the RD design is as strong in internal validity as its randomized experimental alternatives. In practice, however, the validity of the RD design depends directly on how well you can model the true pre-post relationship, certainly a nontrivial statistical problem.

significant. Is this finding interpretable as a treatment effect?" My answer is "Yes." I think the graduate student's desperation-driven intuition to look at order of effects is a sensible one. I would conclude that the reason you did not find statistical effects on the individual variables is that you didn't have sufficient statistical power. (You can find more about this in the discussion on statistical power in Chapter 12.) Of course, the results will be interpretable as a treatment effect only if you can rule out any other plausible factor that could have caused the ordering of outcomes. Nonetheless, the more detailed the predicted pattern and the stronger the correlation to observed results, the more likely it becomes that the treatment effect is the most plausible explanation. In such cases, the expected pattern of results is like a unique fingerprint, and the observed pattern that matches it can only be due to that unique source pattern.

I believe that the pattern-matching notion implicit in the NEDV design opens the way to an entirely different approach to causal assessment, one that is closely linked to detailed prior explication of the program and to detailed mapping of constructs. It suggests a much richer model for causal assessment than one that relies only on a simplistic dichotomous treatment-control model. In fact, I'm so convinced of the importance of this idea that I've staked a major part of my career on developing pattern-matching models for conducting research!

10-3f The Regression Point Displacement (RPD) Design

regression point displacement (RPD)
A pre-post quasi experimental research design where the treatment is given to only one unit in the sample, with all remaining units acting as controls. This design is particularly useful to study the effects of community-level interventions, where outcome data is routinely collected at the community level.

The **regression point displacement (RPD)** design is a simple quasi-experimental strategy that has important implications, especially for community-based research. The problem with community-level interventions is that it is difficult to do causal assessment to determine whether your program made a difference as opposed to other potential factors. Typically, in community-level interventions, program costs preclude implementation of the program in more than one community. You look at pre-post indicators for the program community and see whether there is a change. If you're relatively enlightened, you seek out another similar community and use it as a comparison. However, because the intervention is at the community level, you have only a single unit of measurement for your program and comparison groups.

The RPD design (Figure 10–19) attempts to enhance the single program unit situation by comparing the performance on that single unit with the performance of a large set of comparison units. In community research, you would compare the pre-post results for the intervention community with a large set of other communities. The advantage of doing this is that you don't rely on a single nonequivalent community; you attempt to use results from a heterogeneous set of nonequivalent communities to model the comparison condition and then compare your single site to this model. For typical community-based research, such an approach may greatly enhance your ability to make causal inferences.

I'll illustrate the RPD design with an example of a community-based AIDS education program to be implemented in one particular community in a state, perhaps a county. Assume that the state routinely publishes annual HIV positive rates by county for the entire state. So, the remaining counties in the state

FIGURE 10–19   **The regression point displacement (RPD) design**

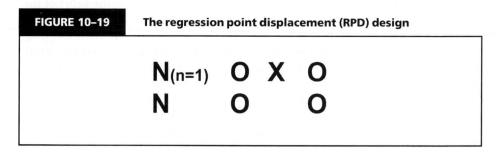

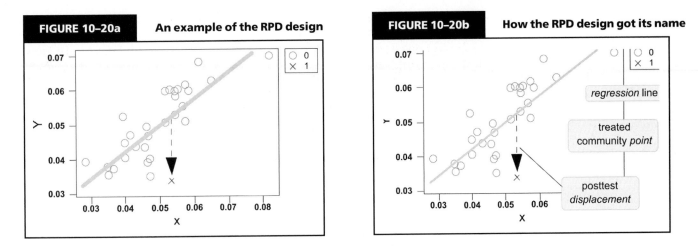

FIGURE 10–20a   An example of the RPD design

FIGURE 10–20b   How the RPD design got its name

function as control counties. Instead of averaging all the control counties to obtain a single control score, you use them as separate units in the analysis. Figure 10–20a shows the bivariate pre-post distribution of HIV positive rates per 1000 people for all the counties in the state. The program county—the one that gets the AIDS education program—is shown as an X and the remaining control counties are shown as Os. You compute a regression line for the control cases (shown in blue on the figure) to model your predicted outcome for a count with any specific pretest rate. To estimate the effect of the program, you test whether the displacement of the program county from the control county regression line is statistically significant.

Figure 10–20b shows why the RPD design was given its name. In this design, you know you have a treatment effect when there is a significant *displacement* of the program *point* from the control group *regression* line.

The RPD design is especially applicable in situations where a treatment or program is applied in a single geographical unit (such as a state, county, city, hospital, or hospital unit) instead of an individual, where many other units are available as control cases, and where there is routine measurement (for example monthly, or annually) of relevant outcome variables.

The analysis of the RPD design turns out to be a variation of the Analysis of Covariance model.

Summary

This chapter introduced the idea of quasi-experimental designs. These designs look a bit like their randomized or true experimental relatives (described in Chapter 9), but they lack their random assignment to groups. Two major types of quasi-experimental designs were explained in detail. Both are pre-post, two-group designs, and they differ primarily in the manner used to assign the groups. In the NEGD, groups are assigned naturally or are used intact; the researcher does not control the assignment. In RD designs, participants are assigned to groups solely on the basis of a cutoff score on the preprogram measure; the researcher explicitly controls this assignment. Because assignment is explicitly controlled in the RD design and not in NEGD, the former is considered stronger with respect to internal validity, perhaps comparable in strength to randomized experiments. Finally, the versatility and range of quasi-experimental design was illustrated through brief presentation of a number of lesser-known designs that illustrate various combinations of sampling, measurement, or analysis strategies.

Login to the Online Edition of your text at www.atomicdog.com to find additional resources located in the Study Guide at the end of each chapter.

Advanced Design Topics

FIGURE 11–7	The basic pre-post randomized experimental design

R   O   X   O
R   O   O

FIGURE 11–8	A randomized experiment expanded with a nonequivalent control group

R   O   X   O
R   O   O
N   O   O

FIGURE 11–9	A randomized experiment expanded with a nonequivalent group to help rule out a testing threat

R   O   X   O
R   O   O
N   O

munication, group rivalry, or demoralization of a group denied a desirable treatment or given an undesirable one to pose threats to the validity of the causal inference. (Social threats to internal validity are covered in Chapter 7.) In such a case, you might add an additional nonequivalent group from a similar institution that consists of persons unaware of the original two groups (Figure 11–8).

In a similar manner, whenever you use nonequivalent groups in a study it is usually advantageous to have multiple replications of each group. The use of many nonequivalent groups helps minimize the potential of a particular **selection bias** affecting the results. In some cases, it may be desirable to include the norm group as an additional group in the design. Norming group averages are available for most standardized achievement tests, for example, and might comprise an additional nonequivalent control group. You can also use cohort groups in a number of ways. For example, you might use a single measure of a cohort group to help rule out a testing threat (Figure 11–9).

In this design, the randomized groups might be sixth graders from the same school year, and the cohort might be the entire sixth grade from the previous academic year. This cohort group did not take the pretest, and if it is similar to the randomly selected control group, it would provide evidence for or against the notion that taking the pretest had an effect on posttest scores. You might also use pre-post cohort groups (Figure 11–10).

Here, the treatment group consists of sixth graders, the first comparison group of seventh graders in the same year, and the second comparison group consists of the following year's sixth graders (the fifth graders during the study year). Strategies of this sort are particularly useful in nonequivalent designs where selection bias is a potential problem and where routinely collected institutional data is available. Finally, one other approach for expanding the groups involves partitioning groups with different assignment strategies. For example, you might randomly divide nonequivalent groups or select nonequivalent subgroups from randomly

selection bias
Any factor other than the program that leads to posttest differences between groups.

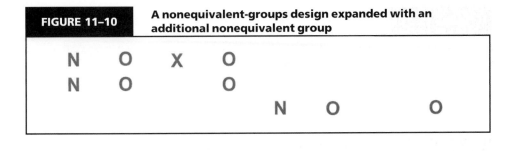

FIGURE 11–10 A nonequivalent-groups design expanded with an additional nonequivalent group

assigned groups. An example of this sort involving the combination of **random assignment** and assignment by a cutoff is discussed in detail in the following section.

11-1c A Simple Strategy for Design Construction

Considering the basic elements of a research design or the possibilities for expansion are not alone sufficient. You need to be able to integrate these elements with an overall strategy. In addition, you need to decide which potential threats are best handled by design rather than by argument, measurement, analysis, or preventive action.

While no definitive approach for designing designs exists, I suggest a tentative strategy based on the notion of expansion discussed previously. First, you begin the designing task by setting forth a design that depicts the simple hypothesized causal relationship. Second, you deliberately overexpand this basic design by expanding across time, program, observations, and groups. At this step, the emphasis is on accounting for as many likely alternative explanations or threats to validity as possible using the design. Finally, you scale back this overexpanded version considering the effect of eliminating each design component. It is at this point that you face the difficult decisions concerning the costs of each design component and the advantages of ruling out specific threats using other approaches.

Several advantages result from using this type of approach to design construction. First, you are forced to be explicit about the decisions you create. Second, the approach is conservative in nature. The strategy minimizes the chance of your overlooking a major threat to validity in constructing your design. Third, you arrive at a design that is tailored to the situation at hand. Finally, the strategy is cost-efficient. Threats you can account for by some other, less costly approach need not be accounted for in the design itself.

11-1d An Example of a Hybrid Design

Some of the ideas discussed in the previous sections can be illustrated in an example. To my knowledge, the design I'm presenting here has never been used, although it has strong features to commend it.

Let us assume that you want to study the effects of a new compensatory education program on subsequent student achievement. The program is designed to help students who are poor in reading improve reading skills. You can begin with the simple hypothesized cause-effect relationship (Figure 11–11).

Here, the X represents the reading program and the O stands for a reading achievement test. Assume you decide that it is desirable to add a pre-program measure so that you might investigate whether the program improves reading test scores. You also decide to expand across groups by adding a comparison group. At this point, you have the typical notation shown in Figure 11–12.

The next problem concerns how to assign the two groups. Since the program is specifically designed to help students who need special assistance in reading, you rule out random assignment because it would require denying the program to students in need. You considered the possibility of offering the program to one

random assignment
Process of assigning your sample into two or more subgroups by chance. Procedures for random assignment can vary from flipping a coin to using a table of random numbers to using the random number capability built into a computer.

FIGURE 11–11	The cause-effect relationship: the starting point for tailoring a design

X   O

FIGURE 11–12	A pre-post, two-group design

O   X   O
O   O

FIGURE 11–13	A randomized experimental design nested within a regression-discontinuity design

C   O   X   O
R   O   X   O
R   O   O
C   O   O

randomly assigned group in the first year and to the control group in the second, but ruled that out on the grounds that it would require 2 years of program expenses and the denial of a potentially helpful program for half of the students for a period of a year. Instead, you decide to assign students by means of a cutoff score on the pretest. All students scoring below a preselected percentile on the reading pretest would be given the program while those above that percentile would act as controls. (The RD design is covered in Chapter 10.) However, experience with this strategy shows that it is difficult to adhere to a single cutoff score for assignment to a group. Of special concern is the fact that teachers or administrators might allow students who score slightly above the cutoff point into the program because they have little confidence in the ability of the achievement test to make fine distinctions in reading skills for children who score close to the cutoff. To deal with this potential problem, you decide to partition the groups using a particular combination of assignment by a cutoff and random assignment as shown in Figure 11–13.

This design has two cutoff points. All those scoring below a certain percentile are assigned to the program group automatically by this cutoff. All those scoring above another higher percentile are automatically assigned to the comparison group by this cutoff. Finally, all those who fall in the interval between the cutoffs on the pretest are randomly assigned to either the program or comparison group.

This strategy has several advantages. It directly addresses the concern to teachers and administrators that the test may not be able to discriminate well between students who score immediately above or below a cutoff point. For example, a student whose true ability in reading would place him or her near the cutoff might have a bad day and therefore might be placed into the treatment or comparison group by chance factors. The design outlined in Figure 11–13 is defensible. You can agree with the teachers and administrators that the test is fallible. Nevertheless, since you need some criteria to assign students to the program, you can argue that the fairest approach would be to assign borderline cases by lottery. In addition, by combining two excellent strategies (the randomized experiment and the regression-discontinuity) you can analyze results separately for each and address the possibility that design factors might bias results.

Many other worthwhile strategies are not mentioned in the previous scenario. For example, instead of using simple randomized assignment within the cutoff interval, you might use a weighted random assignment so that students scoring lower in the interval have a greater probability of being assigned to the program. In addition, you might consider expanding the design in a number of other ways, by including double pretests or multiple posttests; multiple measures of reading skills; additional replications of the program or variations of the programs and additional groups, such as norming groups; controls from other schools; and the like. Nevertheless, this brief example serves to illustrate the advantages of explicitly constructing a research design to meet the specific needs of a particular situation.

11-1e The Nature of Good Design

Throughout the design construction task, it is important to have in mind some endpoint—some criteria that you should try to achieve before finally accepting a design strategy. The criteria discussed in the following sections are only meant to be suggestive of the characteristics found in good research design. It is worth noting that all of these criteria point to the need to individually tailor research designs rather than accepting standard textbook strategies as is.

- *Theory-grounded.* Good research strategies reflect the theories that you are investigating. When you hypothesize specific theoretical expectations, you should then incorporate them into the design. For example, when theory predicts a specific treatment effect on one measure but not on another, the inclusion of both in the design improves discriminant validity and demonstrates the predictive power of the theory.
- *Situational.* Good research designs reflect the settings of the investigation. This was illustrated in the previous section where a particular need of teachers and administrators was explicitly addressed in the design strategy. Similarly, you can assess intergroup rivalry, demoralization, and competition through the use of additional comparison groups not in direct contact with the original group.
- *Feasible.* Good designs can be implemented. You must carefully plan the sequence and timing of events. You need to anticipate potential problems in measurement, adherence to assignment, database construction, and the like. Where needed, you should include additional groups or measurements in the design to explicitly correct for such problems.
- *Redundant.* Good research designs have some flexibility built into them. Often, this flexibility results from duplication of essential design features. For example, multiple replications of a treatment help ensure that failure to implement the treatment in one setting will not invalidate the entire study.
- *Efficient.* Good designs strike a balance between redundancy and the tendency to overdesign. Where it is reasonable, other, less costly strategies for ruling out potential threats to validity are used.

This is by no means an exhaustive list of the criteria by which to judge good research design. Nevertheless, goals of this sort help guide you toward a final design choice and emphasize important components that should be included.

The development of a theory of research methodology for the social sciences has largely occurred over the past half century and most intensively within the past two decades. It is not surprising that in such a relatively recent effort, an emphasis on a few standard research designs has occurred. Nevertheless, by moving away from the notion of design selection and toward an emphasis on design construction, there is much to be gained in our understanding of design principles and in the quality of our research.

11-2 Relationships among Pre-Post Designs

Now that you are getting more sophisticated in understanding the idea of research design, you are ready to think more methodologically about some of the underlying principles that cut across design types. Here I show how the most frequently used design structures can be understood in relation to one another (Figure 11–14).

There are three major types of pre-post program-comparison group designs all sharing the basic design structure shown in Figure 11–14:

- The **RE design**
- The **NEGD design**
- The **RD design**

The designs differ only in the method by which participants are assigned to the two groups. In the RE, participants are assigned randomly. In the RD design, they are assigned using a cutoff score on the pretest. In the NEGD, assignment of participants is not explicitly controlled; they might self-select into either group, or other unknown or unspecified factors might determine assignment.

Because these three designs differ so critically in their assignment strategy, they are often considered distinct or unrelated. However, it is useful to look at them as forming a cor.tinuum, both in terms of assignment and in terms of their strength with respect to internal validity.

You can look at the similarity of the three designs in terms of their assignment by graphing their assignment functions with respect to the pretest variable. In Figure 11–15, the vertical axis is the probability that a specific unit (such as a person) will be assigned to the treatment group. These values, because they are probabilities, range from 0 to 1. The horizontal axis is an idealized pretest score. Each line on the graph is an assignment function for a design.

Let's first examine the assignment function for the simple pre-post randomized experiment. Because units are assigned randomly, the probability that a unit will be assigned to the treatment group is always 1/2 or .5 (assuming equal assignment probabilities are used). This function is indicated by the horizontal red line at .5 in the figure. For the RD design, I've arbitrarily set the cutoff value at the midpoint of the pretest variable and assigned units scoring below that value to the treatment and those scoring at or above that value to the control condition. (The arguments made here would generalize to the case of high-scoring treatment cases as well.) In this case, the assignment function is a simple step function, with the probability of assignment to the treatment = 1 for the pretest scores below the cutoff and = 0 for those above. It is important to note that for both the RE and RD designs, it is an easy matter to plot assignment functions because assignment is explicitly controlled. This is not the case for the NEGD. Here, the idealized assignment function differs depending on the degree to which the groups are nonequivalent on the pretest. If they are extremely nonequivalent (with the treatment group scoring lower on the pretest), the assignment function would approach the step function of the RD design. If the groups are hardly nonequivalent at all, the function would approach the flat-line function of the randomized experiment.

The graph of assignment functions points out an important issue about the relationships among these designs: The designs are not distinct with respect to their assignment functions; they form a continuum (Figure 11–16). On one end of the continuum is the RE design and at the other is the RD. The NEGD can be viewed as a degraded RD or RE depending on whether the assignment function more closely approximates one or the other.

You can also view the designs as differing with respect to the degree to which they generate a pretest difference between the groups.

RE design
The Randomized Experimental (RE) Design is characterized by one essential feature: the random assignment of participants to conditions.

NEGD design
A pre-post twogroup quasi-experimental design structured like a pretest-posttest randomized experiment, but lacking random assignment to group.

RD design
A pretest-posttest, program-comparison group quasi-experimental design in which a cutoff criterion on the preprogram measure is the method of assignment to group.

FIGURE 11–14   **The basic pre-post, two-group design structure**

O   X   O
O   O

FIGURE 11–15   **Probability of assignment to treatment for the RE, NEGD, and RD design**

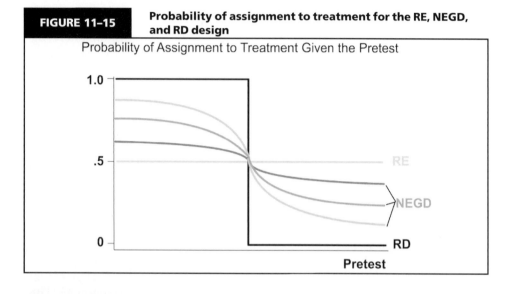

Probability of Assignment to Treatment Given the Pretest

1.0

.5

0

RE

NEGD

RD

Pretest

FIGURE 11–16   **The continuum of pre-post, two-group designs in terms of preprogram equivalence**

Pretest Equivalence

RD   NEGD   RE

Maximally
Nonequivalent   Equivalent

Figure 11–16 shows that the RD design induces the maximum possible pretest difference. The RE design induces the smallest pretest difference (the most equivalent). The NEGD fills in the gap between these two extreme cases. If the groups are extremely nonequivalent, the design is closer to the RD design. If they're extremely similar, it's closer to the RE design.

Finally, you can also distinguish the three designs in terms of the *a priori* knowledge they give about assignment. It should be clear that in the RE design you know perfectly the probability of assignment to treatment; it is .5 for each participant. Similarly, with the RD design, you also know perfectly the probability of assignment. In this case, it is precisely dependent on the cutoff assignment rule. It is dependent on the pretest where the RE design is not. In both these designs, you know the assignment function perfectly, and it is this knowledge that enables you to obtain unbiased estimates of the treatment effect with these designs. This is why I conclude that, with respect to internal validity, the RD design is as strong as the RE design. With the NEGD, however, you do not know the assignment function perfectly. Because of this, you need to model this function either directly or indirectly (for example, through reliability corrections).

The major point is that you should not look at these three designs as entirely distinct. They are related by the nature of their assignment functions and the degree of pretest nonequivalence between groups. This continuum has important implications for understanding the statistical analyses of these designs. (To learn more about statistical analysis, read Chapter 12.)

11-3 Contemporary Issues in Research Design[2]

It is fitting to end this section on research design by reflecting on where the research design endeavor stands today and trying to identify what the major, cutting-edge issues in design currently are. Of course, cutting-edge issues can always turn into a two-edged sword, so let's be careful!

Research design is a relatively recent invention. It really didn't exist in any formal sense prior to the 20th century and didn't really become delineated until the 1950s and 1960s. In the last half of the 20th century, this area has primarily involved explication of two interrelated topics: the theory of the validity of casual inferences and a taxonomy of the research designs that allow the examination of causal hypotheses.

Here I want to make the case that in the past decade traditional thinking has moved beyond the traditional thinking about design as simply a collection of specific designs and threats to validity has been replaced with a more integrated, synthetic view of design as part of a general logical and epistemological framework for research. To support this view that the notion of research design is evolving toward increasing integration, I will present a number of themes that seem to characterize current thinking and that cut across validity typologies and design taxonomies. This list of themes may also be viewed as a tentative description of the advances in thinking about research design in social research.

11-3a The Role of Judgment

One theme that underlies most of the others and that illustrates the increasing awareness of the tentativeness and frailty of research concerns the importance of human judgment in research. I know it's probably obvious to you that the personal subjective judgments of researchers has a major effect on research, but believe it or not, I and a lot of my colleagues really seemed to lose sight of this fact over the past half century and are only rediscovering it now. We were lured by the idea that we might be able to mechanize the research design process, to automate it in a sense to minimize the role of human judgment and (we thought) improve the objectivity of our work. But I think we now realize that objectivity (at least in the old-fashioned positivist sense) isn't all it was cracked up to be and that it is heavily dependent on human judgment itself. Researchers are beginning to think about the psychological components of cause-effect relationships and causal reasoning and are increasingly incorporating models of the judgmental process into their research designs and analyses. And researchers are also recognizing more clearly the sociological bases of scientific thought and the fact that science is at root a human enterprise. We increasingly recognize that scientific communities have social norms and customs and often operate like tribal groups (and, unfortunately, are sometimes as primitive). The positivist, mechanistic view is all but gone from contemporary design thinking, and what remains is a more judgmental and ironically, a more scientifically sensible perspective.

[2]Parts of this section were based on Trochim, W. (Ed.), (1986). Editor's Notes. *Advances in Quasi-Experimental Design and Analysis. New Directions for Program Evaluation Series*, Number 31, San Francisco, CA: Jossey-Bass.

11-3b The Case for Tailored Designs

In the early days, methodologists took a taxonomic approach to design, laying out a collection of relatively discrete research designs and discussing how weak or strong they were for valid causal inference. Presentations of research designs were full of discussions of classification issues and specialized design notation systems (a lot like the *X* and *O* system of notation I present here and which my students fondly refer to as the tic-tac-toe school of design notation). Almost certainly, these early design proponents recognized that there was a virtual infinity of design variations and that validity was more complexly related to theory and context than their presentations implied. Nonetheless, what seemed to evolve was a cookbook approach to design that largely involved picking a design off the shelf and checking off lists of validity threats.

In the past few decades, we've gotten a little more sophisticated than that, constructing tailored research designs as combinations of more elemental units (for example, assignment strategies, measurement occasions) based on the specific contextual needs and plausible alternative explanations for a treatment effect (as described in the first section in this chapter). The implication for you is that you should focus on the advantages of different combinations of design features rather than on a relatively restricted set of prefabricated designs. In writing this text, I try (without always succeeding) to encourage you to break away from this canned, off-the-shelf, taxonomic design mentality, and I emphasize design principles and issues that cut across the traditional distinctions between true experiments, nonexperiments, and quasi-experiments (as in the discussion of the previous section of this chapter).

11-3c The Crucial Role of Theory

Research design has sometimes been criticized for encouraging an atheoretical, black-box research mentality. People are assigned to either complex, convoluted programs, or (often) to equally complex comparison conditions. The machinery of random assignment (or our quasi-experimental attempts to approximate random assignment) are the primary means of defining whether the program has an effect. If you think about it, this comparison group mentality is inherently atheoretical and noncontextual. It assumes that the same design mechanism works in exactly the same way whether you apply it in studies of mental health, criminal justice, income maintenance, or education.

There is nothing inherently wrong with this program-group-versus-comparison-group logic. The problem is that it may be a rather crude, uninformative approach. In the two-group case, you are simply creating a dichotomous input into reality. If you observe a posttest difference between groups, it could be explained by this dichotomous program-versus-comparison-group input or by any number of alternative explanations, including differential attrition rates, intergroup rivalry and communication, initial selection differences among groups, or different group histories. Researchers usually try to deal with these alternative explanations by ruling them out through argument, additional measurement, patched-up design features, and auxiliary analysis.

But we now see that there may be another way to approach research that emphasizes theoretical explanation more and simplistic design structure less. For instance, we have begun to emphasize greater use of patterns in research by using more complex theory-driven predictions that, if corroborated, allow fewer plausible alternative explanations for the effect of a program. (**Pattern matching** is covered in Chapter 10.) Because appropriate theories may not be readily available, especially for the evaluation of contemporary social programs, we are developing methods and processes to help people articulate the implicit theories that program administrators and stakeholder groups have in mind and which presumably guide the formation and implementation of the program.

pattern matching
The degree of correspondence between two data items. For instance, you might look at a pattern match of a theoretical expectation pattern with an observed patten to see if you are getting the outcomes you expect.

11-3d Attention to Program Implementation

A theory-driven approach to research will be futile unless we can demonstrate that the program was in fact carried out or implemented as the theory intended. I know this is obvious to you, but once again, it's astonishing how often people like me forget these basic truths. In the past few decades, we have seen the development of program implementation theory that looks at the process of program execution as an important part of research itself. For instance, one approach emphasizes the development of organizational procedures and training systems that accurately transmit the program and that anticipate likely institutional sources of resistance. Another strategy involves the assessment of program delivery through program audits, management information systems, and the like. This emphasis on program implementation has further obscured the traditional distinction between process and outcome evaluation. At the least, it is certainly clear that good research cannot be accomplished without attending to program processes, and we are continuing to develop better notions of how to combine these two efforts.

11-3e The Importance of Quality Control

Over and over, our experience with research has shown that even the best-laid research plans often go awry in practice, sometimes with disastrous results. Okay, I know this is another one of those things that should have been obvious, but at least we're finally beginning to catch on now. Over the past decade, researchers have begun to pay increasing attention to the integrity and quality of research designs in real-world settings. One way to do this is to go to people who know something about data integrity and quality assurance and incorporate techniques used by these other professions: accounting, auditing, industrial quality control. For instance, double-bookkeeping can be used to keep verifiable records of research participation. Acceptance sampling can be an efficient method for checking accuracy in large data collection efforts where an exhaustive examination of records is impractical or excessive in cost. These issues are particularly important in quasi-experimental research design, where it is especially important to demonstrate that sampling, measurement, group assignment, and analysis decisions do not interact with program participation in ways that can confound the final interpretation of results.

11-3f The Advantages of Multiple Perspectives

Researchers have long recognized the importance of replication and systematic variation in research. In the past few years, we have rediscovered this principle. (There does seem to be an awful lot of rediscovering going on in this discussion, doesn't there?) The emphasis on multiple perspectives rests on the notion that no single point of view will ever be sufficient for understanding a phenomenon with validity. Multiple realizations—of research questions, measures, samples, designs, analyses, replications, and so on—are essential for convergence on the truth (and even then we're lucky if we get there). However, such a varied approach can become a methodological and epistemological Pandora's Box unless researchers apply critical judgment in deciding which multiples to use in a study or set of studies. That's the challenge, and researchers are only beginning to address it.

11-3g Evolution of the Concept of Validity

The history of research design is inseparable from the development of the theory of the validity of causal inference. For decades researchers have been arguing about the definition of validity and debating whether it's more important to the establishment of a cause-effect relationship (internal validity) or whether we should emphasize generalizability (external validity). Some researchers argued that it was more important to nail down the cause-effect relationship even for nonrepresentative people in one place at one time and then worry about generalizing in subsequent studies that attempt to replicate the original study. Others worried that it doesn't make sense to pour our resources into intense rigorous studies of a particular group in one place and at one time because this has no generalizability and little policy relevance. Believe it or not, I remember having numerous intense debates about this dilemma as a graduate student. Of course, the obvious solution—that we want to achieve a balance between internal and external validity, between establishing the cause-effect relationship with precision and sampling broadly enough to have some generalizability—has emerged with painful slowness over time. But, at least we got there. More and more, research design is seen as a balancing act, using judgment to allocate precious and scarce resources to blend different levels of validity.

11-3h Development of Increasingly Complex Realistic Analytic Models

In the past decade, researchers have made considerable progress toward complicating statistical analyses to account for increasingly complex contexts and designs. For all of you who have to take statistics this is, of course, the bad news. In the past 50 years, we have developed more complex statistics for dealing with measurement error, creating dichotomous dependent variables, estimating invisible traits and characteristics, and so on. In fact, I think that many of these advances are among the most important contributions social science has made in the past 50 years. Too bad so few people understand them! Of course, it would help if we could learn how to teach statistics—especially the newer, more complex, and exciting approaches—to real people. Who knows, maybe we'll accomplish that in the next century. In the meantime, those of you who have to slog through advanced stats courses can perhaps take heart that the complexity you're grappling with actually represents a legitimate advance.

Parallel to the development of these increasingly complex, realistic statistical models, cynicism has deepened among researchers about the ability of any single model or analysis to be sufficient. (And that's really saying something because researchers started out as a cynical crowd.) Increasingly researchers are calling for multiple statistical analyses and using the results to bracket the likely true estimates. Researchers have virtually abandoned hope of finding a single correct analysis and have accordingly moved to multiple analyses that are based on systematically distinct assumptional frameworks and that rely in an increasingly direct way on the role of judgment.

Summary

So, where does this leave all of us who do social research? The good news is that all of these advances suggest that researchers have become much more realistic about what research can accomplish. Gone are the heady days of the 1960s and 1970s where we hoped to be able to turn applied social research into a branch of science akin to physics or chemistry. The bad news is that this makes our lives considerably more complicated. Researchers have discovered a lot of problems in our initial approaches to social research and we've invented ever more complicated solutions for them. The overall picture that emerges about contemporary research is that research design is judgmental. It is based on multiple and varied sources of evidence; it should be multiplistic in realization; it must attend to process as well as to outcome; it is better off when theory driven; and it leads ultimately to multiple analyses that attempt to bracket the program effect within some reasonable range.

In one sense, this is hardly a pretty picture. Contemporary views about research design and its role in causal inference are certainly more tentative and critical than they were in

1965 or perhaps even in 1979. But, this more integrated and complex view of research has emerged directly from our experiences in the conduct of such studies. Perhaps the social research community is learning how to do this stuff better. At least, that's the hope.

Login to the Online Edition of your text at www.atomicdog.com to find additional resources located in the Study Guide at the end of each chapter.

Analysis

OUTLINE

By the time you get to the analysis of your data, most of the really difficult work has been done. It's much more difficult to define the research problem; develop and implement a sampling plan; conceptualize, operationalize, and test your measures; and develop a design structure. If you have done this work well, the analysis of the data is usually straightforward.

In most social research, data analysis involves three major steps, performed in roughly this order:

- Data preparation involves checking or logging the data in, checking the data for accuracy, entering the data into the computer, transforming the data, and developing and documenting a database structure that integrates the various measures.
- Descriptive statistics describe the basic features of the data in a study. They provide simple summaries about the sample and the measures. Together with simple graphics analysis, they form the basis of virtually every **quantitative** analysis of data. With descriptive statistics, you are simply describing what is—what the data shows.
- Statistical analysis of the research design tests your research hypotheses. In experimental and quasi-experimental designs, you use statistics to determine whether the program or treatment has a statistically detectable effect.

quantitative
The numerical representation of some object. A quantitative variable is any variable that is measured using numbers.

You should note that the term *statistics* encompasses both descriptive analyses of your data and inferential analyses designed to test formal hypotheses. The descriptive statistics that you actually look at can be voluminous. In most write-ups, you carefully select and organize these statistics into summary tables and graphs that show only the most relevant or important information. After you describe the data, you construct specific analyses for each of the research questions or hypotheses raised in your research design. In most analysis write-ups, it's especially critical that you not miss the forest for the trees. If you present too much detail, the reader may not be able to follow the central line of the results. Often extensive analysis details are appropriately relegated to appendices, reserving only the most critical analysis summaries for the body of the report itself.

This chapter discusses the basics of data analysis. I save the topic of data analysis for your research design for the next chapter. However, I'll warn you right now that this is not a statistics text. I'll cover lots of statistics, some elementary and some advanced, but I'm not trying to teach you statistics here. Instead, I'm trying to get you to think about data analysis and how it fits into the broader context of your research.

conclusion validity
The degree to which conclusions you reach about relationships in your data are reasonable.

I'll begin this chapter by discussing **conclusion validity**, the validity of inferences you draw from your data analyses. This will give you an understanding of some of the key principles involved in any research analysis. Then I'll cover the often-overlooked issue of data preparation. This includes all of the steps involved in cleaning and organizing the data for analysis. I then introduce the basic descriptive statistics and consider some general analysis issues that set the stage for consideration of the analysis of the major research designs in the Chapter 14.

12-1 Conclusion Validity

Of the four types of validity (see also **internal validity**, **construct validity**, and **external validity**), conclusion validity is undoubtedly the least considered and most misunderstood—probably due to the fact that it was originally labeled statistical conclusion validity and you know how even the mere mention of the word *statistics* will scare off most of the human race!

In many ways, conclusion validity is the most important of the four validity types because it is relevant whenever you are trying to decide whether there is a relationship in your observations (and that's one of the most basic aspects of any analysis). Perhaps I should start with an attempt at a definition:

> Conclusion validity is the degree to which conclusions you reach about relationships in your data are reasonable.

For instance, if you're doing a study that looks at the relationship between socioeconomic status (SES) and attitudes about capital punishment, you eventually want to reach some conclusion. Based on your data, you might conclude that there is a positive relationship—that persons with higher SES tend to have a more positive view of capital punishment, whereas those with lower SES tend to be more opposed. Conclusion validity in this case is the degree to which that conclusion or inference is credible or believable.

Although conclusion validity was originally thought to be a statistical-inference issue, it has become more apparent that it is also relevant in **qualitative** research. For example, in an observational field study of homeless adolescents, a researcher might, on the basis of field notes, see a pattern that suggests that teenagers on the street who use drugs are more likely to be involved in more complex social networks and to interact with a more varied group of people than the nondrug users. Although this conclusion or inference may be based entirely on qualitative observational data, you can ask whether it has conclusion validity, that is, whether it is a reasonable conclusion about the relationship inferred from the observations.

Whenever you investigate a relationship, you essentially have two possible conclusions: either there is a relationship in your data, or there isn't. In either case, however, you could be wrong in your conclusion. You might conclude that there is a relationship when in fact, there is not; or you might infer that no relationship exists when in fact one does (but you didn't detect it).

It's important to realize that conclusion validity is an issue whenever you are talking about a relationship, even when the relationship is between some program (or treatment) and some outcome. In other words, conclusion validity also pertains to **causal** relationships. How do you distinguish it from internal validity, which is also involved with causal relationships? Conclusion validity is concerned only with whether there is a relationship; internal validity assumes you have demonstrated a relationship and is concerned with whether that relationship is causal. For instance, in a program evaluation, you might conclude that there is a positive relationship between your educational program and achievement test scores; students in the program get higher scores and students not in the program get lower ones. Conclusion validity is essentially concerned with whether that relationship is a reasonable one or not, given the data. However, it is possible to conclude that, while a relationship exists between the program and outcome, the program didn't cause the outcome. Perhaps some other factor, and not your program, was responsible for the outcome in this study. For instance, the observed differences in the outcome could be due to the fact that the program group was smarter than the comparison group

internal validity
The approximate truth of inferences regarding cause-effect or causal relationships.

construct validity
The degree to which inferences can legitimately be made from the operationalizations in your study to the theoretical constructs on which those operationalizations are based.

external validity
The degree to which the conclusions in your study would hold for other persons in other places and at other times.

qualitative
The descriptive nonnumerical characteristic of some object. A qualitative variable is a descriptive nonnumerical observation.

causal
Pertaining to a cause-effect relationship.

to begin with. Your observed posttest differences between these groups could be due to this initial difference and not be the result of your program. This issue—the possibility that some factor other than your program caused the outcome—is what internal validity is all about. So, it is possible that in a study you can conclude that your program and outcome are related (conclusion validity) and also conclude that the outcome was caused by some factor other than the program (you don't have internal validity).

I'll begin this discussion by considering the major threats to conclusion validity—the different reasons you might be wrong in concluding that there is or isn't a relationship. You'll see that there are several key reasons why reaching conclusions about relationships is so difficult. One major problem is that it is often hard to see a relationship because your measures or observations have low **reliability**; they are too weak relative to all of the noise in the environment. Another issue is that the relationship you are looking for may be a weak one and seeing it is a bit like looking for a needle in the haystack. Sometimes the problem is that you just didn't collect enough information to see the relationship even if it is there. All of these problems are related to the idea of **statistical power**, so I'll spend some time trying to explain what power is in this context. Finally, you need to recognize that you have some control over your ability to detect relationships, and I'll conclude with some suggestions for improving conclusion validity.

12-1a Threats to Conclusion Validity

A **threat to conclusion validity** is any factor that can lead you to reach an incorrect conclusion about a relationship in your observations. You can essentially make two kinds of errors about relationships:

- You can conclude that there is no relationship when in fact there is. (You missed the relationship or didn't see it.)
- You can conclude that there is a relationship when in fact there is not. (You're seeing things that aren't there!)

Most threats to conclusion validity have to do with the first problem. Why? Maybe it's because it's so hard in most research to find relationships in data in the first place that it's not as big or frequent a problem; researchers tend to have more problems finding the needle in the haystack than seeing things that aren't there! So, I'll divide the threats by the type of error with which they are associated.

Type I Error: Finding a Relationship When There Is Not One (or Seeing Things That Aren't There)
In anything but the most trivial research study, the researcher spends a considerable amount of time analyzing the data for relationships. Of course, it's important to conduct a thorough analysis, but most people are well aware of the fact that if you play with the data long enough, you can often turn up results that support or corroborate your hypotheses. In more everyday terms, you fish for a specific result by analyzing the data repeatedly under slightly differing conditions or assumptions.

In statistical analysis, you attempt to determine the probability that your finding is a real one or a chance finding. In fact, you often use this probability to decide whether to accept the statistical result as evidence that there is a relationship. In the social sciences, researchers often use the rather arbitrary value, known as the **.05 level of significance**, to decide whether their result is credible or could be considered a fluke. Essentially, the value .05 means that the result you got could be expected to occur by chance at least 5 times out of every 100 times you ran the statistical analysis.

The probability assumption that underlies most statistical analyses assumes that each analysis is independent of the other. However, that may not be true when you conduct multiple analyses of the same data. For instance, let's say you conduct

---

reliability
The repeatability or consistency of a measure. More technically, reliability is the ratio of the variability in true scores to the variability in the observed scores. In more approximate terms, reliability is the proportion of truth in what you measure as opposed to the proportion of error in measurement.

statistical power
The probability of correctly concluding that there is a treatment or program effect in your data.

threat to conclusion validity
Any factor that can lead you to reach an incorrect conclusion about a relationship in your observations.

.05 level of significance
The significance level. Specifically, alpha is the Type I error, or the probability of concluding that there is a treatment effect when, in reality, there is not.

20 statistical tests and for each one you use the .05 level criterion for deciding whether you are observing a relationship. For each test, the odds are 5 out of 100 that you will see a relationship even if there is not one there. (That's what it means to say that the result could be due to chance.) Odds of 5 out of 100 are equal to the fraction 5/100, which is also equal to 1 out of 20. Now, in this example, you conduct 20 separate analyses. Let's say that you find that of the 20 results, only 1 is statistically significant at the .05 level. Does that mean you have found a statistically significant relationship? If you had done only the one analysis, you might conclude that you found a relationship in that result. However, if you did 20 analyses, you would expect to find one of them significant by chance alone, even if no real relationship exists in the data. This threat to conclusion validity is called the **fishing and the error rate problem**. The basic problem is that you were fishing by conducting multiple analyses and treating each one as though it was independent. Instead, when you conduct multiple analyses, you should adjust the error rate (the significance level) to reflect the number of analyses you are doing. The bottom line here is that you are more likely to see a relationship when there isn't one when you keep reanalyzing your data and don't take your fishing into account when drawing your conclusions.

fishing and the error rate problem
A problem that occurs as a result of conducting multiple analyses and treating each one as independent.

Type II Error: Finding No Relationship When There Is One (or Missing the Needle in the Haystack) When you're looking for the needle in the haystack, you essentially have two basic problems: the tiny needle and too much hay. You can view this as a signal-to-noise ratio problem (Figure 12–1). The signal is the needle—the relationship you are trying to see. The noise consists of all of the factors that make it hard to see the relationship.

There are several important sources of noise, each of which is a threat to conclusion validity. One important threat is *low reliability of measures* (see Section 3-2, Reliability). This can be due to many factors, including poor wording of questions, bad instrument design or layout, illegibility of field notes, and so on. In studies where you are evaluating a program, you can introduce noise through *poor reliability of treatment implementation*. If the program doesn't follow the prescribed procedures or is inconsistently carried out, it will be harder to see relationships between the program and other factors like the outcomes. Noise caused by *random irrelevancies in the setting* can also obscure your ability to see a relationship. In a classroom context, the traffic outside the room, disturbances in the hallway, and countless other irrelevant events can distract the researcher or the participants. The types of people you have in your study can also make it harder to see relationships. The threat here is due to the *random heterogeneity of respondents*. If you have a diverse group of respondents, group members are likely to vary more widely on your measures or

FIGURE 12–1 **The signal-to-noise ratio is analogous to looking for the needle (signal) in the haystack (noise)**

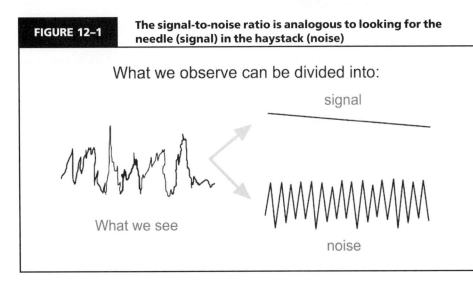

observations. Some of their variability may be related to the phenomenon you are looking at, but at least part of it is likely to constitute individual differences that are irrelevant to the relationship you observe.

All of these threats add variability into the research context and contribute to the noise relative to the signal of the relationship you are looking for. But noise is only one part of the problem. You also have to consider the issue of the signal—the true strength of the relationship. One broad threat to conclusion validity tends to subsume or encompass all of the noise-producing factors mentioned and also takes into account the strength of the signal, the amount of information you collect, and the amount of risk you're willing to take in making a decision about whether a relationship exists. This threat is called *low statistical power*. Because this idea is so important in understanding how to make decisions about relationships, I have included a separate discussion of statistical power later in this chapter.

Problems That Can Lead to Either Conclusion Error Every analysis is based on a variety of assumptions about the nature of the data, the procedures you use to conduct the analysis, and the match between these two. If you are not sensitive to the assumptions behind your analysis, you are likely to draw erroneous conclusions about relationships. In quantitative research, this threat is referred to as the *violated assumptions of statistical tests*. For instance, many statistical analyses are based on the assumption that the data is distributed normally—that the population from which it is drawn would be distributed according to a normal or bell-shaped curve. If that assumption is not true for your data and you use that statistical test, you are likely to get an incorrect estimate of the true relationship. It's not always possible to predict what type of error you might make—seeing a relationship that isn't there or missing one that is.

I believe that the same problem can occur in qualitative research as well. There are assumptions, some of which you may not even realize, behind all qualitative methods. For instance, in interview situations you might assume that the respondents are free to say anything they wish. If that is not true—if the respondent is under covert pressure from supervisors to respond in a certain way—you may erroneously see relationships in the responses that aren't real and/or miss ones that are.

The threats discussed in this section illustrate some of the major difficulties and traps that are involved in one of the most basic areas of research—deciding whether there is a relationship in your data or observations. So, how do you attempt to deal with these threats? Section 12-1c details a number of strategies for improving conclusion validity through minimizing or eliminating these threats.

12-1b Statistical Power

Warning! I am about to launch into some technical, statistical gibberish. I think I can explain statistical power in a way that is understandable, but you will need to have a little patience. This is probably a good section for you read while intermittently applying some classic relaxation techniques—deep breathing, meditation, and so on. I highly recommend reading this in small doses with frequent meditative breaks. So here goes . . .

Four interrelated components influence the conclusions you might reach from a statistical test in a research project:

- *Sample size*, or the number of units (people) accessible to the study
- *Effect size*, or the salience of the treatment relative to the noise in measurement
- **Alpha level** (α, or significance level), or the odds that the observed result is due to chance
- *Power*, or the odds that you will observe a treatment effect when it occurs

If you know the values for any three of these components, it is possible to compute the value of the fourth. For instance, you might want to determine what a

alpha level
The significance level. Specifically, alpha is the Type I error, or the probability of concluding that there is a treatment effect when, in reality, there is not.

FIGURE 12–2   The statistical inference decision matrix

In reality → / What we conclude ↓	Null true Alternative false In reality... • There is no real program effect • There is no difference, gain • Our theory is wrong	Null false Alternative true In reality... • There is a real program effect • There is a difference, gain • Our theory is correct
Accept null **Reject alternative** We <u>say</u>... • There is no real program effect • There is no difference, gain • Our theory is wrong	$1 - \alpha$ (e.g., .95) **THE CONFIDENCE LEVEL** The odds of saying there is <u>no</u> effect or gain when in fact there is none # of times out of 100 when there is <u>no</u> effect, we'll say there is none	β (e.g., .20) **TYPE II ERROR** The odds of saying there is <u>no</u> effect or gain when in fact there is one # of times out of 100 when there <u>is</u> an effect, we'll say there is none
Reject null **Accept alternative** We <u>say</u>... • There is a real program effect • There is a difference, gain • Our theory is correct	α (e.g., .05) **TYPE I ERROR** The odds of saying there <u>is</u> an effect or gain when in fact there is none # of times out of 100 when there is <u>no</u> effect, we'll say there is one	$1 - \beta$ (e.g., .80) **POWER** The odds of saying there <u>is</u> an effect or gain when in fact there is one # of times out of 100 when there <u>is</u> an effect, we'll say there is one

reasonable sample size would be for a study. If you could make reasonable estimates of the effect size, alpha level, and power, it would be simple to compute (or, more likely, look up in a table) the sample size. Fortunately, there are conventional guidelines to give you a starting point for your alpha level and power. These will be presented later in this chapter. However, since the advent of a research synthesis strategy called *meta-analysis* in the late 1970s, the importance of carefully considering effect sizes in both the planning and interpretive stages of research has been elevated considerably. In addition, there is much more appreciation of the distinction between practical or clinical significance and statistical significance. You will learn more about these matters when you get to Chapter 16, but for now I advise you to look carefully at prior studies in your topic area to see if there might be any consensus about what constitutes a meaningful change on a measure you are considering using, or how strong a relationship between constructs would be predicted by a reasonable theory or prior studies.

Some of these components are easier to manipulate than others, depending on the project's circumstances. For example, if the project is an evaluation of an educational program or counseling program with a specific number of available consumers, the sample size is set or predetermined, or, if the drug dosage in a program has to be small due to its potential negative side effects, the effect size may consequently be small. The goal is to achieve a balance of the four components that allows the maximum level of power to detect an effect if one exists, given programmatic, logistical, or financial constraints on the other components.

Figure 12–2 shows the basic decision matrix involved in any statistical conclusion. What do I mean by a *decision matrix*? It is a table that shows what decisions or conclusions you can reach from any statistical analysis and how these are related to reality. All statistical conclusions involve constructing two mutually exclusive hypotheses, termed the null (labeled H_0) and alternative (labeled H_1) hypothesis (see Chapter 1). Together, the **hypotheses** describe all possible outcomes with respect to the inference. The central decision involves determining which hypothesis to accept and which to reject. (Because the two are mutually exclusive and

hypothesis
A specific statement of prediction.

exhaustive, you will always have to accept one and reject the other.) For instance, in the typical case, the null hypothesis might be:

H_0: Program Effect $= 0$

whereas the alternative might be:

H_1: Program Effect $<> 0$

When you conduct a statistical analysis to test this hypothesis, you have to accept one of these: either your program works (H_1) or it doesn't (H_0). When you accept one, you automatically reject the other. This is what you conclude, but things are a little more complicated than this. Just because you conclude something doesn't make it true. (Remember your parents telling you this at some point?) Reality often has a way of being different from what we think it is. So, the other aspect of your decision has to do with the reality of the conclusion. Like your statistical conclusion, this can be expressed in only two ways—the null hypothesis is true or the alternative one is true. That's it. Those are the only options.

You should now be getting an inkling of where I am going with this somewhat convoluted presentation. The statistical decision matrix shown in Figure 12–2 shows the four possible options made by combining each possible conclusion with each possible reality.

Figure 12–2 is a complex figure that you should take some time to study. In fact, I think you should prop it up on a table, sit down in front of it cross-legged, and just stare at it for a few hours.

First, look at the header row (the shaded area). This row depicts reality—whether there really is a program effect, difference, or gain. Of course, the problem is that you never know for sure what is really happening (unless you're God). Nevertheless, because you have set up mutually exclusive hypotheses, one must be right and one must be wrong. Therefore, consider this the view from God's position, knowing which hypothesis is correct—isn't it great to get a chance to play God? The first column of the 2 × 2 table shows the case where the program does not have an effect; the second column shows where it does have an effect or make a difference.

The left header column describes the world mortals live in. Regardless of what's true, you have to make decisions about which of your hypotheses is correct. This header column describes the two decisions you can reach—that your program had no effect (the first row of the 2 × 2 table) or that it did have an effect (the second row).

Now, let's examine the cells of the 2 × 2 table. The first thing to recognize is that two of the cells represent a correct conclusion and two of them represent an error. If you say there is no relationship or effect (accept the null) and there is in reality no relationship or effect, you're in the upper-left cell and you are correct. If you say a program effect exists (accept the alternative) and there is in reality a program effect, you're in the lower-right cell and you are correct. Those are the two possible correct conclusions. Now consider the two errors. If you say there is a relationship or effect and there is not, you're in the cell on the lower left and you're wrong. We call this type of error a Type I error. (Pretty original, huh?) It is like seeing things that aren't there (as described earlier in this chapter). You're seeing an effect but you're wrong. If you say there is no effect and in fact there is an effect, you're in the cell on the upper right and you're wrong. We call this type of error—guess what—a Type II error. This type of error is like not seeing the needle in the haystack as described earlier in this chapter. There is an effect in reality, but you couldn't see it.

Each cell shows the Greek symbol used to name that cell. (You knew there had to be Greek symbols here. Statisticians can't even write their own names without using Greek letters.) Notice that the columns sum to 1 ($\alpha + (1 - \alpha) = 1$ and $\beta + (1 - \beta) = 1$). (Having trouble adding in Greek? Just keep in mind that $\alpha - \alpha = 0$, no matter what language you use for the symbol α.) Why can you sum down the columns, but not across the rows? Because if one column is true, the other is irrelevant; if the program has a real effect (the right column), it can't, at the same time, not have one. Reality can be in only one column or the other (even though, given the reality, you could be in either row). Therefore, the odds or probabilities have to sum to 1 for each column because the two rows in each column describe the only possible decisions (accept or reject the null/alternative) for each possible reality.

Below the Greek symbol is a typical value for that cell. You should especially note the values in the bottom two cells. The value of α is typically set at .05 in the social sciences. A newer, but growing, tradition is to try to achieve a standard for statistical power of at least .80. Below the typical values is the name typically given for that cell (in caps). If you weren't paying attention a few paragraphs ago, I'll give you one more chance to note that two of the cells describe errors—you reach the wrong conclusion—and in the other two cells, you reach the correct conclusion. Sometimes it's hard to remember which error is Type I and which is Type II. If you keep in mind that Type I is the same as the α, or significance level, it might help you remember that both involve seeing things that aren't there. People are more likely to be susceptible to a Type I error because they almost always want to conclude that their program works. If they find a statistical effect, they tend to advertise it loudly. On the other hand, people probably check more thoroughly for Type II errors because when they find that the program was not demonstrably effective, they immediately want to find out why. (In this case, you might hope to show that you had low power and high β—that the odds of saying there was no treatment effect even when there was were too high.) Following the capitalized common name are two ways of describing the value of each cell: one in terms of outcomes and one in terms of theory testing. In italics, I give an example of how to express the numerical value in words.

To better understand the strange relationships between the two columns, think about what happens if you want to increase your power in a study. As you increase power, you increase the chances that you are going to find an effect if it's there (wind up in the bottom row). However, if you increase the chances of winding up in the bottom row, you must, at the same time, increase the chances of making a Type I error! Although you can't sum to 1 across rows, there is clearly a relationship. Since you usually want high power *and* low Type I error, you should be able to appreciate that you have a built-in tension here. (Now might be a good moment for a meditation break. Reread the last paragraph over and over until it begins to make sense!)

We often talk about alpha (α) and beta (β) using the language of higher and lower. For instance, you might talk about the advantages of a higher or lower α level in a study. You have to be careful about interpreting the meaning of these terms. When you talk about *higher* α levels, you mean that you are *increasing* the chance of a Type I error. Therefore, a *lower* α level actually means that you are conducting a *more rigorous* test.

With all of this in mind, let's consider a few common associations evident in the table. You should convince yourself of the following (each of these is it's own little meditation exercise):

- The lower the α, the lower the power. The higher the α, the higher the power.
- The lower the α, the less likely it is that you will make a Type I error (reject the null when it's true).
- The lower the α, the more rigorous the test.
- An α of .01 (compared with .05 or .10) means the researcher is being relatively careful and is willing to risk being wrong only 1 in a 100 times in rejecting the null when it's true (saying there's an effect when there really isn't).
- An α of .01 (compared with .05 or .10) limits the chances of ending up in the bottom row, of concluding that the program has an effect. This means that statistical power and the chances of making a Type I error are lower.
- An α of .01 means there is a 99 percent chance of saying there is no difference when there in fact is no difference (being in the upper-left box).

- Increasing α (for example from .01 to .05 or .10) increases the chances of making a Type I error (saying there is a difference when there is not), decreases the chances of making a Type II error (saying there is no difference when there is), and decreases the rigor of the test.
- Increasing α (for example from .01 to .05 or .10) increases power because you will be rejecting the null more often (accepting the alternative) and consequently, when the alternative is true, there is a greater chance of accepting it (power).

12-1c Improving Conclusion Validity

So let's say you have a potential problem ensuring that you reach credible conclusions about relationships in your data. What can you do about it? Here are some general guidelines you can follow in designing your study that will help improve conclusion validity.

- *Good statistical power.* The rule of thumb in social research is that you want statistical power to be greater than 0.8 in value (see the previous discussion on statistical power). That is, you want to have at least 80 chances out of 100 of finding a relationship when there is one. As pointed out in the discussion of statistical power, several factors interact to affect power. One thing you can usually do is collect more information—use a larger sample size. Of course, you have to weigh the gain in power against the time and expense of having more participants or gathering more data. The second thing you can do is increase your risk of making a Type I error—increase the chance that you will find a relationship when it's not there. In practical terms, you can do that statistically by raising the alpha level. For instance, instead of using a 0.05 significance level, you might use 0.10 as your cutoff point. Finally, you can increase the effect size. Since the effect size is a ratio of the signal of the relationship to the noise in the context, there are two broad strategies here. To raise the signal, you can increase the salience of the relationship itself. This is especially true in experimental contexts where you are looking at the effects of a program or treatment. If you increase the dosage of the program (for example, increase the hours spent in training or the number of training sessions), it will be easier to see the effect when the treatment is stronger. The other option is to decrease the noise (or, put another way, increase reliability).
- *Good reliability.* Reliability (see Section 3-30) is related to the idea of noise or error that obscures your ability to see a relationship. In general, you can improve reliability by doing a better job of constructing measurement instruments, by increasing the number of questions on a scale, or by reducing situational distractions in the measurement context. When you improve reliability, you reduce noise, which increases your statistical power and improves conclusion validity.
- *Good implementation.* When you are studying the effects of interventions, treatments, or programs, you can improve conclusion validity by ensuring good implementation. You accomplish this by training program deliverers and standardizing the protocols for administering the program.

12-2 Data Preparation

Data preparation involves checking or logging the data in, checking the data for accuracy, entering the data into the computer, transforming the data, and developing and documenting a database structure that integrates the various measures.

12-2a Logging the Data

In any research project, you might have data coming from several different sources at different times as in the following examples:

- Mail survey returns
- Coded-interview data
- Pretest or posttest data
- Observational data

In all but the simplest of studies, you need to set up a procedure for logging the information and keeping track of it until you are ready to do a comprehensive data analysis. Different researchers differ in how they keep track of incoming data. In most cases, you will want to set up a database that enables you to assess, at any time, which data is already entered and which still needs to be entered. You could do this with any standard computerized database program (such as Microsoft Access or Claris Filemaker), although this requires familiarity with such programs, or you can accomplish this using standard statistical programs (for example, SPSS, SAS, Minitab, or Datadesk) and running simple descriptive analyses to get reports on data status. It is also critical that the data analyst retain the original data records—returned surveys, field notes, test protocols, and so on—for a reasonable time. Most professional researchers retain such records for at least 5 to 7 years. For important or expensive studies, the original data might be stored in a data archive. The data analyst should always be able to trace a result from a data analysis back to the original forms on which the data was collected. A database for logging incoming data is a critical component in good research record keeping.

12-2b Checking the Data for Accuracy

As soon as you receive the data, you should screen it for accuracy. In some circumstances, doing this right away allows you to go back to the sample to clarify any problems or errors. You should ask the following questions as part of this initial data screening:

- Are the responses legible/readable?
- Are all important questions answered?
- Are the responses complete?
- Is all relevant contextual information included (for example, date, time, place, and researcher)?

In most social research, quality of measurement is a major issue. Ensuring that the data collection process does not contribute inaccuracies helps ensure the overall quality of subsequent analyses.

12-2c Developing a Database Structure

The database structure is the manner in which you intend to store the data for the study so that it can be accessed in subsequent data analyses. You might use the same structure you used for logging in the data; or in large complex studies, you might have one structure for logging data and another for storing it. As mentioned previously, there are generally two options for storing data on computer: database programs and statistical programs. Usually database programs are the more complex of the two to learn and operate, but they allow you greater flexibility in manipulating the data.

In every research project, you should generate a printed **codebook** that describes the data and indicates where and how it can be accessed. At a minimum, the codebook should include the following items for each variable:

- Variable name
- Variable description

codebook
A written description of the data that describes each variable and indicates where and how it can be accessed.

- Variable format (number, data, text)
- Instrument/method of collection
- Date collected
- Respondent or group
- Variable location (in database)
- Notes

The codebook is an indispensable tool for the analysis team. Together with the database, it should provide comprehensive documentation that enables other researchers who might subsequently want to analyze the data to do so without any additional information.

12-2d Entering the Data into the Computer

You can enter data into a computer in a variety of ways. Probably the easiest is to just type the data in directly. To ensure a high level of data accuracy, you should use a procedure called **double entry**. In this procedure, you enter the data once. Then, you use a special program that allows you to enter the data a second time and checks the second entries against the first. If there is a discrepancy, the program notifies you and enables you to determine which is the correct entry. This double-entry procedure significantly reduces entry errors. However, these double-entry programs are not widely available and require some training. An alternative is to enter the data once and set up a procedure for checking the data for accuracy. For instance, you might spot-check records on a random basis.

After you enter the data, you will use various programs to summarize the data that enable you to check that all the data falls within acceptable limits and boundaries. For instance, such summaries enable you to spot whether there are persons whose age is 601 or whether anyone entered a 7 where you expect a 1 to 5 response.

12-2e Data Transformations

After the data is entered, it is almost always necessary to transform the raw data into variables that are usable in the analyses. This is often accomplished by using a transformation, that is, by transforming the original data into a form that is more useful or usable. There are a variety of transformations that you might perform. The following are some of the more common ones:

- *Missing values.* Many analysis programs automatically treat blank values as missing. In others, you need to designate specific values to represent missing values. For instance, you might use a value of −99 to indicate that the item is missing. You need to check the specific program you are using to determine how to handle missing values.
- *Item reversals.* On scales and surveys, the use of reversal items (see Chapters 4 and 5) can help reduce the possibility of a response set. When you analyze the data, you want all scores for scale items to be in the same direction, where high scores mean the same thing and low scores mean the same thing. In these cases, you have to reverse the ratings for some of the scale items. For instance, let's say you had a 5-point response scale for a self-esteem measure where 1 meant strongly disagree and 5 meant strongly agree. One item is "I generally feel good about myself." If respondents strongly agree with this item, they will put a 5, and this value would be indicative of higher self-esteem. Alternatively, consider an item like "Sometimes I feel like I'm not worth much as a person." Here, if a respondent strongly agrees by rating this a 5, it would indicate low self-esteem. To compare these two items, you would reverse the scores. (Probably you'd reverse the latter item so that high values always indicate higher self-esteem.) You want a transformation where if the original value was 1, it's changed to 5; 2 is changed to 4; 3 remains the same; 4 is changed to 2; and 5 is

double entry
An automated method for checking data-entry accuracy in which you enter data once and then enter it a second time, with the software automatically stopping each time a discrepancy is detected until the data enterer resolves the discrepancy. This procedure assures extremely high rates of data entry accuracy, although it requires twice as long for data entry.

changed to 1. Although you could program these changes as separate state-ments in most programs, it's easier to do this with a simple formula like the following:

$$\text{New Value} = (\text{High Value} + 1) - \text{Original Value}$$

In our example, the *high value* for the scale is 5; so to get the new (trans-formed) scale value, you simply subtract the *original value* on each reversal item from 6 (that is, 5 + 1).

- *Scale totals.* After you transform any individual scale items, you will often want to add or average across individual items to get a total score for the scale.
- *Categories.* You will want to collapse many variables into categories. For instance, you may want to collapse income estimates (in dollar amounts) into income ranges.

12-2f Dealing with Missing Data

Missing data can be a major threat to conclusion validity, depending on how much data is missing and why it is missing. As always, prevention is better than cure, and when it comes to research, good planning can help prevent missing data from becoming a major issue. If you have carefully planned your study so that it is feasible (for example, you have good access to your sample and your study is not too long, boring, or difficult, and might even be rewarding in some way), then you may have an inconsequential problem and can proceed with your analysis as planned (for example, 5 percent or fewer missing cases from a well-powered large study). If your study is at the other extreme and you end up with a relatively sparse representation of your sampling frame, then it will be difficult to convince anyone that what you find in your data is a valid representation of the sample much less the population, no matter how clever your analysis is. In that case you might want to go back to the design drawing board and consider this a valuable pilot. More often than not, you will be somewhere in the middle, in a situation where you have invested available resources and think you have enough data to analyze. The questions that need to be addressed in such cases are: "Who or what is missing, why, and what effect might it have on the results of the analysis?" So in effect you have to address an empirical question about the quality of your data before you address the substantive questions of your study.

There are many reasons that data may be missing, and you may find missing data issues at the level of the item (for example, some items might not be relevant, may be badly worded, or may be so sensitive that people do not want to answer) or at the level of the case (for example, data forms may have been missing or lost; some respondents may have limited reading ability or be fatigued, ill, or disabled; or some may have low motivation to help). For example, imagine the challenges of getting complete data if you happen to want to study a 10-session method of ther-apy for families with troubled adolescents. In such a study, you may have to deal with missing data for certain questions, forms, therapists, dates, families, or individ-ual family members. It is wise to examine early returns on a study, especially a longi-tudinal study. In addition to alerting you to any potential abnormalities in data **distributions**, you may detect an obvious problem (for example, the last page of a questionnaire). If you have found such an issue early in the data collection process, you can possibly take steps to correct it.

If there is nothing that can be done procedurally to get more complete reports, then you must work with what you have. Fortunately, methodologists have provided us with some good ideas about how to assess the impact of "missingness" as well as procedures for replacing missing values with estimates. The essential issue is whether the missing data can be considered to be randomly missing. That is, if there is a systematic pattern in the missing data related to important characteristics of your sample or relationships among variables, then your conclusions will be

distribution
The manner in which a variable takes different values in your data.

biased (less valid). This type of situation is often referred to as one of *nonignorable missing data*. The default mechanism for handling missing data in most statistical programs is to delete all cases that have missing data on any variable. This procedure, known as *listwise deletion*, leaves you with just the complete cases to analyze. If the resulting complete cases are essentially a random subsample of your entire dataset, then you can proceed with the analysis you planned to do and not worry about introducing bias. This may be the rare case, however, and most researchers will want to consider alternatives to use as many cases as possible. Let's first consider the case of the missing scale item, and then the situation when one or more variables have missing data.

If you are using well-developed multi-item scales and have the scoring manuals or original articles describing the measure, then you may already have a standardized way to estimate the total score from the items that were completed. However, if you do not have the benefit of standardized procedures for handling missing data for a particular scale, or if your missing data is related to individual items that are not part of larger summary scales, you will need to examine the pattern of missingness in your data and consider your options. SPSS includes a missing values analysis module that allows you to examine patterns of data completion in a descriptive way, and it also includes a test that will allow you to see if your data significantly depart from the missing completely at random assumption (Little's MCAR test). If the chi-square test statistic is not significant, then you can assume that the data are missing completely at random and proceed with confidence using the listwise deletion procedure.

If it appears that the missing data are not random, then a method of substituting an estimate can be considered. Substituting an estimated value is called **imputation**. Many people have heard the rule of thumb advising that you "plug in the **mean**," but research has shown that this method is biased, as are other methods, with some important exceptions. Two methods that can provide relatively unbiased estimates for missing values are maximum likelihood procedures and multiple imputation methods (Allison, 2002). Popular software, such as SPSS and SAS, include procedures for generating substitute values based on one or both of these methods. Finally, structural equation modeling programs such as AMOS can be used to generate unbiased estimates.

imputation
Substituting an estimated value for a missing one so that an analysis can include the variable.

12-3 Descriptive Statistics

Descriptive statistics describe the basic features of the data in a study. They provide simple summaries about the sample and the measures. Together with simple graphics analysis, they form the basis of virtually every quantitative analysis of data.

Descriptive statistics present quantitative descriptions in a manageable form. In a research study, you may have many measures, or you might measure a large number of people on any given measure. Descriptive statistics help you summarize large amounts of data in a sensible way. Each descriptive statistic reduces data into a simpler summary. For instance, consider a simple number used to summarize how well a batter is performing in baseball—the batting average. This single number is the number of hits divided by the number of times at bat (reported to three significant digits). A batter who is hitting .333 is getting a hit one time in every three at bats. One batting .250 is hitting one time in four. The single number describes a large number of discrete events. Or consider the scourge of many students—the grade point average (GPA). This single number describes the general performance of a student across a potentially wide range of course experiences.

Every time you try to describe a large set of observations with a single indicator, you run the risk of distorting the original data or losing important detail. The batting average doesn't tell you whether batters hit home runs or singles. It doesn't tell whether they've been in a slump or on a streak. The GPAs don't tell you whether

descriptive statistics
Statistics used to describe the basic features of the data in a study.

the students were in difficult courses or easy ones, or whether the courses were in their major field or in other disciplines. Even given these limitations, descriptive statistics provide a powerful summary that enables comparisons across people or other units.

A single variable has three major characteristics that are typically described as follows:

- Distribution
- **Central tendency**
- **Dispersion**

In most situations, you would describe all three of these characteristics for each of the variables in your study.

12-3a The Distribution

The distribution is a summary of the frequency of individual values or ranges of values for a variable. The simplest distribution lists every value of a variable and the number of persons who had each value. For instance, a typical way to describe the distribution of college students is by year in college, listing the number or percent of students at each of the four years. Or, you describe gender by listing the number or percent of males and females. In these cases, the variable has few enough values that you can list each one and summarize how many sample cases had the value. But what do you do for a variable like income or GPA? These variables have a large number of possible values, with relatively few people having each one. In this case, you group the raw scores into categories according to ranges of values. For instance, you might look at GPA according to the letter grade ranges, or you might group income into four or five ranges of income values.

One of the most common ways to describe a single variable is with a **frequency distribution**. Depending on the particular variable, all of the data values might be represented, or you might group the values into categories first. (For example, with age, price, or temperature variables, it is usually not sensible to determine the frequencies for each value. Rather, the values are grouped into ranges and the frequencies determined.) Frequency distributions can be depicted in two ways, as a table or as a graph. Figure 12–3a shows an age frequency distribution with five categories of age ranges defined. The same frequency distribution can be depicted in a graph, as shown in Figure 12–3b. This type of graph is often referred to as a histogram or bar chart.

central tendency
An estimate of the center of a distribution of values. The most usual measures of central tendency are the mean, median, and mode.

dispersion
The spread of the values around the central tendency. The two common measures of dispersion are the range and the standard deviation.

frequency distribution
A summary of the frequency of individual values or ranges of values for a variable.

FIGURE 12–3a	A frequency distribution in table form

Category	Percent
Under 35	9%
36 - 45	21%
46 - 55	45%
56 - 65	19%
66 +	6%

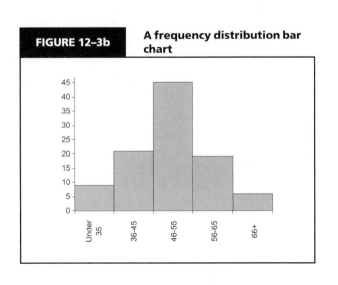

FIGURE 12–3b A frequency distribution bar chart

Distributions can also be displayed using percentages. For example, you could use percentages to describe the following:

- Percentage of people in different income levels
- Percentage of people in different age ranges
- Percentage of people in different ranges of standardized test scores

12-3b Central Tendency

The central tendency of a distribution is an estimate of the center of a distribution of values. There are three major types of estimates of central tendency:

- Mean
- Median
- Mode

mean
A description of the central tendency in which you add all the values and divide by the number of values.

The **mean**, or average is probably the most commonly used method of describing central tendency. To compute the mean, all you do is add up all the values and divide by the number of values. For example, the mean, or average, quiz score is determined by summing all the scores and dividing by the number of students taking the exam. Consider the test score values:

15, 20, 21, 20, 36, 15, 25, 15

The sum of these eight values is 167, so the mean is $167/8 = 20.875$.

median
The middle number in a series of numbers or the score found at the exact middle or fiftieth percentile of the set of values. One way to compute the median is

The **median** is the score found at the exact middle of the set of values. One way to compute the median is to list all scores in numerical order and then locate the score in the center of the sample. For example, if there are 500 scores in the list, score number 250 would be the median. If you order the eight scores shown previously, you would get

15, 15, 15, 20, 20, 21, 25, 36

There are eight scores and score number 4 and number 5 represent the halfway point. Since both of these scores are 20, the median is 20. If the two middle scores had different values, you would have to interpolate to determine the median.

mode
The most frequently occurring value in the set of scores.

The **mode** is the most frequently occurring value in the set of scores. To determine the mode, you might again order the scores as shown previously and then count each one. The most frequently occurring value is the mode. In our example, the value 15 occurs three times and is the mode. In some distributions, there is more than one modal value. For instance, in a bimodal distribution, two values occur most frequently.

Notice that for the same set of eight scores, we got three different values—20.875, 20, and 15—for the mean, median, and mode, respectively. If the distribution is truly normal (bell-shaped), the mean, median, and mode are all equal to each other.

12-3c Dispersion or Variability

range
The highest value minus the lowest value.

Dispersion refers to the spread of the values around the central tendency. The two common measures of dispersion are the **range** and the **standard deviation**. The range is simply the highest value minus the lowest value. In the previous example distribution, the high value is 36 and the low is 15, so the range is $36 - 15 = 21$.

standard deviation
The spread or variability of the scores around their average in a *single sample*. The standard deviation, often abbreviated sd, is mathematically the square root of the variance. The standard deviation and variance both measure dispersion, but because the standard deviation is measured in the same units as the original measure and the variance is measured in squared units, the standard deviation is usually more directly interpretable and meaningful.

The standard deviation is a more accurate and detailed estimate of dispersion because an outlier can greatly exaggerate the range (as was true in this example where the single outlier value of 36 stands apart from the rest of the values). The standard deviation shows the relation that set of scores has to the mean of the sample. Again, let's take the set of scores:

15, 20, 21, 20, 36, 15, 25, 15

To compute the standard deviation, you first find the distance between each value and the mean. You know from before that the mean is 20.875. So, the differences from the mean are:

$$15 - 20.875 = -5.875$$
$$20 - 20.875 = -0.875$$
$$21 - 20.875 = +0.125$$
$$20 - 20.875 = -0.875$$
$$36 - 20.875 = +15.125$$
$$15 - 20.875 = -5.875$$
$$25 - 20.875 = +4.125$$
$$15 - 20.875 = -5.875$$

Notice that values that are below the mean have negative discrepancies and values above it have positive ones. Next, you square each discrepancy:

$$-5.875 \times -5.875 = 34.515625$$
$$-0.875 \times -0.875 = 0.765625$$
$$+0.125 \times +0.125 = 0.015625$$
$$-0.875 \times -0.875 = 0.765625$$
$$+15.125 \times 15.125 = 228.765625$$
$$-5.875 \times -5.875 = 34.515625$$
$$+4.125 \times +4.125 = 17.015625$$
$$-5.875 \times -5.875 = 34.515625$$

Now, you take these squares and sum them to get the sum of squares (SS) value. Here, the sum is 350.875. Next, you divide this sum by the number of scores minus 1. Here, the result is 350.875/7 = 50.125. This value is known as the **variance**. To get the standard deviation, you take the square root of the variance (remember that you squared the deviations earlier). This would be = 7.079901129253.

Although this computation may seem convoluted, it's actually quite simple. To see this, consider the formula for the standard deviation shown in Figure 12–4.

In the top part of the ratio, the numerator, notice that each score has the mean subtracted from it, the difference is squared, and the squares are summed. In the bottom part, the denominator, you take the number of scores minus 1. The ratio is

variance
A statistic that describes the variability in the data for a variable. The variance is the spread of the scores around the mean of a distribution. Specifically, the variance is the sum of the squared deviations from the mean divided by the number of observations minus 1.

FIGURE 12–4	Formula for the standard deviation

$$\sqrt{\frac{\Sigma(X - \bar{X})^2}{(n-1)}}$$

where:
X = each score
$\bar{X}$ = the mean or average
n = the number of values
Σ means we sum across the values

TABLE 12–3	Descriptive Statistics for Correlation Calculation Example						
	Variable Mean	Std. Dev.	Variance	Sum	Minimum	Maximum	Range
Height	65.4	4.40574	19.4105	1308	58	75	17
Self-esteem	3.755	0.426090	0.181553	75.1	3.1	4.6	1.5

FIGURE 12–6	Histogram for the self-esteem variable in the example correlation calculation

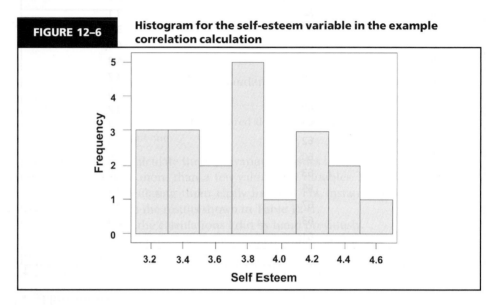

FIGURE 12–7	Bivariate plot for the example correlation calculation

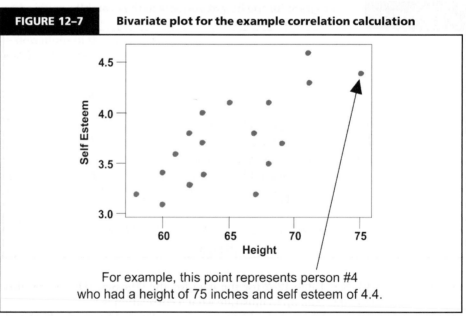

For example, this point represents person #4 who had a height of 75 inches and self esteem of 4.4.

correlation is nothing more than a quantitative estimate of the relationship, you would expect a positive correlation.

What does a positive relationship mean in this context? It means that, in general, higher scores on one variable tend to be paired with higher scores on the other and that lower scores on one variable tend to be paired with lower scores on the other. You should confirm visually that this is generally true in the plot in Figure 12–7.

FIGURE 12–8   The formula for the correlation

$$r = \frac{N\Sigma xy - (\Sigma x)(\Sigma y)}{\sqrt{[N\Sigma x^2 - (\Sigma x)^2][N\Sigma y^2 - (\Sigma y)^2]}}$$

where:

N = number of pairs of scores
Σxy = sum of the products of paired scores
Σx = sum of x scores
Σy = sum of y scores
Σx^2 = sum of squared x scores
Σy^2 = sum of squared y scores

TABLE 12–4   Computations for the Example Correlation Calculation

Person	Height (x)	Self-Esteem (y)	xy	x^2	y^2
1	68	4.1	278.8	4624	16.81
2	71	4.6	326.6	5041	21.16
3	62	3.8	235.6	3844	14.44
4	75	4.4	330	5625	19.36
5	58	3.2	185.6	3364	10.24
6	60	3.1	186	3600	9.61
7	67	3.8	254.6	4489	14.44
8	68	4.1	278.8	4624	16.81
9	71	4.3	305.3	5041	18.49
10	69	3.7	255.3	4761	13.69
11	68	3.5	238	4624	12.25
12	67	3.2	214.4	4489	10.24
13	63	3.7	233.1	3969	13.69
14	62	3.3	204.6	3844	10.89
15	60	3.4	204	3600	11.56
16	63	4.0	252	3969	16
17	65	4.1	266.5	4225	16.81
18	67	3.8	254.6	4489	14.44
19	63	3.4	214.2	3969	11.56
20	61	3.6	219.6	3721	12.96
Sum =	1308	75.1	4937.6	85912	285.45

Calculating the Correlation Now you're ready to compute the correlation value. The formula for the correlation is shown in Figure 12–8.

The symbol r stands for the correlation. Through the magic of mathematics, it turns out that r will always be between -1.0 and $+1.0$. If the correlation is negative, you have a negative relationship; if it's positive, the relationship is positive. (Pretty clever, huh?) You don't need to know how I came up with this formula unless you want to be a statistician. But you probably will need to know how the formula relates to real data—how you can use the formula to compute the correlation. Let's look at the data you need for the formula. Table 12–4 shows the original data with the other necessary columns.

FIGURE 12–9	The parts of the correlation formula with the numerical values from the example

$$N = 20$$
$$\Sigma xy = 4937.6$$
$$\Sigma x = 1308$$
$$\Sigma y = 75.1$$
$$\Sigma x^2 = 85912$$
$$\Sigma y^2 = 285.45$$

FIGURE 12–10	Example of the computation of the correlation

$$r = \frac{20(4937.6) - (1308)(75.1)}{\sqrt{[20(85912) - (1308 * 1308)][20(285.45) - (75.1 * 75.1)]}}$$

$$r = \frac{20(4937.6) - (1308)(75.1)}{\sqrt{[1718240 - 1710864][5709 - 5640.01]}}$$

$$r = \frac{521.2}{\sqrt{[7376][68.99]}}$$

$$r = \frac{521.2}{\sqrt{508870.2}}$$

$$r = \frac{521.2}{713.3514}$$

$$r = .73$$

The first three columns are the same as those in Table 12–2. The next three columns are simple computations based on the height and self-esteem data in the first three columns. The bottom row consists of the sum of each column. This is all the information you need to compute the correlation. Figure 12–9 shows the values from the bottom row of the table (where $N = 20$ people) as they are related to the symbols in the formula:

Now, when you plug these values into the formula in Figure 12–8, you get the following. (I show it here tediously, one step at a time in Figure 12–10.

So, the correlation for the 20 cases is .73, which is a fairly strong positive relationship. I guess there is a relationship between height and self-esteem, at least in this made-up data!

Testing the Significance of a Correlation   After you've computed a correlation, you can determine the probability that the observed correlation occurred by chance. That is, you can conduct a significance test. Most often, you are interested in determining the probability that the correlation is a real one and not a chance occurrence. When you are interested in that, you are testing the mutually exclusive hypotheses:

$H_0 : r = 0$

$H_1 : r \neq 0$

The easiest way to test this hypothesis is to find a statistics book that has a table of critical values of r. (Most introductory statistics texts would have a table like this.) As in all hypothesis testing, you need to first determine the significance level you will use for the test. Here, I'll use the common significance level of $\alpha = .05$. This

TABLE 12–5		Hypothetical Correlation Matrix for 10 Variables								

	C1	C2	C3	C4	C5	C6	C7	C8	C9	C10
C1	1.000									
C2	0.274	1.000								
C3	−0.134	−0.269	1.000							
C4	0.201	−0.153	0.075	1.000						
C5	−0.129	−0.166	0.278	−0.011	1.000					
C6	−0.095	0.280	−0.348	−0.378	−0.009	1.000				
C7	0.171	−0.122	0.288	0.086	0.193	0.002	1.000			
C8	0.219	0.242	−0.380	−0.227	−0.551	0.324	−0.082	1.000		
C9	0.518	0.238	0.002	0.082	−0.015	0.304	0.347	−0.013	1.000	
C10	0.299	0.568	0.165	−0.122	−0.106	−0.169	0.243	0.014	0.352	1.000

means that I am conducting a test where the odds that the correlation occurred by chance are no more than 5 out of 100. Before I look up the critical value in a table, I also have to compute the **degrees of freedom (df)**. The *df* for a correlation is simply equal to $N - 2$ or, in this example, $20 - 2 = 18$. Finally, I have to decide whether I am doing a one-tailed or two-tailed test (see the discussion in Chapter 1). In this example, because I have no strong prior theory to suggest whether the relationship between height and self-esteem would be positive or negative, I'll opt for the two-tailed test. With these three pieces of information—the significance level ($\alpha = .05$), degrees of freedom ($df = 18$), and type of test (two-tailed)—I can now test the significance of the correlation I found. When I look up this value in the handy little table at the back of my statistics book, I find that the critical value is .4438. This means that if my correlation is greater than .4438 or less than −.4438 (remember, this is a two-tailed test), I can conclude that the odds are less than 5 out of 100 that this is a chance occurrence. Since my correlation of .73 is actually quite a bit higher, I conclude that it is not a chance finding and that the correlation is statistically significant (given the parameters of the test). I can reject the null hypothesis and accept the alternative—I have a statistically significant correlation.

degrees of freedom (df)
A statistical term that is a function of the sample size. In the *t*-test formula, for instance, the df is the number of persons in both groups minus 2.

The Correlation Matrix

All I've shown you so far is how to compute a correlation between two variables. In most studies, you usually have more than two variables. Let's say you have a study with 10 interval-level variables and you want to estimate the relationships among all of them (between all possible pairs of variables). In this instance, you have 45 unique correlations to estimate (more later on how I knew that). You could do the computations just completed 45 times to obtain the correlations, or you could use just about any statistics program to automatically compute all 45 with a simple click of the mouse.

I used a simple statistics program to generate random data for 10 variables with 20 cases (persons) for each variable. Then, I told the program to compute the correlations among these variables. The results are shown in Table 12–5.

This type of table is called a **correlation matrix**. It lists the variable names (in this case, C1 through C10) down the first column and across the first row. The diagonal of a correlation matrix (the numbers that go from the upper-left corner to the lower right) always consists of ones because these are the correlations between each variable and itself (and a variable is always perfectly correlated with itself). The statistical program I used shows only the lower triangle of the correlation matrix. In every correlation matrix, there are two triangles: the values below and to the left of the diagonal (lower triangle) and above and to the right of the diagonal (upper triangle). There is no reason to print both triangles because the two triangles of a correlation matrix are always mirror images of each other. (The correlation of variable

correlation matrix
A table of correlations showing all possible relationships among a set of variables. The diagonal of a correlation matrix (the numbers that go from the upper-left corner to the lower right) always consists of 1s because these are the correlations between each variable and itself (and a variable is always perfectly correlated with itself). Off-diagonal elements are the correlations of variables represented by the relevant row and column in the matrix.

TABLE 12–8	Hypothetical Cross-Tabulation of Two Variables with Row and Column Percentages Added

			Grades		
			A	B	Total
Gender	Female	Count	5	5	10
		% within gender	50.0%	50.0%	100.0%
		% within grades	71.4%	38.5%	50.0%
		% of total	25.0%	25.0%	50.0%
	Male	Count	2	8	10
		% within gender	20.0%	80.0%	100.0%
		% within grades	28.6%	61.5%	50.0%
		% of total	10.0%	40.0%	50.0%
Total		Count	7	13	20
		% within gender	35.0%	65.0%	100.0%
		% within grades	100.0%	100.0%	100.0%
		% of total	35.0%	65.0%	100.0%

TABLE 12–9	Observed and Expected Frequencies

			Grades		
			A	B	Total
Gender	Female	Count	5	5	10
		Expected count	3.5	6.5	10.0
	Male	Count	2	8	10
		Expected count	3.5	6.5	10.0
Total		Count	7	13	20
		Expected count	7.0	13.0	20.0

The expected cell frequency is calculated by multiplying the observed row total by the observed column total and dividing by the total *N*. For example, in this table the expected count of males obtaining *A*s is 3.5, which is (7 × 10)/20.

statistical way to state this question would be: Do the observed percentages (or frequencies or proportions) differ from those that would be expected to occur by chance?

Several statistics could be used to summarize the strength of this relationship and to test whether it is statistically significant, but by far the most frequently used statistic in this situation is the chi-square test. The chi-square statistic directly tests whether the observed frequencies differ from those that would be expected to occur by chance. The idea of the test is very straightforward. Calculate the average difference between the observed and expected frequencies across all of the cells and then compare this number to the critical value associated with a particular probability level, given the degrees of freedom for your data. The degrees of freedom for a chi-square test is the product of the number of rows times minus 1 times the number of columns minus 1 [in our example: $(2 - 1)(2 - 1) = 1$]. In Table 12–9, the observed and expected frequencies are shown and the calculation of the expected frequency for one of the cells is highlighted. I imagine that you now have the idea but are very curious about the final result. It turns out that the critical value for this analysis (1 degree of freedom, at the .05 level of significance) is 3.84, but the computed value of chi-square for this data is only 1.98 with an associated probably of .16, above our .05 cutoff. So we have to conclude that for this data, the pattern observed does not differ from that expected by chance. This example demonstrates a basic way to examine a simple two-variable situation. Of course, there are far more complex possibilities and many more ways to examine relationships between nominal variables, including multivariate model-building techniques.

The expected cell frequency is calculated by multiplying the observed row total by the observed column total and dividing by the total N. For example, in this table the expected count of males obtaining As is 3.5, which is $(7 \times 10)/20$.

12-4 Exploratory Data Analysis and Graphics

John Tukey provided us with important ways of obtaining mathematical, verbal, and graphic insight about our data. He coined the term **exploratory data analysis** (EDA) to describe methods that would reestablish the exploration of data as a necessary companion to the confirmatory statistical techniques that became dominant in the second half of the last century. (Tukey also coined the term *software* and is regarded as one of the great minds of the 20th century, especially in statistics.) I present the topic of EDA and graphics toward the end of this chapter, but that does not imply it should be done last or least. In fact, if I have not done some EDA and graphic analysis of a dataset I'm working on, then I cannot convince *myself* of the conclusion validity of any other analysis I might have done let alone anyone else. EDA is as much an attitude of wanting to understand your data, to see below the surface, as it is mastering the tools. The goal is to effectively describe patterns in data so that you will understand what meaning there may be. Simplicity and clarity are valued over complexity and abstraction. We have already used some of the most common graphic methods when we examined the histogram (Figures 12–5 and 12–6) and scatterplot (Figure 12–7). In this section, I will review only some of the classic techniques, but I encourage you to explore every variable carefully before conducting your formal hypothesis tests. You may have even practiced some of these techniques early in your education because people who design curricula for elementary and secondary math courses realize how important they are in facilitating understanding of data and relationships.

exploratory data analysis
The use of graphic and other methods to examine relationships in a data set. EDA is especially helpful when trying to develop hypotheses about relationships and when examining distributions of variables by themselves or in relation to other variables.

12-4a The Stem and Leaf Plot

Earlier in the chapter you read about ways of summarizing central tendency and variability with statistical indicators such as the mean and standard deviation. Tukey created a graphic approach that allows us to see both dimensions of a variable, called the **stem and leaf diagram**. In Figure 12–12, you will see a stem and leaf diagram for the previously studied height data. The left-hand column represents the "stem," which is the unique part of each value after removing the last digit. The last digit for every value is then shown with the other "leaves" on the right side of the figure. Note that you can see the "big picture" on this variable while retaining every single case. This particular figure was done using SPSS and gives you the frequency count for each row as well as a legend to help interpret the figure at the bottom.

stem and leaf diagram
In a stem-and-leaf plot, each observed value is divided into two components—leading digits (the stem) and trailing digits (the leaves). Like the histogram, it shows the entire distribution of a variable, but in addition preserves all of the individual values in the display. The stem-and-leaf plot is one of the many graphic techniques developed by John Tukey.

12-4b The Boxplot (or Box and Whisker Plot)

The **boxplot** is another way to effectively display several characteristics of a variable in a simple graphic format. In Figure 12–13, you see a boxplot of the height data. This plot shows you all of the following about height in this sample: (1) the median

boxplot
A boxplot (or box and whisker plot) is a graphic display invented by John Tukey that summarizes the distribution of a numeric variable by showing the median and quartiles as a box, and the extreme values as "whiskers" extending from the box.

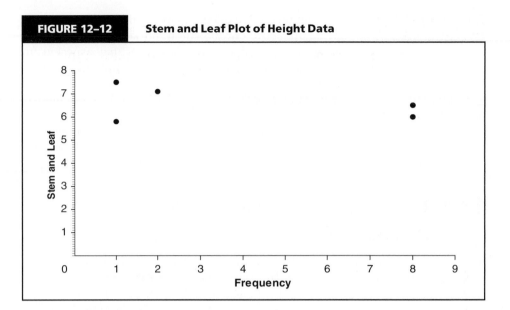

FIGURE 12–12   Stem and Leaf Plot of Height Data

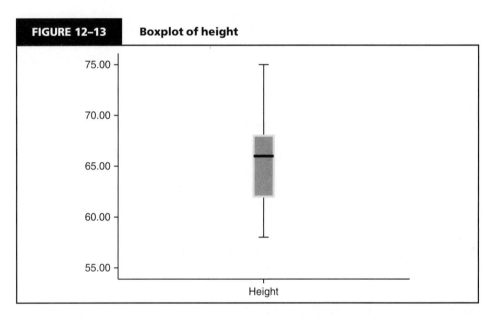

FIGURE 12–13   Boxplot of height

(the black line in middle of the box); (2) the 25th and 75th percentile values (the bottom and top boundaries of the box); (3) the interquartile range (the middle 50% of the values represented by the box itself); and (4) the highest and lowest values (the "whiskers"; the ends of the lines extending from the box). If the variable had extreme values (outliers), then you could also add these to the plot as dots (or other symbols) beyond the end of the whiskers. The boxplot can also be used to explore subgroups on variables. For example, in Figure 12–14, you can see the self-esteem variable broken down by gender and grades. What do you notice about this figure? I hope you notice that quite a bit of information about the relationship of three variables can be gleaned from this one picture, including the central tendencies, variability, and very likely some ideas about what may be going on below the surface of the data, as Professor Tukey would say.

12-4c Anscombe's Quartet

Anscombe's quartet is a dataset that clearly illustrates the importance of looking at your data graphically, and not just assuming that summary statistics tell the whole

FIGURE 12–14	Boxplot of self-esteem by gender and grades

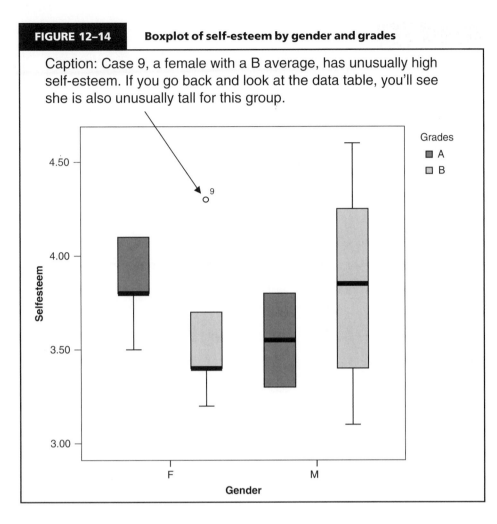

Caption: Case 9, a female with a B average, has unusually high self-esteem. If you go back and look at the data table, you'll see she is also unusually tall for this group.

TABLE 12–10	Anscombe's Quartet with Summary Statistics

x1	y1	x2	y2	x3	y3	x4	y4
10.00	8.04	10.00	9.14	10.00	7.46	8.00	6.58
8.00	6.95	8.00	8.14	8.00	6.77	8.00	5.76
13.00	7.58	13.00	8.74	13.00	12.74	8.00	7.71
9.00	8.81	9.00	8.77	9.00	7.11	8.00	8.84
11.00	8.33	11.00	9.26	11.00	7.81	8.00	8.47
14.00	9.96	14.00	8.10	14.00	8.84	8.00	7.04
6.00	7.24	6.00	6.13	6.00	6.08	8.00	5.25
4.00	4.26	4.00	3.10	4.00	5.39	19.00	12.50
12.00	10.84	12.00	9.13	12.00	8.15	8.00	5.56
7.00	4.82	7.00	7.26	7.00	6.42	8.00	7.91
5.00	5.68	5.00	4.74	5.00	5.73	8.00	6.89

Summary statistics for all X-Y pairs:

— Mean of the x values = 9.0

— Mean of the y values = 7.5

— Equation of the least-squared regression line is: $y = 3 + 0.5x$

— Sums of squared errors (about the mean) = 110.0

— Regression sums of squared errors (variance accounted for by x) = 27.5

— Residual sums of squared errors (about the regression line) = 13.75

— Correlation coefficient = 0.82

— Coefficient of determination = 0.67

FIGURE 12–15   **Scatterplots of Anscombe's quartet**

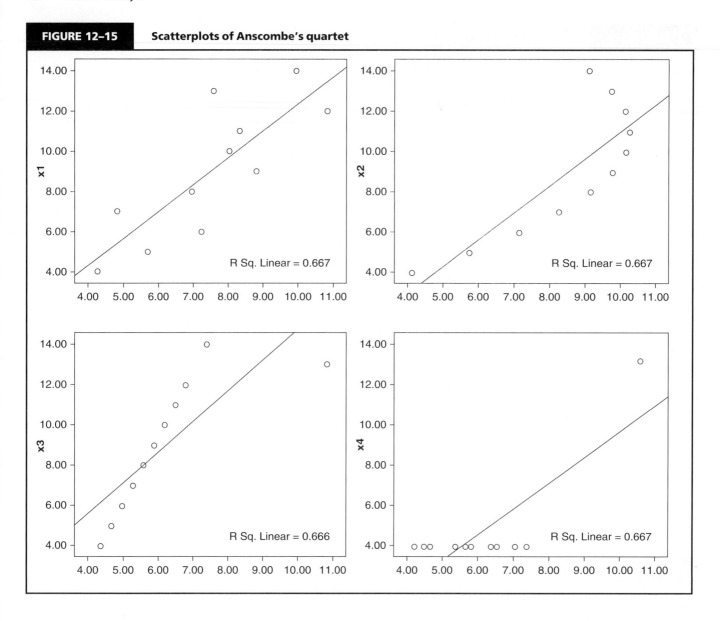

story. Anscombe published the data in 1973, and it was later utilized very effectively by Edward Tufte in his book, The Visual Display of Quantitative Information (2001), one of the most insightful and frankly beautiful books I've ever seen (his Web site is listed at the end of this chapter, too). In Table 12–10 (see p. 279), you'll see four X-Y pairs. Remarkably, the summary statistics for all for X-Y pairs are equivalent. The lesson from Anscombe's quartet is seen strikingly when we plot the data. In Figure 12–15, scatterplots of all of the data pairs are shown.

Summary

This chapter introduced the basics involved in data analysis. Conclusion validity is the degree to which inferences about relationships in data are reasonable. Conclusions from data involve accepting one hypothesis and thereby rejecting its mutually exclusive and exhaustive alternative, and in reaching a conclusion, you can either be correct or incorrect. You can make two types of errors. A Type I error occurs when you conclude there is a relationship when in fact there is not (seeing something that's not there). A Type II error occurs when you conclude there is no effect when in fact there is (missing the needle in the haystack). Data preparation involves checking or logging the data in, checking the data for accuracy, entering the data into the computer, transforming the data, and developing and documenting a database structure that integrates the various measures. Missing data should be assessed before any analysis, especially whether the missing data is random. Descriptive statistics describe the basic features of the data in a study. The basic descriptive statistics include descriptions of the data distributions, measures of central tendency and dispersion or variability, and the different forms of correlation. EDA and statistical graphics can greatly enhance your understanding of your data as well as your ability to communicate that understanding to others.

Login to the Online Edition of your text at www.atomicdog.com to find additional resources located in the Study Guide at the end of each chapter.

CHAPTER 13

Qualitative and Mixed Methods Analysis

constant comparison
content analysis
data reduction

grounded theory
open-coding
theoretical saturation

data reduction
The systematic process undertaken to convert a set of raw data to a coded or summary form.

In general terms, the goal of any analysis is to answer the research question by some sequence of data processing steps (usually some form of **data reduction**) and inference. By data reduction, I mean the translation of raw data into a form that represents the original data in summary, indexed, graphic, or other coded form. In qualitative analysis, just as in quantitative analysis, the data processing and analysis strategies chosen should be a function of the original purpose of the study as well as the nature of the data. Several systematic approaches to qualitative and mixed methods data analysis have been developed, and new variations are regularly introduced and adapted to particular study goals and contexts. But it is unlikely that you will ever see a "qualitative cookbook" that provides you with probabilistic looking procedures and formulas (Eisner, 1991).

In their introduction to the first textbook on qualitative data analysis, Miles and Huberman (1984) noted that in attempting to provide a comprehensive guide to analysis of qualitative data, they invented or reinvented most of the methods in the book. They reported that doing so was a straightforward and enjoyable process, and predicted that the future of qualitative analysis would include such an "inventive, method-creating stance" (p. 17). The intervening years have shown that their prediction has been largely accurate, as evidenced by the second edition of their text (1994) as well as the diversity of methods and gradual acceptance by more academic journals and granting agencies in more recent years.

In conducting qualitative analysis, a creative investigative mind-set based in a responsible, ethically enlightened, participant-in-context-respecting attitude, is as necessary as an explicit set of analytic strategies. Such an attitude is difficult to learn from a textbook but can probably become well established through a combination of study and practice in the company of like-minded scholars, ideally a qualitative or mixed methods research team.

This chapter will provide an overview of some of the more classic methods as well as an introduction to some of the ways that computing has enhanced the range of possibilities for qualitative analysis. The examples in this chapter are only a brief and inadequate introduction to the richness of qualitative and mixed methods analysis and further reading is highly recommended.

13-1 Grounded Theory

grounded theory
A theory rooted in observation about phenomena of interest. Also, a method for achieving such a theory.

As noted in the discussion of qualitative design in Chapter 8, analysis from a **grounded theory** perspective is an iterative process directed toward the development of a theory describing or explaining a phenomenon of interest. The method was first used by Glaser and Strauss in their 1965 book *Awareness of Dying*, a landmark study both because of its subject matter and its methods. In this study, the researchers used a natural field setting to observe how situational conditions, particularly variations in level of patient awareness of likely mortality, influenced the experience of dying. In the process, they developed what later became known as the *method of constant comparative analysis* (Glaser & Strauss, 1967). Constant comparative analysis includes a relatively well-defined set of activities for studying the qualitative dataset resulting from observations, interviews, or other methods generating narratives. The data is usually studied in transcript form obtained from video or audio recordings. New methods of computerized analysis are making the study of

FIGURE 13–1   **Grounded theory analysis (constant comparison)**

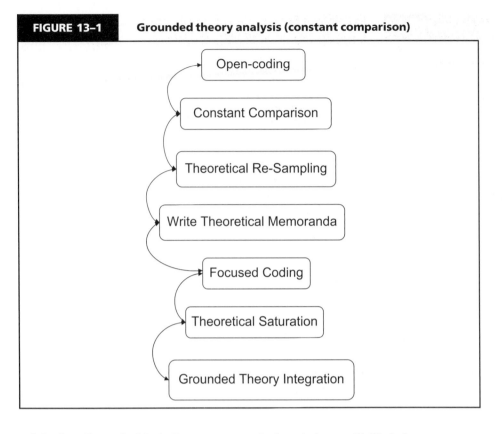

original audio and video clips more practical and these will likely become more common in grounded theory and other qualitative studies.

In Figure 13–1, the typical steps in a grounded theory analysis are shown. The data may originate from any of the qualitative measurement strategies described in Chapter 6, including interviews, focus groups, narratives, video or audio recordings, or other qualitative or unobtrusive methods. The steps are shown to connect with double-headed arrows, intended to indicate that the phases are dynamic and that moving back and forth is acceptable and common practice.

Open-coding refers to the analyst's attempt to review the raw data and identify key aspects that can be used as an index or code in relating a particular passage to other facets of the dataset. Or, in less academic terms, open coding involves making up categories that you can assign chunks of text to. The coding is considered "open" in that the process involves discovery. In contrast, you can think of a codebook for a quantitative analysis as a kind of closed coding system because all variables and values are specifically defined.

The **constant comparison** process involves the continuous sorting and contrasting of the elements of the dataset. The elements may include comments of participants, variations of higher-order concepts, and tentative theoretical propositions. The constant comparison process may occur at any point in the data collection and analysis and may stimulate particular kinds of inquiries during the study that add to the data and further stimulate the comparison process. The back-and-forth process often includes returning to the original participants to confirm the accuracy of the interpretation of the data.

The analysis continues to a point referred to as **theoretical saturation**. This is the point where the analyst recognizes redundancy in the constant comparison process and where new data no longer stimulates revision of the conceptual framework. Practical limits are often imposed on the analysis as well. Sometimes access is limited to participants and settings. Nearly always, time and money will be finite. The context of the analysis is usually reported, including the researcher's sense of how the study results may have been limited by practical contingencies.

open-coding
A phase of the grounded theory method where you consider the data in minute detail while developing some initial categories.

constant comparison
The iterative and sequential process used when analyzing qualitative data that involves refinement of categories and interpretations based on increasing depth of understanding.

theoretical saturation
The point at which the analyst or analysts agree that new data no longer adds new meaning. The analysis is then saturated in the sense that it is complete and sufficient.

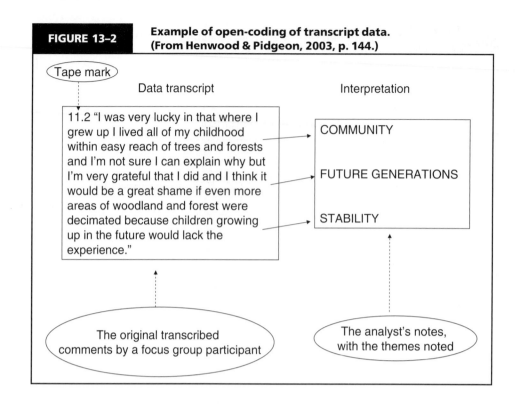

FIGURE 13-2   **Example of open-coding of transcript data. (From Henwood & Pidgeon, 2003, p. 144.)**

Henwood and Pidgeon (2003) illustrated the use of grounded theory with a study they conducted on personal significance of trees, woods, and forests among the residents of northern Wales. Their study will be described here to provide a sense of the big picture in grounded theory analysis as well as some insight into specific steps in such an analysis and how investigators adapt them to their own needs and preferences.

In this study, the data were generated in focus groups. The focus group participants were asked to talk about the personal and cultural significance of woodlands (for example, "What specific meanings attached to forests, woods, and trees in discussions of their cultural role and significance?") (p. 142). The goal of the study was to add another level of meaning to policy discussions of environmental issues that had typically been largely restricted to economic analyses.

The focus groups were audio-recorded. The analysis began when the investigators listened to all recordings independently and jointly. They then proceeded with development of transcripts and open-coding of comments. In this study, the authors found that they could make the coding process more efficient by transcribing specific parts of the discussion rather than the entire sessions as their analysis proceeded. This procedure illustrates the flexibility that tends to come with qualitative analysis, and it also shows the importance of reporting on procedures and the thinking that may have influenced judgments about procedures. In this case, the authors noted that the partial transcript allowed them to meet deadlines by saving time that would have been needed for transcribing the entire group discussion. They also noted that the process of listening to tapes separately and together was helpful. And they recommended doing one's own transcription as "a way for researchers to start early on the path of thinking analytically about the data and its properties" (p. 142).

A sample of transcript contents and coding from this study is shown in Figure 13-2. On the left side of the figure you see the verbatim comment of a participant, beginning with a notation as to the point in the tape where the comment was made. Then in the box on the right, three themes are noted. This example shows how coding of a simple and uninterrupted passage can be accomplished. In Figure 13-3, a more complex example from the same study is shown.

FIGURE 13–3 | **Example of more complex coding of transcript data.**
(From Henwood & Pidgeon, 2003, p. 144.)

Participant code

Data transcript   Interpretation

12.7 M1"would it be pompous to say that one of the parts of the human condition is that we have a natural affinity with nature and possibly a non-natural affinity with man-made artifacts like cities and towns so the loss of trees forestation vegetation is much more fundamental than say the loss of buildings or whatever?" M2 [Welsh participant – ironic/mocking?] "sounds dead cool" [laughter] M3 "there have around for many years" M4 "symbolic of country living isn't it the tree" M1 "it's more fundamental than that we all lived in the country one time and urban living is a relatively new thing?"

NATURAL/ARTIFICIAL

{Memo by NP – is nature more fundamental than man-made artifacts?}

TREES SYMBOLIZE NATURE

{Memo by NP – M1 and M4 both ex-city dwellers and incomers. My feeling was the NW participants, e.g., M2 – were far more skeptical of this stereotype of 'things country'}

Contextual notes added by analyst   Memos added by analyst

In Figure 13–3, we see how the analysts handled what appears to be a quick back-and-forth discussion along with some significant notes about the tone of the comments as well as information about the background of the participants. The analysts' notes reveal the beginning of a theoretical theme regarding the importance of "insider" and "outsider" perspectives. The authors reported that this was an unanticipated discovery that led to thinking about the implications of labeling participants in these terms as well as sensitivity to some political attitudes possibly underlying the comments of participants. The analysts' memos also serve the important function of documenting the thought process that influenced the coding and interpretation of data.

Once the transcripts had been reviewed and the initial open-coding completed, a sequence of analyses that represent the process of constant comparison was initiated in order to identify higher-order concepts. The constant comparison involved review and discussion across and within sessions in order to develop theoretical hunches that could be further pursued. In most studies, this includes returning to the participants with new questions based on the accumulated understanding. The questions become increasingly differentiated as the theoretical understanding evolves. This is one of the defining features and advantages of the approach, and it is why such analysis can rightly be labeled "rich". In the Henwood and Pidgeon analysis, the next steps included developing themes based on the codes and verbatim excerpts as well as keeping track of the contribution of each to study conclusions. An example of the correspondence of higher-order themes, raw data, and study conclusions from Henwood and Pidgeon's study is shown in Table 13–1. This table is consistent with the dynamic nature of constant comparison in that a relationship between participant report and analyst interpretation is evident. They employed additional analytic steps and later collected additional data from other locations to examine geographic variation in attitudes and values.

As the authors noted, their study should not be considered the model for all grounded theory inquiry, but it does illustrate the basic approach. The ongoing discussions about the purpose and procedures of grounded theory make it unlikely that any particular study will satisfy all points of view on best practices in grounded theory analysis.

TABLE 13–1   **Grounded Theory Example of Correspondence of Themes, Data, and Study Conclusions**

Higher-Order Theme	Original Illustrative Data from Transcripts	Study Conclusion
Protection of wildlife/ biodiversity	"trees belong to the earth they belong to the animals . . . a lot of humans treat them in a way they shouldn't . . . they are supposed to be there just for a home and for food (for the animals)"	"Valuing woods and trees as wildlife habitats often simultaneously expressed older style conservationist beliefs and more recent environmental discourses; a dislike of human domination of nature is often featured, but this dislike is countered by fears of the chaotic potential of nature and a more modern (sometimes entrepreneurial) tolerance of the blurring of the boundaries between nature, human intervention, and culture."

Excerpt from table by Henwood & Pidgeon, 2003, p. 147.

13-2 Content Analysis

content analysis
The analysis of text documents. The analysis can be quantitative, qualitative, or both. Typically, the major purpose of content analysis is to identify patterns in text.

Content analysis is an extremely broad area of research. Content analysis is the systematic analysis of text (Krippendorff, 2004). The analysis can be quantitative, qualitative, or both. Typically, the major purpose of content analysis is to identify patterns in text. In Chapter 8, you read about the Hsieh and Shannon's (2005) distinctions in various purposes of content analysis (that is, conventional, directed, and summative content analysis).

Content analysis typically includes several important steps or phases. First, when there are many texts to analyze (for example, newspaper stories, organizational reports), the researcher often has to begin by sampling from the population of potential texts to select the ones that will be used. Second, the researcher usually needs to identify and apply the rules that are used to divide each text into segments or "chunks" that will be treated as separate units of analysis in the study, a process referred to as *unitizing*. For instance, you might extract each identifiable assertion from a longer interview transcript. Third, the content analyst constructs and applies one or more codes to each unitized text segment, a process called *coding*. The development of a coding scheme is based on the themes that you are searching for or uncover as you classify the text. Finally, you analyze the coded data, very often both quantitatively and qualitatively, to determine which themes occur most frequently, in what contexts, and how they might be correlated.

Content analysis has several potential limitations that you should keep in mind. First, you are limited to the types of information available in text form. If you were studying the way a news story is being handled by the news media, you probably would have a ready population of news stories from which you could sample. However, if you are interested in studying people's views on capital punishment, you are less likely to find an archive of text documents that would be appropriate. Second, you have to be especially careful with sampling to avoid bias. For instance, a study of current research on methods of treatment for cancer might use the published research literature as the population. This would leave out both the writing on cancer that was not published for one reason or another (publication bias), as well as the most recent work that has not yet been published. Finally, you have to be

| **FIGURE 13–4** | **Schilling's (2006) qualitative content analysis spiral** |

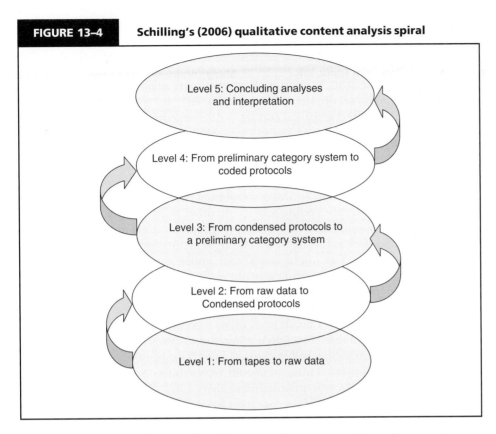

careful about interpreting results of automated context analyses. A computer program cannot always determine what someone meant by a term or phrase. It is relatively easy in a large analysis to misinterpret a result because you did not take into account the subtleties or context of meaning. However, content analysis has the advantage of being unobtrusive and, depending on whether automated methods exist, can be a relatively rapid method for analyzing large amounts of text.

Schilling (2006) sought to bring some order to the diversity of analytic procedures for content analysis with the "spiral" model reproduced in Figure 13–4. Schilling's model is an attempt to address the frequent criticism of qualitative methods that there is a lack of systematic procedures that would allow replication by other researchers using the same data. The model is described as providing a more rules-based and transparent method of analysis. For example, prior to engaging in formal analysis, he advised that explicit rules for anonymizing participants should be written. That is, how will any part of the text that might compromise the anonymity of participants (assuming it has been promised by the researcher) be handled? A simple rule for recoding such text will facilitate the preparation for analysis, and reporting it in the methods section of the write-up will allow others to replicate the study. For example, if you know that one and only one of your participants had a job that was well known by the public, then transcripts could be reviewed to convert all references that might reveal the job and therefore the person's identity to a disguised form prior to the analysis and write-up. Being able to assure such a participant of this aspect of the study would have both ethical and methodological benefits.

13-3 Computerized Qualitative Data Analysis

Computerized qualitative data analysis is attractive because computers are so helpful in organizing, searching, sorting, and otherwise processing large amounts of data in systematic, rule-based ways. Programs make it possible to examine large amounts of text efficiently for overall patterns as well as specific instances of particular kinds of words or phrases.

As an example of the power of the computer in qualitative analysis, think of the index at the end of this book (or any other book) as a kind of coding scheme for the major ideas in the text. The index shows you every major or nontrivial occurrence of the key ideas in the text. Now imagine that you are doing a qualitative study and have completed an initial coding of 10 transcripts, have developed your preliminary coding of key themes, but still have 500 more transcripts to study. Your initial coding is like a draft of a book index, but it covers only a tiny fraction of your whole dataset. You might never be able to complete the analysis of all of your data by hand, but with the help of a computer program, you could expedite the analysis of the rest of the transcripts by applying your initial coding scheme to them rather than continuing to evolve the coding scheme. In other words, you can sample a subset of transcripts (hopefully a subset that represents the variety of viewpoints in all the transcripts) and then apply the initial coding scheme much more rapidly to the rest of the population. You might quickly recognize the inherent limit in this approach: What if your initial coding scheme is somehow biased or overly narrow? Expect that developing your coding scheme will require a very significant investment of time and brain power as you tinker with it.

You will probably need to be an even more careful and critical thinker if you use a computer program than if you do not because, as you probably all know, Murphy's Law (what can go wrong, will go wrong) must have been written shortly after the invention of computers. Thus, we should never think that the computer will "do the analysis for us." As with quantitative analysis, careful and deliberate analysis requires that we maintain some level of direct involvement with the data and double check every step.

The software options available to qualitative researchers are many and constantly growing. Most have at their core systems for coding and locating units of text, audio, or video, and some have added features to enable data management, open-coding, theory building, and reporting. There are numerous commercially available programs and a good number of free ones as well.

A project in the United Kingdom has been initiated to support computerized qualitative data analysis. The Computer-assisted Qualitative Data Analysis (CAQDAS) project (http://caqdas.soc.surrey.ac.uk/) provides support, training, and information on a great variety of freely available and commercial software. At present, nearly 40 programs are listed in their links section, a large but not completely exhaustive list (which would be impossible given the continuing changes in the field). The project has recently published the fifth edition of their online guide to qualitative analysis software (Lewins & Silver, 2006, downloaded September, 2006, from http://caqdas.soc.surrey.ac.uk/ChoosingLewins&SilverV5July06.pdf).

I wholeheartedly agree with Lewins and Silver's comment that there is no one "best" program and that an informed choice should be based on the needs and resources available for a particular study. This is no doubt obvious, and it applies to evaluation of all computer programs, from statistical to musical. The CAWDAS guide provides a nice overview of the features and functionality of many popular programs, some of which are free, including ATLAS.ti 5, HyperRESEARCH 2.6, MAXqda2, N6, NVivo2, NVivo7, QDA Miner, Qualrus, and Transana. The site also provides links to freely available programs, including AnSWR and CDC-EZ-Text, developed and supported by the Centers for Disease Control and Prevention. Most software developers have made demonstration versions or limited licenses available for users to "try before you buy."

13-4 Mixed Methods Analysis

I begin this brief section on mixed methods analysis with a quote from a previously cited (Chapter 8) qualitative researcher and methodologist, Elliot Eisner. In a

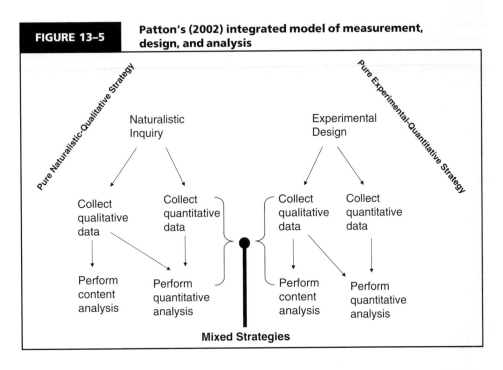

FIGURE 13–5   Patton's (2002) integrated model of measurement, design, and analysis

chapter on sources and kinds of qualitative data, he said, "... I feel compelled to say that in qualitative inquiry *numbers are okay*" (1991, p. 186). He repeated the comment for emphasis and went on to make the point that we should use whatever represents our phenomena in context best, including words, number, graphs, pictures, and so on. This perspective is very helpful in mixed methods analysis, because there should be clear thinking about what the contribution of any and all quantitative and qualitative indicators may be to answering the research question.

One way to envision the possibilities for combining qualitative and quantitative analysis is Patton's model of measurement, design, and analysis reproduced in Figure 13–5. In the figure, we see that methods can be construed on a continuum from a pure naturalistic-qualitative approach at one end to a pure experimental-quantitative design at the other, with possibilities for mixing methods emanating from a point in the center of the continuum. It would be relatively simple to use this model as a base for considering options as well as a study schema once decisions on design have been rendered.

Patton's model and many of the other resources developed for qualitative analysis have more of a heuristic than prescriptive quality. That is, they can stimulate thinking about analysis possibilities more effectively than providing a formula to follow. In this sense, qualitative and mixed methods analysis is both art and science. There are few limits as to what might be considered "good data," including letters, emails, blogs, films, poems, music, portraits, photographs, tests and papers, conversations, and virtually any other reflection of lived experience. The range of possibilities for analysis is also very wide, and I encourage you to read qualitative studies to get a sense of the integrated character of measurement, design, analysis, and reporting. I also encourage you to review sources such as Miles and Huberman's (1994) handbook and to download trial or free versions of qualitative analysis programs to get a first hand (I could say *qualitative!*) sense of the possibilities.

Summary

This chapter provided a brief overview of qualitative and mixed methods analysis. The integration of measurement, design and analysis, based on the study purpose, was emphasized. Grounded theory, one of the best-known qualitative methods, was illustrated with a review of

causal
Pertaining to a cause-effect relationship.

relationship
Refers to the correspondence between two variables.

descriptive statistics
Statistics used to describe the basic features of the data in a study.

hypothesis
A specific statement of prediction.

random assignment
Process of assigning your sample into two or more subgroups by chance. Procedures for random assignment can vary from flipping a coin to using a table of random numbers to using the random number capability built into a computer.

inferential statistics
Statistical analyses used to reach conclusions that extend beyond the immediate data alone.

quasi-experimental research design
Research designs that have several of the key features of randomized experimental designs, such as pre-post measurement and treatment-control group comparisons, but lack random assignment to a treatment group.

The heart of the quantitative data analysis—the part where you answer the major research questions in a quantitative study—is inextricably linked to the research design. Especially in **causal** research, the research design frames the entire endeavor, specifying how the measures and participants are brought together. So, it shouldn't surprise you that the research design also frames the data analysis, determining the type of analysis that you can and cannot do.

This chapter describes the **relationship** between design and analysis. I begin with inferential statistics, which differ from **descriptive statistics** in that they are explicitly constructed to address a research question or **hypothesis**. I then present the general linear model (GLM). Even though each specific design has its own design quirks and idiosyncrasies, things aren't as confusing or distinct as they may at first seem. The GLM underlies all of the analyses presented here, so if you get a good understanding of what that's all about, the rest should be a little easier to handle. (Note that I said a little easier. I didn't say it was going to be easy.) I then move on to consider the basic randomized experimental designs, starting with the simplest—the two-group, posttest-only experiment—and moving to more complex designs. Finally, I take you into the world of quasi-experimental analysis where the quasi nature of the design leads to all types of analytic problems (some of which may even make you queasy). You'll learn that you pay a price, analytically speaking, when you move away from **random assignment**. By the time you're through with all of this, you'll have a pretty firm grasp on how analysis is crafted to your research design and about the perils of applying the analysis that seems most obvious to the wrong design structure.

14-1 Inferential Statistics

Inferential statistics is the process of trying to reach conclusions that extend beyond the immediate data. You are trying to use the data as the basis for drawing broader inferences (thus, the name) rather than just describing the data. For instance, you use inferential statistics to try to infer from the sample data what the population might think. Or, you use inferential statistics to make judgments about the probability that an observed difference between groups is a dependable one or one that might have happened by chance in your study. Thus, you use inferential statistics to make inferences from your data to general conditions; you use descriptive statistics simply to describe what's going on in the data.

In this chapter, I concentrate on inferential statistics, which are useful in experimental and **quasi-experimental research design** or in program-outcome evaluation. To understand inferential statistics there are two issues I need you to consider, one somewhat general and theoretical and the other more concrete and methodological. You should also know that this presentation differs from what you typically see in a statistics text. Here we are taking a top-down approach, that is, going from the big picture to the specific test situation. In most statistics textbooks, you start with the relatively simple analyses such as the *t*-test and work your way up to the more complex statistical modeling approaches. Imagine that instead of teaching you how to analyze data, I was trying to teach you how to make beer. If that was the case (pun intended), I would start with the big picture about what beer is made from and how you go from water, malt, hops, and yeast to a particular kind of beer. So here we start with the most general model and then consider some specific kinds of analysis that are derived from it. For the following discussion, you may actually find that a beer or two will help you along.

First, virtually all the major inferential statistics come from a general family of statistical models known as the general linear model (GLM). You can't get much more general than the GLM. This includes the *t*-test, analysis of variance (ANOVA), analysis of covariance (ANCOVA), regression analysis, (all of which are described later in this chapter), and many of the multivariate methods like factor analysis, multidimensional scaling, cluster analysis, discriminant function analysis, and so on. Given the importance of the GLM, it's a good idea for any serious social researcher to become familiar with it. The discussion of the GLM here is elementary and considers only the simplest straight-line model, but it will familiarize you with the idea of a **linear model** and help prepare you for the more complex analyses described in the rest of this chapter.

Second, on a more concrete and methodological note, you can't truly understand how the GLM is used to analyze data from research designs unless you learn what a dummy variable is and how it is used. The name doesn't suggest that you are using **variables** that aren't smart or, even worse, that the analyst who uses them is a dummy! Perhaps these variables would be better described as proxy variables. Essentially a dummy variable is one that uses discrete numbers, usually 0 and 1, to represent different groups in your study in the equations of the GLM. The concept of dummy variables is a simple idea that enables some complicated things to happen. For instance, by including a simple dummy variable in a model, you can model two separate lines (one for each treatment group) with a single equation. All this will be clarified here.

14-1a Significance Testing

Remember that in Chapter 2 in this text you learned that in most research situations, we do not study the entire population of interest by measuring everyone; instead, we attempt to study a sample and then see what we can infer from the data about the whole population. But how do we decide whether to make those inferences? Surely not every result is as important as every other result. The guidelines for significance testing help us make those decisions, and the more recent (more recently taken seriously, that is) guidelines about **confidence intervals** and **effect size** help us interpret the precision and magnitude of our results. There has been a very important reformation in statistical methods in the past 10 years, including standards for reporting results. This is related to common misunderstanding of what was meant by a "*p* **value**" and the procedures for **null hypothesis** significance testing generally. Here I'll introduce these ideas, and then I'll expand on the discussion of confidence intervals and effect sizes in Chapter 16.

Sir Ronald Fisher remains one of the most important statisticians in history for many reasons, one of which is that his work established the basic guidelines used to determine whether the results of a statistical test were worth paying attention to, or "significant." Sir Ronald suggested the notion that a statistical result could be considered significant if it could be shown that the probability of the result being due to chance was 5 percent or less. For those of you who just connected this to the discussion of statistical power and conclusion validity in Chapter 12, congratulations,

---

t-test
A statistical test of the difference between the means of two groups, often a program and comparison group. The *t*-test is the simplest variation of the one-way analysis of variance (ANOVA).

linear model
Any statistical model that uses equations to estimate lines.

variables
Any entity that can take on different values. For instance, age can be considered a variable because age can take on different values for different people at different times.

confidence intervals
Technically, 1-alpha. The confidence interval is the probability of correctly concluding that there is no treatment effect.

effect size
An estimate of the effect of a treatment or program. The effect size is a signal to noise ration where the numerator (top) represents the effect you are trying to assess (e.g., a difference in averages between two groups) and the denominator (bottom) represents the variability or noise in the data.

p value
The estimate of the probability for a test of an hypothesis. Usually the p value is compared to the significance level when testing a hypothesis. If the p-value exceeds the designated significance level the alternative hypothesis is accepted; if it does not, the null hypothesis is accepted.

null hypothesis
The hypothesis that describes the possible outcomes other than the alternative hypothesis. Usually, the null hypothesis predicts there will be no effect of a program or treatment you are studying.

in schools (by grade, school, school district etc.). HLM allows researchers to examine the direct influence of such variables as well as their interactions.

14-2c Dummy Variables

dummy variable
A variable that uses discrete numbers, usually 0 and 1, to represent different groups in your study in the equations of the GLM.

control group
A group, comparable to the program group, that did not receive the program.

A **dummy variable** is a numerical variable used in regression analysis to represent subgroups of the sample in your study. It is not a variable used by dummies. In fact, you have to be pretty smart to figure out how to use dummy variables. In research design, a dummy variable is typically used to distinguish different treatment groups. In the simplest case, you would use a 0,1 dummy variable, where a person is given a value of 0 if placed in the **control group** or a 1 if in the treated group.

Dummy variables are useful because they enable you to use a single regression equation to represent multiple groups. This means that you don't need to write out separate equation models for each subgroup. The dummy variables act like *switches* that turn various parameters on and off in an equation. Another advantage of a 0,1 dummy-coded variable is that even though it is a nominal-level variable, you can treat it statistically like an interval-level variable. (If this made no sense to you, you probably should refresh your memory on levels of measurement covered in Section 3-3, Levels of Measurement.) For instance, if you take an average of a 0,1 variable, the result is meaningful—the proportion or percentage of 1s in the distribution.

To illustrate dummy variables, consider the simple regression model for a posttest-only two-group randomized experiment shown in Figure 14–2. This model is mathematically identical to conducting a *t*-test on the posttest means for two groups or conducting a one-way ANOVA (as described later in this chapter). The key term in the model is β_1, the estimate of the difference between the groups. To see how dummy variables work, I'll use this simple model to show you how dummy variables can be used to pull out the separate subequations for each subgroup. Then I'll show how to estimate the difference between the subgroups by subtracting their respective equations. You'll see that you can pack an enormous amount of information into a single equation using dummy variables. All I want to show you here is that (β_1) is the difference between the treatment and control groups.

To see this, the first step is to compute what the equation would be for each of the two groups separately (Figure 14–3). For the control group, $Z = 0$. When you substitute that into the equation, and recognize that by assumption the error term averages to 0, you find that the predicted value for the control group is β_0, the intercept. Now, to figure out the treatment-group line, you substitute the value of 1 for Z, again recognizing that by assumption, the error term averages to 0. The equation for the treatment group indicates that the treatment group value is the sum of the two beta values.

FIGURE 14–2	Use of a dummy variable in a regression equation

$$y_i = \beta_0 + \beta_1 Z_i + e_i$$

where:

y_i = outcome score for the ith unit

β_0 = coefficient for the *intercept*

β_1 = coefficient for the *slope*

Z_i = 1 if i^{th} unit is in the treatment group

　　　0 if i^{th} unit is in the control group

e_i = residual for the ith unit

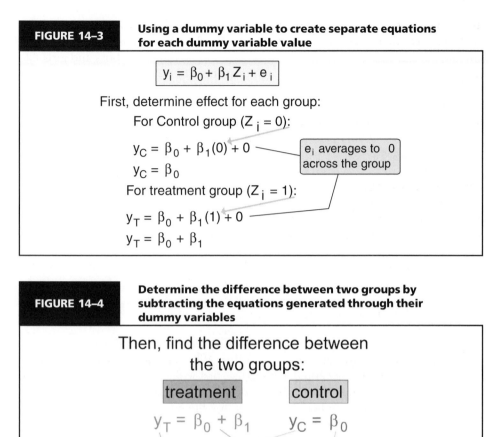

FIGURE 14–3 **Using a dummy variable to create separate equations for each dummy variable value**

$$y_i = \beta_0 + \beta_1 Z_i + e_i$$

First, determine effect for each group:

For Control group ($Z_i = 0$):

$$y_C = \beta_0 + \beta_1(0) + 0$$

$$y_C = \beta_0$$

e_i averages to 0 across the group

For treatment group ($Z_i = 1$):

$$y_T = \beta_0 + \beta_1(1) + 0$$

$$y_T = \beta_0 + \beta_1$$

FIGURE 14–4 **Determine the difference between two groups by subtracting the equations generated through their dummy variables**

Then, find the difference between the two groups:

treatment   control

$$y_T = \beta_0 + \beta_1 \qquad y_C = \beta_0$$

$$y_T - y_C = (\beta_0 + \beta_1) - \beta_0$$

$$y_T - y_C = \cancel{\beta_0} + \beta_1 - \cancel{\beta_0}$$

$$y_T - y_C = \beta_1$$

Now you're ready to move on to the second step—computing the difference between the groups. How do you determine that? Well, the difference must be the difference between the equations for the two groups that you worked out previously. In other words, to find the difference between the groups, you find the difference between the equations for the two groups! It should be obvious from Figure 14–4 that the difference is β_1. Think about what this means. The difference between the groups is β_1. Okay, one more time just for the sheer heck of it: The difference between the groups in this model is β_1 in the equation at the top of Figure 14–3!

Whenever you have a regression model with dummy variables, you can always see how the variables are being used to represent multiple subgroup equations by following the two steps described in Figures 14–3 and 14–4 as follows:

- Create separate equations for each subgroup by substituting the dummy values (as in Figure 14–3).
- Find the difference between groups by finding the difference between their equations (as in Figure 14–4).

14-3 Experimental Analysis

I turn now to the discussion of the experimental designs and how they are analyzed. Perhaps one of the simplest inferential tests is used when you want to compare the average performance of two groups on a single measure to see whether there is a

randomized block designs (RD)
Experimental designs in which the sample is grouped into relatively homogeneous subgroups or blocks within which your experiment is replicated. This procedure reduces noise or variance in the data.

difference. This simple two-group, posttest-only randomized experiment is usually analyzed with the simple *t*-test, which is actually just the simplest variation of the one-way ANOVA. You might want to know whether eighth-grade boys and girls differ in math test scores or whether a program group differs on the outcome measure from a control group. The factorial experimental designs are usually analyzed with the ANOVA model. **Randomized block designs (RD)** use a special form of the ANOVA-blocking model that uses dummy-coded variables to represent the blocks. The analysis of covariance experimental design uses, not surprisingly, the analysis of covariance (ANCOVA) statistical model.

14-3a The *t*-Test

To analyze the two-group, posttest-only randomized experimental design you need an analysis that meets the following requirements:

- Has two groups
- Uses a post-only measure
- Has two distributions (measures), each with an average and variation
- Assesses treatment effect = statistical (non-chance) difference between the groups

The *t*-test fits the bill perfectly. The *t*-test assesses whether the means of two groups are *statistically* different from each other. Why is it called the *t*-test? Because when the statistician who invented this analysis first wrote out the formula, he used the letter "*t*" to symbolize the value that describes the difference between the groups. Why? Beats me. You remember the formula for the straight line from your high school algebra? You know, the one that goes $y = mx + b$? Well, using the name *t*-test is like calling that formula the *y*-formula. Maybe the statisticians decided they would come up with more interesting names later. Maybe they were in the same fix as the astronomers who had so many stars to name they just assigned temporary numbers until someone noteworthy enough came along. Whatever the reason, don't lose any sleep over it. The *t*-test is just a name and, as the bard says, what's in a name?

Before you can proceed to the analysis itself, it is useful to understand what we mean by the term "difference" in the question, "Is there a difference between the groups?" Each group can be represented by a bell-shaped curve that describes the group's distribution on a single variable. You can think of the **bell curve** as a smoothed histogram or bar graph describing the frequency of each possible measurement response.

Figure 14–5 shows the distributions for the treated (dotted line) and control (solid line) groups in a study. Actually, the figure shows the idealized or smoothed

bell curve
Smoothed histogram or bar graph describing the expected frequency for each value of a variable. The name comes from the fact that such a distribution often has the shape of a bell.

| FIGURE 14–5 | Idealized distributions for treated and control group posttest values |

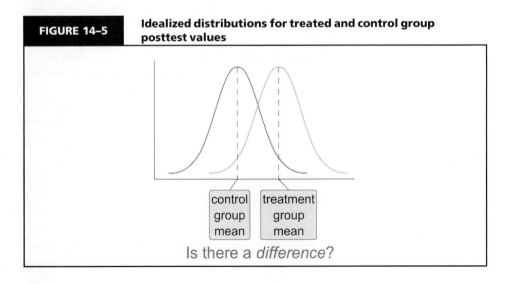

control group mean   treatment group mean

Is there a *difference*?

FIGURE 14–6 **Three scenarios for differences between means**

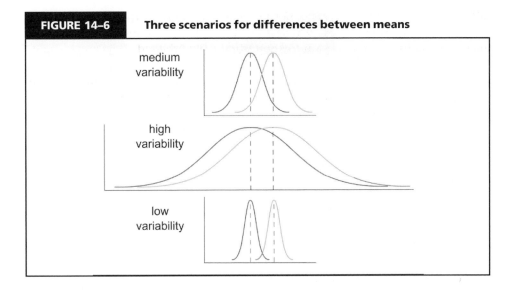

distribution—the actual distribution would usually be depicted with a histogram or bar graph. The figure indicates where the control and treatment group means are located. The question the *t*-test addresses is whether the means are statistically different.

What does it mean to say that the averages for two groups are statistically different? Consider the three situations shown in Figure 14–6. The first thing to notice about the three situations is that *the difference between the means is the same in all three.* But, you should also notice that the three situations don't look the same; they tell different stories. The top example shows a case with moderate variability of scores within each group. The second situation shows the high-variability case. The third shows the case with low variability. Clearly, you would conclude that the two groups appear most different or distinct in the bottom or low-variability case. Why? Because there is relatively little overlap between the two bell-shaped curves. In the high-variability case, the group difference appears least striking (even though the difference between groups is identical) because the two bell-shaped distributions overlap so much.

This leads to an important conclusion: When you are looking at the differences between scores for two groups, you have to judge the difference between their means relative to the spread or variability of their scores. The *t*-test does just this.

Statistical Analysis of the *t*-Test
So how does the *t*-test work? The formula for the *t*-test is a ratio. The top part of the ratio is the difference between the two means or averages. The bottom part is a measure of the variability or dispersion of the scores. This formula is essentially another example of the signal-to-noise metaphor in research; the difference between the means is the signal that, in this case, you think your program or treatment introduced into the data; the bottom part of the formula is a measure of variability that is essentially noise that might make it harder to see the group difference. The ratio that you compute is called a ***t*-value** and describes the difference between the groups relative to the variability of the scores in the groups. Figure 14–7a shows the formula for the *t*-test and how the numerator and denominator are related to the distributions.

The top part of the formula is easy to compute—just find the difference between the means. The bottom part is called the **standard error of the difference**. To compute it, take the **variance** (see Chapter 12) for each group and divide it by the number of people in that group. You add these two values and then take their square root. The specific formula is given in Figure 14–7b. Remember, that the variance is simply the square of the **standard deviation**. The final formula for the *t*-test is shown in Figure 14–7c.

t-value
The estimate of the difference between the groups relative to the variability of the scores in the groups.

standard error of the difference
A statistical estimate of the standard deviation one would obtain from the distribution of an infinite number of estimates of the difference between the means of two groups.

variance
A statistic that describes the variability in the data for a variable. The variance is the spread of the scores around the mean of a distribution. Specifically, the variance is the sum of the squared deviations from the mean divided by the number of observations minus 1.

standard deviation
The spread or variability of the scores around their average in a *single sample*. The standard deviation, often abbreviated SD, is mathematically the square root of the variance. The standard deviation and variance both measure dispersion, but because the standard deviation is measured in the same units as the original measure and the variance is measured in squared units, the standard deviation is usually more directly interpretable and meaningful.

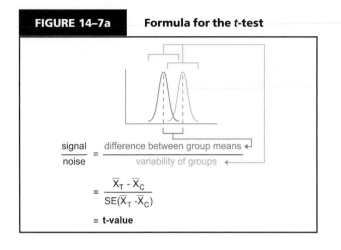

FIGURE 14–7a   **Formula for the *t*-test**

$$\frac{signal}{noise} = \frac{\text{difference between group means}}{\text{variability of groups}}$$

$$= \frac{\overline{X}_T - \overline{X}_C}{SE(\overline{X}_T - \overline{X}_C)}$$

$$= \textbf{t-value}$$

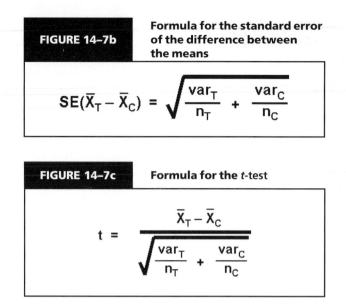

FIGURE 14–7b   **Formula for the standard error of the difference between the means**

$$SE(\overline{X}_T - \overline{X}_C) = \sqrt{\frac{var_T}{n_T} + \frac{var_C}{n_C}}$$

FIGURE 14–7c   **Formula for the *t*-test**

$$t = \frac{\overline{X}_T - \overline{X}_C}{\sqrt{\dfrac{var_T}{n_T} + \dfrac{var_C}{n_C}}}$$

alpha level
The significance level. Specifically, alpha is the Type I error, or the probability of concluding that there is a treatment effect when, in reality, there is not.

degrees of freedom (*df*)
A statistical term that is a function of the sample size. In the *t*-test formula, for instance, the df is the number of persons in both groups minus 2.

The *t*-value will be positive if the first mean is larger than the second value and negative if it is smaller. After you compute the *t*-value, you have to look up the probability or *p*-value associated with your *t*-value (many statistical programs automatically provide the *p*-value) in a table of significance to test whether the *t*-ratio is large enough to say that the difference between the groups is not likely to have been a chance finding. To test the significance, you need to set a risk level (called the **alpha level**, as described in Chapter 12). In most social research, the rule of thumb is to set the alpha level at .05. This means that 5 times out of 100, you would find a statistically significant difference between the means even if there were none (meaning by chance). You also need to determine the **degrees of freedom (*df*)** for the test. In the *t*-test, the *df* is the sum of the persons in both groups minus 2. Given the alpha level, the *df*, and the *t*-value, you can look the *t*-value up in a standard table of significance to determine the *p*-value. By comparing the *p*-value with the significance level or alpha you can determine whether the *t*-value is large enough to be significant. If it is, you can conclude that the difference between the means for the two groups is different (even given the variability). Fortunately, statistical computer programs routinely print the significance test results and save you the trouble of looking them up in a table.

You can estimate the treatment effect for the posttest-only randomized experiment in three ways. All three yield mathematically equivalent results, a fancy way of saying that they give you the exact same answer. So why are there three different ones? In large part, these three approaches evolved independently and only after that was it clear that they are essentially three ways to do the same thing. So, what are the three ways? First, you can compute an independent *t*-test as described here. Second, you could compute a one-way ANOVA between two independent groups. Finally, you can use regression analysis to regress the posttest values onto a dummy-coded treatment variable. Of these three, the regression analysis approach is the most general. In fact, I describe the statistical models for all the experimental and quasi-experimental designs in regression-model terms. You just need to be aware that the results from all three methods are identical. Okay, so here's the statistical model for the *t*-test in regression form (Figure 14–8).

Look familiar? It is identical to the formula I showed in Figure 14–2 to introduce dummy variables. Also, you may not realize it (although I hope against hope that you do), but essentially this formula is the equation for a straight line with a random error term (e_i) thrown in. Remember high school algebra? Remember high school? Okay, for those of you with faulty memories, you may recall that the equation for a straight line is often given as follows:

$$y = mx + b$$

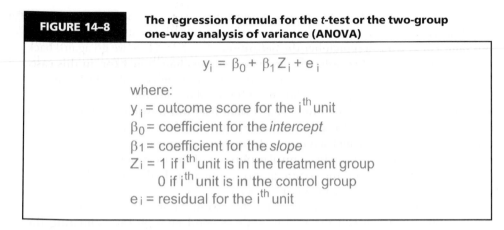

FIGURE 14–8   **The regression formula for the *t*-test or the two-group one-way analysis of variance (ANOVA)**

$$y_i = \beta_0 + \beta_1 Z_i + e_i$$

where:

y_i = outcome score for the ith unit

β_0 = coefficient for the *intercept*

β_1 = coefficient for the *slope*

Z_i = 1 if i^{th} unit is in the treatment group

　　 0 if i^{th} unit is in the control group

e_i = residual for the ith unit

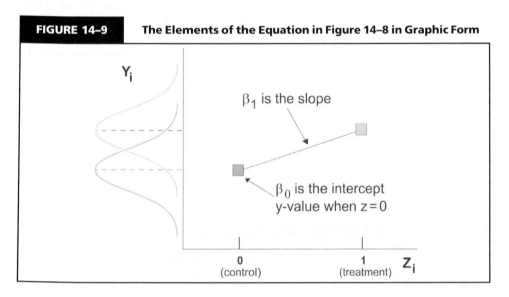

FIGURE 14–9   **The Elements of the Equation in Figure 14–8 in Graphic Form**

which, when rearranged can be written as follows:

$$y = b + mx$$

(The complexities of the commutative property make you nervous? If this gets too tricky, you may need to stop for a break. Have something to eat, make some coffee, or take the poor dog out for a walk.) Now you should see that in the statistical model y_i is the same as y in the straight line formula, β_0 is the same as b, β_1 is the same as m, and Z_i is the same as x. In other words, in the statistical formula, β_0 is the intercept and β_1 is the slope (Figure 14–9).

It is critical that you understand that the slope, β_1, is the same thing as the posttest difference between the means for the two groups. How can a slope be a difference between means? To see this, you have to look at a graph of what's going on, which I provide for you in Figure 14–9. The graph shows the posttest on the vertical axis. This is exactly the same as the two bell-shaped curves shown in Figures 14–5 and 14–6 except that here they're turned on their sides and are graphed on the vertical dimension. On the horizontal axis, the Z variable is plotted. This variable has only two possible values: a 0 if the person is in the control group or a 1 if the person is in the program group. This kind of variable is a dummy variable because it is a stand-in variable that represents the program or treatment conditions with its two values (see the discussion of dummy variables earlier in this chapter). The two points in the graph indicate the average posttest value for the control ($Z = 0$) and treated ($Z = 1$) cases. The line that connects the two dots is included only for visual enhancement purposes; because there are no Z values between 0 and 1, there can

15-1 Envisioning the Write-up

So now that you've completed the research project, what do you do? I know you won't want to hear this, but your work is still far from done. In fact, this final stage—writing up your research—may be one of the most difficult—and most important. Dr. Robert Day's book on scientific writing concludes with a very clear statement about just how important writing the research report is: "What I have said in this book is this: Scientific research is not complete until the results have been published. Therefore, a scientific paper is an *essential* part of the research process" (p. 184, 1998).

Developing a good, effective, and concise report is an art form in itself, and in many research projects, you will need to write multiple reports that present the results at different levels of detail for different audiences. In this chapter you'll get an overview of the various kinds of reports you might eventually write, as well as a more detailed treatment of the most common kind of report using the most general format.

15-1a The Type of Report

The course in which you are studying this book is most likely devoted to helping you write two important kinds of papers before you have any data: the literature review and the research proposal. But if you do a systematic and careful job with your literature review and proposal, then any subsequent write-up of the complete study will be much easier to adapt to the purpose of the particular version of your study you need to write. Here is a list of some of the types of papers you may end up writing about any given research project: summary for study participants, report to the internal review board, paper for a class, abstract of the study to be submitted as a proposal for a conference paper or poster, thesis or dissertation, report to funding agency, summary for campus newspaper, technical report for distribution at a conference or on the Internet, peer-reviewed article for electronic or paper journal publication, chapter in a book, or a complete monograph reporting a series of studies. Each of these kinds of reports involves some common general considerations to keep in mind while planning your write-up.

15-1b The Audience

Who is going to read the report? Reports will differ considerably depending on whether the audience will want or require technical detail, whether they are looking for a summary of results, or whether they are about to examine your research in a Ph.D. examination.

15-1c The Story Line

I believe that every research project has at least one major story in it. Sometimes the story centers around a specific research finding. Sometimes it is based on a methodological problem or challenge. When you write your report, you should attempt to tell the story to your reader. Even in formal journal articles where you will be required to be concise and detailed at the same time, a good story line can help make an otherwise dull report interesting to the reader. The manner in which the story is told may be depend on whether your study is qualitative, quantitative, or a mixed methods study, but in all cases a well-written report will have a story that flows in a coherent and interesting way.

The hardest part of telling the story in your research is finding the story in the first place. Usually when you come to writing up your research you have been steeped in the details for weeks or months (and sometimes even for years). You've been worrying about sampling responses, struggling with operationalizing your measures, dealing with the details of design, and wrestling with the data analysis. You're a bit like the ostrich that has its head in the sand. To find the story in your research, you have to pull your head out of the sand and look at the big picture. You have to try to view your research from your audience's perspective. You may have to let go of some of the details that you obsessed so much about and leave them out of the write-up or bury them in technical appendices or tables.

15-1d The Writing Style

Are you writing a research report to submit for publication in a journal? If so, you should be aware that every journal requires articles that follow specific formatting guidelines. Thinking of writing a book? Again, every publisher requires specific formatting. Writing a term paper? Most faculty members require you to follow specific guidelines. Doing your thesis or dissertation? Every university I know of has strict policies about formatting and style. There are legendary stories that circulate among graduate students about the dissertation that was rejected because the page margins were a quarter inch off or the figures weren't labeled correctly.

Further guidance on writing style can be found in a variety of books written to help students in various disciplines with major writing tasks. For example, former American Psychological Association President Robert Sternberg, one of the most prolific writers in the field, produced a very helpful guide to scientific writing that covers many of the basics of good writing, as well as professional issues such as finding a book publisher (2003). Locke, Spirduso, and Silverman's (2000) book on proposal writing, now in the fourth edition, remains a very popular guide across disciplines and includes examples of experimental, quasi-experimental, and qualitative study proposals, as well as a funded grant proposal. In addition, a growing number of books have been written to integrate advice on coping with the challenges of graduate school with specific guidance on writing the thesis and dissertation (for example, Heppner & Heppner, 2004; Rudestam & Newton, 2001).

15-1e Quantitative, Qualitative and Mixed Methods Write-ups*

If you browse some journals in your field that are primarily quantitative, and then browse some journals in your field that are primarily qualitative, you will notice some obvious differences in the papers published. These differences include the degree to which writers appear to take an objective versus subjective stance, the kinds of goals expressed, the use of numbers versus quotes or other "raw data," and so on. The

---

*Krathwohl, D.R. and Smith, N.L., (2005). *How To Prepare A Dissertation Proposal: Suggestions For Students In Education and the Social and Behavioral Sciences.* Syracuse, NY: Syracuse University Press.

differences should not make you think that there are no commonalities. Gilgun (2005) encouraged qualitative researchers to write with "grab," Glaser's term for writing that is memorable and interesting. I think the concept of writing with grab applies well to all kinds of writing, although you have to be a little careful about this when writing for technical or scientific journals where the norm is to stick to a straightforward presentation of the facts and a dispassionate rendering of your conclusions.

As you learned in a previous chapter, mixed methods designs are in a formative stage and norms for writing are not yet well established. But I can say without hesitation that writing a mixed methods report requires first and foremost a clear statement of purpose and a coherent rationale tying the choices made in framing questions to the choices made in the methods used to generate answers. One of the best ways to communicate a clear message about purpose and procedures is to use a study schema.

15-1f The Study Schema

study schema
A graphic display showing the procedural steps of a study and indicating the number of participants at each step.

Graphic **study schemas** can be very helpful in communicating the overall plan and flow of a study, whether the study includes mixed methods, or solely qualitative or quantitative procedures. One of the most important examples of the use of such graphics in communication is the CONSORT (Consolidated Standards of Reporting Trials) statement. The CONSORT group was formed by a scientists and editors who were concerned about the lack of uniformity in reporting of clinical trials and the introduction of bias in the report of studies that resulted from the variability in reporting. The group maintains a Web site (http://www.consort-statement.org) and periodically updates their recommendations. The CONSORT guidelines have now been adopted by dozens of leading scientific journals. The current CONSORT flowchart for reporting studies is shown in Figure 15–1. Qualitative researchers make extensive use of graphics to illustrate study processes as well as outcomes, although as you might expect, they tend to do so in a less structured manner than quantitative reporters.

15-1g Distribution Media

distribution media
In the context of research, it is the universe of possibilities for sharing a research report including all paper and electronic forms.

reference database program
A specialized kind of database program designed to help writers keep track of citations. It may include special tools for managing references from the point when a researcher downloads a citation from a bibliographic database to the writing of a manuscript.

digital repository
A publicly shared electronic archive for research reports and data.

As of this writing, you cannot download a research paper from *iTunes*, but you can do so from virtually any journal Web site. You can also organize personal databases of electronic references, abstracts, and even figures and tables with programs such as *EndNote*, a powerful **reference database program** for researchers that may be the research equivalent of *iTunes* in terms of organizing your own personal knowledge base. Most likely you will have obtained much of your background literature from electronic sources, and you may find that your own work will be published in an electronic journal or accessible from some other Web-based portal. Most leading journals produce both paper and electronic versions, and increasingly, electronic-only journals are becoming accepted in academic circles. The Internet is also home to a variety of specialized knowledge bases, such as government, university, and private Web sites. For example, DSpace (http://dspace.org/index.html), an open-source program created as a joint venture of MIT and Hewlett Packard, is a "**digital repository**" for papers, data, programs, and other research materials. Any organization can establish its own repository, which is linked to all others. In a sense, it is like *EndNote* in that it provides a way to organize and index a large and growing volume of knowledge, except on a public rather than personal scale. Technological developments will continue to affect the way we report studies, but I hope there will be a purpose beyond the mere application of technology—to speed the dissemination of findings in order to improve practice, thus improving quality of life for as many people as possible.

15-2 Key Elements of the Research Report

To illustrate what a set of research report specifications might include, I present in this section general guidelines for the formatting of a research write-up for a class term

| FIGURE 15–1 | **The CONSORT flowchart** |

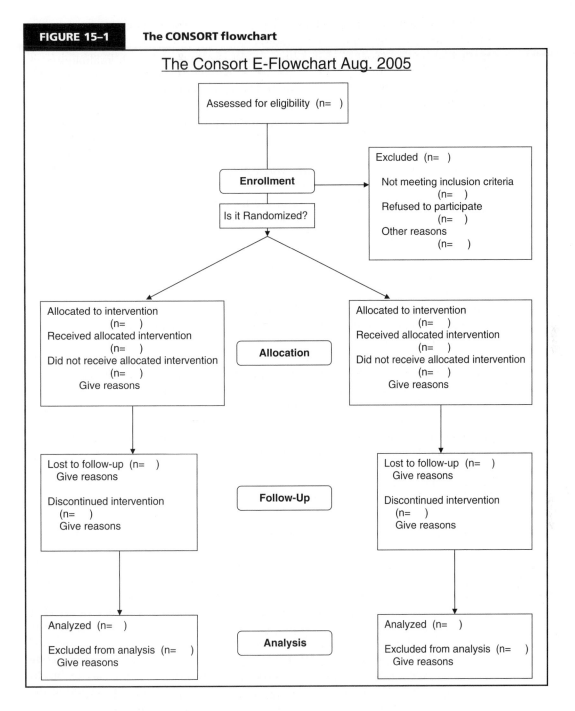

The Consort E-Flowchart Aug. 2005

paper. These guidelines are similar to the types of specifications you might be required to follow for a journal article. However, you need to check the specific formatting guidelines for the report you are writing; the ones presented here are likely to differ in some ways from any other guidelines that may be required in other contexts.

Following you will see the elements or criteria that you must typically address in a research paper, like the one I typically require from students in my courses. The assumption here is that you are addressing a causal hypothesis in your paper.

I. Introduction

1. *Statement of the problem:* State the general problem area clearly and unambiguously. Discuss the importance and significance of the problem area.

cause-effect relationship
A cause effect relationship. For example, when you evaluate whether your treatment or program causes an outcome to occur, you are examining a causal relationship.

hypothesis
A specific statement of prediction.

sample
The actual units you select to participate in your study.

external validity
The degree to which the conclusions in your study would hold for other persons in other places and at other times.

generalizability
The degree to which study conclusions are valid for members of the population not included in the study sample.

scaling
The branch of measurement that involves the construction of an instrument that associates qualitative constructs with quantitative metric units.

reliability
The degree to which a measure is consistent or dependable; the degree to which it would give you the same result over and over again, assuming the underlying phenomenon is not changing.

construct validity
The degree to which inferences can legitimately be made from the operationalizations in your study to the theoretical constructs on which those operationalizations are based.

design
The design of a study is the specification of how the research question will be answered. A research design should specify how the selection of participants, method of assignment, and choice of measures and time frame work together to accomplish the study objectives.

internal validity
The approximate truth of inferences regarding cause-effect or causal relationships.

2. *Statement of causal relationship:* Clearly state **cause-effect relationship** to be studied and relate it sensibly to the problem area.
3. *Statement of constructs:* Explain each key construct in the research/evaluation project (minimally, both the cause and effect). Ensure that explanations are readily understandable (that is, jargon-free) to an intelligent reader.
4. *Literature citations and review:* Cite literature from reputable and appropriate sources (such as professional journals and books, and not *Time, Newsweek*, and so on). Condense the literature in an intelligent fashion and include only the most relevant information. Ensure that all citations are in the correct format. Describe the search procedures you used, including databases and keywords (Cooper, 1998).
5. *Statement of hypothesis:* Clearly state the **hypothesis** (or hypotheses) and specify what the paper predicts. The relationship of the hypothesis to both the problem statement and literature review must be readily understood from reading the text.

II. Methods

Sample section:
1. *Sampling procedure specifications:* Describe the procedure for selecting units (such as subjects and records) for the study and ensure that it is appropriate. State which sampling method you used and why. Describe the population and sampling frame. In an evaluation, the program participants are frequently self-selected (volunteers) and if so, should be described as such.
2. *Sample description:* Describe the **sample** accurately and ensure that it is appropriate. Anticipate problems in contacting and measuring the sample.
3. **External validity** *considerations:* Consider **generalizability** from the sample to the sampling frame and population.

Measurement section:
1. *Measures:* Describe each outcome measurement construct briefly. (A minimum of *two* outcome constructs is required.) For each construct, briefly describe the measure or measures and include an appropriate citation and reference (unless you created the measure). Describe briefly any measure you constructed and *provide the entire measure* in an appendix. The measures that are used are relevant to the hypotheses of the study and are included in those hypotheses. Wherever possible, use multiple measures of the same construct.
2. *Construction of measures:* Clearly word questionnaires, tests, and interviews. They should be specific, appropriate for the population, and follow in a logical fashion. Follow the standards for good questions. For archival data, describe original data collection procedures adequately and construct indices (for example, combinations of individual measures) correctly. For scales, you must describe briefly which **scaling** procedure you used and how you implemented it. Describe the procedures you used for collecting the qualitative measures in detail.
3. *Reliability and validity:* You must address both the **reliability** and validity of *all* of your measures. For reliability, you must specify what estimation procedure(s) you used. For validity, you must explain how you assessed **construct validity**. Wherever possible, you should minimally address both convergent and discriminant validity. The procedures that are used to examine reliability and validity are appropriate for the measures.

Design and Procedures section:
1. *Design:* Clearly present the **design** in both notational and text form. Ensure that the design is appropriate for the problem and addresses the hypothesis.
2. *Internal validity:* Discuss threats to **internal validity** and how they are addressed by the design. Also consider any threats to internal validity that are not well controlled.

3. *Description of procedures:* Include an overview of how the study will be conducted. Describe the sequence of events and ensure that it is appropriate to the design. Include sufficient information so that the essential features of the study could be replicated by a reader.

III. Results

1. *Statement of Results:* State the results concisely and ensure that they are plausible for the research described.
2. *Tables:* Format a table (or tables) correctly to present part of the analysis accurately and concisely.
3. *Figures:* Design figure(s) clearly to accurately describe a relevant aspect of the results.

IV. Conclusions, Abstract, and Reference Sections

1. *Implications of the study:* Assuming the expected results are obtained, discuss the implications of these results. Briefly mention any remaining problems that you anticipate in the study.
2. *Abstract:* The **abstract** is 125 words or less and presents a concise picture of the proposed research. Include major constructs and hypotheses. The abstract is the first section of the paper.
3. *References:* Include all **citations** to each **reference** in the correct format and ensure that they are appropriate for the study described.

Stylistic Elements

I. **Professional Writing**
Avoid first person and sex-stereotyped forms. Present material in an unbiased and unemotional (for example, no feelings about things), but not necessarily uninteresting, fashion.

II. **Parallel Construction**
Keep tense parallel within and between sentences (as appropriate).

III. **Sentence Structure**
Use correct sentence structure and punctuation. Avoid incomplete and run-on sentences.

IV. **Spelling and Word Usage**
Make sure that spelling and word usage are appropriate. Correctly capitalize and abbreviate words.

V. **General Style**
Ensure that the document is neatly produced and reads well, and that the format for the document has been correctly followed.

15-3 Formatting

In this section, I discuss formatting a research article or a research report. This discussion follows the formatting requirements stated in the *Publication Manual of the American Psychological Association* (American Psychological Association [APA], 2001), often referred to as APA formatting. Although APA formatting is widely followed in the social sciences, it is not universally required. However, virtually every publisher adheres to some set of format guidelines. Please consult the specific guidelines that are required by the publisher for the type of document you are producing.

In APA format, for example, all sections of a research paper are typed, double-spaced on white 8 ½-by 11-inch paper with 12-point typeface with all margins set to 1 inch. Every page has a header in the upper-right corner with the running header right-justified on the top line and the page number right-justified and double-spaced

abstract
A concise description of a research study, usually displayed at the beginning of a research publication as a summary.

citation
A brief reference in the text of a research write-up to a specific source used in the article, such as another research article, website, book, etc. Each citation in a write-up should have a complete reference included in the reference section at the end of the article.

reference
A complete description of a source (such as another research article, website, book, etc.) that is relevant to your research, including authors, title, date, publisher, page numbers and location. References for a research write-up are usually all listed at the end of the article.

have to confirm your hypotheses. In fact, the common experience in social research is the finding of no effect.

15-3k Conclusions

Here you should describe the conclusions you reach (assuming you got the results described in the Results section). You should relate these conclusions back to the level of the construct and the general problem area that you described in the introduction. You should also discuss the overall strength of the research proposed (for example, a general discussion of the strong and weak validity areas) and should present some suggestions for possible future research that would be sensible based on the results of this work.

15-3l References

There are really two parts to a reference citation. First, there is the way you cite the item in the text when you are discussing it. Second, there is the way you list the complete reference in the reference section in the back of the report.

Reference Citations in the Text of Your Paper Cited references appear in the text of your paper and are a way of giving credit to the source of the information you quoted or used in your paper. They generally consist of the following bits of information:

> The author's last name, unless first initials are needed to distinguish between two authors with the same last name. If there are six or more authors, the first author is listed followed by the term, et al., and then the year of the publication is given in parenthesis. The year of publication appears in parentheses. Page numbers are given with a quotation or when only a specific part of a source was used.

> "To be or not to be" (Shakespeare, 1660, p. 241)

One Work by One Author:
> Rogers (1994) compared reaction times . . .

One Work by Multiple Authors:
> Wasserstein, Zappulla, Rosen, Gerstman, and Rock (1994) [first time you cite in text].
> Wasserstein et al. (1994) found [subsequent times you cite in text].

Reference List in Reference Section There are a wide variety of reference citation formats. Before submitting any research report, you should check to see which type of format is considered acceptable for that context. If there is no official format requirement, the most sensible thing is for you to select one approach and implement it consistently. (There's nothing worse than a reference list with a variety of formats.) Here, I'll illustrate by example some of the major reference items and how they might be cited in the reference section.

The references list all the articles, books, and other sources used in the research and preparation of the paper and cited with a parenthetical (textual) citation in the text. These items are entered in alphabetical order according to the authors' last names; if a source does not have an author, alphabetize according to the first word of the title, disregarding the articles *a*, *an*, and *the* if they are the first word in the title.

Examples

Book by One Author:
Jones, T. (1940). *My life on the road.* New York: Doubleday.

Book by Two Authors:
Williams, A., & Wilson, J. (1962). *New ways with chicken.* New York: Harcourt.

Book by Three or More Authors:
Smith, J., Jones, J., & Williams, S. (1976). *Common names.* Chicago: University of Chicago Press.

Book with No Given Author or Editor:
Handbook of Korea (4th ed.). (1982). Seoul: Korean Overseas Information, Ministry of Culture & Information: Author.

Two or More Books by the Same Author:
Oates, J. C. (1990). *Because it is bitter, and because it is my heart.* New York: Dutton.
Oates, J. C. (1993). *Foxfire: Confessions of a girl gang.* New York: Dutton.

Note: Entries by the same author are arranged chronologically by the year of publication, the earliest first. References with the same first author and different second and subsequent authors are listed alphabetically by the surname of the second author, and then by the surname of the third author. References with the same authors in the same order are entered chronologically by year of publication, the earliest first. References by the same author (or by the same two or more authors in identical order) with the same publication date are listed alphabetically by the first word of the title following the date; lower case letters (*a*, *b*, *c*, and so on) are included after the year, within the parentheses.

Book by a Corporate (Group) Author:
President's Commission on Higher Education. (1977). *Higher education for American democracy.* Washington, DC: U.S. Government Printing Office.

Book with an Editor:
Bloom, H. (Ed.). (1988). *James Joyce's Dubliners.* New York: Chelsea House.

A Translation:
Dostoevsky, F. (1964). *Crime and punishment* (J. Coulson, Trans.). New York: Norton (Original work published 1866).

An Article or Reading in a Collection of Pieces by Several Authors (Anthology):
O'Connor, M. F. (1975). *Everything that rises must converge.* In J. R. Knott, Jr., & C. R. Raeske (Eds.), *Mirrors: An introduction to literature* (2nd ed., pp. 58–67. San Francisco: Canfield.

Edition of a Book:
Tortora, G. J., Funke, B. R., & Case, C. L. (1989). *Microbiology: An introduction* (3rd ed.). Redwood City, CA: Benjamin/Cummings.

Diagnostic and Statistical Manual of Mental Disorders:
American Psychiatric Association. (1994). *Diagnostic and statistical manual of mental disorders* (4th ed.). Washington, DC: Author.

A Work in Several Volumes:
Churchill, W. S. (1957). *A history of the English speaking peoples: Vol. 3. The age of revolution.* New York: Dodd, Mead.

Encyclopedia or Dictionary
Cockrell, D. (1980). Beatles. In *The new Grove dictionary of music and musicians* (6th ed., Vol. 2, pp. 321–322). London: Macmillan.

Article from a Weekly Magazine:
Jones, W. (1970, August 14). Today's kids. *Newseek, 76,* 10–15.

Article from a Monthly Magazine:
Howe, I. (1968, September). James Baldwin: At ease in apocalypse. *Harper's, 237,* 92–100.

Article from a Newspaper:
Brody, J. E. (1976, October 10). Multiple cancers termed on increase. *New York Times (national ed.),* p. A37.

Article from a Scholarly Academic or Professional Journal:
Barber, B. K. (1994). Cultural, family, and personal contexts of parent-adolescent conflict. *Journal of Marriage and the Family, 56,* 375–386.

Government Publication:
U.S. Department of Labor. Bureau of Labor Statistics. (1980). *Productivity.* Washington, DC: U.S. Government Printing Office.

Pamphlet or Brochure:
Research and Training Center on Independent Living. (1993). *Guidelines for reporting and writing about people with disabilities* (4th ed.) [Brochure]. Lawrence, KS: Author.

15-3m Tables

Any tables should have a heading with "Table #" (where # is the table number), followed by the title for the heading that describes concisely what is contained in the table. Tables and figures are typed on separate sheets at the end of the paper after the references and before the appendices. In the text you should put a reference where each table or figure should be inserted using this form: "Insert Table 1 about here."

15-3n Figures

Figures are drawn on separate sheets at the end of the paper after the references and tables, and before the appendices. In the text you should put a reference where each figure will be inserted using this form: "Insert Figure 1 about here."

15-3o Appendices

Appendices should be used only when absolutely necessary. Generally, you will use them only for presentation of extensive measurement instruments, for detailed descriptions of the program or independent variable, and for any relevant supporting documents that you don't include in the body. Even if you include such appendices, you should briefly describe the relevant material in the body and give an accurate citation to the appropriate appendix (for example, "see Appendix A").

A Checklist for Reviewing Your Paper (or Critically Reviewing Any Other Study) One of the best ideas for improving the quality of your writing is to have it proofread by others. Ask a colleague or two for feedback about all aspects of the paper, from writing style to ethics to science. To help you get your paper ready for such an informal review, as well as the more formal evaluation of your professor or anonymous journal reviewers, I suggest you consider every question on the list in Table 15–1. In fact, this checklist can be used in reviewing any scientific report, but

TABLE 15–1	Some Questions to Ask When Critically Reviewing a Research Report*

Title/Abstract:
1. Does the title suggest the important constructs and relationships in the study?
2. Does the abstract provide sufficient information for you to make a decision about whether to read the full article?
3. Is the purpose of the study clearly stated?
4. Does the introduction make the purpose of the study easy to understand?

Introduction/Literature Review
1. Is the topic of the study introduced in terms of what is already known about the subject?
2. Have the authors described relevant theories? Do they propose any problems with existing theories that they will address in their study?
3. Have conflicting findings from previous studies been discussed? Was any insight provided as to how to explain the conflicting results?
4. Were decisions about the design and procedures of the present study justified in terms of prior studies?
5. Were the study goals or hypotheses clearly stated?

Method—Participants
1. Were the subjects treated in an ethically enlightened manner?
2. Was the study reviewed by an ethics committee/board?
3. Is there a clear explanation of why these particular subjects were sampled?
4. What was the selection process?
5. Was random selection or assignment used?
6. Was a power analysis done?
7. Is there any evidence of bias due to poor sampling or non-response (missing data)? Are details of non-participants or dropouts given?

Method—Design
1. Was a specific research design named?
2. Are the primary variables defined?
3. Have any particular validity threats been identified?
4. Have any particular validity threats been overlooked?
5. If this is a longitudinal study are the number and timing of observations justified?
6. If this is an intervention study, have treatment procedures been clearly described?

Method—Measures
1. Are all of the instruments used well described and referenced?
2. Has reliability and validity data been presented for each instrument?
3. Are there any researcher-constructed instruments in the study? Have they been pilot tested?
4. Does the study report the exact protocol used for obtaining measures?
5. Have scoring procedures been described? Are there any deviations from standard scoring procedures?

Method—Data Analysis
1. Have the data analysis procedures been described in detail?
2. Do they fit the questions being asked?
3. Have assumptions of statistical tests been checked?
4. To what extent have data been explored for irregularities such as non-random missingness and outliers?
5. How was missing data handled?

(continued)

TABLE 15-1	**Some Questions to Ask When Critically Reviewing a Research Report** (*Continued*)

6. Have references been given for any statistical software used?
7. Is practical or clinical significance described?
8. Are effect sizes and confidence intervals given?
9. Are exact p values provided?
10. Have the authors "gone fishing"?

Results and Discussion
1. Do the study conclusions relate directly to the results, or do they range beyond the results into speculation?
2. Do the study conclusions relate directly to the purpose and hypotheses of the study?
3. Are the results linked in the discussion to prior knowledge?
4. Are limitations of the study discussed?
5. Have the authors given you an adequate answer to the question, "So what?"

Figures
1. Does the figure caption clearly identify the variables?
2. Are the figure axes clearly labeled?
3. Does the figure "stand alone," or do you have to refer to text to understand it?

Tables
1. Does the title clearly indicate which variables or categories of variables are included in the table?
2. Are the rows and columns clearly labeled?
3. Are significance tests noted?
4. Does the table "stand alone," or do you have to refer to text to understand it?

References
1. Are the references appropriately formatted?
2. Do the references include key sources by leading researchers in the area?

Writing Style
1. Is a particular writing style consistently used?
2. What is the overall quality of the writing? (Consider technical aspects of style as well as your overall impression of the paper with regard to quality of writing.)

---

* Some items adapted from Locke, Silverman, and Spirduso (2000) and Fink (2004).

if you get in the habit of systematically asking these kinds of questions about your own work, your critical thinking skills are likely to develop nicely.

Summary

This chapter discussed the last step in a typical research project—the write-up. I outlined the key elements that typically must be included somewhere in a standard research write-up—the introduction, methods, results, and conclusions—and described what should be included in each of these sections. I described the major style issues you should watch out for when writing the typical report, and I presented one way to format a research paper appropriately, including how to cite other research in your report. Even though formatting rules can vary widely from one field to another, once you see how a set of rules guides report writing, it's a simple matter to change the formatting for a different audience or editorial policy.

So, with the write-up, the formal part of the research process is complete. You've taken the journey down the research road, from the initial plan for your trip, through all of the challenges along the way, and now with the write-up, on to your final destination. Now what? If you're a researcher, you don't stay in one place for very long. The thrill of the journey is just too much to resist. You begin pulling out the road maps (formulating research questions and hypotheses) and thinking about how you'd like to get to your next destination. There's a certain restlessness, a bit of research-based wanderlust that sets in. And there are all the lessons you've learned from your previous research journeys. Now, if on this next trip you can only avoid the potholes! After you've done research for a while, you might actually start thinking about how the research can be utilized or related to practice, how you can do research (like evaluation) in more immediately practical contexts, and how we might look across multiple research studies to assess what is goin on (i.e., meta-analysis). Each of these topics is introduced in Chapter 16.

I hope that when you set out on your own research journey, you'll take this book along. Consider it a brief guidebook, a companion that might help point the way when you're feeling lost. And be sure to watch out for those bumps in the road.

Login to the Online Edition of your text at www.atomicdog.com to find additional resources located in the Study Guide at the end of each chapter.

CHAPTER 16

Evaluation, Research Synthesis, Meta-analysis, and Evidence-Based Practice

KEY TERMS

evidence-based practice
meta-analysis
research synthesis
effect size
meta-analysis
secondary analysis
cost-effectiveness and cost-benefit
analysis
impact evaluation
outcome evaluations

process evaluation
implementation evaluation
structured conceptualization
evaluability assessment
needs assessment
summative evaluations
formative evaluation
evaluation
evolutionary epistemology

16-1 Background and Context

This book was primarily written to help you navigate the road to research and perhaps feel that you were in the company of a trusted guide along the way. Most of the stops on the research road have been places where you would meet ideas about such things as measurement, design, and analysis. I tried to pay some attention to where we'd been and where we were going in linking the chapters together, but mainly our view has been up-close to the matter at hand, topic by topic, study by study, chapter by chapter, step by step. But, then what? How can we use our research skills to address real-world problems and generate practically useful results that affect decision-making and policy development? We consider such applied uses of research methods in the section in this chapter on *evaluation*. Furthermore, imagine that the research road you've been on has come to a surprising turn: You can now see the entire journey for your research project, and you can see the projects and paths that others have taken in their research projects, too. Imagine the view as from a mountaintop, where you can see all of the terrain and take it in as a whole. Wouldn't that be something? Well, in this chapter we're also going to introduce you to this broader perspective. *Research synthesis, meta-analysis,* and *evidence-based practice* are all terms that reflect this mountaintop view.

This chapter addresses some of the most important innovations in contemporary research methods over the past decade, although most have histories that stretch way back to the late 1800s. Evaluation research is a subfield of social science that not only addresses the evidence-based practice question of "what works," but also has a long-standing focus on how things work and how well. Research synthesis is a systematic approach used to integrate the results of multiple studies, including qualitative and mixed methods approaches. Meta-analysis is a specific type of research synthesis that can be used when quantitative results are available from multiple studies. These methods are part of a new movement of "evidence-based practice" that encourages that practice in the form of research and that we make more effective use of research in practice. This movement holds the promise of a new era in the way our society integrates research into the way we live.

16-2 An Evolutionary, Ecological, Systems View of Research

This volume so far has emphasized how we would conduct a single research study. But what difference does a single study make? How do we use the results of a study

16-5

In this se
our curre
value of t
produce t

1. The d
   bases.
2. Recog
   empha
3. Intern
   and ex
   to be a
4. Innova
   tions a
   and Ru
   (1998
   (2006)
   sis and

We b
culture, a
and evide

16-6

Since its i
(USDA)
central t
service (h
the origi
as part of
shall con
(Dunifor
tember
the focu
related t
curity (p
view fro
tler, and
ogy, a fie

16-7

Evaluati
also has
and how
ical area
research
social re
tional co
sitivity t
not rely
and som

to advance knowledge? It should be clear by now that no study by itself can ever be considered perfect. Every study will have some threats to validity that cannot be completely addressed. So, how do we build our understanding and knowledge, a firm evidence base, from an imperfect, fallible study? The short answer to this question is that we don't. No single study is likely to resolve the complexities of a topic of interest. And that's the key to the answer—we don't rely on a single study to establish knowledge. Ultimately, we look at multiple studies. Research synthesis of multiple studies, meta-analysis of quantitative results as part of research synthesis, the dissemination and of the resulting evidence-based interventions, and the evaluation of their effects, are all essential to the building of our knowledge in science and in applied social research.

At the root of how a single study fits into the larger endeavor of human knowledge acquisition is a philosophical framework, a perspective about what we are trying to accomplish in research, a view that is based on the ideas of evolution and ecological systems thinking. Let's start with a basic idea, that of evolution. Just as species evolve, philosophers also have come to believe that ideas evolve. This is a notion called **evolutionary epistemology** (Campbell, 1974, 1988; Popper, 1985), the idea that our knowledge about the world evolves according to the same principles that describe the evolution of all life. In evolutionary theory generally we believe that there is variation among organisms. If the organism survives its environment, its unique variations have a higher chance of being preserved and passed on to others. If not, they become extinguished along with the organism. A similar process occurs with ideas. New ideas are suggested that are invariably based in some way on previous thinking. Sometimes they take hold. Other times they are criticized and rejected, or simply ignored altogether. There is, in effect, an evolutionary process of natural selection for ideas just as there is for species. A research project is simply the examination of one or more ideas (the questions or hypotheses). The results of our research might be accepted, be criticized and rejected, or ignored altogether. Biologists will tell you that evolution operates on populations of species. In each generation of a species there will be variation and some of this variation may be selected for and survive, and be promulgated through the species more broadly over time. The same thing might be said for research. For any given issue or problem we may over time generate a population of studies, a collection of studies that all differ slightly from each other (at the very least they are done with different people, in different settings and at different times). We want to look at these studies and try to decide which variations or studies are telling us something valuable, which should "survive" to contribute to our knowledge about the issue.

Research synthesis and its quantitative sub-field of meta-analysis are designed to look at populations of studies to determine what they say as a species or group. In essence, research methods contribute studies that form this population and research synthesis and meta-analysis are critically important tools for the selection of survivor ideas in the evolution of our knowledge. Evidence-Based Practice is the process of disseminating or encouraging the use of the surviving knowledge or evidence from synthesis and meta-analysis. Evaluation can be viewed as the process of assessing or providing feedback about the effects of using programs that we established as potentially applicable in previous research. In addition, multiple evaluations on similar programs contribute to the ecology and provide more variation for us to use in understanding what works and evolving better knowledge and solutions to problems.

When we situate research as an evolutionary endeavor, and a research study as one of a population of similar studies that accrue over time to address some central problem or question, we are viewing a research project as part of an ecology of research, one element in a system of how people come to understand the world around us. This leads us to think a little differently about a specific research project. Increasingly, we are recognizing how important it is to see our research within an ecological and systems framework and to apply systems thinking principles and perspectives to our stand-alone research studies.

evolutionary epistemology
A philosophical position that holds that all knowledge evolves through evolutionary processes of natural selection.

16-8 The Rise of Research Synthesis, Meta-Analysis, and Evidence-Based Practice in Medicine, Social Science, and Education

In one of his early films, *Sleeper*, Woody Allen played a person who wakes up in the future after years of slumber. Among his first experiences upon waking was hearing a radio report proclaiming that a new study had shown that red meat was extremely good for you, the opposite, the announcer said, of what had long believed to be true. We haven't quite heard that report yet, but we have all had the experience of hearing or reading about some surprising new study that reports something different than what had been "common knowledge" until that point.

Woody's film and our everyday experience of news reports suggests that progress in research is a sort of all-or-nothing process in which truth is revealed by the latest p value but also suggesting that we shouldn't have much faith in the durability of the individual products of science. In the preface of their book, *Summing Up*, a classic in the field of research synthesis, Light and Pillemer (1984) cited a typically incisive comment from Mark Twain that captures the problem: "The thirteenth stroke of a clock is not only false itself, but casts grave doubts on the credibility of the preceding twelve" (p. viii). Thus, to counter the sense of doubt we need a valid method of taking all of the evidence into account; that is, to synthesize prior research.

As you begin to research the prior knowledge base in your topic area, there is a reasonable chance that you will come across "contradictory findings" that others have used to motivate their studies, and it is also reasonably likely that at the end of the study, further studies are advised. Once again, from this perspective it is reasonable to see research as a pretty disappointing enterprise, short on definitive answers and long on contradictions and controversies.

This situation may reflect the inevitable pace of an evolutionary process based on deliberate but flawed methods. But researchers going all the way back to Karl Pearson knew that some kind of summative accounting of data must be possible and that such an analysis would help overcome the inevitable limits of the individual study in terms of sampling, measures, and conclusions. It took until the latter part of the 1900s for research synthesis, meta-analysis, and evidence-based practice to come of age, in part because of controversies over some of the most basic practices in research.

16-9 Problems with Null Hypothesis Significance Testing

Kline (2004) recently wrote a text to help us move beyond the controversies about null hypothesis significance testing. The controversy essentially has revolved around the over-reliance on null hypothesis testing, particularly the misuse of probability values associated with statistical tests. As Kline and others (for example, Wilkinson and the Task Force on Statistical Inference, 1999) have noted, a p value indicates only the probability of an observed result, *assuming that the null hypothesis is true*. It does not "prove" the null or alternative hypothesis, it does not provide a measure of the likelihood of the result being replicated, and perhaps most critically, it does not tell us how big the result is or how important it is in practical or clinical terms. And as you know from our prior discussion of statistical power, a significance test result has much to do with sample size as well as the size of the effect. A large enough sample will always produce a statistically significant result. To more accurately report on the results of a study, we should report effect sizes with confidence intervals in order to gauge the precision of the estimates and should provide a contextual interpretation that includes attention to practical and/or clinical significance as much as possible.

16-10 Effect Sizes and Confidence Intervals

The fundamental idea of meta-analysis and research synthesis is the **effect size** (Lipsey & Wilson, 2001). An effect size is a signal-to-noise ratio that expresses the size of a relationship or a difference in a standardized way. By translating findings from different studies into a common metric, summary effect sizes (weighted by sample sizes and taking into account methodological strengths and weaknesses) can be calculated. These effects might be represented in a statistic such as Cohen's *d*, which reflects the standardized mean difference between groups across multiple studies. Or an effect size might be constructed using the correlation or variance accounted for. No matter the index of effect uses, it is very important to calculate and report a confidence interval to give a sense of the precision of the effect size. The confidence interval allows the reader to know the likely upper and lower bounds of the estimated effect.

effect size
An effect size is a signal-to-noise ratio that expresses the size of a relationship or a difference in a standardized way. Effect sizes are important in planning studies so that we can estimate sample sizes accurately, in comparing results across studies, and in synthesizing research results as in meta-analysis.

16-11 Statistical, Practical, and Clinical Significance

Commentators from medicine, social science, and education have all recognized the importance of providing effect sizes and confidence intervals along with a contextual interpretation, and different fields have adapted to the circumstances of their problems and populations. For example, in medicine, an effect size might be expressed in an index known as the *Number Needed to Treat (NNT)*, that is, the number of patients a doctor has to treat in order to expect a "benefit" to be observed. The NNT is considered an index of clinical significance because it impacts clinical decision making. The benefit is often put into practically significant terms so that both patient and doctor can discuss such practical issues as the likelihood of being able to resume a vocation after treatment. Kline's book (2004) provides a detailed and very readable guide to computation of effect sizes and confidence intervals for most of the designs introduced in this text. But the determination of clinical and practical significance is very much in its infancy in most fields. As in our previous discussion of power analysis, researchers may use pilot data, prior published studies, and expert judgment to estimate clinically or practically significant effects.

16-12 Research Synthesis

Research synthesis, the process of producing integrative summaries of a body of research, has become a primary activity in science and applied social science. This is not only because of the oft-cited "explosive growth" in virtually every field but also because of a very practical issue: Before we plan a new study we should have a reasonable idea about where things stand. In the past, this was accomplished through the narrative literature review, a process now regarded as less systematic and more subjective than is possible or desirable. In addition, we need a systematic way to evaluate both the positives and the negatives in the history of a research problem.

research synthesis
A structured empirical process of producing integrative summaries of a body of research.

Most of the published research syntheses are based on quantitative data and are specifically called *meta-analysis*. But there are qualitative synthesis methods as well, although there is less standardization in procedures, similar to the state of things in the primary qualitative research. First we will consider meta-analysis (quantitative synthesis), and then move on to qualitative and mixed methods.

16-12a Meta-analysis

meta-analysis
A structured empirical analysis that integrates and summarizes results of multiple research studies or evaluations.

Cooper (1998) described a general stage model for **meta-analysis** or quantitative research synthesis. A similar model was later proposed by Lipsey and Wilson (2001) who added helpful details on quantitative procedures, including appendices with Effect Size formulas and Excel routines to conduct the analyses.

The basic stages of the model are shown in Figure 16–1. The most important and perhaps obvious characteristic of the model is that research synthesis turns literature review into a replicable scientific study. That is, instead of the subjective narrative review with variability in selection of studies, evaluation of evidence, and summary conclusions, we have a set of well-defined steps that clearly show how the synthesis of study findings was accomplished. That is not to say that the model makes research synthesis easy. In each stage, there are formidable challenges as an extensive methodological literature on the topic shows (Cooper & Hedges, 1994).

The first step of a research synthesis is to define the problem to be studied. As in a primary study, this may involve a statement of a hypothesis regarding a particular effect to be estimated (for example, Cooper has extensively examined the effect of homework on academic achievement) or may be more exploratory (for example, what is the best treatment for gambling addiction?). In either case, as in a primary study, the constructs of interest must be identified and defined. The synthesist will often encounter variations in definitions as well as the measures that have been used in prior studies. Decisions on which constructs and measures to include versus exclude must be documented, as well as the justification for such decisions.

In the literature search phase, the research synthesist encounters more decisions, including what studies to include in the review and how they will be accessed. Meta-analysts need to carefully specify inclusion criteria and document their efforts to explore the multiple channels available in study retrieval. Study inclusion criteria should be explained to the reader so that the tradeoffs between broad inclusiveness and a more restricted but higher quality set of studies are clear to the reader. The search procedures should be exhaustive and show efforts to retrieve studies via database searches as well as government documents, citation indexes, relevant journal, conference proceedings and consultation with well-known experts in the field (Lipsey & Wilson, 2001).

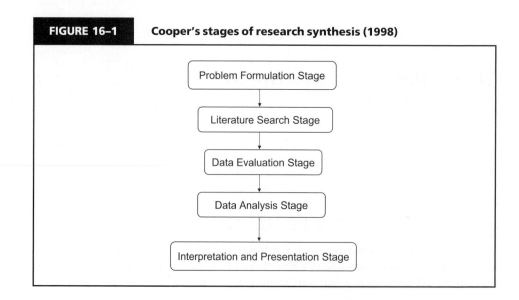

| **FIGURE 16–1** | **Cooper's stages of research synthesis (1998)** |

In addition, the development of a coding scheme is a major task. The coding scheme will enable systematic review of each study and typically includes study identification information, characteristics of the design such as type of design, sample, and measures, and detailed recording of all of the statistical outcomes reported. One of the key issues to be aware of in the search as well as the data evaluation stage is the "file drawer problem." It is well known that researchers are more likely to submit studies for publication if the results appear to be "significant," and it is also known that journal editors favor studies with "significant" results (Begg, 1994), again making the thoroughness of the search procedures a critical feature of the quality of the meta-analysis.

The data evaluation stage involves critical review of the yield of the literature search. In this phase, criteria may be applied that limit which kinds of designs will be included in the subsequent analysis. Cooper (1998) provided a set of possible guidelines for the critique, including a "threats to validity" perspective that is quite consistent with the emphasis of this text.

The next stage, data analysis, occurs when the analyst has extracted the statistical results from the studies and mathematically combines them into the overall effect size. This process involves assessing the variability of the observed effect sizes. If there is large variability (and there are statistics, most notably the Q statistic, to tell you), then consideration of what might account for that variability must be given. Quite often, such consideration includes study of potential moderators of effect sizes. Moderators are variables that interact with other study variables to influence outcomes. These may either have to do with the substantive area being studied or the designs used in the sample of studies. The data analysis stage has been facilitated by the emergence of computer programs. These include complete systems, such as *Comprehensive Meta-Analysis* (http://www.meta-analysis.com/), as well as guides such as Lipsey and Wilson's (2001), that provide examples of routines that can be run in common software such as Excel and SPSS.

The reporting stage should be handled as with any other scientific report. That is, sufficient information on all procedures and analyses should be included so that others may critically review or replicate the study. Graphic plots, such as the forest plot showing the effect size and confidence interval for all studies, are extremely helpful in communicating the results of a meta-analysis. Cooper also advised reporting on all possible threats to validity of study conclusions and his book provides numerous practical suggestions for assessing and reducing threats to validity of a research synthesis.

16-13 Qualitative Meta-Synthesis

Most of what has been written about research synthesis has focused on quantitative studies. But there is increasing interest in developing methods for synthesizing qualitative research as well. For example, Jensen and Rodgers (2001) described case study research as a goldmine waiting to be discovered. Similarly, Stake (2006) has recently produced a text that shows a method of cross-case analysis. These and other qualitative synthesis methods are in an early stage of development. Perhaps they have most in common with content analysis, reviewed in Chapter 13. In addition, it is fair to say that mixed methods research is at its core a synthetic approach because in most cases the goal of the study is to integrate results across more than one method within the single study.

16-14 Evidence-Based Practice

Medicine, perhaps motivated by the tremendous stakes for individuals and society as a whole, has been central to the development of **evidence-based practice** based on research synthesis. Sackett and colleagues (2000) described the history of

evidence-based practice
Evidence-based practice means the use of the best available programs or treatments based on careful evaluation using critically reviewed research.

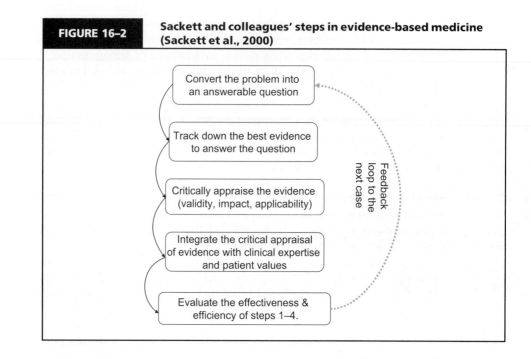

FIGURE 16–2 **Sackett and colleagues' steps in evidence-based medicine (Sackett et al., 2000)**

evidence-based medicine (EBM) in their concise guide. Beginning with the leadership of Professor Gordon Guyatt at McMaster University in Ontario, Canada, EBM has grown into a worldwide phenomenon, changing the culture of medical science, practice, and training profoundly. Sackett and colleagues defined EBM as "the integration of the best research with clinical expertise and patient values" (p. 1). Note that this is a three-part definition, giving weight to clinical judgment and patient preferences.

Sackett and colleagues developed the five-step model of EBM practice shown in Figure 16–2. The process was specifically designed for the clinical practice of medicine, but it can be generalized as a strategy for evidence-based practice. The first step is to put the problem into the form of an answerable question or questions. This means that the problem should be framed in terms that empirical inquiry may possibly help us with. Sackett and colleagues differentiated between background questions that address general aspects of a disorder such as causes and foreground questions that focus on the particular patient and possibilities for treatment, and they encouraged the evidence-based practitioner to include both kinds of questions.

The second step, tracking down the best evidence, has been transformed by computing technology and the efforts of professional groups to organize research synthesis so that it is widely accessible. Internet access to such databases means that in moments a doctor can find the most current research evidence, including synthesis, available. In addition to the main academic databases like *MedLine* and *PsychINFO*, there are evidence-based centers such at the *Cochrane Collection* in health care research (http://www.cochrane.org/) and the *Campbell Collaboration* for social science research (http://www.campbellcollaboration.org/), There are also specific evidence-based journals such as *Evidence-based Mental Health* that provide continuous updates on clinical problems.

The third step, critical appraisal of the evidence, is where the clinician's expertise as both a scientist and practitioner really kick in. At this step, Sackett and colleagues advise that the found evidence be appraised for three aspects: (1) validity, the apparent truth of the evidence based on the strength of the research; (2) impact, or the size of the effect reported in the research; and (3) applicability, or utility for the particular patient and setting.

Next, the clinical-scientist assesses the patient's values and preferences, discussing possible outcomes of treatments and side effects. In fields such as education, this may involve consultation with parents and other teachers and school personnel regarding a child's personality, abilities, interests, home situation, and so on. The relevant data on the individual case is then combined with the research evidence via a clinical judgment process in which parameters for a trial of a particular treatment, including how the outcome will be evaluated, are established.

Finally, the implementation and results are evaluated, with the goal of not only assessing the current status of the individual, but also feeding back into the cycle of evidence-based practice. In this sense, the evidence includes both that garnered from the research literature and from the lived experience of the practitioner with the patient, student, client, or other.

16-15 Conclusion: An Evaluation Culture

The ideas and methods introduced in this chapter suggest an important and implicit aspect of applied social research, the capacity for reflection and self-evaluation. Upon reflection, it is clear that we exist in a community of social researchers, a culture of its own. What are the values of the culture? Or, perhaps more important, what *should* its values be? Here I provide a vision of the types of values I would like to see become an integral part of 21st century thought in general, and of the applied research community in particular. There is no special order of importance to the way these ideas are presented; I'll leave that ordering to subsequent efforts. As you read this discussion, ask yourself how similar these values are to your own. What values do you think the applied research community should adopt? Here are my views.

First, an evaluation culture will embrace an *action-oriented* perspective that actively seeks solutions to problems, trying out tentative ones, weighing the results and consequences of actions, all within an endless evolutionary cycle of supposition-action-evidence-revision that characterizes good science and good management. This activist evaluation culture will encourage innovative approaches at all levels. However, well-intentioned activism by itself is not enough and may at times be risky, be dangerous, and lead to detrimental consequences. In an evaluation culture, you won't act for action's sake; you'll always attempt to assess the effects of your actions.

This evaluation culture will be an accessible, *teaching-oriented* one that emphasizes the unity of formal evaluation and everyday thought. Most evaluations will be simple, informal, efficient, practical, low-cost, and easily carried out and understood by nontechnicians. Evaluations won't just be delegated to one person or department; everyone will be encouraged to become involved in evaluating what they and their organizations do. Where technical expertise is needed experts will be encouraged to also educate others about the technical side of what they do, trying to find ways to explain their techniques and methods adequately for nontechnicians. Considerable resources will be devoted to teaching others about evaluation principles.

An evaluation culture will be *diverse, inclusive, participatory, responsive,* and *fundamentally nonhierarchical.* World problems cannot be solved by simple silver-bullet solutions. There is growing recognition in many arenas that the most fundamental problems are systemic, interconnected, and inextricably linked to social and economic issues and factors. Solutions will involve husbanding the resources, talents, and insights of a wide range of people. The formulation of problems and potential solutions needs to involve a broad range of constituencies. More than just research skills will be needed. Especially important will be skills in negotiation and consensus-building processes. Evaluators are familiar with arguments for greater diversity and inclusiveness; they've been talking about stakeholder, participative, multiple-constituency research for nearly two decades. No one that I know is seriously debating anymore whether there should be a move to more inclusive participatory approaches. The real question seems to be how such work might best be accomplished, and despite all the rhetoric about the importance of participatory methods, there is a long way to go in learning how to accomplish them effectively.

An evaluation culture will be a *humble, self-critical* one. Researchers will openly acknowledge limitations and recognize that what is learned from a single evaluation study, however well designed, will almost always be equivocal and tentative. In this regard, I believe cowardice in research is too often undervalued. I find it wholly appropriate that evaluators resist being drawn into making decisions for others, although certainly evaluation results should help inform decision makers. A cowardly approach helps prevent the evaluator from being drawn into the political context, helping ensure the impartiality needed for objective assessment, and it protects the evaluator from taking responsibility for making decisions that should be left to those who have been duly authorized and who have to live with the consequences. Most program decisions, especially decisions about whether to continue a program or close it down, must include more input than an evaluation alone can ever provide. While evaluators can help elucidate what has happened in the past or might happen under certain circumstances, it is the responsibility of the organization and society as a whole to determine what ought to happen. The debate about the appropriate role of an evaluator in the decision-making process is an extremely intense one right now in evaluation circles, and my position advocating a cowardly reluctance of the evaluator to undertake a decision-making role may well be in the minority. This issue needs to be debated vigorously, especially for politically complex, international-evaluation contexts.

An evaluation culture will need to be an *interdisciplinary* one, doing more than just grafting one discipline onto another through constructing multidiscipline research teams. Such teams are needed, of course, but I mean to imply something deeper, more personally internalized—a need to move toward being nondisciplinary, consciously putting aside the blinders of peoples' respective specialties in an attempt to foster a more whole view of the phenomena being studied. As programs are being evaluated, it will be important to speculate about a broad range of implementation factors or potential consequences. It should be possible to anticipate some of the organizational and systems-related features of these programs, the economic factors that might enhance or reduce implementation, their social and psychological dimensions, and especially whether the ultimate utilizers can understand or know how to utilize and be willing to utilize the results of evaluation work. It should also be possible to anticipate a broad spectrum of potential consequences: system-related, production-related, economic, nutritional, social, and environmental.

This evaluation culture will also be an honest, *truth-seeking* one that stresses accountability and scientific credibility. In many quarters in contemporary society, it appears that people have given up on the ideas of truth and validity. An evaluation culture needs to hold to the goal of getting at the truth while at the same time honestly acknowledging the revisability of all scientific and research-based knowledge. It is important to be critical of those who have given up on the goal of getting it right about reality, especially those among the humanities and social sciences who argue that truth is entirely relative to the knower, objectivity an impossibility, and reality nothing more than a construction or illusion that cannot be examined publicly. For them, the goal of seeking the truth is inappropriate and unacceptable, and science a tool of oppression rather than a road to greater understanding. Philosophers have, of course, debated such issues for thousands of years and will undoubtedly do so for thousands more. In the evaluation culture it will be important to check in on their thinking from time to time, but until they settle these debates, it is necessary to hold steadfastly to the goal of getting at the truth—the goal of getting it right about reality.

This evaluation culture will be prospective and *forward looking*, anticipating where evaluation feedback will be needed rather than just reacting to situations as they arise. Simple, low-cost evaluation and monitoring information systems will be constructed when new programs or technology are initiated; it will not do to wait until a program is complete or a technology is in the field before turning attention to its evaluation.

Finally, the evaluation culture I envision is one that will emphasize fair, open, *ethical, and democratic* processes. This will require moving away from private ownership of and exclusive access to data. The data from all evaluations needs to be accessible to all interested groups, allowing more extensive independent, secondary analyses and opportunities for replication or refutation of original results. Open commentary and debate regarding the results of specific evaluations should be encouraged. Especially when multiple parties have a stake in such results, it is important for reporting procedures to include formal opportunities for competitive review and response. An evaluation culture must continually strive for greater understanding of the ethical dilemmas posed by research. The desire for valid, scientific inference will at times cause conflicts with ethical principles. The situation is likely to be especially complex in international-evaluation contexts where evaluations may involve multiple cultures and countries that are at different stages of economic development and have different value systems and morals. It is important to be ready to deal with potential ethical and political issues posed by research methodologies in an open, direct, and democratic manner.

Do you agree with the values I'm describing here? What other characteristics might this evaluation culture have? You tell me. There are many more values and characteristics that ought to be considered. For now, the ones mentioned previously, and others in the literature, provide a starting point for the discussion. I hope you will add to the list, and I encourage each of you to criticize these tentative statements I've offered about the extraordinary potential of the evaluation culture that is in the process of evolving today.

Summary

And so we come to the end of our journey, at least for this volume. This chapter takes a view from the mountaintop back at the research path we follow in a particular study and at the aggregate of paths made up of the many studies that we accomplish collectively as our knowledge evolves. We looked at the general idea of synthesizing across multiple research studies, and the specific quantitative approaches to meta-analysis of results. We then looked at the connection of research to practice in the recent development of the evidence-based practice movement. We introduced the idea of evaluation and evaluation research both as an endeavor for conducting a practical research study that can be utilized and to generate multiple studies for later synthesis. Finally, we sketched out the value system that might underlie a culture of evaluation within which research methodology is a central component. We wish you the best on your own research journeys and hope we have provided you with the basics you will need to accomplish them successfully.

Login to the Online Edition of your text at www.atomicdog.com to find additional resources located in the Study Guide at the end of each chapter.

GLOSSARY

.05 level of significance. The significance level. Specifically, alpha is the Type I error, or the probability of concluding that there is a treatment effect when, in reality, there is not.

A

abstract. A concise description of a research study, usually displayed at the beginning of a research publication as a summary.

alpha level. The significance level. Specifically, alpha is the Type I error, or the probability of concluding that there is a treatment effect when, in reality, there is not.

alternative hypothesis. A specific statement of prediction that usually states what you expect will happen in your study.

analysis of covariance (ANCOVA). An analysis that estimates the difference between the groups on the posttest after adjusting for differences on the pretest.

anonymity. The assurance that no one, including the researchers, will be able to link data to a specific individual.

attribute. A specific value of a variable. For instance, the variable sex or gender has two attributes: male and female.

B

bell curve. Smoothed histogram or bar graph describing the expected frequency for each value of a variable. The name comes from the fact that such a distribution often has the shape of a bell.

boxplot. A boxplot (or box and whisker plot) is a graphic display invented by John Tukey that summarizes the distribution of a numeric variable by showing the median and quartiles as a box, and the extreme values as "whiskers" extending from the box.

C

case study. An intensive study of a specific individual or specific context.

causal. Pertaining to a cause-effect relationship.

causal relationship. A cause effect relationship. For example, when you evaluate whether your treatment or program causes an outcome to occur, you are examining a causal relationship.

cause construct. Your abstract idea or theory of what the cause is in a cause-effect relationship you are investigating.

cause-effect relationship. A cause effect relationship. For example, when you evaluate whether your treatment or program causes an outcome to occur, you are examining a causal relationship.

census. A kind of survey that involves a complete enumeration of the entire population of interest.

central tendency. An estimate of the center of a distribution of values. The most usual measures of central tendency are the mean, median, and mode.

citation. A brief reference in the text of a research write-up to a specific source used in the article, such as another research article, website, book, etc. Each citation in a write-up should have a complete reference included in the reference section at the end of the article.

cluster or area random sampling. A sampling method that involves dividing the population into groups called *clusters*, randomly selecting clusters, and then sampling each element in the selected clusters. This method is useful when sampling a population that is spread across a wide geographic area.

codebook. A written description of the data that describes each variable and indicates where and how it can be accessed.

coding. The process of categorizing qualitative data.

compensatory equalization of treatment. A social threat to internal validity that occurs when the control group is given a program or treatment (usually, by a well-meaning third party) designed to make up for or "compensate" for the treatment the program group gets.

compensatory program. A program given to only those who need it on the basis of some screening mechanism.

compensatory rivalry. A social threat to internal validity that occurs when one group knows the program another group is getting and, because of that, develops a competitive attitude with the other group.

concept mapping. Two dimensional graphs of a group's ideas where ideas that are more similar are located closer together and those judged less similar are more distant. Concept maps are often used by a group to develop a conceptual framework for a research project.

concurrent validity. An operationalization's ability to distinguish between groups that it should theoretically be able to distinguish between.

confidence intervals. Technically, 1-alpha. The confidence interval is the probability of correctly concluding that there is no treatment effect.

confidentiality. An assurance made to study participants that identifying information about them acquired through the study will not be released to anyone outside of the study.

confirmability. The degree to which others can confirm or corroborate the results in qualitative research.

constant comparison. The iterative and sequential process used when analyzing qualitative data that involves refinement of categories and interpretations based on increasing depth of understanding.

construct validity. The degree to which inferences can legitimately be made from the operationalizations in your study to the theoretical constructs on which those operationalizations are based.

constructivists. Constructivist are people who hold a philosophical position that maintains that reality is a conceptual construction. In constructivism, the emphasis is placed on understanding how we construe the world. Constructivists may be realists (believe there is an external reality that we imperfectly apprehend and construct our view of) or subjectivists (believe that all constructions are mediated by subjective experience).

content analysis. The analysis of text documents. The analysis can be quantitative, qualitative, or both. Typically, the major purpose of content analysis is to identify patterns in text.

content validity. A check of the operationalization against the relevant content domain for the construct.

control group. A group, comparable to the program group, that did not receive the program.

convergent validity. The degree to which the operationalization is similar to (converges on) other operationalizations to which it should be theoretically similar.

correlation. A single number that describes the degree of relationship between two variables.

correlation matrix. A table of correlations showing all possible relationships among a set of variables. The diagonal of a correlation matrix (the numbers that go from the upper-left corner to the lower right) always consists of 1s because these are the correlations between each variable and itself (and a variable is always perfectly correlated with itself). Off-diagonal elements are the correlations of variables represented by the relevant row and column in the matrix.

correlational relationship. Two variables that perform in a synchronized manner.

cost-effectiveness and cost-benefit analysis. Economic assessments of the costs of achieving specific outcomes and of these costs weighed against the estimated benefits.

covariate. Variables you adjust for in your study.

covariation of the cause and effect. A criterion for establishing a causal relationship that holds that the cause and effect must be related or co-vary.

credibility. Establishing that the results of qualitative research are believable from the perspective of the participant in the research.

criterion-related validity. The validation of a measure based on its relationship to another independent measure as predicted by your theory of how the measures should behave.

critical realism. The belief that there is an external reality independent of a person's thinking (realism) but that we can never know that reality with perfect accuracy (critical).

Cronbach's alpha. One specific method of estimating the reliability of a measure. Although not calculated in this manner, Cronbach's alpha can be thought of as analogous to the average of all possible split-half correlations.

cross-sectional. A study that takes place at a single point in time.

cross-tabulation. A table that describes the frequency and/or percentage for all combinations of two or more nominal or categorical variables.

D

data audit. A systematic assessment of data and data collection procedures conducted to establish and document the credibility of data collection processes and potential inaccuracies in the data.

data reduction. The systematic process undertaken to convert a set of raw data to a coded or summary form.

deductive. Top-down reasoning that works from the more general to the more specific.

degrees of freedom (df). A statistical term that is a function of the sample size. In the *t*-test formula, for instance, the df is the number of persons in both groups minus 2.

dependability. In qualitative research, the degree to which the research adequately describes the continuously changing context and its effects on conclusions.

dependent variable. The variable affected by the independent variable; for example, the outcome.

descriptive statistics. Statistics used to describe the basic features of the data in a study.

design. The design of a study is the specification of how the research question will be answered. A research design should specify how the selection of participants, method of assignment, and choice of measures and time frame work together to accomplish the study objectives.

dichotomous question. A question with two possible responses.

dichotomous response scale. A question with two possible responses. The better term to use is dichotomous response *format.*

diffusion or imitation of treatment. A social threat to internal validity that occurs because a comparison group learns about the program either directly or indirectly from program group participants.

digital repository. A publicly shared electronic archive for research reports and data.

direct observation. The process of observing a phenomenon to gather information about it. This process is distinguished from participant observation in that a direct observer does not typically try to become a participant in the context and does strive to be as unobtrusive as possible so as not to bias the observations.

discriminant validity. The degree to which concepts that should not be related theoretically are, in fact, not interrelated in reality.

dispersion. The spread of the values around the central tendency. The two common measures of dispersion are the range and the standard deviation.

distribution. The manner in which a variable takes different values in your data.

distribution media. In the context of research, it is the universe of possibilities for sharing a research report including all paper and electronic forms.

double entry. An automated method for checking data-entry accuracy in which you enter data once and then enter it a second time, with the software automatically stopping each time a discrepancy is detected until the data enterer resolves the discrepancy. This procedure assures extremely high rates of data entry accuracy, although it requires twice as long for data entry.

double-pretest design. A design that includes two waves of measurement prior to the program.

dummy variable. A variable that uses discrete numbers, usually 0 and 1, to represent different groups in your study in the equations of the GLM.

E

ecological fallacy. Faulty reasoning that results from making conclusions about individuals based only on analyses of group data.

effect construct. Your abstract idea or theory of what the outcome is in a cause-effect relationship you are investigating.

effect size. An effect size is a signal-to-noise ratio that expresses the size of a relationship or a difference in a standardized way. Effect sizes are important in planning studies so that we can estimate sample sizes accurately, in comparing results across studies, and in synthesizing research results as in meta-analysis.

An estimate of the effect of a treatment or program. The effect size is a signal to noise ration where the numerator (top) represents the effect you are trying to assess (e.g., a difference in averages between two groups) and the denominator (bottom) represents the variability or noise in the data.

empirical. Based on direct observations and measurements of reality.

epistemology. Is the philosophy of knowledge or of how you come to know.

error term. A term in a regression equation that captures the degree to which the line is in error (that is, the residual) in describing each point.

ethnography. Study of a culture using qualitative field research.

evaluability assessment. A structured empirical process of assessing whether a formal evaluation is feasible in any specific context.

evaluation. The systematic acquisition and assessment of information to provide useful feedback about some object

evidence-based practice. Evidence-based practice means the use of the best available programs or treatments based on careful evaluation using critically reviewed research.

The use of the best available programs or treatments based on careful evaluation using critically reviewed research.

evolutionary epistemology or natural selection theory of knowledge. A theory that ideas have survival value and that knowledge evolves through a process of variation, selection, and retention.

evolutionary epistemology. A philosophical position that holds that all knowledge evolves through evolutionary processes of natural selection.

exception dictionary. A dictionary that includes all nonessential words like *is*, *and*, and *of*, in a content analysis study.

exception fallacy. A faulty conclusion reached as a result of basing a conclusion on exceptional or unique cases.

exhaustive. The property of a variable that occurs when you include all possible answerable responses.

expert sampling. A sample of people with known or demonstrable experience and expertise in some area.

exploratory data analysis. The use of graphic and other methods to examine relationships in a data set. EDA is especially helpful when trying to develop hypotheses about relationships and when examining distributions of variables by themselves or in relation to other variables.

external validity. The degree to which the conclusions in your study would hold for other persons in other places and at other times.

F

face validity. A type of validity that assures that "on its face" the operationalization seems like a good translation of the construct.

factorial designs. Designs that focus on the program or treatment, its components, and its major dimensions and enable you to determine whether the program has an effect, whether different subcomponents are effective, and whether there are interactions in the effects caused by subcomponents.

feasibility. In qualitative research, the "doability" of the design—the degree to which each part of the study is realistic and appears to have a high probability of success in implementation.

field research. A research method in which the researcher goes into the field to observe the phenomenon in its natural state.

filter or contingency question. A question you ask the respondents to determine whether they are qualified or experienced enough to answer a subsequent one.

fishing and the error rate problem. A problem that occurs as a result of conducting multiple analyses and treating each one as independent.

focus group. A qualitative measurement method where input on one or more focus topics is collected from participants in a small-group setting where the discussion is structured and guided by a facilitator.

formative evaluation. Evaluations that strengthen or improve the object being evaluated. Formative evaluations are used to improve programs while they are still under development.

frequency distribution. A summary of the frequency of individual values or ranges of values for a variable.

fully crossed factorial design. A design that includes the pairing of every combination of factor levels.

P

p value. The estimate of the probability for a test of an hypothesis. Usually the p value is compared to the significance level when testing a hypothesis. If the p-value exceeds the designated significance level the alternative hypothesis is accepted; if it does not, the null hypothesis is accepted.

participant observation. A method of qualitative observation in which the researcher becomes a participant in the culture or context being observed.

pattern matching. The degree of correspondence between two patterns. For instance, you might look at a pattern match of a theoretical expectation pattern with an observed pattern to see if you are getting the outcomes you expect or if your measures intercorrelate the way you would theoretically predict they would.
The degree of correspondence between two data items. For instance, you might look at a pattern match of a theoretical expectation pattern with an observed pattern to see if you are getting the outcomes you expect.

pattern-matching NEDV design. A single-group pre-post quasi- experimental design with multiple outcome measures where there is a theoretically specified pattern of expected effects across the measures. To assess the treatment effect, the theoretical pattern of expected outcomes is correlated or matched with the observed pattern of outcomes as measured.

Pearson product moment correlation. A particular type of correlation used when both variables can be assumed to be measured at an interval level of measurement.

phenomenology. A philosophical perspective as well as an approach to qualitative methodology that focuses on people's subjective experiences and interpretations of the world.

plausible alternative explanation. Any other cause that can bring about an effect that is different from your hypothesized or manipulated cause.

population parameter. The mean or average you would obtain if you were able to sample the entire population.

population. The group you want to generalize to and the group you sample from in a study.

positive relationship. A relationship between variables in which high values for one variable are associated with high values on another variable, and low values are associated with low values.

positivism. The philosophical position that the only meaningful inferences are ones that can be verified through experience or direct measurement. Positivism is often associated with the stereotype of the hardheaded, lab-coat scientist who refuses to believe in something if it can't be seen or measured directly.

post-positivism. The rejection of positivism in favor of a position that one can make reasonable inferences about phenomena based upon theoretical reasoning combined with experience-based evidence.

posttest-only nonexperimental design. A research design in which only a posttest is given. It is referred to as nonexperimental because no control group exists.

posttest-only randomized experiment. An experiment in which the groups are randomly assigned and receive only a posttest.

pre-post nonequivalent groups quasi-experiment. A research design in which groups receive both a pre- and posttest, and group assignment is not randomized, and therefore, the groups may be nonequivalent, making it a quasi-experiment.

predictive validity. A type of construct validity based on the idea that your measure is able to predict what it theoretically should be able to predict.

probabilistic equivalence. The notion that two groups, if measured infinitely, would on average perform identically. Note that two groups that are probabilistically equivalent would seldom obtain the exact same average score in a real setting.

probability sampling. Method of sampling that utilizes some form of random selection.

process evaluation. A structured empirical assessment of the process of delivering a program or technology.

propensity score analysis. A statistical modeling approach for adjusting for selection bias by estimating the probability or "propensity" of assignment to treatment given a set of pre-program variables.

proportional quota sampling. A sampling method in which you sample until you achieve a specific number of sampled units for each subgroup of a population, where the proportions in each group are the same.

proximal similarity model. A model for generalizing from your study to another context based upon the degree to which the other context is similar to your study context.

proxy-pretest design. A post-only design in which, after the fact, a pretest measure is constructed from preexisting data. This is usually done to make up for the fact that the research did not include a true pretest.

Q

qualitative. The descriptive nonnumerical characteristic of some object. A qualitative variable is a descriptive nonnumerical observation.

qualitative data. Data in which the variables are not in a numerical form, but are in the form of text, photographs, sound bytes, and so on.

qualitative measures. Data not recorded in numerical form.

qualitative variable. A variable that is not in numerical form.

quantitative. The numerical representation of some object. A quantitative variable is any variable that is measured using numbers.

quantitative data. The numerical representation of some object. A quantitative variable is any variable that is measured using numbers.

quantitative variable. Data in the form of numbers.

quasi-experimental design. Research designs that have several of the key features of randomized experimental designs, such as pre-post measurement and treatment-control group comparisons, but lack random assignment to a treatment group.

quasi-experimental research design. Research designs that have several of the key features of randomized experimental designs, such as pre-post measurement and treatment-control group comparisons, but lack random assignment to a treatment group.

quota sampling. Any sampling method in which you sample until you achieve a specific number of sampled units for each subgroup of a population.

R

random assignment. Process of assigning your sample into two or more subgroups by chance. Procedures for random assignment can vary from flipping a coin to using a table of random numbers to using the random number capability built into a computer.

random sampling. Process or procedure that assures that different units in your population are selected into a sample by chance.

random selection. Process or procedure that assures that the different units in your population are selected by chance.

randomized block designs (RD). Experimental designs in which the sample is grouped into relatively homogeneous subgroups or blocks within which your experiment is replicated. This procedure reduces noise or variance in the data.

range. The highest value minus the lowest value.

reference database program. A specialized kind of database program designed to help writers keep track of citations. It may include special tools for managing references from the point when a researcher downloads a citation from a bibliographic database to the writing of a manuscript.

reference. A complete description of a source (such as another research article, website, book, etc.) that is relevant to your research, including authors, title, date, publisher, page numbers and location. References for a research write-up are usually all listed at the end of the article.

regression artifact. *See* regression threat.

regression line. A line that describes the relationship between two or more variables.

regression point displacement design (RPD). A pre-post quasi experimental research design where the treatment is given to only one unit in the sample, with all remaining units acting as controls. This design is particularly useful to study the effects of community-level interventions, where outcome data is routinely collected at the community level.

regression threat. A statistical phenomenon that causes a group's average performance on one measure to regress toward or appear closer to the mean of that measure than anticipated or predicted. Regression occurs whenever you have a nonrandom sample from a population and two measures that are imperfectly correlated. A regression threat will bias your estimate of the group's posttest performance and can lead to incorrect causal inferences.

regression to the mean. *See* regression threat.
See regression threat.

regression-discontinuity (RD). A pretest-posttest program-comparison group quasi-experimental design in which a cutoff criterion on the preprogram measure is the method of assignment to group.

relationship. Refers to the correspondence between two variables.

relevance. In qualitative research, the degree to which a study may make a practical contribution to a substantive area as well as the goodness of fit of methods to the study goals in all aspects of the design.

reliability. The degree to which a measure is consistent or dependable; the degree to which it would give you the same result over and over again, assuming the underlying phenomenon is not changing.
The repeatability or consistency of a measure. More technically, reliability is the ratio of the variability in true scores to the variability in the observed scores. In more approximate terms, reliability is the proportion of truth in what you measure as opposed to the proportion of error in measurement.

repeated measures. Two or more waves of measurement over time.

Requests for Proposals (RFPs). RFPs, published by government agencies and some companies, describe some problem that the agency would like researchers to address. Typically, the RFP describes the problem that needs addressing, the contexts in which it operates, the approach the agency would like you to take to investigate the problem, and the amount the agency would be willing to pay for such research.

research question. The central issue being addressed in the study, which is typically phrased in the language of theory.

research synthesis. A structured empirical process of producing integrative summaries of a body of research.

resentful demoralization. A social threat to internal validity that occurs when the comparison group knows what the program group is getting and becomes discouraged or angry and gives up.

residuals. The vertical distance from the regression line to each point. The residual in regression analysis refers to the portion of the outcome or dependent variable that you cannot predict with your regression equation.

response. A specific measurement value that a sampling unit supplies.

response brackets. A question response type that includes groups of answers, such as between 30 and 40 years old, or between $50,000 and $100,000 annual income.

response format. A response format that has a number beside each choice where the number has no meaning except as a placeholder for that response.

response scale. A sequential numerical response format, such as a 1-to-5 rating format.

right to service. The ethical issue involved when participants do not receive a service that they would be eligible for if they were not in your study. For example, members of a control group might not receive a drug because they are in a study.

rigor. In qualitative research, the soundness of the methods chosen and degree to which the design has accounted for potential problems in any stage of the research.

S

sample. The actual units you select to participate in your study.

W–Z